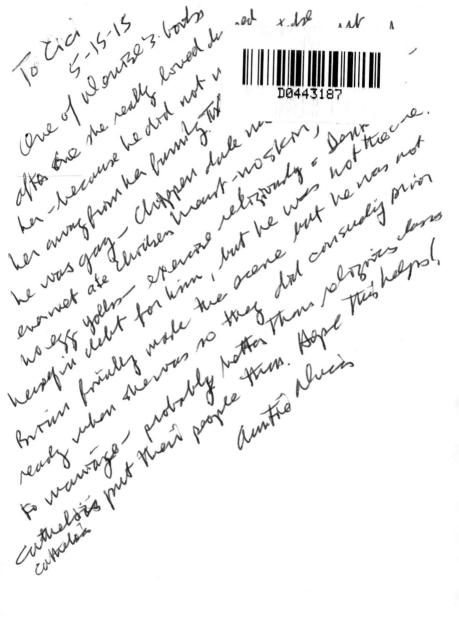

To Cici
5-15-15

One of Wendle's 3 books
after one she really loved...
her — because he did not...
her away from her family. Tho
he was gay — Chippendale...
ever met ate Chicken breast - no skin,
no egg yolks — exercise religiously — Don't
happen... debt for him, but he was not
running friendly made the scene but he was not
ready when she was so they did conscudy prior
to marriage — probably hotter than... religious dawn
Catholics put their people thru. Hope this helps!,

Auntie Alice

D0443187

ARE YOU THE ONE FOR ME?

REAL MOMENTS

BARBARA De ANGELIS, Ph.D.

TWO
NEW YORK
TIMES
BESTSELLERS
IN ONE
VOLUME

MJF BOOKS
NEW YORK

mjf

Published by MJF Books
Fine Communications
Two Lincoln Square
60 West 66th Street
New York, NY 10023

Library of Congress Catalog Card Number 97-75442
ISBN 1-56731-241-1

Manufactured in the United States of America on acid-free paper

MJF Books and the MJF colophon are trademarks of Fine Creative Media, Inc.

10   9   8   7   6   5   4   3   2   1

BARBARA
DE ANGELIS, PH.D.

ARE YOU THE ONE FOR ME?

KNOWING WHO'S RIGHT & AVOIDING WHO'S WRONG

I dedicate this book
to my mother, Phyllis Garshman,
and my stepfather, Daniel Garshman,
▼
For loving me unconditionally,
for always being there when I needed you
and for showing me, by your example,
how wonderful love can be
when you're with the right person.

ACKNOWLEDGMENTS

▼▼▼

I want to express my gratitude to the following people:

To my incredible staff at the Los Angeles Personal Growth Center—April Whitney, Linda Boswell, Marla Campbell, Alicia Smith, and Jill Cresap: Thank you for sharing my vision, for working so hard to manifest it, and for trusting me so completely. I feel so fortunate to have each of you in my life.

To my assistants staff for Making Love Work Seminars over the past two years: Maria Talamini, Dennis Cohen, Madelon Cohen, Steve and Wendy Vitalich, David Davison, Suzi Ogulnick, Judy Murphy, Victoria Pruett, Rebecca Gerber Kahane, Stephanie Livingston, Dave Pearson, Mike Handron, Paul Belanger, Fred Balch, Chris McRae, John Heaviside, Kathy Elliott, Steve Hargett, and especially Kevin Roesch. Thank you for your continued love and support; for merging your dreams of healing the planet with mine and making them a reality month after month. What a joy to be traveling together!!

To Harvey Klinger, my literary agent: Thank you for believing in me, for knowing exactly what I need, always getting it for me, and for coming up with the title for this book! You are the best there is!

To David Sams, my business partner and manager: Thank you for always holding the big picture and supporting me in taking the time off from our projects to write this book. I am so grateful for all you've done for me, and mostly for your friendship.

To Mark Fisher, my business manager: Thank you for always watching over me and my business with such a loving eye, and for being true family.

To everyone at Delacorte Press: Especially Carole Baron—Thank you for trusting me so completely with this book; Roger Bilheimer— Thank you for always being there for me; and Jill Lamar—Thank you for your sensitive editing.

To Ruth Cruz: Thank you for always taking such good care of me and my home so I can do things like write this book. I feel blessed to have you in my life.

To the thousands of men and women who have shared their pain and growth with me on the radio, through letters, and through my seminars: Thank you for showing me that I needed to write this book, and for having the courage to heal your heart.

To my best friend and animal companion "Bijou," who sat or slept next to me for every one of the thousands of hours I spent at my computer writing this book, never leaving my side: Thank you, precious puppy, for showing me such total love and devotion, for being a never-ending source of comfort, for knowing just when I'd had enough and taking me for a walk, and for reminding me about what really matters.

And most of all, to my heart's true companion, Jeffrey James: "Thank you" does not begin to express my gratitude for your love, your kindness, your patience, and your loyalty. Without you I could not have written this book, for I wouldn't have had the experience of a healthy relationship to talk about. Thank you for being my teacher, my light, and my anchor. Thank you for loving me not just when I'm beautiful, but when I'm sitting at the computer in my bathrobe and glasses for hours on end. Thank you for helping me heal the frightened little girl inside me by not going away. I love you always.

CONTENTS

▼

UNDERSTANDING
YOUR LOVE CHOICES

▼

▼

AVOIDING WHO'S WRONG

▼

▼

KNOWING WHO'S RIGHT

▼

UNDERSTANDING
▼
YOUR
▼
LOVE
▼
CHOICES

▼▼▼

You are lying in the dark next to the person you love. You can tell by his breathing that he's asleep, and as you gaze at the outlines of his face, you wonder about the future of this relationship. You know he wants to marry you. You love him; you can't imagine living without him, but the thought of marrying him scares you to death. What if you make the commitment and find out later that there's someone you're more compatible with? *How can you be sure he's really the one for you?*

You and your husband are eating pizza and watching a movie on television. This is the first chance you've had to be alone together all week. It's hard to believe that next month will be your tenth wedding anniversary. It's been a good ten years, and although there are no big problems in the marriage, sometimes you wonder if you made the right choice. You love him, but don't feel as "in love" as when you met. You glance over at him sitting on the couch and ask yourself whether you're really fulfilled, or just "comfortable." *Would you be happier with someone else? Is he really your perfect partner?*

You're sitting in your attorney's office, looking down at your divorce papers. Once you sign them, your marriage will be officially over. The pen trembles in your hand, and your eyes fill with tears as dozens of memories flood into your mind: the first time he kissed you; the night he asked you to marry him; the joy you felt on your wedding day; the fun you had fixing up your first home; the closeness you felt when your children were born; the safety you felt in his arms; the hopes and dreams and plans for the future. Never in your wildest dreams did you imagine that it would turn out this way. You were so sure it would work, so confident that he was the right person for you. But now, as your signature severs the marriage forever, you ask yourself, "**Why didn't I see it?** *How could I have known it wouldn't last? Why did I make the wrong choice?*"

1

▼▼▼

LOVE IS
NOT ENOUGH

▼▼▼

Falling in love is a magical and powerful experience. Each kiss, each conversation, each moment in the beginning seems so right, so perfect. But soon attraction and infatuation become a "relationship," and we are brought down to earth with the challenging realities of sharing our life with another human being. And as those first enchanted weeks turn into months, one day we find ourselves asking: *"Is this person right for me?"*

If you've ever been in a serious relationship, you've asked yourself this question—before you made a commitment, before you got married, or, if the relationship didn't work, before you decided to leave for good.

I used to hear this question every day when I had a radio talk show in Los Angeles. I received more phone calls about this problem than any other.

▶ *"I love my boyfriend, but I'm afraid to make a commitment and marry him. What if I meet someone I love more in a few years? How can I tell if we're compatible enough?"*

▶ *"I've been dating a woman for two years, but she has children I don't get along with. Do you think this relationship can work?"*

▶ *"My husband and I argue all the time. He refuses to go to counseling, and we hardly ever have sex anymore. I love him and don't want to hurt the children, but I'm totally miserable. How can I be sure it's really over before I leave?"*

▶ *"I've just come out of a very painful relationship. I want to find a partner to share my life with, but I'm afraid of getting hurt again. How can I tell the next time if I'm with someone who is wrong for me* before *my heart gets broken?"*

I understand the pain and turmoil these people are going through, because I've been through it, too. Since my first serious relationship at seventeen, and, until recently, I fell in love without giving serious consideration to whether the person was right for me, let alone whether they loved me enough. Someone showed up, and if he had something lovable about him, I would start a relationship. I'd convince myself he was "*the one,*" only to find out that we were incompatible and watch the relationship fail. Then I would feel sorry for myself and wonder what I was doing wrong.

After too many heartbreaks, I was forced to face the sad truth: **In spite of my experience, education, and my intense desire to be happy, I continually chose partners who were not right for me. I was falling in love with the wrong people for the wrong reasons.**

I'm happy to say, I've spent the past five years of my life learning how to help myself and others make better love choices, and the results have been truly amazing. When it was time to choose a topic for my third book, I knew right away what it would be. My first two books were about *how* to love; this book is about *whom* to love. It's about knowing when someone is right for you, and avoiding those who are wrong. I hope that what you learn in this book will give you the understanding and support you need to create the passionate and fulfilling relationship you deserve.

HOW COULD I HAVE BEEN SO BLIND?

We all want to be happy in our love life, and we want our relationships to work. So, obviously, none of us deliberately sets out to choose partners who are wrong for us. We truly believe we are making the right decision when we select a mate. But the sad reality is that, more often than not, those choices turn out to be painful mistakes.

▼
Many of us are choosing the wrong partners and wondering why our relationships are not working.
▲

Have you ever thought or said the following about one of your relationships?

▶ "How could I have been so blind? Why didn't I see what he/she was really like?"

▶ "I felt so sure that, this time, it would work. Where did I go wrong?"

▶ "He seemed so wonderful when we first met. I can't figure out why he changed into someone I can't stand."

▶ "All the signs were there from the beginning that she didn't feel the way I did. I guess I just ignored them and convinced myself things would get better."

▶ "We loved each other, but we couldn't agree on anything, and all we did was argue."

▶ "I was so sure he was different from the other men I'd been with. It took me almost two years to find out that I'd picked the same type of guy all over again! How could I have wasted so much time?"

▶ "I remember feeling really in love with her at the time, but the truth is, I never told anyone we were together because I was embarrassed to admit I was even involved with a woman like that."

▶ "Everything about him seemed so perfect; I kept telling myself that I should be happy with him, but there just wasn't any chemistry between us."

There is an old saying, "Hindsight has 20/20 vision." It's always so much easier to look back and see things clearly that we could not see at all then. It's much easier to be wiser about the mistakes we made yesterday than the ones we are in the process of making today. Yet, I've always lived by the philosophy that there are no "mistakes"—only opportunities for growth and learning. And learning from the past gives meaning, and even purpose, to some of the pain and heartache collected along the way.

This book contains everything I have learned about choosing the right partner, from my own experiences and those of the men and women I have counseled and worked with. It's about understanding why you make the love choices you do, and learning how to make more fulfilling ones. It answers the questions, "How could I have been so blind?" and "How can I tell if I'm with the right person?" and hopefully will give you the vision you need to see the truth about your own love life.

> **IF YOU ARE SINGLE,** I hope this book will give you tools and guidelines for making healthy, successful choices in your partner for your next relationship.
>
> **IF YOU ARE RECOVERING FROM A BROKEN HEART,** I hope this book will help you understand why your relationship choices were not good ones for you, and will give you information that will help you make much wiser and less painful choices next time.
>
> **IF YOU ARE UNMARRIED BUT IN A RELATIONSHIP,** I hope this book will support you in getting clear about whether your relationship is right for you, so you don't have to waste time and energy on a relationship that won't work.
>
> **IF YOU ARE IN A COMMITTED RELATIONSHIP OR MARRIAGE,** I hope this book will show you that many of the conflicts you and your partner experience may stem not from lack of love, but lack of compatibility, and that understanding your differences can help you live more peacefully and passionately together.

WHY SOME RELATIONSHIPS DON'T WORK

Relationships don't work for one of two reasons:

1. **You are with the right person but *you are loving wrong*.**
   ▶ You and your partner have poor communication habits.
   ▶ You don't know how to create real intimacy.
   ▶ You don't ask for what you want, and end up feeling resentful.
   ▶ You neglect the relationship.

or

2. **You are with the *wrong person*.**
   ▶ Your love or life-style is incompatible with your partner's.
   ▶ You do not share enough common values and commitments.
   ▶ Your partner has "fatal flaws" that make having a successful relationship impossible.
   ▶ You can't give each other enough of what you need.

Several years ago I wrote my first book, *How to Make Love All the Time,* as a manual to help people learn how to love one another in a way that creates healthy, passionate, fulfilling relationships. The book was really about how to stop loving the wrong way and start loving the right way, reason number one above. But that information, as valuable as it has been to millions of my readers around the world, is incomplete without the material I've included in this book, because **if you are loving the wrong person, loving the right way won't make a difference.**

▼

***WHOM* YOU CHOOSE TO LOVE IS AS IMPORTANT AS *HOW* YOU CHOOSE TO LOVE.**

▲

WHY WE FALL IN LOVE

Ask most people why they fell in love with their partners, past or present, and you'll probably hear answers like this:

▶ "I met Kathy at the gym where I work out. Something about the way she got so into that aerobics class and gave it so much energy really appealed to me."

▶ "Donna was a bridesmaid at my cousin's wedding. She looked so beautiful in this pink strapless dress—I knew on the spot I was going to fall in love with her."

▶ "Jo Anne and I knew each other since we were kids. Everyone always said we'd probably get married when we grew up, and I guess I never even questioned it—it seemed like the right thing to do."

▶ "Alex and I were assigned to work together on a project in our office. I think it was watching him problem-solve—he is so creative—that attracted me to him."

▶ "I've always been a sucker for music, so when I heard Fred play the guitar at a friend's house, I knew he was the one for me."

▶ "This sounds terrible, but I always had this fantasy of a tall, dark-haired man with a mustache. Dennis looked exactly like that, and nothing else really mattered."

▶ "My ex-husband was so selfish and controlling. After my divorce, I think I was attracted to Stan because he was such a nice guy. He always seemed so sweet and considerate."

These may seem like good reasons to start a relationship, but they are NOT:

▶ All Kathy's boyfriend knows about her is that she has a lot of physical energy.

▶ All Donna's boyfriend knows about her is that she looks good in pink chiffon.

▶ Jo Anne's husband has been so influenced by what his friends and family think that he doesn't even know why he loves her.

▶ Alex's girlfriend is enthralled with his business skills but has no idea what his emotional skills are.

▶ Fred's partner has fallen under a musical spell—she knows nothing about him except for the romantic personality she assumes all guitar players have.

▶ Dennis's girlfriend likes the way he looks—she is attracted to a fantasy, but doesn't know anything about the person underneath.

▶ And all Stan's wife knows is that Stan is definitely different from her ex-husband. But whether he is what she wants and needs is a different story.

None of these people thought they were making the wrong decision. They all sincerely believed that they were making intelligent, sensible choices in their partners. But the frightening truth is that **many of them will discover in a month, or six months, or six years that they are in a relationship with the wrong person.**

▼

MOST PEOPLE PUT MORE TIME AND EFFORT INTO DECIDING WHAT KIND OF CAR OR VIDEO PLAYER TO BUY THAN THEY DO INTO DECIDING WHOM TO HAVE A RELATIONSHIP WITH.

▲

Is it any wonder, then, that our relationships don't turn out the way we want them to, that our hopes and dreams turn into heartache, disappointment, and despair?

TEST YOUR LOVE IQ

Part of the reason why so many people choose to be in a relationship with the wrong person is that they have what I call a low "Love IQ." Your Love IQ is based on how much you know about creating and maintaining a healthy relationship with another person. Therefore, whether your Love IQ is high or low determines how good or how bad your choice in partner will be. If you have a high Love IQ and are "Love Smart," you will probably still make some mistakes in love, but not as many as if you have a low Love IQ. Then you are "Love Stupid."

Here is a quiz to help you determine your Love IQ. It contains ten statements about love. **Grade yourself according to how much each statement describes the way you have felt about love, now or in the past, and how often this belief has affected your life.**

If the belief about how love should feel expressed in the statement has affected you in your past or present relationships:

Very frequently . . . . **Give yourself 0 points**
Often . . . . **Give yourself 4 points**
Occasionally . . . . **Give yourself 8 points**
Rarely or never . . . . **Give yourself 10 points**

WARNING:

You will be tempted to take this quiz from the perspective of how you think you should feel about love and romance, instead of being honest about how you actually felt in your past. Don't respond to each statement only on the basis of your present attitudes and all you have learned; respond honestly, based on a summary of all of your relationships throughout your life.

Why is this important? For instance, let's take the first statement in the quiz:

"If my partner and I really love one another enough, none of our problems or personality differences will threaten the existence of our relationship."

Perhaps you're in a new relationship, where, for the first time, you're being honest about problems rather than avoiding them. You might feel that this statement doesn't apply to how you feel now at all. You want to answer "Rarely or Never" and give yourself a quick 10 points. But let's say that in your previous relationships, you've ignored conflicts and flaws by telling yourself you loved the person so much that none of his or her hurtful or unloving behavior mattered. From that point of view, this statement applies very much to how you felt. So you should answer "Very Frequently" and give yourself 0 points!

The reason you may be tempted to answer from the point of view of your new understanding of love, rather than how your relationships have really been in the past, could be that you just don't want to appear unenlightened or messed up. As a member of my office put it, "Can't I just answer from the past six months of my life? Do I have to include all those years when I didn't know what I was doing?" My answer is, "If you want to be honest with yourself, and learn from your mistakes, *yes,* you must include your past."

YOUR LOVE IQ QUIZ

1. If my partner and I really love one another enough, none of our problems or personality differences will threaten the existence of our relationship.

2. If I am finally with the right person, I won't ever be really attracted to someone else, because I will be so in love.

3. If it's really true love, I'd know the moment I see the person for the first time.

4. The right relationship will always be interesting and exciting.

5. If it's really true love, I won't feel complete and whole when I'm not with my partner.

6. The sex in a relationship can't be really fabulous unless it is true love.

7. My perfect partner will give me everything I need and will fill in all the empty spaces in my life—I won't really need anyone else.

8. If I'm really in love, I'll feel excited and nervous each time I see my partner; being with him/her will give me goose bumps.

9. If I'm with the right person, we will be so in tune with each other, we'll always know how the other person is feeling.

10. If I'm in the right relationship, it will feel naturally harmonious, and we won't have to work that hard to make it work.

Now total your points:

▶ **80–100 POINTS: CONGRATULATIONS! YOU HAVE A HIGH LOVE IQ.** You are realistic in your understanding of relationships and realize that love is not enough to make a relationship work— it takes communication, compatibility, and hard work. To avoid future problems, work on those areas in which you have a low score.

▶ **60–79 POINTS: YOUR LOVE IQ ISN'T BAD, BUT IT COULD BE BETTER.** You are still letting your romantic ideals and fantasies determine your attitudes about relationships. Pay more attention to how you are feeling and not to how you want the relationship to look. Don't be so afraid of conflict. Remind yourself that true love doesn't mean things have to be "perfect" all the time. The exercises in this book will help you raise your Love IQ.

▶ **40–59 POINTS: WARNING!** *Your Love IQ is dangerously low, but you probably already know this because you have been hurt so much in relationships.* The reason you continue to be disappointed in love is that you don't pay enough attention to whom you are with. You put your partners on a pedestal and are more "in love with love" than with them. If you want to stop suffering and be happier, you will need to make some major changes in the way you choose and behave in relationships. Use the information in the rest of this book to become much smarter about love.

▶ **0–39 POINTS: EMERGENCY!** *Your Love IQ is so low that you are guaranteed to get your heart broken over and over again.* Your love life needs immediate attention. It's time to grow up and leave your fantasy world behind. Your relationships can work, but only if you commit yourself to understanding what you've been doing wrong and learn how to make better choices for yourself. Stop blaming the partners who have let you down and take a good, hard look at how you set up relationships to fail from the beginning. The rest of this book will help you find the answers you need to create healthy relationships.

If you ended up with a very low Love IQ, don't feel too badly. When I first devised this quiz and took it myself, I scored a meager 28 points! Obviously I knew that these ten statements about love were unhealthy attitudes, but I tried to be totally honest with myself about how I have viewed love in my past, and that's how I scored 28 points. By the time you finish reading this book, your Love IQ will be much higher and your confidence in your ability to make successful love choices will be much greater.

UNCOVERING YOUR LOVE MYTHS

▶ Have you ever convinced yourself you were in love when you were really in lust?

▶ Have you ever been involved with a partner who was all wrong for you and not realized it until months or even years later?

▶ Do you ignore the problems in your relationship because you don't want to "rock the boat"?

▶ Have you had a habit of mistaking drama and tension for true love?

▶ Have you ever talked yourself into staying with someone who was mistreating you because your relationship "looks good" on the outside?

▶ Do you ever question a really healthy relationship because you don't feel head over heels in love with your partner all the time?

▶ Do you suspect that you choose partners with whom you are not compatible and ignore the people with whom you could be truly compatible?

If you answered yes to any of these questions, it's because you've been affected by what I call:

THE FIVE DEADLY MYTHS ABOUT LOVE

Love myths are beliefs many of us have about love and romance that actually prevent us from making intelligent love choices. These beliefs or attitudes are false notions about relationships that we develop from:

▶ **watching television and movies**

▶ **reading romantic novels**

▶ **never being taught about love**

Consciously and unconsciously, we base our decisions in relationships on these Love Myths. Let's look at five of the most deadly Love Myths. As you read each one, think not only of your present relationship but about your past relationships as well.

---

1. **TRUE LOVE CONQUERS ALL.**
2. **WHEN IT'S REALLY TRUE LOVE, YOU WILL KNOW IT THE MOMENT YOU MEET THE OTHER PERSON.**

3. **THERE IS ONLY ONE TRUE LOVE IN THE WORLD WHO IS RIGHT FOR YOU.**
4. **THE PERFECT PARTNER WILL FULFILL YOU COMPLETELY IN EVERY WAY.**
5. **WHEN YOU EXPERIENCE POWERFUL SEXUAL CHEMISTRY WITH SOMEONE, IT MUST BE LOVE.**

LOVE MYTH

▼　　▼　　▼　　▼　**1**　▼　　▼　　▼　　▼

True Love Conquers All

Deep in our hearts, we all secretly believe this myth about love—that if we really love our partner, we will be able to make the relationship work. **No problem, no conflict, no set of circumstances is insurmountable if we just love enough.**

Exercise: Think back to your past relationships, or to problems in your present relationship, and fill in the blank to this sentence for yourself. Make a list of *at least a dozen responses* that refer to different partners you have had.

► **If I love my partner enough, it won't matter that (problem)**

► **If I love my partner enough, it won't matter that _____**

► **If I love my partner enough, it won't matter that _____**

_____

_____

_____

_____

_____

_____

_____

_____

EXAMPLE: **If I love my partner enough, it won't matter that:**

▶ he drinks
▶ our sex life isn't great
▶ she criticizes me all the time
▶ we fight constantly over how to raise the children
▶ he is a strict Catholic and I am Jewish
▶ I'm not really sexually attracted to her
▶ he doesn't have a job and hasn't worked in two years
▶ she has a terrible temper and blows up all the time
▶ he constantly flirts with other women
▶ I don't get along with her children
▶ he has a hard time telling me how he feels
▶ his family doesn't accept me
▶ I want children and he doesn't
▶ she still hasn't gotten over her ex-boyfriend
▶ he's thirty years older than I am
▶ we live on opposite sides of the country

Here are the consequences of believing in Love Myth #1:

1. You avoid facing your relationship problems, or seeking solutions to those problems, by telling yourself: "If we love each other enough, none of these conflicts or personality differences will matter."

Dennis, thirty-seven, called me on my radio talk show one day and explained that he was Jewish and his fiancée, Alice, thirty-five, was Catholic. They had been dating for two years, and although they talked about their difference in religion, they never really resolved their feelings about it. "I always worried that one day it would be a problem," Dennis confessed, "but we got along so well in so many other ways, and I didn't want to rock the boat. Then Alice and I started to talk about marriage. When I thought about my future, and about having children, I realized that I wanted my kids to be brought up in the Jewish faith, and that there were things about Alice not being Jewish that I also missed but had never told her. I asked her to convert, but she refused. She is a pretty strict Catholic, and says she wants to be married in the Church by a priest, which means she couldn't marry a practicing Jew. I keep feeling like our love should conquer these differences, but they don't seem to go away."

The love Alice and Dennis felt for one another was not enough to overcome their lack of religious compatibility. Although many couples can make interfaith marriages work, Alice and Dennis were each too deeply entrenched in their own religions to compromise. No matter how much they cared about one another, they could not be happy and true to their own beliefs by staying together. But they had put off facing these problems by telling themselves, **"If we really love one another, our differences won't matter."** They kept trying to love and accept each other more, never facing the obvious until the very end.

2. You stay in unloving and unfulfilling relationships even when they are not working by telling yourself, "If I just love him more, he will change."

Kimberly, twenty-eight, and her husband David, thirty, came to me in hopes of saving their marriage. They had been together for six years but couldn't seem to get along without constant arguing. "I love David so much," Kimberly explained with tears in her eyes, "but I am constantly criticizing him. It's driving him crazy, and I hate myself for doing it." I asked Kimberly to list her complaints about her husband. "David is a quiet type of guy. He's pretty introspective, and not much for socializing with a lot of people. I'm totally the opposite—very outgoing and talkative, and I love having fun, being with friends, and living life passionately. I hate to say this, but I feel bored a lot of the time with him. It seems like we don't have anything to talk about, and I feel like I'm always pulling him out of his shell."

"I've told Kim that this is the way I am," David responded tensely. "I want to make her happy, but I feel like she is asking me to be someone I am not. I've always been low-key, and I really don't want to change."

As we talked more, I learned that Kimberly married David because she was looking for stability after having been cheated by a college boyfriend. She was so concerned with making sure he was a nice guy that she never asked herself whether they would be compatible together. *Kimberly and David had so many differences in life-style, temperament, and personality that living together harmoniously was next to impossible. They loved one another very much, but it was not enough to make their relationship work.*

But Kimberly believed Love Myth #1, that true love conquers all, and continued to stay with David, hoping that if she just loved him more, he would change. She never considered the possibility that David wasn't changing because David didn't want to change. She just kept trying to be the perfect wife, believing her love would transform David from the man he was into the man she wanted him to be.

Sadly, belief in this Love Myth can cause you heartache, pain, and even physical harm because it convinces you to stay in relationships that are not healthy. *People with very low self-esteem or a childhood history of neglect or abuse often set themselves up in toxic relationships they find difficult to leave, convincing themselves that if they just loved their partner more, his/ her harmful behavior would disappear and be replaced with love and affection.* This is a trap. Your partner's dysfunctional behavior is determined by forces that have nothing to do with how loving you are.

3. You beat yourself up emotionally when a relationship doesn't work, telling yourself, "If I had only loved him/her more, I know I could have saved it."

Eileen, fifty-four, was married to Raoul, sixty, for thirty-one years. Raoul was an alcoholic whose rages and irresponsibility had tortured Eileen and her three children throughout their lives. After pleading with her husband to get some help, and facing his total denial of the problem, Eileen found the courage to leave. Two years after their divorce, she came to me for help with her feelings of depression. When I asked Eileen what she thought was bothering her, she replied, "I guess I feel guilty."

"Guilty about leaving your husband?"

"Not just about leaving him," Eileen said with tears in her eyes, "but guilty for not trying harder to make it work. I feel like I abandoned him. Maybe if I had gone to more Al-Anon meetings myself, I would have understood him better, and he would have stopped drinking. Or maybe if I had been more affectionate, or satisfied him more, he would have given up the alcohol."

The more we talked, the more obvious it was that Eileen was still punishing herself for what she saw as her failure to save her marriage. Eileen's mother had always told her that "a good wife stands by her man through thick and thin," and so Eileen felt that she was an inadequate wife. Eileen's depression was brought on by her belief in Love Myth #1—that if she had just loved Raoul more, their marriage would have worked. The reality of love is very different from the myth. Of course, love is the foundation for a good relationship. But if a relationship is going to survive and grow, it needs a lot more than love.

Here's the reality about Love Myth #1:

▼

LOVE IS NOT ENOUGH TO MAKE A RELATIONSHIP WORK — IT NEEDS COMPATIBILITY AND IT NEEDS COMMITMENT.

▲

The sad truth is, very few relationships end because the two partners do not love each other; they end because they are not compatible partners.

I know this from my own painful experience in several of my past relationships. Like many people with the wrong partner, I attempted to make up for the lack of compatibility by trying extra hard and loving with added intensity. But in the end, we were not compatible enough to live peacefully and happily together. For years I blamed myself, thinking that if I had loved more, the differences wouldn't have mattered. Now I know I was wrong. Differences do matter, sometimes just enough to make a relationship challenging, but often enough to make it unhealthy and unfulfilling. Throughout the rest of the book we'll look in more detail at how to tell if you are compatible with another person.

LOVE MYTH

▼　　▼　　▼　　▼　　2　　▼　　▼　　▼　　▼

When It's Really True Love, You Will Know It the Moment You Meet the Other Person

When you watch a romantic film, you see it.
When you listen to a romantic song, you hear about it.
When you are single and lonely, you dream about it.

LOVE AT FIRST SIGHT

I think we all secretly believe in "love at first sight," the idea that if it is really true love, you will know it the moment you meet the other person. Oh, there may be other kinds of love, but according to this Love Myth, *true love* will strike you like lightning.

I remember first hearing this myth as a young girl, and I longed to be swept away during a powerfully romantic moment in which I'd look into a man's eyes and know instantly, and without a doubt, that this was my lifelong soulmate! I dreamed about "some enchanted evening," as the famous ballad from the play and movie *South Pacific* described it, when I would "find [my] true love . . .

across a crowded room." Anything less than this kind of intense emotional recognition seemed a pale imitation of what I was sure true love should feel like.

You can call it "love at first sight" or "instant chemistry," but the possible problems are the same if you believe in Love Myth #2:

1. You dwell on the intense connection or chemistry and avoid examining the rest of the relationship.

Skip, thirty-two, is a very successful entrepreneur, who met Marcia, a twenty-seven-year-old accountant, at a wedding. "My first thought when I saw her," he told me, "was, 'God, she is beautiful,' and my second thought was, 'I'm going to marry this woman.' That night was probably the most romantic night of my life. It was a beautiful summer evening, and we danced together on an outdoor patio under the stars. Marcia even caught the bridal bouquet, and everyone kidded us about being next.

"We dated each other for the next ten months, and then she told me she wanted me to make more of a commitment—in other words, to propose to her. I told her I needed more time, that I didn't want to rush things, but she kept pressuring me until one day she gave me an ultimatum: marry her or she'd leave.

"I knew something was wrong, because I just wasn't happy, but whenever I'd question whether I was making a mistake, a little voice in my head would say, 'How could she be wrong for you if you had "that feeling" when you first saw her?' I couldn't answer that question, and I kept remembering how crazy I'd been about Marcia in the beginning. I told myself that my concerns were born from my unwillingness to grow up. So I married her."

"Are you still married?" I asked Skip.

"No," he answered with a sad grimace. "I left Marcia after two years. The truth was, our relationship didn't live up to that first magical evening—Marcia is beautiful, but she is also very angry. She controlled me with her rages, and she drank too much, which made the blowups all too frequent. I put off breaking up with her for much longer than I should have, because I kept doubting my own feelings and thinking about how perfect things were when we met. I didn't want to see the truth; the romantic picture was much nicer."

Skip was a victim of Love Myth #2—he hid behind his intense first impressions of Marcia, and used them to fuel his fantasy of their relationship, rather than facing the reality of how unhappy he really was.

ARE YOU A "LOVE-AT-FIRST-SIGHT JUNKIE"?

2. You get addicted to flashy beginnings and miss opportunities for real, lasting love.

Alexia was a petite, striking thirty-six-year-old woman who owned a children's clothing store. She came to me to decide what to do about her relationship with Kent. "I'll tell you right away that in the past, my relationships haven't been great," Alexia began. "I seem to have been attracted to these flashy, exciting men who end up leaving me or cheating on me or somehow hurting me. These relationships always seem so powerful when they start, and I feel so wildly and desperately in love, and then—POW!—I get hurt.

"Last year I decided to swear off men entirely, and then I met Kent. He is the cousin of a good friend of mine, and a bunch of us started spending time together on the weekends. I liked Kent from the moment I met him, but never considered dating him because he wasn't 'my type.' We became really good friends, talking for hours on the phone at night, sharing things with one another we'd never told anyone else. It got to the point where we called each other several times a day and spent most of our free evenings together.

"Suddenly one night while we were driving back from seeing a movie, Kent leaned over and kissed me on the lips. At first I was shocked and thought, 'You shouldn't be kissing him—he's your friend!' But then I started getting into the kiss and realized that I liked it. Kent looked at me and confessed that he'd been wanting to kiss me for months and that he thought he was falling in love with me."

"How did you feel about that?" I asked Alexia.

"Totally confused. Excited, frightened, all mixed up. Kent was supposed to be just a friend, not a lover. He's not the kind of guy that I picture myself with."

"And what kind of guy is that?"

Alexia looked a little embarrassed as she replied sarcastically, "Oh, you know, the kind that sweeps me off my feet and then knocks me down again."

"Alexia," I answered, "your relationship with Kent sounds *healthy*. I don't think you've ever known what healthy love is supposed to feel like."

Alexia believed so strongly in the Love Myth of love-at-first-sight that she was invalidating her growing feelings for Kent. She couldn't imagine that love could be real if it didn't hit her over the head in the first five minutes of the relationship. **Like many "love-at-first-**

sight junkies," Alexia was addicted to the instant high of infatuation and therefore couldn't even recognize the real love that had developed in her relationship. She almost sabotaged the first healthy romance in her life.

Being a "love-at-first-sight junkie" is one of the most deadly ways in which we lower our "Love IQ."

"LOVE-AT-FIRST-SIGHT JUNKIES" OFTEN LOOK FOR ALL THE WRONG QUALITIES IN A MATE AND OVERLOOK THE RIGHT QUALITIES.

WHAT IS LOVE AT FIRST SIGHT?

Just what is it that you feel when you meet someone and have that instant feeling of falling in love? If it isn't love at first sight, what is it?

▶ **Lust-At-First-Sight:** You experience raw, sexual chemistry between you and another person, and assign more emotion to the bond than there actually is. *You can't stop thinking about the person,* **not** *because you are in love with them, but because you are turned on by them.* Intense physical attraction, especially with someone who fits your mental picture of the "perfect" partner, can easily be mistaken for love, especially if you are looking for an instant high. But the high of lust-at-first-sight is often followed by the low of the disappointment you feel when the relationship doesn't turn out the way you hoped it would. (See Chapter Four for more about "Lust Blindness.")

▶ **Infatuation with their image: Sometimes when you think you are falling in love with someone, you are actually 'in love' with their image:** how they look; their profession; how much money they have; the car they drive; the things they've done in their life. You build a fantasy relationship in your head, telling yourself, "My boyfriend is a doctor," or "I'm dating a woman with the perfect body," and thus you ignore the real person.

In spite of these dangers, is it possible to feel at the moment you meet someone that this is the perfect partner for you, and to be correct? What about those couples married for thirty years who say they knew they were right for one another on their first date? Wasn't that love at first sight? I like to think that they experienced a powerful attraction and emotional connection that grew into a strong and successful relationship. *They recognized something special in one another at "first sight," but the true love developed over time.*

Here's the reality about Love Myth #2:

IT TAKES JUST A MOMENT TO EXPERIENCE INFATUA-TION, BUT TRUE LOVE TAKES TIME.

Imagine sitting in a cabin on a cold, snowy night. You decide to build a fire to keep yourself warm. You have a choice of using newspapers for the fire, or logs. If you know anything about fire, you know the answer to this puzzle—the newspaper would create a big blaze quickly but would die out just as quickly. The logs would take longer to catch, but would burn slowly and steadily for a very long time.

I've seen so many people, including myself, make the mistake of looking for that instant blaze at the beginning of a relationship rather than looking for a partner with whom they can build a solid and lasting relationship. I'm not saying you can't have both, just as you can use newspaper and logs to build a strong fire. But if you have found yourself choosing inappropriate partners over and over again, perhaps you'd be better off looking for Mr. (or Ms.) Log instead of Ms. or Mr. Flammable!

HOW I ALMOST MISSED OUT ON THE BEST RELATIONSHIP OF MY LIFE

In case you haven't guessed by now, I was a "love-at-first-sight-junkie" myself. The more infatuated I felt with someone, the more credibility I gave my feelings about him and my new relationship. I'll share more about my own mistakes in the following chapters of this book, but first let me tell you about how my search for instant chemistry came close to ruining my chances for true romantic happiness.

About four years ago I was in the process of ending an extremely painful relationship with a man I had loved for a long time. I was fortunate enough to have two best friends, both male, named Kevin and Jeffrey. I originally met Kevin and Jeffrey through my seminar work, and they eventually became facilitators in my organization. Through their support I found the courage to admit to myself that I wasn't getting what I wanted in my relationship, and to face the fact that I needed to leave.

During the many months over which I came to terms with my decision, Jeffrey and I became very close. We talked every day on the phone. We worked on many projects together. We joked around that we were really like brother and sister, since we look alike. I knew women really found Jeffrey attractive, although I told myself he wasn't my "type," and he would often kid me and say if he could find a woman like me, he'd take her. I found myself making excuses to see or talk to him, but I told myself it was just because I was going through such a hard time. I noticed we were finding more reasons to hug or touch one another, but I convinced myself it was because we felt so safe together.

One evening as Kevin, Jeffrey, and I were in a meeting discussing some seminar business, Kevin looked at us and said, "What's going on with the two of you?"

"What do you mean? Nothing's going on," I responded quickly.

"Well, it's just that when you are together, you look like you are in love," he answered.

"Don't be silly," said Jeffrey. "We are just great friends. You can't actually believe that we would be any more than that, can you?"

"All I know is that when I'm around you, it sure feels like more than friends," Kevin said with a smile. "Look, I'm going to leave the room now, so you can both talk about it." And with that, Kevin walked out.

Jeffrey and I sat across from each other on the couch in silence. For a moment we looked into each other's eyes, and then we both started to cry, for Kevin had put something into words that we had both avoided talking about, or even admitting to ourselves: We were indeed falling in love.

Jeffrey reached out and took my hands. "I can't believe this is happening," he said. "We are supposed to be just friends."

"Maybe it is just something temporary," I answered in a frightened voice. "Maybe we just think we feel this way, but it will pass."

And in that moment, I truly wanted to believe that my feelings for Jeffrey would fade, because I couldn't totally accept the fact that I loved *him*. Dozens of questions forced their way into my mind all at once: If I loved him, why hadn't I known about it until tonight? How could I feel so close to someone I hadn't been attracted to initially? Since it hadn't been love at first sight, did that mean the relationship would be passionless?

Like many "Love-At-First-Sight junkies," I didn't trust my feelings for someone unless they hit me over the head. *I looked for all the wrong signals to determine whether I was "in love"—drama,*

intensity, fear of loss or abandonment, extreme highs and lows—
all signs of an unhealthy relationship. For the first time in my life I
had developed an emotional connection with a man based on
friendship, trust, openness, safety, consistency, and true caring, and
I hadn't even recognized it because

it felt too peaceful to be love.

For several months I struggled with my emotions: One day I'd
want to go ahead with the relationship, and the next day I'd decide
that I was kidding myself and should break it off. There were many
moments in which I questioned whether my feelings for Jeffrey were
strong enough, all because the relationship had crept up on me
rather than arriving all at once. I put poor Jeffrey through hell with
my lack of certainty and came close to losing him for good. It took
me almost a year to let go of my Love Myth about the way we should
have met and the way I should have felt, and to finally appreciate the
depth and the joy of how I did feel. That was four years ago, and
looking back, I thank God that Jeffrey was so patient and that I didn't
throw away the best thing that ever happened to me. Instead I threw
away the Love Myth that had gotten me into one dysfunctional
relationship after another.

A first impression of someone is not enough to determine
whether he or she will be a healthy and loving partner. You need a
second, third, fourth, and fifth impression. You need time to discover
someone's character, not just their exterior.

Remember: Falling in love is the easy part, but building a
healthy relationship takes hard work.

LOVE MYTH

▼   ▼   ▼   ▼   **3**   ▼   ▼   ▼   ▼

There Is Only One True Love in the World
Who Is Right for You

There comes a time in every relationship when we ask ourselves
this question:

"Is he the one for me?"
or
"Is she the one for me?"

Part of the problem we have answering this question is the phrase "the one." It assumes that *for each person in the world, there is one and only one right partner, and we need to find that person or we will never be happy*. No imposters will do, no imitations. We must make sure we have fallen in love with our real soulmate.

So when we are single, we walk through life suspiciously scrutinizing each potential partner, cataloging every flaw as evidence that this is *not* "the one." **The one** would be a better dancer; **the one** wouldn't have two children from a previous marriage; **the one** would be making more money; **the one** wouldn't be ten pounds overweight. But in our attempt to avoid making a mistake and missing out on our one true love, we often deprive ourselves of experiencing truly wonderful relationships.

And when we are in a relationship, especially during rough times, we secretly ask ourselves, "I wonder if _____ is really my perfect mate? I wonder if there is someone else out there somewhere who I would be happier with?"

Here are the consequences of believing Love Myth #3:

1. You compare your partner to your fantasy picture of "the one" and miss out on appreciating their uniqueness.

Tammy was a very attractive, outgoing thirty-four-year-old flight attendant who came to one of my seminars in hopes of figuring out why she couldn't develop a serious relationship with a man. "I don't know what's wrong with me," she began, "but all of my friends are either married or engaged or at least in love, and I can't seem to find anyone who's right for me."

"Do you date a lot?" I asked.

"That's just it—I meet guys all the time who are interested in me, and at first I feel really enthusiastic about them. But within a month or two I get turned off and stop seeing them. Last year I thought I'd finally found someone I could really spend my life with. We went together for eight months. And for the first four or five, everything was perfect. But then little things about him started to bother me, and for the last few months of our relationship we fought all the time until I finally broke it off."

As I talked more with Tammy, I discovered that she thought a relationship was working only when things were "perfect," and to her "perfect" meant no conflict, no differences, and most important, nothing about her partner she didn't like. Tammy had grown up believing in Love Myth #3, that somewhere out there in the world, this "perfect" man was waiting for her, and that he and only he would make her happy. So at the first sign of challenge in her relationships, she bailed out, unconsciously comparing her boy-friends with Mr. Perfect. Naturally, they all flunked the test. And in the process she never had an opportunity to truly appreciate the individual she was with and to fall in love with him.

I worked with Tammy to help her understand the origin of her fantasy picture of men and how it prevented her from having any real relationships. Three months later she wrote me a letter to let me know she was dating her old boyfriend again. "I can't believe how different it feels," she marveled. "He is the same person, but I've stopped expecting him to be perfect, and it's making it so much easier to love him as he is."

2. It prevents you from being open to a new relationship after one has ended.

The second problem with believing Love Myth #3 is that it can inhibit you from starting over again after the relationship you hoped would last a lifetime ends through breakup, divorce, or death. If you really believe in one true love, and you lose that person, you are left facing the rest of your life with a lonely heart, sure that no one could replace your mate.

Several years ago, I met a woman through a mutual friend I'll call Doris. Doris was sixty-one years old at the time and had been widowed for two years after almost forty years of marriage. Her husband had fought a long battle with cancer, and Doris had spent the past few years adjusting to life without him. Now, her family and friends were encouraging her to date again, but she was resistant and reluctant.

"I had the love of my life," she explained to me over lunch. "We had many wonderful years together. Why should I run around trying to find someone who doesn't exist to replace my husband? You only get one true love like that in a lifetime."

I explained to Doris that a new partner would never replace her deceased husband but would offer her an opportunity to experience a totally different relationship. "I don't know," Doris said hesitantly. "I think I'm too old for that kind of thing."

Six months passed, and I received a phone call from Doris. "I think I need some help!" she begged. Doris had met a sixty-four-year-old gentleman named Saul through a charity she was involved with. Saul had been divorced for fifteen years but had never found a partner he wanted to share the rest of his life with, until Doris. "He's crazy about me!" Doris explained. "And the scary part is, I think I'm crazy about him, too. We've been seeing each other for four months. At first I thought of him as an escort or companion to social engagements, but lately I can't stand to be without him. Now he's talking about marriage, and when he brings up the subject, I feel like I can't breathe. I keep thinking about how different this relationship is from my marriage, and feeling like I already have a husband, so what am I doing with him?"

"You're loving him," I answered with a smile, "not in the same exact way you loved your husband, but in a new and different way. That's what is so wonderful about love—you can experience it in so many different expressions."

"You mean it is okay for me to love him?" Doris asked sheepishly.

"It's okay, Doris," I reassured her.

Two months later, Doris and Saul were married. They are gloriously happy together, and from time to time Doris calls to tell me how she is doing. "I can't get over this relationship!" she always says. "I loved my first husband so much, but I love Saul just as much, only in different ways. Who would have thought a grandmother would get a second chance!"

Doris almost missed out on a wonderful life with Saul by believing in Love Myth #3, that there is only one true love.

THERE ARE MANY RIGHT PARTNERS FOR YOU

The love reality for Love Myth #3 is:

▼

IT IS POSSIBLE TO EXPERIENCE TRUE LOVE WITH MORE THAN ONE PERSON—THERE ARE MANY POTENTIAL PARTNERS YOU COULD BE HAPPY WITH.

▲

I can't tell you that there are X number of potential partners for each of us roaming around the earth, but I do know that the possibilities of your experiencing happiness in love are not limited to one person. I know from my own experience that the human heart has a tremendous capacity for loving, and that we limit the amount of love we allow ourselves to enjoy because of the Love Myths we believe. I believe that if you selected just about any two people in the world and stranded them alone on a deserted island for the rest of their lives, they would probably become romantic partners. While this may not be your romantic fantasy, it illustrates the point that the act of loving itself is inherently so enjoyable, that if given the opportunity we find ways to love people we thought we couldn't.

Each true love we have stretches our heart in a different direction, and each relationship serves us in a different way. Does this mean that it really doesn't matter who you are with? Of course not—in fact, it makes the issue of compatibility even more important. *Finding a partner with whom you are compatible, as well as one you love, is the formula for a healthy, lasting relationship.*

LOVE MYTH

▾ ▾ ▾ ▾ 4 ▾ ▾ ▾ ▾

The Perfect Partner Will Fulfill You Completely in Every Way

Imagine sitting in a job interview for a position you are interested in.

"Could you tell me about this job?" you ask the person who would be hiring you to work for him.

"Basically, I expect you to fulfill my every need. I expect you to know what I want, even when I don't tell you what I want. I want you to read my mind and know all of my secret expectations and deliver them. I want you to have the answers for me when I am confused, cheer me up when I am down, and make me love myself more when I don't feel confident. You will, of course, entertain me constantly so I never get bored, and enjoy all of my hobbies and interests so you can be the perfect companion."

I'm sure you agree that these expectations are outlandish and that no amount of money could tempt you to put yourself in such a highly pressured and impossible situation. And although this story is slightly exaggerated, the truth is **that many of us walk into relationships unconsciously expecting our partner to fulfill our every need, and when they do not, we become resentful and disillusioned.** I call this "setting someone up," especially because you may be unconscious of what some of those needs are and therefore can't articulate them to the person you love.

Here are the negative consequences of believing in Love Myth #4:

1. You fail to recognize a good relationship because your partner isn't fulfilling the needs you should be filling yourself.

"I think I should divorce my husband," Andrea proclaimed as we sat in my office. She had made an appointment with me to discuss her relationship, which was in major crisis. Andrea was twenty-seven, cute, and very athletic-looking. She had been married to Benjamin for almost two years.

"What's the problem?" I asked.

"I don't know," Andrea answered. "I'm just not happy. I thought marriage would be better than this, would change things for me, but it hasn't seemed to make any difference, and I'm disappointed."

"What did you think marriage would change?"

"I guess I wanted to feel more confidence, more clear about my life and where it is going; instead, I just feel confused."

"Let's talk about the rest of your life. What do you do?" I inquired.

"Well, not anything right now. I had a job six months ago, but I quit because I didn't like it. I don't really know what I want to do. I keep thinking that if I get out of this marriage, I'll feel better."

"Is there a particular complaint you have about Benjamin?"

Andrea thought for a minute and then replied: "No, not exactly. He's really loving and sweet to me. He just doesn't make me happy."

After talking to Andrea for a while, it was obvious to me that the problem in her relationship wasn't her husband, but herself. Andrea had no direction, no goals in her life. She married Benjamin hoping he would fill that empty place inside her, the place where she harbors her low self-esteem. But that was Andrea's job, not Benjamin's. And instead of pursuing a career or getting an education,

Andrea spent her days going to the gym and working out, or watching television.

Andrea was a self-indulgent woman who had never really grown up. But no matter how much Benjamin loved Andrea, he couldn't fill that void inside her. Because she felt empty, she assumed the marriage was not fulfilling her. The truth was, Benjamin was a good husband to Andrea, but Andrea wasn't very good to Andrea. *Her dissatisfaction wasn't with her marriage—it was with herself.*

The fantasy that your true love will "make everything okay" is a deadly one. It can cause you to end a perfectly good relationship because you expect your partner to do for you what you should be doing for yourself.

IF YOU FEEL EMOTIONALLY EMPTY BEFORE YOU START A RELATIONSHIP, YOU WILL FEEL JUST AS EMPTY ONCE YOU ARE IN A RELATIONSHIP.

---

2. You resent your partner for not giving you what you should be finding elsewhere.

Another pitfall of believing that your perfect partner will fulfill all your needs is the pressure you put on him or her to be everything to you. How many times have I heard women complain that they wish their husbands would go shopping with them, or spend a Saturday browsing for antiques, or cared more about how they redecorated the house! It took me years to figure out that there are needs we have as women that men just can't and shouldn't have to fulfill—not basic needs like those for love, affection, friendship, etc., but needs women have to enjoy themselves. Face it, ladies: Most husbands are never going to enjoy coordinating the decorations for your child's birthday party, sorting through fabric samples for the new couch, or spending hours roaming the mall for sales as much as most women do. These are needs better fulfilled by other women.

Men seem to have lower expectations in these areas than women, but men, too, experience their share of disappointment that we aren't fulfilling them in every way. Jeffrey went through this stage a few years into our relationship and began to doubt whether I was right for him. Naturally I was scared to death, but as we talked about it, his concerns focused on one area: sports. He is very athletically talented and loves sports of all kinds. Although I enjoy them, I tend to make other things a priority in my life. The more we discussed this issue, the more Jeffrey realized that his Love Myth told him that the "right woman" would want to go out and throw a baseball around with him, play racquetball every weekend, and do some serious bodybuilding. Jeffrey was depriving himself of doing these things himself because he wanted me to do them, too. "I guess I've been resenting you for depriving me of enjoying my interests," he confessed. We agreed that I would make an effort to share more athletic activities with him but that he would fulfill *himself* by joining a softball team, making workout dates with friends, and taking the time he needed to do what he enjoyed.

Here's the truth about Love Myth #4:

▼

THE RIGHT PARTNER WILL FULFILL MANY OF YOUR NEEDS BUT NOT ALL OF THEM.

▲

We each have our "wish list" of what we want in a perfect partner, but here is the point: There are some needs only your partner should fulfill. But there are others that your family, friends, and acquaintances can fulfill for you.

IT'S IMPORTANT TO DISTINGUISH BETWEEN WHAT YOU WOULD *LIKE* IN A PARTNER AND WHAT YOU REALLY *NEED* IN A PARTNER.

If Jeffrey hadn't challenged Love Myth #4, he might have ended our relationship and gone in search of Miss Junior Athlete of 1992, leaving behind the deep and powerful connection we have.

LOVE MYTH

▼   ▼   ▼   ▼   **5**   ▼   ▼   ▼   ▼

When You Experience Powerful Sexual Chemistry with Someone, It Must Be Love

Have you ever convinced yourself that you really loved someone as an excuse to continue having sex with them?

Have you ever been in a relationship where the only time you got along really well was in bed?

Have you ever pursued someone, telling yourself that you were madly in love, and after consummating the relationship sexually, realized it wasn't love, but lust?

Boy, does this Love Myth get us in trouble! It has its basis in the inherent guilt many of us in our culture feel about acknowledging and enjoying our sexuality. *Since society, our upbringing, and our morality often don't give us "permission" to be sexual for its own sake, we imagine that we have romantic feelings for partners we simply have the hots for!*

I call this the "Lust into Love Formula." Here's how it works:

THE LUST INTO LOVE FORMULA

1. First, you feel powerful sexual chemistry with someone or, in raw terms, *lust*.
2. Next, you act on those urges and have sex with that person.
3. Then you experience some guilt or discomfort having been so sexually intimate with someone you aren't that emotionally connected with.
4. Finally you create a relationship with that person to legitimize your lust.

Obviously I'm *not* saying that every time you form a relationship with someone you are following the Lust into Love Formula. However, if you are a strong believer in Love Myth #5, you may find yourself in this situation more often than you'd like to admit.

Here are the negative consequences of believing in Love Myth #5:

1. You get involved with people you are not compatible with.

Ann is a twenty-six-year-old buyer for a clothing store. Here is her story about how Love Myth #5 got her in real emotional trouble:

"Brian and I met while we were both skiing in Colorado. I guess being away from home combined with the cold and how cute he looked on skis took precedence over my better judgment, and I slept with him on our second date. Maybe it was the altitude, but I'd never had such exciting sex in my life. Brian prided himself on being a great lover, and he was. I was sure I had fallen head over heels.

"Our vacation ended—he went back to Seattle, I returned to San Francisco. We talked on the phone every few days, and I told him how I felt about him. For six months we spent every other weekend together, and, you guessed it, most of the time we were in bed. *The physical passion between us was spectacular, and so I assumed I must love him very much to feel that way.* We even began talking about marriage.

"That summer, we both decided to take two weeks off from our jobs and spend it together at my house. I could hardly wait for Brian to arrive. The first few days were wonderful, as usual. But then things began to fall apart. We started arguing about everything. First it was Brian's smoking—I'd known he smoked, but we were in bed so much that it wasn't that frequent. Now that we had more time together, he seemed to be smoking constantly. And I'd never realized how negative he was. He found something bad to say about my friends, the way I'd decorated my house, even the way I drive. Things got progressively worse until we weren't having sex at all, and I could hardly wait for him to leave.

"The night he went back to Seattle, I lay in bed crying my heart out. I was so confused, and I felt like my dreams were shattered before my eyes. I spent the next few days really thinking about my relationship with Brian, and suddenly everything became clear: *I'd never had a relationship with Brian. All we ever did was make love.* Our meeting was a romantic fling, and the six months afterward were filled either with phone calls that consisted of a lot of flirting and joking, or short visits during which we were in bed the whole time. I'd never seen Brian as a person, just a sexual partner. Once I did, I didn't even *like* him very much!"

Ann had never had really good sex with any of her previous boyfriends. So when she met Brian and the sparks flew, she assumed it must be love. It was also hard for her to admit that she could be that sexually turned on with someone she didn't love or wouldn't marry. She learned the hard way that passion doesn't always come from love. All she and Brian had in common was that they loved to ski and loved sex—enough for a fling, but not enough to make a long-term relationship work.

2. You stay in relationships longer than you should, and have a hard time letting go of partners who are not right for you.

Jamal approached me after a seminar in which I talked about

Love Myths. "You were describing me!" he exclaimed. Jamal is thirty-eight, divorced, and a teacher. Here is his story:

"I got married when I was really young to my high-school girlfriend. I was pretty inexperienced sexually, and she had never been with anyone but me, so it took me a while to realize that we were sexually incompatible. As the years passed, I lost all attraction to her, though I loved her very much. We had three children, and I tried to make it work for them, but finally when I was thirty-one I left and we got a divorce.

"I was on the dating scene for the first time since I was nineteen years old, and I was ready to roll. I promised myself that I'd never end up in some sexless relationship again, and I have to admit I was pretty wild for those first few years. I was so afraid I'd fall in love with someone I wasn't attracted to that I would only date women I felt totally and immediately turned on by.

"That's how I met Sabrina. We were at a jazz coffeehouse, and she was sitting at the bar. The first thing I noticed about her was her body—she looked like my fantasy woman. We started talking, then dancing, and I could hardly keep it together until we went back to her place and got it on. Man, I thought I had died and gone to heaven. She was like a wild pony. It felt the way I always thought it should be with a woman.

"I had promised myself that I wouldn't get involved again until I was completely sure of the relationship, but my resolve was shot to pieces. Sabrina would purr and wrap herself around me until she got her way. I ended up moving into her place within a month, and that's when the trouble began. I found out Sabrina had no money—she'd been supported by an ex-boyfriend, and she had a stack of unpaid bills. I was under her spell, so I agreed to help her out until she got back on her feet.

ESCAPING THE PRISON OF SEXUAL PARADISE

Jamal continued: "Six months passed, and our relationship was like a roller coaster—one minute we'd be fighting and the next we'd be having wild sex. Sabrina was like a spoiled, irresponsible child. She never even looked for a job, and was draining me of all of my energy. I knew I had to get out, but each time I told her I was leaving, she would seduce me and I'd end up staying.

"Finally, one day when Sabrina came home with a thousand dollars' worth of new clothes, I couldn't take it anymore, and I left. I felt free for the first time in months. Unfortunately, that feeling didn't last. Sabrina would call me at my new place and show up dressed in what I call a 'screw me' outfit, and I'd lose my willpower. We'd see each other a few days, then I'd break it off again for a month or two. Then one night she'd call me, tell me she was lonely, and I'd find myself back in bed with her again. I was disgusted with myself.

"I hate to admit this, but I was so hooked into the great sex it took me two years to finally let go of Sabrina."

Jamal's story is dramatic but not that uncommon. He was sure that if sex with Sabrina was that good, she was the right woman for him. It took several years of drama and humiliation to teach Jamal that good sex didn't necessarily mean healthy love.

Here's the reality about Love Myth #5:

GOOD SEX HAS NOTHING TO DO WITH TRUE LOVE, BUT MAKING LOVE DOES.

If you have fantastic sex with a partner:

▶ it does not necessarily mean you love them
▶ it does not necessarily mean you are meant to be together
▶ it does not necessarily mean you have a good relationship

It does mean:

▶ you have good sexual chemistry
▶ one or both of you are skilled lovers

It might mean:

▶ you have a strong attraction that can be the basis for a healthy, whole relationship *if you are compatible in other areas outside the bedroom*

THE TRUTH ABOUT LOVE

You have probably been able to relate to one or all of these five Love Myths. Isn't it amazing to realize how they've contributed to some of the mistakes you've made in love?

Here are the five Love Myths again, and the five love realities we came up with:

LOVE MYTH	LOVE REALITY
1 True love conquers all.	Love is not enough to make a relationship work—it needs compatibility and commitment.
2 When it's really true love, you will know it the moment you meet the other person.	It takes just a moment to experience infatuation, but true love takes time.
3 There is only one true love in the world who is right for you.	It is possible to experience true love with more than one person—there are many potential partners you could be happy with.
4 The perfect partner will fulfill you completely in every way.	The right partner will fulfill many of your needs but not all of them.
5 When you experience powerful sexual chemistry with someone, it must be love.	Good sex has nothing to do with true love, but making love does.

CREATING THE LOVE YOU DESERVE

I recently gave a public lecture to a large group of people, and as I was autographing books at the end of the evening, a young woman approached me with tears in her eyes. "I am so inspired by everything you said," she began. "I attended the seminar you and your boyfriend gave last month as well, and I just hope one day I am lucky enough to have a relationship as good as yours."

There was a line of about fifty people waiting to speak with me, and normally I would have thanked this woman and gone on to talk to the next person. But something made me stop and take her hands. "I want you to know something," I said, looking into her eyes. "I do feel very blessed to have such a wonderful man in my life. **But luck had nothing to do with it.** I've made so many unhealthy love choices in my past. I've found men and tried to change them into who I wanted them to be. I've had partners I was totally incompatible with, and told myself it didn't matter. I've loved men for all the wrong reasons. **It's not luck that is making this relationship work—I finally chose the right person,** and together we've worked very hard to create the kind of closeness and harmony we have. And you can have the same thing in your life!"

Perhaps you, too, have felt unlucky in love, and have lost the hope of having the kind of relationship you dream of. Or perhaps you do have someone special in your life but want to feel closer and more loving and aren't quite sure how. I'm happy that you've found this book and have chosen to read it. I know it will help you find the power and wisdom that wait within you to guide your heart toward love that is healthy, joyous, and real.

2

▼▼▼

WHY WE CHOOSE
THE PEOPLE WE LOVE

▼▼▼

► Have you ever wanted a responsible, mature partner, only to end up with an irresponsible, unreliable person who drove you crazy?

► Have you ever told yourself you were ready for a long-term, committed relationship, and were looking for someone who felt the same way, only to end up falling in love with someone who was unavailable or incapable of making a commitment?

► Have you ever vowed never again to get involved with someone who was emotionally shut down and distant, only to find yourself hopelessly infatuated with someone who couldn't love you back the way you deserved to be loved?

► Have you ever wondered why you've ended up with the partners you've had?

We all think we know what we want in a mate. We don't want any unhealthy or negative qualities, just lots of great ones. So we get frustrated and disappointed when we end up in a relationship with someone different from, and usually much less wonderful than, our ideal.

I'm sure you've read the "Personals" in magazines and newspapers, those columns of ads where single people advertise for the kind of mate they would like to meet. If you had to write an Emotional Want Ad describing the kind of partner you were looking for, it would probably sound something like this:

WANTED:

Attractive, sensitive, caring person for permanent relationship. Must be emotionally open, able to talk about feelings, unafraid of intimacy. Successful but not a workaholic, with a great sense of humor. Knows how to make me feel really loved and appreciated. If you are healthy, honest, faithful, and ready for a commitment, I'm the one for you!

The truth is, if you had to match your Emotional Want Ads to the partners you have actually ended up with, they might read more like these:

WANTED:

Self-absorbed, damaged *loser* who has lots of potential and is doing nothing with it. Must be immature, irresponsible, and lazy. Low sex drive a bonus. No skills, background, or success required. If you are looking for someone to make empty promises to and like to blame others for your failures, call me now. Note: Men with jobs need *not* apply.

WANTED:

Are you married? Engaged? Unable to make a commitment? Then I'm the woman for you. I'm looking for an unavailable man for a long, painful, and frustrating relationship. No time or energy required. I'll do all the work. Call anytime, day or night; I'll be waiting. If you like being dishonest, stringing me along, and thinking only about yourself, you're my type of guy.

Obviously none of us would ever write ads like these last two or even agree to accept these kinds of relationships into our lives. And yet, we often end up with partners who fit these descriptions.

This chapter is designed to help you understand why you have chosen the partners you've been with, or the one you are with now.

CHARTING YOUR LOVE CHOICES

The following exercise will give you an overview of the relationships you have been in. I've taught this process for years in my seminars, and it is always an eye-opener for each person who does it. **NOTE: This is one of the most important exercises you will learn in this book. Please read the instructions carefully, and take all the time you need to complete each portion.**

Here's how it works:

STEP 1 On a blank piece of paper, list the names of each partner you have had a significant relationship with, including the one you are with now. *Don't* include someone you dated only a few times. *Do* include anyone to whom you were very emotionally attached. Leave space after each name so you have room to write. If you have had only one partner in your life, just put down that name.

STEP 2 After each person's name, make a list of their *most negative qualities*, those parts of their personality you dislike the most. Don't write a whole sentence—rather, sum up the quality in a word or two. *Example: Marcy's boyfriend could never keep a job during their four years together. So Marcy should write "jobless" on her list.* **Do *not*** list positive qualities.

STEP 3 Once you have finished, read over all of your lists and circle any words or qualities that seem to repeat themselves from one person to another.

STEP 4 Make a *"summary list"* of those words or qualities you used more than once or that stood out to you.

STEP 5 Take some time to think about your summary list and your individual lists. Ask yourself the following questions:
- ► Are there some patterns in my relationships of which I need to be aware?
- ► Is there a trend I can see in my relationships over time? Getting healthier? Getting worse? Getting better and then a relapse?
- ► Were some partners easier to list negative qualities about than others?
- ► Is my present partner significantly different from previous partners? Better? Worse? The same?

Example #1. Ann's Love Choices Chart

EDDIE
- Dishonest
- Manipulative
- Space case (lives in dream world)
- Impractical
- Controlling
- Self-absorbed
- Explosive temper
- Sexually dysfunctional
- Moody
- Uses me for money
- Can't keep a job

DAVID
- Low sex drive
- Moody
- Deceptive
- Explosive temper
- Stubborn
- Can't talk about feelings
- Unfaithful
- Impractical
- Self-absorbed

JERRY
- Space case
- Moody
- Self-absorbed
- Unromantic
- Explosive temper
- Impractical
- Professionally passive

SEAN (ex-husband)
- Angry
- Unfaithful
- Critical
- Moody
- Jobless
- Deceptive
- Controlling
- Low sex drive
- Emotionally distant
- Self-absorbed
- Rebellious
- Hates talking about feelings
- Uses me for money

ADAM (husband)
- Not romantic enough
- Low sex drive
- Hard time talking about feelings
- Temper
- Rebellious
- Serious

Ann, thirty-nine, has listed five important men in her life. She is married to one now (Adam), another previously (Sean), and the other three men were long-time partners. When Ann looked over her list, several things were obvious:

1. Her list of negative qualities about Sean was the *longest*, accu-

rately reflecting that this had been the most painful relationship in her life.

2. Her list about her present husband, Adam, was the *shortest*, accurately reflecting that this is the healthiest and most satisfying relationship in her life.

3. There was an enormous contrast between her relationship with Sean and her present husband, Adam, indicating some real growth on her part.

In Step 3 of the exercise, Ann circled similar qualities that seemed to repeat themselves on the lists and then made a summary list.

STEP 4: ANN'S SUMMARY LIST OF SIMILAR OR COMMON QUALITIES

Angry
Dishonest
Moody
Irresponsible and unreliable
Sexually dysfunctional
Self-absorbed
Jobless
Hates talking about feelings
Controlling

"This is embarrassing," Ann complained as she read her summary list. "I never realized these men had these traits in common. I always told myself how 'different' each new one was from the last. I guess they looked different on the outside, but they were very similar. At least I've improved over the years, and married a loving, reliable man."

Ann's Love Choices Chart helped her understand exactly why her relationships didn't work. Once it was on paper, it was easy for her to see what kind of men she had been attracting and why she had been so unhappy.

Example #2. Mitchell's Love Choices Chart

Mitchell is a thirty-six-year-old attorney who wanted to figure out why he couldn't find the right woman to marry. "I'm looking for a powerful, independent woman who won't smother me in a relationship," he explained, "But somehow I end up with the opposite."

<u>VALERIE</u>
Emotionally unstable
Insecure
Drama queen
Clinging
Irrational
Obsessive (looks)
Victim
Whiny
Manipulative
Childish
Helpless
Sexually damaged

<u>LINDA</u>
Manipulative
Drama queen
Temper
Controlling
Always tense
Whiny
Emotionally unavailable
Sexually repressed
Frightened
Too attached to parents

<u>SHERYL</u>
Domineering
Critical
Selfish
Addicted/food
Drama queen
Complainer
Negative
Nervous
High-strung
Closed-minded
Victim
Draining

STEP 4: MITCHELL'S SUMMARY LIST OF SIMILAR OR COMMON QUALITIES
Drama queen
Controlling
Obsessive
Victim
Emotionally unstable
Immature
Sexually damaged

When Mitchell looked at his summary list, he was amazed. "I found these women so compelling," he admitted, "but for all the wrong reasons. I'm obviously attracting weak, little-girl types with a victim mentality and a real addiction to drama. You can imagine how turbulent these relationships are. The women fall apart and go from one crisis to the next, and I try to rescue them and fix everything."

Mitchell learned several things from his Love Choices Chart:

▶ He not only attracts women who are addicted to drama, but he himself is obviously addicted to drama, since he puts up with this kind of behavior.
▶ He gets to feel superior to his partners by choosing women who are a mess, and helping them get their lives together.
▶ Even though he says he wants a strong, independent woman, he finds women who are dependent and not self-sufficient, and once again he gets to feel needed and important.

CREATING YOUR EMOTIONAL WANT AD

Now that you've made your Love Choices Chart and worked on your summary list, it's time for you to face the truth about the kinds of partners you've chosen in your life.

▼

TO FIND OUT WHAT KIND OF PERSON YOU'VE BEEN SEEKING, LOOK AT THE KIND OF PARTNERS YOU'VE ENDED UP WITH.

▲

▶ **You don't end up with your mates by accident.**
▶ **You don't attract someone because you have bad luck.**
▶ **You don't find the same type of person over and over again by coincidence.**

You get what you ask for!

I believe that we get back what we put out, that our unconscious mind has certain "agendas" or needs, and based on these needs, we choose particular partners in our lives. Ann could insist to herself and her friends that she truly wanted a loving, open, stable, responsible man, but in truth, and as shown by her summary list, she attracted men who were angry, unreliable, self-absorbed, jobless, and sexually dysfunctional. Mitchell claimed he longed to find a strong, independent woman, and yet he continually attracted immature, overly dramatic women who needed rescuing.

One of the most effective ways to sum up the kind of person you've been unknowingly seeking, whether in your past or today, is to create your own Emotional Want Ad. You've actually already found the ingredients for your want ad in your Love Choices summary list.

Here's what to do:

Write a want ad using the characteristics you have on your summary list. Make the ad as direct and as humorous as you can. It's okay to make fun of yourself and your past choices. *In fact, the more dramatic and outrageous your ad is, the more it can help you to break free from the negative emotional patterns that have been hurting your love life.*

Here is Ann's Love Choices summary list once more:

Angry
Dishonest
Moody
Irresponsible and unreliable
Sexually dysfunctional
Self-absorbed
Jobless
Hates talking about feelings
Controlling

Now here is how Ann's Emotional Want Ad might sound:

WANTED:

Angry, unemployed control freak for long, demeaning relationship. **Must be moody, manipulative, and an expert at making me tiptoe around in fear, because that's what I like. The more you keep me guessing, the happier I'll be. Men with ambition or a clean credit record need not apply. If you are looking for someone to love you no matter how unavailable and obnoxious you become, then I'm the girl for you. Chronic lateness and lying are real pluses. Don't worry if you can't get it up—I'll pretend you're normal and won't ever complain. Call whenever *you* want to—after all, you're the boss.**

Here is Mitchell's Love Choices summary list once more:

Drama queen
Controlling
Obsessive
Victim
Emotionally unstable
Immature
Sexually damaged

Here's how Mitchell's Emotional Want Ad might sound:

WANTED:

Do you hate yourself? Do you hate the world? Do you like to blame everyone else for what's gone wrong in your life? I'm looking for an immature, sexually damaged woman who will whine and complain twenty-four hours a day. Eating disorders, drug addiction, or other obsessions are definite pluses. You must be good at jumping out of moving cars, hanging up on me on the phone, and throwing temper tantrums in expensive restaurants. Hate being touched? Then you are perfect for me! If you call your parents less than once a day, don't bother applying, because I'm not looking for a grown-up. Call me in the middle of the night, or better yet, at work during an important meeting. Don't worry about interrupting— nothing is as important as you and your latest crisis.

Writing your Emotional Want Ad can be very confrontational, because it forces you to look at the message you've been giving out about the kind of partner you are willing to accept. *But it is a powerful way to break your own negative programming by taking what has been unconscious and making it conscious.*

DON'T SKIP THIS EXERCISE, EVEN IF IT IS UNCOMFORTABLE. WORK ON YOUR WANT AD UNTIL IT IS SO STRONG THAT IT MAKES YOU LAUGH.

Here are a couple more samples written by some of the participants at my seminars:

Cynthia was married for thirty-two years before she divorced her husband. She wrote this want ad based on her list formulated from their relationship:

WANTED:

Moody asshole who doesn't know how to talk. Sign language O.K. I'm looking for a man to glue himself to the couch, watch sports day and night, and belch. The more boring you are, the more I like you. No need to shave or shower frequently. I like to be disgusted. Denial a must. Don't ever admit that we have any problems. Erections not necessary.

Carl, thirty-six, keeps attracting women who don't think he is good enough for them. Here is his want ad:

WANTED:

I know you are out there. You: gorgeous, superficial, obsessed with money, cars, and being seen by the right people. Me: not good enough for you. Together we'll be perfect. You'll constantly put me down, and I'll love it. I need a woman who will make me feel inadequate. Humiliation in public a big plus, especially around your friends. If you spend hours getting dressed and putting on makeup and haven't read a book in years, you are just what I am looking for. Please call—I need you to make me feel worthless.

Francine, forty-three, has a history of attracting charming but cruel men. Here is her want ad:

WANTED:

Hey There! Do you like hurting the one you love? Are you interested in a long, drawn-out, painful relationship fraught with multiple breakups and reconciliations? I'm looking for someone to make me miserable. I'm not picky; addictions welcome. Call any time day or night. My good night's sleep is nothing compared to the pure pleasure of hearing from you. Your thoughtless impulse to call after an evening of drinking and whoring will be viewed as the ultimate in attentiveness and a compliment to my desirability as a woman. Hurry. There are many men even more troubled than yourself applying at this very moment.

Over the years I've helped thousands of people understand more about their relationships through making Love Choices Charts and Emotional Want Ads. Remember: **We're not looking at the positive qualities in your partners, but the pattern of negative or undesirable qualities.**

▼

LOCATING THE PERSISTENT, NEGATIVE PATTERNS IN YOUR RELATIONSHIPS IS THE FIRST STEP TOWARD ELIMINATING THOSE PATTERNS.

▲

Understanding Your Emotional Programming

Have you ever wondered:

► why you've stayed in relationships with people you knew weren't good for you?

► why you've attracted the same kind of person over and over again?

► why the very characteristics you dislike in a person are the ones your partner possesses?

As the saying goes, **"If I'm so smart, how did I end up in such a dumb relationshp?"**

The answer lies in understanding why you've chosen the partners you have in your life.

▼

WHEN YOU UNDERSTAND WHY YOU'VE MADE THE LOVE CHOICES YOU HAVE, YOU WILL THEN BE FREE TO MAKE NEW AND BETTER LOVE CHOICES.

▲

The rest of this chapter is dedicated to helping you gain insight into your relationship choices, past and present. As you read, remind yourself of your summary list of negative characteristics and your Emotional Want Ad. This will keep you focused on the particular issues you'd like to know more about.

As I said earlier, it is not by accident, nor by virtue of your bad luck that you've ended up with the partners you have. Rather, it is due to your *emotional programming.* **Your emotional programming is simply a set of decisions and beliefs you made about yourself, others, and the world in general when you were growing up.** Each day that you are alive, you collect experiences, and each experience helps you form decisions about yourself, about people, and about life. In the same way you would program a computer with basic information, so you program your mind with these beliefs. For the rest of your life this "program" affects how you think and behave.

In other words, your **life experiences** cause you to make certain **decisions** about yourself and others. The combination of all of these decisions is your **emotional programming,** which in turn causes you to make certain **love choices** as an adult.

Life Experiences → Decisions →
Emotional Programming → Love Choices

Here's something else to be aware of: The majority of this emotional programming occurs when you are still very young. Psychologists estimate that:

▶ **Between birth and five years of age—you receive 50 percent of your emotional programming.**

▶ **Between five and eight years of age—you receive 30 percent of your emotional programming.**

That means, by the age of eight, you are 80 percent programmed, psychologically.

In other words, 80 percent of your decisions about yourself and others have already been made.

▶ **Between the ages of eight and eighteen—you receive 15 percent more of your emotional programming.**

So by the time you are eighteen years old, you're 95 percent done! That leaves 5 percent left for the rest of your life. This may not seem like much, but it's that 5 percent that I work with when I help people make changes in their lives. And the good news is that you can use that 5 percent to understand and change the other 95 percent.

Perhaps now you can better understand why, even though the 5 percent of your mind that is conscious says, "I want a wonderful partner who loves me and treats me well," the 95 percent of your mind that is *unconscious* is responsible for making your poor love choices.

*Once you understand **why** you've been doing what you've been doing, you will be free to change your behavior permanently.*

▼

YOUR UNCONSCIOUS EMOTIONAL PROGRAMMING IS RESPONSIBLE FOR MUCH OF THE PAIN YOU EXPERIENCE IN YOUR LOVE LIFE.

▲

DISCOVERING YOUR DECISIONS ABOUT LOVE

Your next step is to understand your own emotional programming, as if you were reading a computer manual for your brain. Here's an exercise that will help you:

Exercise: Making Your Emotional Programming Map

STEP 1 Make a list of the most painful realities or experiences you can recall from childhood, up until you left home. Include things such as ongoing situations (a parent's alcoholism, for instance), or particular events (being punished or ridiculed by a parent).

Sample situations

My parents were divorced.

Mom and Dad always fought.

I was always compared to my "perfect" sister.

I was overweight and always teased.

Dad was never home and cheated on Mom.

We had eight kids in the family and not enough time or money to go around.

Mom was a rageaholic and very moody.

Dad never showed affection or praised me.

Mom died of cancer when I was ten.

I had a stepfather who hated me.

We had a strict religious upbringing and lived in constant fear of sin.

Dad molested me.

Sample events

Younger brother was born and I was ignored.

My parents put my dog to sleep without telling me.

Dad promised to come to my birthday party and never showed up.

I saw Dad beat up my brother.

I found Mom drunk and unconscious.

I thought Mom left me behind in a store.

My parents didn't believe me when I told them my brother had molested me.

My father let go of me in the ocean and I almost drowned.

My best friend dropped me and told everyone she hated me when I was eleven.

STEP 2 Think carefully about each item on your list, and ask yourself, "*What descisions did I make about myself, others, or life because of this experience?*" Then write down your decisions next to the appropriate memory. Take your time doing this, and if you get stuck on one, go on to another and come back to the first one later.

Don't be surprised if many of the decisions you made when you were young are similar.

Examples:

SITUATION OR EVENT	DECISION
My parents were divorced.	I'm not lovable enough.
Dad molested me.	I'm bad and dirty and men who love me control me.
Mom and Dad always fought.	I have to be good so I don't make people mad—it's not okay for me to be angry.
I was overweight and always teased.	I'm not okay the way I am so I have to try extra hard to get people to like me.
Dad was never home and cheated on Mom.	Men can't be trusted, and women are doormats.
Mom was a rageaholic and very moody.	It's not safe to express myself—I can't make people upset.
Dad never showed affection or praised me.	I'm not lovable—I have to work hard to get people to love me.
Mom died of cancer when I was ten.	I have to take care of everyone.
I had a stepfather who hated me.	People who love me (Mom) abandon me.
We had a strict religious upbringing and lived in constant fear of sin.	It's not okay to have fun or be sexual.
Dad promised to come to my birthday party and never showed up.	Men are irresponsible and I can't count on them.
I saw Dad beat up my brother.	I have to be good so I don't get hurt/I can't protect the people I love.
My parents didn't believe me when I told them my brother had molested me.	My feelings don't count so I should just keep them to myself.

STEP 3 After thinking about the decisions you made due to a particular experience or circumstance, *write down how this emotional programming has affected your love choices and the kinds*

of partners you choose. This is the hardest portion of this exercise, but the most important. You may want to think about this over a period of days, and talk with close friends or your partner to help clarify your ideas. Keep adding to your list as new revelations surface.

We've been talking about Ann throughout this chapter, and earlier we saw her summary list and her Emotional Want Ad: *"WANTED: Angry, unemployed control freak for demeaning relationship."* Now look at her emotional programming table.

Ann's Emotional Programming Table

SITUATION OR EVENT	DECISION	LOVE CHOICE
Dad made promises he didn't keep. Let me down constantly, didn't show up when he was supposed to.	People I love will disappoint me. Men can't be trusted.	Men whom I put on a pedestal and then they disappoint me. Men who are irresponsible.
Never told Mom and Dad were having problems. Wasn't told they were getting divorced until right before.	People I love will lie to me, so I can't trust them.	Men who are dishonest with themselves and with me.
Never saw Dad loving and affectionate toward Mom. Dad cheated on Mom with other women.	Men aren't turned on by their own wives. Women are starved for love.	Men with low sex drive who don't show me they want me. Men who are attracted to other women.
Sick with high fevers as young child. Dad doesn't come home. Mom left alone with me.	I can't count on men to be there for me. I have to take care of myself.	Men with no jobs whom I have to support. Men who are impractical and don't take care of me.

Neither Mom nor Dad will talk about divorce or how sad they are feeling afterward. Act like everything is fine.	It's not safe for me to share my feelings. People I love don't want to talk about feelings.	Men who have a difficult time discussing feelings and hate my being emotional. Men who refuse to look at our problems.

Ann's comments: "I never realized how much these childhood events affected me. All along I've known I was choosing the wrong men, but I couldn't figure out why. Reading down that column of decisions I made as a little girl was frightening, but I could feel in my heart that part of me really still believes those things. *I attracted men who made me feel the same way I felt with my father—angry, discounted, betrayed.* The worst part is, I didn't even recognize the pattern because I was so used to having those feelings in childhood."

Now that Ann understands more about why she has attracted the wrong partners, she can begin making changes to attract the right partner.

▼

ONCE YOU BECOME AWARE OF YOUR UNCONSCIOUS DECISIONS ABOUT LOVE, YOU CAN MAKE NEW, HEALTHY DECISIONS.

▲

Later we'll talk more about how to "reprogram" your mind so you can break free from the unhealthy habits of the past.

Here are some more samples of the kinds of love choices you might have made based on childhood events and the decisions about love that followed:

SITUATION OR EVENT	DECISION	LOVE CHOICE
Mom was a rageaholic and very moody.	It's not safe to express myself. I can't make people upset.	Moody partners with bad tempers. Partners who hate when I get upset or emotional and won't talk about feelings.

Dad molested me.	I'm bad and dirty, and men who love me control me.	Partners who are sexually obsessed and very domineering.
I was overweight and always teased.	I'm not okay the way I am, so I have to try extra hard to get people to like me.	Partners who are unavailable or like me as friends, whom I pursue and feel rejected by.
Dad was never home and cheated on Mom.	Men can't be trusted, and women are doormats.	Partners who aren't there for me emotionally, who are workaholics or who are still in love with their ex.
Dad never showed affection or praised me.	I'm not lovable—I have to work hard to get people to love me.	Unemotional partners who don't make me feel special.
My parents were divorced.	People who love me abandon me.	Partners I test by behaving badly and who end up leaving me.
I saw Dad mistreat Mom.	I have to be good so I don't get hurt. I can't protect the people I love.	Partners who have problems I try to fix.

WHY YOU CHOOSE THE PEOPLE YOU LOVE

There are many ways in which your emotional programming can have an effect on whom you choose to love. Here are some of the reasons you might end up with a particular partner.

THE "GOING HOME" SYNDROME

As human beings, we gravitate toward the familiar. We like to sleep on the same side of the bed each night, to park in the same space at work, to go back to our favorite vacation spot. *Returning to the familiar* is a basic instinct that gives our lives a sense of continuity and safety in a chaotic and changing universe. Unfortunately, this instinct can work against us.

▼

WE OFTEN SEEK OUT EMOTIONAL SITUATIONS THAT ARE SIMILAR TO THOSE WE EXPERIENCED IN CHILD-HOOD, REGARDLESS OF WHETHER THOSE EXPERI-ENCES WERE POSITIVE OR NEGATIVE.

▲

I call this pattern *"going home."* Here's how it works:

When you were a young child, your home was the main source of love and safety in your life. Even if there was violence or chaos in your household, it was still "home"—it was where you were fed and had a place to sleep and received some sort of attention. So you associate **love** with **home.** You also associate **home** with other characteristics, based on your experiences at home. For instance, if your parents fought a lot, you might have an equation in your mind that says **home = chaos.** If you weren't shown much love or affection, your equation might be **home = loneliness.** If one of your parents was abusive, it might be **home = fear.**

Remember your basic math from school, where you learned:

$$\text{If } A = B, \text{ and } B = C, \text{ then } A = C$$

Let's use this same principle to illustrate "going home":

▶ If love = home, and home = chaos, then **love = chaos.**

▶ If love = home, and home = loneliness, then **love = loneliness.**

▶ If love = home, and home = fear, then **love = fear.**

▼

YOUR MIND WILL EQUATE WHATEVER ASSOCIATIONS YOU HAVE ABOUT "HOME" WITH WHAT LOVE IS SUP-POSED TO FEEL LIKE.

▲

So if home felt like chaos, you might seek unstable partners who will help you create dramatic, chaotic relationships. If home felt like loneliness, you might seek a partner who doesn't give you enough love, affection, or attention, so that you end up feeling lonely. If home felt like fear, you might attract someone who always criticizes you, threatens to leave, or makes you jealous, so that you always feel fearful. You unconsciously choose what is familiar—**you are going home.**

Obviously, we all have positive associations with home as well, which we also seek to reproduce in our adult life. I've found, however, that *it is the more painful associations that can cause the most trouble, because they are usually unconscious.* In other words, if you came from a home where your parents showed you a lot of affection but criticized one another, you might consciously seek a partner who was very loving, but unconsciously attract someone who was critical.

HOW ANN WAS "GOING HOME" IN HER RELATIONSHIPS

We've been following Ann throughout this chapter. Ann is a thirty-nine-year-old woman with a history of attracting irresponsible, emotionally distant men. Ann is now happily married to Adam, but still finds herself afraid to trust completely because of her past experiences. Reading Ann's emotional programming list, you can see how she went "home" in most of her relationships with men. When I asked Ann to write down her negative associations with home, here is what she came up with:

HOME = **Disappointment**
Denial
Lack of communication about feelings
Betrayal
Inadequacy
Dishonesty
Abandonment

Substitute the word **love** for **home,** and you see Ann's unconscious associations regarding **love:**

LOVE = **Disappointment**
Denial
Lack of communication about feelings
Betrayal
Inadequacy
Dishonesty
Abandonment

Ann was amazed at how similar her negative description of her childhood was to her negative description of her adult relationships. All of her love affairs included the same emotions she felt as a little girl. **Ann had left home physically, but she hadn't left home emotionally.** She continued to re-create the same emotional circumstances, because, as unpleasant as they might have been, they were what she was used to. The good news was that in her marriage to Adam, Ann felt very few of those old, familiar feelings. Unlike Ann's previous partners, Adam was responsible, successful, and emotionally open. "It looks like I'm finally leaving home!" she remarked. "Adam is helping me change many of the negative decisions I'd made about love. Even though there are times when Adam reminds me of my father, we can talk about my reactions together, which allows me to heal."

I asked Ann to redefine her concepts of **home** and **love** by turning each negative quality into its opposite and adding others.

Ann's new list:

HOME & LOVE = **Trust**
Honesty
Communication about feelings
Fidelity
Reliability
Consistency
Safety
Support

WHY MITCHELL CHOSE WOMEN WHO WERE EMOTIONAL BASKET CASES

Remember Mitchell, the thirty-six-year-old attorney who kept attracting women who smothered him and depended on him to fix their lives? Here is his list about **home** and **love**:

HOME & LOVE = **Drama**
Lack of stability
Responsibility
Mom's pain
Crisis
No childhood

Mitchell's mother was an alcoholic who couldn't function as an adult half of the time. When she wasn't passed out, she was on an emotional roller coaster. Mitchell's dad was a quiet, passive man whose method of dealing with his wife's disease was denial. As the oldest child in the family, Mitchell ended up taking on much of the responsibility that should have been his mother's—cooking, cleaning, caring for his younger sisters and brother. In this way, he really had no childhood.

Mitchell's biggest burden, however, was the emotional one he took on in trying to fix his mother. "I loved my mom so much," Mitchell shared, "but nothing I could do would get her to stop drinking. I felt like I was her only hope. No wonder I don't realize how screwed up these women are when I meet them," he exclaimed. "Emotionally unstable, dramatic women seem 'normal' to me. It feels familiar—just like home. It's what I experienced every day of my life."

Does becoming aware of his emotional programming completely eradicate it for Mitchell? Of course not. But now that he is conscious of his "weakness" for rescuing messed-up women, he can be much more vigilant about making sure to choose self-sufficient, healthy partners.

Now it's your turn to look at your emotional programming about **home** and **love**.

Exercise: Defining "Love" and "Home":

STEP 1 Make a list of the negative associations you have with the word "home" from childhood. Try to use a word or phrase, as in the examples above, rather than a long description.

STEP 2 Substitute the word "love" for "home" to understand more about your unconscious programming regarding love.

STEP 3 Compare your "love =" list to your summary list of negative qualities in partners. Notice the similarities, and determine if you've been "going home" by loving the partners you have chosen.

COMPLETING UNFINISHED EMOTIONAL BUSINESS FROM CHILDHOOD

The second way in which your emotional programming affects whom you choose to love is by unconsciously motivating you to complete unfinished emotional business from childhood. Here's how it works. Every child has two basic instincts, or agendas:

▶ They want to feel happy and loved, especially by their parents.

▶ They want to see their parents happy and loved.

If you go through your childhood and these agendas, or desires, aren't met, it is as if you have unfinished psychological business that is left hanging. You somehow feel incomplete, as if something is not right. *Your mind "remembers" that these desires are important to you, and will create circumstances in your adult life to "help" you accomplish these unconscious goals.*

▼

YOUR UNCONSCIOUS MIND WILL SEEK TO COMPLETE ITS UNFINISHED EMOTIONAL BUSINESS FROM CHILDHOOD BY GETTING YOU TO "CHOOSE" PEOPLE WHO WILL HELP YOU RE-CREATE YOUR CHILDHOOD DRAMAS.

▲

Here are some of the ways in which you may be completing unfinished childhood business:

▶ **If you didn't get the love/attention you wanted from a parent, you might** attract a partner who, like your parent, doesn't give you the love you want and makes you work hard to try and get it.

▶ **Or, if you are really angry at that parent, you might** attract a partner who, unlike your parent, *does* give you the love you want, and you reject him, hurt him, or make him work hard to get your love (i.e., retaliation).

ARE YOU FALLING IN LOVE WITH YOUR MOM OR DAD?

Michelle, twenty-nine, is a perfect example of a woman who was unconsciously using the men in her life to complete some emotional business from her childhood. Michelle came to me complaining that she always attracted very critical, controlling men who made her feel she wasn't good enough for them. She found partners who'd tell her she wasn't skinny enough, smart enough, or motivated enough. She'd had three long-term relationships in which each of her boyfriends tried to change her into someone else. Michelle even went so far as to have plastic surgery to increase her bust size because her last boyfriend told her her boobs were too small!

I gave Michelle an assignment—to write out a complaint list about each of her parents, and then to compare the list to her complaint list about her boyfriends. Here is what she came up with:

DAD	MOM
unavailable	critical
passive	demanding
nonexpressive	sarcastic
serious	moody
cold	perfectionist
workaholic	angry

"I can't believe this," Michelle told me. *"I've been falling in love with my mother."* Michelle's mom was a highly critical, caustic woman. Nothing Michelle ever did as a child met her mother's standards. She was always fussing over her daughter and comparing her to other children, both in appearance and behavior. Michelle's dad was a real absentee father, but when he was around, he didn't disapprove or approve—he was just there. Michelle received a lot of attention from her mom, but it was negative attention. Even as an adult, when Michelle calls home with news of a job promotion, or a trip she's planning, her mother still questions Michelle's judgment and makes her feel inadequate.

By attracting men who constantly put her down, Michelle is re-creating a relationship with her mother in which she tries hard to be smart enough, pretty enough, and good enough. It's as if a part of her mind thinks, "Maybe this time I'll get him to think I'm beautiful," or "I know he will love me if I can just be more of what he wants me to be." The little girl inside her has never released her need for Mommy's approval, so she makes poor love choices.

If you suspect that you may be "falling in love with a parent," complete the exercise I gave Michelle: Make a complaint list about your parents, and compare it to your summary list earlier in this chapter. The similarities can be frightening, but you will definitely gain some insight.

ARE YOU PUNISHING MOM OR DAD?

If you didn't feel loved as a child, and you have a lot of suppressed anger about it, you might act out a second option—*finding a partner like your parent and unconsciously setting out to hurt him.* Louisa, forty-one, has been married to Fredric, forty-three, for four years. This was Louisa's third marriage, and they came to me on the verge of divorce. "I feel like I'm seeing the past flash before my eyes," Louisa admitted with a frightened look on her face. "In each of my marriages, I've ended up feeling completely turned off to my husband. The last two times, I've cheated on them, and our breakups were ugly. I love Fredric, and when we got married, I vowed I would never make the same mistakes again, but for the past six months I can't seem to do anything but criticize him."

The key to understanding Louisa's pattern lay in her relationship with her father. Louisa's parents were divorced when she was five. Her father moved to another city, wrote or called infrequently, and visited even less. All through her childhood, Louisa lived for a scrap of love and attention from her dad, and never expressed anything but adoration for him. But the rage she was feeling inside began to manifest itself when she hit puberty and started dating. Louisa became a heartbreaker: She'd find some guy who was crazy about her, get involved with him only long enough to be sure he really loved her; then she'd cheat on him, break up suddenly, or treat him shamelessly. **Louisa was "punishing" her father for abandoning her by abandoning all the men in her life.** It was as if she were saying, "See how bad it feels to be rejected? Now you know what I went through!"

▼

IF YOU ARE STILL ANGRY AT ONE OF YOUR PARENTS FOR HURTING YOU, YOU MIGHT ATTRACT PARTNERS WHOM YOU HURT.

▲

ARE YOU TRYING TO RESCUE MOM OR DAD?

Here's another way in which we often unconsciously finish childhood business:

If your parent wasn't happy and loved, you might:

▶ attract a partner just like your parent to love, regardless of whether he is good for you or not, to "prove" to Mom or Dad that you do love them, even if their spouse didn't

▶ attract a partner like your parent and try to fix or rescue him, to try to make that parent happy

▶ attract a relationship that isn't any better than your parents' marriage, in order not to be any happier than Mommy and Daddy

CASE #1: *How Tammy Tried to Rescue Her Father*

"I am so sick of falling in love with alcoholics!" Tammy complained to me. "Why do I keep finding these guys with addictions and staying with them?" Tammy was a bright, thirty-two-year-old advertising executive with lousy taste in men. No matter how hard she tried, she attracted one addictive man after another. Even though *she* didn't drink, smoke, or do drugs, she somehow managed to fall in love with men who did. Her current boyfriend, Todd, was typical— a charming, successful business owner with a big ego and a big drinking problem.

Tammy's pattern wasn't hard to figure out. She'd grown up on a farm, the youngest of three girls, Daddy's favorite. Tammy's father was a hardworking, affectionate man and an alcoholic. Though no one in Tammy's family ever used that word, everyone knew that living with Dad meant accepting his "crazy times." Tammy spent her childhood watching her mother try to cover up for her husband's problem, and watching her dad suffer financial loss and eventually severe physical disease—all brought on by his drinking. Tammy felt helpless—she loved her daddy so much, but didn't know how to encourage him to stop hurting himself. As a little girl, she used to hide his liquor bottles under the hay in the barn, hoping he wouldn't find them, but he always did.

Soon after Tammy moved away from her home state to a large city, her father was diagnosed with liver cancer and died. Tammy was devastated. Inside, she felt as if somehow she should have been able to prevent his tragic end. At about this time she began falling in love with alcoholics, all of whom she desperately tried to heal. Todd was her latest "case." "I know you are going to tell me to leave him," she told me, "but he really needs me. He had the worst childhood, and I really believe if I'm just there for him, he will finally stop."

To Tammy, leaving Todd would be like abandoning her father and her mission to save him. Tammy was trapped in a self-destructive cycle. *Like all people who have an unconscious emotional program to save Mom or Dad, or to make them happy, she was a prisoner of her past, and her love choices weren't based on who was good for her but who she could help.*

Case #2: *How Jeremy Married His Mother*

When I first met Jeremy, a forty-five-year-old plumbing contractor, he seemed like a really nice guy. Married for twenty-four years to Becky, Jeremy was in turmoil because he didn't feel in love with his wife but couldn't bring himself to leave. "I've known Becky since college," he told me, "and she's the sweetest person in the world. She's a wonderful mother to our four kids, and a devoted wife. If I'm honest with myself, I have to admit that I've been unhappy with our relationship for most of our marriage. It's not that she does anything wrong, because she's perfect, but I'm not attracted to her as a lover, and except for the children, we have very little in common."

As I worked with Jeremy to understand how his childhood may have affected his relationship with Becky, he began to see why he had been willing to sacrifice his own happiness in order to keep his wife happy for so long. Jeremy's father had deserted his wife and children by running off with his secretary. Jeremy's mother was devastated, and felt totally inadequate as a woman. She never dated or married again. Jeremy was eleven at the time, and the only boy in the family. Though he didn't understand all the details of the scandal, he was sensitive enough to know that his mother felt insecure and rejected. At that point in his life, Jeremy made several unconscious decisions: *to prove to his mother that she was good enough by trying to fill her emptiness with his love, and to prove to his father that he had been wrong to leave by never leaving a woman himself.*

When Jeremy met Becky in college, he felt instantly drawn to her: She was insecure, vulnerable, and afraid of men, just like Mom. From the first, he felt a profound sense of responsibility to protect Becky and make her feel loved. This feeling grew until he asked her to marry him. Only after years of thinking about what made Becky happy did Jeremy finally begin to admit to himself that he wasn't happy. But his emotional programming didn't allow him even to consider doing anything that would hurt Becky, so he stayed in the relationship, feeling more and more trapped with each passing year. To Jeremy, the idea of leaving Becky was unthinkable: It would make him just like his father, and he would be saying to his mother, "Dad was right to leave you because you didn't fulfill his needs, just as Becky doesn't fulfill mine."

I pointed out to Jeremy that it wasn't his love for Becky that was keeping him a prisoner, but his anger at his father and his protection of his mother. His unfinished childhood business had held him hostage for almost thirty years. Jeremy hadn't ever fully

*been in a relationship with his wife, because he was still emotion-
ally bound to his mother.*

**Give yourself permission to have a wonderful, loving
person in your life.**

I believe that we all have some unfinished emotional business
from childhood, but if you aren't happy with your relationship
choices and suspect you may still be held hostage by your childhood
feelings, spend some time thinking about all you've read and look
for some connections between your past and your present.

FEAR OF INTIMACY

► **Do you attract people who can't make a commitment?**

► **Do you feel frightened or smothered when someone expresses strong feelings of love toward you?**

► **Do you find yourself pushing people away, even when
they're giving you what you want?**

If you answered yes to any of these questions, you may be
affected by the third way in which your emotional programming can
determine your love choices: It gives you a fear of intimacy.

▼

**IT'S NOT INTIMACY WE FEAR,
IT'S THE *CONSEQUENCES* OF INTIMACY.**

▲

Here's how it works: Let's say that, as a child, someone with
whom you were intimate, such as a parent, sibling, or relative, hurt
you in some way. Maybe you loved your mother and she died when
you were a child. Your mind makes an association between intimacy
and that painful experience.

Intimacy = Loss of Intimacy = Shame of Intimacy = Pain

In other words, you associate intimacy with a negative consequence.

Years pass. You consciously tell yourself you want a loving,
intimate relationship with a partner, but your emotional programming associates intimacy with something undesirable. *So your unconscious mind makes choices in partners who will "protect" you*

from intimacy because they are either unavailable or uncomfortable with intimacy themselves. "Why can't I attract someone who will give me the love I want?" you complain. The answer: Because you don't want to be loved that way. You don't trust it. It caused you pain in the past, and you are afraid it will again.

Suzanne is a thirty-eight-year-old graphic artist who attended a women's seminar I gave. "My biological clock is running out," Suzanne told us. "All I want is to find a husband, settle down, and have a family. I've been looking for the right man for years, but I keep finding the wrong ones—married men, men who don't want kids, men who are afraid to feel. Why aren't there any good men out there?"

I listened to Suzanne complain about her love life, and had a feeling there was something else to it. A few hours later, after an emotional exercise, I found out what it was. "I've never realized this before," she began with a shaky voice and tears in her eyes, "but I don't think I ever forgave my father for leaving me and my mother. My parents got divorced when I was three years old, and my father moved to another state. I only saw him a few times after that. I remember my mom telling me that we were better off without him, and I think I convinced myself that she was right. I've tried for years to block him out of my mind, to tell myself his leaving didn't affect me, but I know it must have. Ever since I walked into this workshop, I haven't been able to stop thinking about it, and I'm tired of pretending that it was okay. I'm tired of feeling so numb."

Suzanne continued to attract unavailable or unsuitable men into her life because she was petrified of intimacy. *To Suzanne, intimacy meant loss, fear, mistrust, pain, and disappointment. Consciously she wanted a man in her life, but unconsciously she was emotionally programmed to avoid intimacy at all costs.* Before she could have a healthy relationship with a man, Suzanne would have to purge herself of the pain she had avoided feeling for so long, and create a new, positive picture of intimacy.

Exercise: *Write down any negative words you have associated with intimacy. Think about why you may have made those decisions about what intimacy means, and ask yourself if those decisions have been affecting your choices in partners.*

LOW SELF-ESTEEM

There's a popular concept in many metaphysical philosophies that says:

YOU GET WHAT YOU THINK YOU DESERVE.

Not only do I believe this, but I have seen it manifest itself in my own life and the lives of thousands of people I have worked with. For many of us, the problem is that we don't think we deserve a lot when it comes to love. This is the fourth way your emotional programming can affect your love life: It unconsciously tells you that you don't deserve the love you consciously think you want.

I could write a whole book on self-esteem, but here's the important point:

IF YOU WERE TOLD OR CONCLUDED THAT YOU WERE NOT LOVABLE AS A CHILD, YOU MAY HAVE A DIFFICULT TIME ATTRACTING LOVE.

As children we believe what our parents tell us, because we love them and because they are the only authorities we know. So if your parents told you you weren't good enough, or smart enough, or likable enough, part of you believed them. Even if they didn't actually use these words, but treated you in an unloving way, you probably still concluded that you were unlovable. **When you grow up, you either attract people into your life who can't love you, or mistreat you, or you have a difficult time finding partners at all.**

The big problem with low self-esteem is that you may not even realize you aren't being treated well in your relationships. *People with self-esteem problems typically either make excuses for why their partner isn't loving them enough or blame themselves for their partner's behavior.*

CASE #1

Craig, twenty-seven, is dating a woman who constantly breaks dates, shows up late or not at all, and doesn't call to explain. It's obvious to his friends that she doesn't really care about Craig, but he doesn't see it that way. "Patrice is just really busy," he insists. "She is dedicated to her career, and sometimes things come up at the last minute she needs to do." Craig grew up with a father who told him he would never amount to anything, and a silent mother who was afraid to interfere. Craig is used to being ignored and treated like he is unimportant, so Patrice's behavior doesn't seem strange to him.

DO YOU FEEL TOO GUILTY TO BE LOVABLE?

Sometimes it isn't our parents' influence that destroyed our self-esteem, but repressed feelings of guilt or shame we've been carrying with us since childhood.

▼

IF YOU'VE DONE SOMETHING YOU HAVEN'T FORGIVEN YOURSELF FOR, OR FEEL IN SOME WAY RESPONSIBLE FOR SOMEONE ELSE'S PAIN, YOUR EMOTIONAL PROGRAMMING MIGHT HAVE CONCLUDED THAT YOU DON'T DESERVE TO BE LOVED.

▲

CASE #2

Joanie was a vivacious thirty-two-year-old nurse who couldn't seem to meet men, let alone start a relationship. I was surprised to hear Joanie describe her lonely life, since she was so outgoing and attractive. "I don't know what it is about me," she complained, "but no matter what I do, I can't find someone to love. All of my friends are either married or have boyfriends. What's wrong with me?"

As we worked to uncover her emotional programming, we came up against something from Joanie's childhood that she had never connected with her vacant love life. Joanie had a younger sister named Stephanie who was born severely handicapped. As a young girl, Joanie remembered helping carry her little sister everywhere, because she couldn't walk, and helping to feed her, because she couldn't coordinate her limbs. Stephanie was confined to a wheelchair at age five, and eventually was put into a home for children with special needs.

"I remember lying in bed as a child next to Stephanie," Joanie reminisced, "and looking at her beautiful face. I couldn't understand why God did this to my little sister. She was my only sibling—my parents didn't have any children after that—and I felt like she was taken from me. Everyone used to tell me how lucky I was to be healthy, but that only made me feel more . . . well, I guess 'guilty' is the right word. I felt guilty to be so normal when poor Steph was so damaged."

Joanie broke down and cried tears of grief and love for her little sister. We talked about the decisions she had made as a child—*that she didn't deserve to be happy if Stephanie wasn't happy; that she didn't deserve to have a husband and a normal love life, since Stephanie would never be able to have one.* Joanie hadn't been aware of what a powerful effect her guilt had on her as an adult. Somehow her feelings translated into behavior that kept men away from her. She was emotionally programmed *not* to fall in love. Now that she was aware of the source of her pattern, Joanie could begin to heal her feelings of guilt and give herself permission to be twice as happy—one dose for herself, and one dose for Stephanie.

USING YOUR PAST TO CREATE A LOVING FUTURE

I'm sure you have been able to relate to some if not many parts of this chapter. Don't be surprised if your personal experience is a *combination* of several things: Maybe you concluded that you've been "going home" by choosing partners who don't make you feel special, because that's what your childhood was like, *and* have been falling in love with men or women just like Mom or Dad in order to rescue them. You may even have to read this chapter over several times before you can digest all of the information it contains. Here are some suggestions that will help:

▶ **Make sure to do all of the exercises I've included.** They really work. Don't avoid the ones that are scary—they are probably the ones you need to do most.

▶ **Write down all of the realizations and insights you have about yourself and your love choices.** Putting your thoughts into words will help make them more tangible and will start the process of helping you change your emotional programming.

▶ **If you are in a relationship, share your insights with your partner, and ask him or her to read the book and do the same.** If you are *not* in a relationship, do this with a close friend. THE MORE YOU TALK ABOUT YOUR NEW REALIZATIONS, THE LESS YOU WILL TEND TO FORGET THEM.

This chapter is titled "Why We Choose the People We Love." We've talked about emotional programming, completing childhood business, trying to rescue Mom or Dad, and other unhealthy motivators for choosing a mate.

But what about healthy reasons for falling in love? Don't they exist? *Is it possible to choose a partner because we simply love them?* The answer, of course, is YES. That magical feeling of connection called "love" can draw us to someone. **What's important to remember, however, is that even in the best of relationships, many unhealthy patterns may manifest themselves.** For instance, you could be in a very happy relationship but notice that you have a tendency to try to fix your partner, or rebel against your mate's demands for intimacy. These behaviors probably have their source in that emotional programming we discussed.

So if you are in a good relationship, and have discovered that some of the reasons you are together have to do with your emotional programming, don't panic and think you need to break up or get divorced. Every relationship has some elements of healing in it, and there is nothing better than having a partner with whom you feel safe. You can work together to heal the wounded parts in each of you.

And if you are in a relationship you suspect is not healthy, read Chapter Eleven in this book to help you determine whether to stay in a relationship.

I know this can be a painful, though enlightening, chapter to read, and I'm proud of you for having had the courage to finish it! There is a wonderful quote by George Santayana:

> *"Those who cannot remember the past are*
> *condemned to repeat it."*

None of us can ever fully escape from the influence of our past. I truly believe, however, that by remembering, we can turn the pain of our poor choices into wonderful lessons that help us create the healthy and loving relationships we desire.

3

▼▼▼

FALLING IN LOVE
FOR ALL
THE WRONG REASONS

▼▼▼

A person doesn't need a reason to fall in love.
The experience itself is reason enough.
BARBARA DE ANGELIS, AGE 17
JOURNAL ENTRY

▼▼▼

When I was seventeen and hope-
lessly romantic, I lived in a philosophical world of idealism and
fantasy. The year was 1968. My favorite book was *The Little Prince*
by Antoine de Saint-Exupéry, my favorite song "The Impossible
Dream" from the Broadway musical *Man of La Mancha.* I used to
listen to that song ten times a day because it helped me believe
anything was possible; I believed in people; I believed in the hope of
world peace. And most of all, I believed in love. To me, falling in love
had to be the highest human experience there was. As you can see
from the above quote, I didn't really care about whether a relationship was good or bad, whether the person was right for me or not. I
was fascinated with the mere idea of being in love.

Many years and many lessons later, I have learned that what
should be the joy of falling in love can quickly turn into sorrow if

you are falling in love for the wrong reasons. Can there be wrong reasons for falling in love? In spite of what I thought at seventeen, the answer is yes.

▼

GETTING INVOLVED WITH SOMEONE FOR THE WRONG REASONS IS ONE OF THE WAYS IN WHICH WE CREATE UNHEALTHY AND UNFULFILLING RELATIONSHIPS.

▲

There are many reasons why people decide to have relationships other than being in love. This chapter talks about seven wrong reasons to have a relationship. As you read each one, ask yourself if you've made one or more of these mistakes in your past, or if you're making them in your life even now. *The more of these patterns you recognize, the more you'll understand why some of your past relationships caused you so much pain and disappointment, and the more you'll be able to avoid recreating these patterns in your future relationships.*

▼

SEVEN WRONG REASONS TO BE IN A RELATIONSHIP:

1. **Pressure (age, family, friends, etc.)**
2. **Loneliness and desperation**
3. **Sexual hunger**
4. **Distraction from your own life**
5. **To avoid growing up**
6. **Guilt**
7. **To fill up your emotional or spiritual emptiness**

▲

WRONG REASON

▼　▼　▼　▼　**1**　▼　▼　▼　▼

Pressure

▶ Are most of your friends part of a couple, but you are still single?

▶ Are you unmarried and over thirty?

▶ Are you the last person in your family to "settle down"?

▶ Are you recently divorced?

If you answered yes to any of these questions, you probably already know about pressure. Pressure is the influence that your friends, family, society, and your own programming place upon you that gives the message, **"You should be in a relationship, and if you're not, something is wrong with you."** When we feel pressured by those outside influences or our own internal ones, we may choose to get involved in relationships we normally would not choose.

Here are some of the different kinds of pressure people commonly experience:

Age Pressure

▶ A woman meets a thirty-seven-year-old man who has never been married, and calls up her friend to share her excitement. Her friend's first reaction is "He's thirty-seven and unmarried. What's wrong with him?"

▶ You attend the wedding of your first cousin. During the reception, you hear the same thing from each of your relatives: "So you're almost thirty. Why aren't you married?"

This is age pressure—the attitude that if you are over a certain age and not seriously involved with someone, you aren't "normal." Of course, just what that age is varies from person to person. Whether you're conscious of it or not, you probably have an age by which you think you should be married, or in a permanent relationship. That number might have come from things your family talked about when you were growing up, or what ages your older brothers and sisters were when they got married, or just an image of at what age a person is really grown up.

To understand the origins of age pressure, we need to go back thousands of years in history. The economic and physical survival of a family was based on how many children there were. Sons could help with hunting, farming, and protecting the family against enemies. Daughters could help with chores and be valuable assets if desired by other males for mates. The sooner a young man or woman married and started his or her own family, the better. It strengthened the family group, or clan, by adding to their number and, in families who owned property, guaranteed that there would be inheritors to keep what the ancestors accumulated. And remember, life expectancy was less than half of what ours is now in the twentieth century. So a girl of fourteen might have had only another twenty or, at most, thirty years left to live. By the time she was in her twenties, she was middle-aged! Therefore it was natural for her family to want her married in her early teens, so she could start having children right away.

Although we've come a long way from those ancient times, we are still influenced by some of the thinking our forebears lived by. So when your Aunt Mabel pulls you aside at Thanksgiving dinner and says, "Sweetheart, I know it's not my business, but why don't you find a nice guy and settle down?" she is voicing a sentiment that has its roots in historical realities.

Whether the pressure comes from your family, your friends, or from your own sense of urgency, the result is the same: **You may compromise your standards for an acceptable partner just to have a relationship with someone.**

ROSEANN'S HIGH-SCHOOL REUNION TRAUMA

RoseAnn had just turned twenty-eight when she received an invitation to her ten-year high-school reunion. "That's when the impact of being single really hit me," she explained. "I'd been wanting to find someone special for a long time, but I was so busy starting my own business that I guess I didn't stop to think about how I was feeling. When I opened up that invitation and thought of seeing all of my old friends, I got so depressed. I had these fantasies of showing up at the hotel, greeted by all of my girlfriends and their husbands carrying piles of baby pictures, and me the only unmarried one there."

"That's when I met Sandy. A friend introduced us, and I didn't really think he was my type, but decided to give him a chance. Before I knew what happened, we were in a relationship. Looking back, I can see that from the beginning, there were big problems. I kept finding things wrong with Sandy, and wanting to improve him. I didn't like his taste in lots of things—clothes, food, movies. Even the way he kissed bugged me. But I found myself tolerating all of this stuff and telling everyone how happy I was.

"Five months after the reunion, I woke up and admitted to myself that I didn't want to be in this relationship with Sandy. I wanted to be in a relationship, period, and the combination of turning twenty-eight and facing the reunion put tremendous pressure on me to find someone so I didn't look like I was alone. Breaking up with him was painful, because there was double pressure—all my friends and family had already been asking, When's the wedding?, and now I had to disappoint them as well as Sandy."

RoseAnn is a perfect example of someone who got involved with a partner to lessen the pressure, not because she was really in love.

Pressure from Family and Friends

Some people are very susceptible to the opinions of their family and friends and allow themselves to be pressured to get into or stay in relationships that aren't making them happy. If you don't have a strong sense of yourself, or if you are very enmeshed with your family members, you could end up having a relationship because everyone else thinks you should, not because you truly want to be with that person.

HOW LENNY LET HIMSELF BE PRESSURED INTO MARRIAGE

Lenny sat with his head in his hands. "I've let everyone down," he said with a moan. "What am I going to do?" Lenny, forty-four, and his wife, Krista, forty-three, had known each other since grade school. Their families belonged to the same church and were good friends, so when Lenny and Krista began dating in junior high, their parents were delighted. "I can't remember a time when it wasn't just assumed that Krista and I would get married one day. Everyone talked about it like it had already happened—Mom would make comments like, When you and Krista get older, Grandma's china will be passed down to you, or Dad would say to Krista's father, You know, Samuel, I always did feel like you were family, and hopefully one day, you will be. And Krista had been trying out my last name with hers for years.

"When I graduated from high school, I went into the Navy, again because my dad thought it would be good experience for me. Everyone seemed to think that when I got out, I'd ask Krista to marry me, and I did. If I look back now, I don't remember deciding to do it. It was just the thing I was supposed to do. You can imagine how happy they all were. That's when I started going numb. It's not that I didn't love Krista; I did, in a certain way. But I wasn't ready to marry her, or anyone.

"It's been almost twenty years, three kids, and four affairs later, and I just can't handle it anymore. I'm so lost, I'm hurting my wife and children, and letting everyone I love down."

I watched Lenny weep like a frightened little boy, and felt so much empathy for this man who had been under pressure for so long to live up to everyone else's expectations of how his life was supposed to be. **The truth was that Lenny had been *letting himself down* for years by not listening to his own heart, by making decisions others thought were best, not because he thought they were.** In doing what his friends and family thought he should, Lenny had robbed himself of a chance to experience true love and happiness.

When you make a decision to be with someone because of the pressure you feel (from yourself or others) rather than because the person seems right for you, you are giving your power away and ensuring an unhappy end to your love story. If you have been in this position often, or are in it now, ask yourself what *you* want and need, and give that first priority over what anyone else thinks.

WRONG REASON

▼ ▼ ▼ ▼ **2** ▼ ▼ ▼ ▼

Loneliness and Desperation

► You're lying in bed at night, alone. It's been a long time since you've been in love, let alone made love. Your body feels empty, your heart hurts. Your mind thinks back to your ex, and the one before him, and remembers the happy times when you had someone to hold you and make you feel special. And then you hear yourself say, "Maybe I should just call him up and tell him I miss him. It can't hurt, can it? Maybe it wasn't so bad after all."

► It's Friday afternoon, and once again you have nothing exciting planned for the weekend. You are tired of being single. You're beginning to dread Saturday nights, renting a video and sitting home without anyone to share it with. Then you remember the guy you met at the car wash who asked you out for Saturday night. You told him you would get back to him today when you found out if you were free. Of course you're free. But do you want to go out with him? He seemed kind of boring. You decide to call him. After all, it's better than a date with the video store.

► You're out on a date with a woman you've seen a couple of times.

You know she likes you, but she isn't really that appealing. You finish dinner, and she invites you over to her apartment. On the way there in the car, she puts her hand on your thigh. She obviously likes you. You aren't really attracted to her, but it's been over five months since you've been with a woman, and you miss the closeness. So what if you decide to sleep with her. It doesn't mean you have to marry her, does it?

We can all relate to these stories, because we have all experienced loneliness, periods in our lives when we felt so emotionally empty that we were desperate for someone, anyone to love. But unfortunately, what starts out as a lonely act of reaching out to another human being can end in a very complicated and hurtful relationship.

Take the woman in the first story above. She'll call up her ex-boyfriend and tell him she is lonely. He'll decide to come over and "cheer her up," and they'll end up in bed. Suddenly they're involved again—except he neglected to tell her he's seeing someone else. She'll go through months of "back and forth" with him until they finally break up, this time for good. All of that pain from one desperate night of loneliness.

The woman in the second story will end up going out with the guy she's not really interested in. Six months later, when they're still involved, she'll meet someone she really cares for. Now she has to hurt the first man, whom she was really only using, and tell him she doesn't want to see him anymore because she has met a man she loves more.

The man in the third story may think he is in for a simple one-night stand, but this girl may have other things in mind. By always being there for him, making it easy for him to be in the relationship, she may indeed end up getting him to marry her. One day he'll wake up and finally admit he isn't in love with his wife, break her heart, upset their families, and feel like a heel.

These three people didn't just end up in these unfortunate circumstances because of bad luck; they got involved with people for the wrong reasons, and doomed their relationships to unhappy endings.

WHEN YOU ARE FEELING LONELY OR DESPERATE, YOU ARE MUCH MORE LIKELY TO MAKE POOR LOVE CHOICES AND END UP IN UNFULFILLING RELATIONSHIPS.

HOW RHONDA'S LONELINESS ALMOST KILLED HER

The story of Rhonda is a sad example of the pain we can create for ourselves and others when we choose love out of desperation. Rhonda, thirty-five, had been overweight as a child. While her friends were dating in junior high school, Rhonda stayed home and absorbed herself in her schoolwork. Because of her tremendous scholastic achievements, Rhonda won a scholarship to a private university in the Northeast. She arrived at college never having been on a date in her life.

In her first year of school, Rhonda lost fifty pounds (she says it was getting away from her mother's cooking). She could hardly believe what she saw when she looked in the mirror: She actually looked attractive. And when young men began to ask her out, Rhonda knew her transformation was real. She went out on one or two dates before she met Karl.

Karl was a senior in college and from a very wealthy family. He was athletic, good-looking, and very domineering. When he asked Rhonda out, she was sure he'd made a mistake. She never expected anyone that handsome to be interested in her. In fact, Rhonda had no idea what to expect in a relationship. She'd never been in one. So as the months passed, and they began dating exclusively, Rhonda was so overjoyed she didn't pay much attention to some of Karl's characteristics that were, to say the least, a bit strange. For instance, Karl liked to gamble—not just small amounts of money, but also large ones. He also liked his sex rough and dirty, and needed to push Rhonda around to get really turned on. And when he wasn't with Rhonda, he frequented porno film theaters and strip bars.

Rhonda was a smart girl—in the back of her mind, she knew something wasn't right. But she didn't want to lose Karl. After all, he was the only man who had ever really wanted her. So she ignored the problems and worked hard to please him. And when Karl suggested they get married, Rhonda was sure her dreams were finally coming true.

When Rhonda came to me fifteen years later, she was on the verge of a nervous breakdown. Her dream of a happy marriage had quickly become a nightmare. Karl was a compulsive gambler and a sexaholic with a violent temper. His behavior had progressively deteriorated until he'd gambled away most of his family inheritance, and like many men who link sex and anger together, his need for violent sex increased until he would beat Rhonda before he slept with her. The fat little girl who lived inside Rhonda was so afraid of losing Karl that she put up with this treatment until the night before she called me, when, for the first time, Rhonda fought back against Karl's abuse and he raped her. Fearing for her life, she fled with her two small children to a friend's house.

Rhonda's healing was not just in leaving Karl, but in forgiving herself for staying with him for so long. She needed to work hard to understand that her desperation to be loved had driven her to tolerate such inhumane treatment by her husband.

Rhonda's case is extreme, but the pattern is not. If you suspect that you've allowed your emotional vulnerability to influence your choice of partners, and you have ended up in unhappy relationships, you should be excited to know that happy relationships are just a decision away. The solution for you is to **BE MUCH PICKIER. DON'T LOWER YOUR STANDARDS JUST BECAUSE YOU'RE FEELING TIMES ARE TOUGH. YOU'RE NOT A STORE TRYING TO GET RID OF OLD MERCHANDISE THAT PUTS IT ON SALE—YOU ARE A VALUABLE, LOVABLE HUMAN BEING WHO DESERVES TO HAVE THE KIND OF RELATIONSHIP YOU WANT, NOT JUST THE KIND YOU THINK YOU CAN GET.**

WRONG REASON

▼　　▼　　▼　　▼　　**3**　　▼　　▼　　▼　　▼

Sexual Hunger

▶ Have you ever been so horny that you talked yourself into believing you cared much more for someone than you actually did?

▶ Have you ever overlooked things in a partner you didn't like so you could prolong your relationship and keep having sex?

You know what I'm talking about—it's been a while since you've had sex, and you get involved with someone you normally wouldn't be with, because you feel "the hunger." Eventually you face the fact that the relationship is not what you want, and have to admit to yourself that you were probably just horny. How embarrassing! How humiliating! But how common.

I've heard countless stories of people who ended up in relationships simply because they wanted the intimacy of physical touching and the release of sex so badly that they took whomever they could get. When you are feeling this kind of sexual pressure, you become good at having a relationship with just about anyone, and at making tremendous compromises to convince yourself you are doing the right thing.

Here's an important point: I'm *not* talking about falling in love with someone because you have intense sexual chemistry. I call that "Lust Blindness," and we'll talk about it in Chapter Four. With sexual hunger you may not even feel attracted to the person you get involved with. You just want to be with *someone*.

HOW LONNIE'S SEXUAL HUNGER LEFT HER STARVING FOR LOVE

"I'm disgusted with men," Lonnie complained to me. She'd called my radio talk show to ask my advice on a pattern in her life. "I'm twenty-four years old and I've had eight relationships in five years," she began. "I have really bad luck. I meet these men and have a brief affair with them, but when we stop seeing one another, they go out, find a woman, and get married. I'm not kidding, Dr. Barbara, all eight of them got married after being with me. I can't figure out what I'm doing wrong."

My first question to Lonnie was, "Where do you meet these guys?" When she answered "in bars," I saw part of the problem. My second question was, "How long do you know them before you sleep together?" When she answered "one night to a week," I saw more of the problem. Then I asked her what she'd been taught about sex growing up. "My mom told me that all men want women for is our bodies," Lonnie said. Now I saw the whole problem.

"There is no such thing as bad luck, Lonnie," I told her. **"But there is such a thing as bad choices, and you keep making them.** You have such a strong need to be loved by a man, and you think that means a man who wants you sexually, you'll take anyone who'll sleep with you, which is just about any man. You don't love them, or even like them—you like *the attention* they are giving you. They fill up that empty place inside your soul. Then, when they leave to find a complete relationship, you feel angry and rejected. You set the whole thing up as a way to hurt yourself."

Lonnie was getting involved for all the wrong reasons, and her self-esteem was paying the price.

THE HIGH PRICE NICHOLAS PAID FOR BEING HORNY

"I'm in big trouble, Dr. Barbara," Nicholas said with a pained expression on his face. Nicholas was a nice-looking thirty-five-year-old dentist attending a lecture series of mine. "I met this woman, Jackie, three months ago. She was an ex-girlfriend of a friend of mine, and I wasn't really that attracted to her. But it had been over a year since I'd slept with a woman. A year! I felt like something was wrong with me. I felt like people could just look at me and say, 'Hey, that guy looks like he hasn't gotten laid in a long time.' I just hadn't met anyone I really liked, and the months went by. So when Jackie came along, I thought, what the hell, I don't really like her, but at least I'll break the cycle.

"We went out once or twice and ended up sleeping together. The big joke was, the sex wasn't even that good. I knew it was going nowhere, but I figured since I didn't know when I'd have sex again, I might as well stock up now. I know it sounds awful, but it gets worse. Six weeks passed, and I'm geting disgusted with myself, so one day I decided to tell Jackie that night that we really shouldn't see each other anymore. That afternoon I got an emergency call at my office in the middle of fitting a patient for dentures—it was Jackie, and she had to talk to me immediately. When I picked up the phone I heard her say, 'Nicholas, I'm pregnant.' I was so shocked, I dropped the man's teeth right on the floor.

"That night I went over to Jackie's house and we talked about everything. Dr. Barbara, she wants to keep the baby. I told her I didn't love her, that I didn't even like her, that it was wrong of me to sleep with her and lead her on, and she told me that she didn't care how I felt. She loved me and wanted my child. I can't believe this is happening to me."

Nicholas didn't plan on paying such a high price for his sexual hunger. Jackie had his child, and Nicholas pays child support and sees his daughter fairly frequently. He has a lot of anger at Jackie, and even more anger at himself, especially for not insisting on using birth control. And although he claims he wants to find a woman to love, he hasn't found anyone yet.

WHAT'S YOUR SEXUAL HUNGER LIMIT?

Do you have a Sexual Hunger Limit (SHL), a period of time beyond which you feel "something is wrong" because you haven't been sexually active? If you're single, ask yourself what your limit is—a few months or a year or more. You might have to look back through your calendar or datebook to figure it out, but it's well worth the effort. Remember, I'm not talking about what makes you physically uncomfortable, but what time period makes you psychologically uncomfortable. It's good to know your **Sexual Hunger Limit.** *You might want to put it on your calendar as the time approaches, so you can be careful to avoid getting involved with someone for the wrong reason!*

WRONG REASON

▼   ▼   ▼   ▼   *4*   ▼   ▼   ▼   ▼

Distraction from Your Own Life

Have you ever thought about how distracting it is to be in love? You think about how the other person is feeling, what they need, what makes them happy, how your behavior affects theirs, just to name a few examples. **It's no wonder, then, that we often get into relationships *not* because we have found the right person but as an excuse to avoid our own life.**

▼

Are You Using Relationships To Avoid Dealing with Your Own Life?

Read each of the following statements and ask yourself if it applies to you now, or if it has applied to you in the past:

▶ I have a history of unfulfilling relationships.
▶ I don't go for long periods of time without being in a relationship.
▶ The relationships I get involved in are very time-consuming.
▶ There are many areas of my own life that are not operating the way I'd like them to.
▶ There are projects or dreams I've had for a while that I haven't followed through with.
▶ When I'm in a relationship, I devote less time to my own interests and friends.

► I tend to become romantically involved with my partners rather quickly.
► As a rule, I don't enjoy spending time alone, and would rather be with other people.
► When I am working on a task or project, I tend to become easily distracted by phone calls, unimportant errands, other people's needs, etc.
► I find it easier to motivate others to solve their problems than to motivate myself to solve my own.

───────────────────────── ▲ ─────────────────────────

If you relate to several of these statements, you may be using relationships to avoid taking care of your own life. What you have been thinking is your obsession with love could very well be your addiction to not facing yourself and your problems. After all, if you are busy loving someone else and working full time to make them happy and meet their needs, you won't have much time left to meet your own needs or realize your own dreams.

Some people have relationships because they are bored with the lack of passion and purpose in their lives, and rather than looking within to find out why they feel that way, they get involved in a love affair and make that their purpose. These relationships never work *because you aren't in love with the person—you're in love with the distraction.* And when the relationship ends, you're left with yourself once more.

WHY MARY BETH NEEDED TO GO ON A "RELATIONSHIP FAST"

Mary Beth stood up in one of my seminars and announced that she was suffering from "relationship burnout," a syndrome I wrote about in *How to Make Love All the Time.* "I am so sick of going from one man to another," she complained. "I feel like moving to the mountains and becoming a nun. I get in these stupid relationships and stay until I can't take it anymore, and then I leave. For a few weeks I am so happy to be on my own. I clean up my apartment; I do the things I've been wanting to do but didn't have time to when I was seeing my latest guy. But all of a sudden I start to feel restless, and before I know it I'm at a party or a bar and getting fixated on some new man."

I asked Mary Beth what she did professionally, and noticed that she instantly became uncomfortable. "Well, right now I'm doing hair in a salon downtown, but that's just until I start my own business."

Mary Beth had a dream of being an interior decorator. But as I questioned her, it became clear that she had never done anything about it. She kept telling herself she should go back to school and get a degree, or look for a job with someone in interior design. Yet she never did. Each time she would be single again, she'd get excited about her goals for a few days or weeks. Then she'd come up against her fear of failure. And suddenly she was on the prowl for a partner again. *She used each new relationship to keep her from facing her procrastination.*

I pointed out to Mary Beth that she was using the men in her life as distractions in the same way that some men use women for sex. She agreed to go on a *"Relationship Fast"* for six months—no dates, no bar-hopping, nothing. During that time she would start to develop a relationship with herself and embrace her dreams again. Once she focused on getting her life in order, she wouldn't need to hide behind her love affairs, and she could take her time looking for a partner with whom she could have a healthy, long-term relationship.

If you suspect you've been using relationships to avoid dealing with yourself, try going on a *"Relationship Fast."* It may be difficult at first, but it will force you to face all the issues in your life that you've been avoiding.

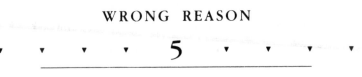

WRONG REASON

▼　　▼　　▼　　▼　　**5**　　▼　　▼　　▼　　▼

To Avoid Growing Up

Some people get into relationships not because they are ready to share the fullness of their own life with someone *but because they want to be taken care of.* These men and women are trying to avoid growing up, so they find partners who will play "Mommy" and "Daddy" roles for them. These relationships are not about learning and growing together—they are about *dependence.* You may be in this kind of relationship when:

▶ There is a big age difference between you and your partner.

► There is a big difference in the financial and professional success of you and your partner.

► There is a big contrast in the life experience level of you and your partner.

► One partner is always looking to the other for help and advice.

In these relationships you convince yourself you are in love when, in reality, you have simply found a replacement for Mom or Dad.

Katrina, a twenty-five-year-old actress, is a classic example of a woman who had a habit of falling in love for all the wrong reasons, and her favorite reason was to avoid growing up. She came to me for help when her two-year relationship with Simon, a thirty-four-year-old attorney, was in major trouble. Simon had become disenchanted with their romance and was thinking of leaving, and Katrina was in an emotional panic. "Simon is my whole life," she cried. "I can't function without him. I'll do anything to get him to stay."

I listened to Katrina describe her relationship with Simon, and realized that although she loved the way Simon had been taking care of her, she didn't really love *him*. When she talked about their time together, she would detail what he bought her, where he took her on vacation, how he gave her career advice, and how good he was at helping her with her problems. I don't even think Katrina knew Simon that well. He was just "Daddy," who'd be there for her no matter what. Katrina's own father had left when she was four, and she'd seen him only twice since. She was hungry for strong, male caretaking energy, and that's what she'd found in Simon. Her two prior boyfriends were also older and more mature. Katrina fooled herself in thinking, "I guess I just like older men."

When I met with Simon, I found myself talking to a sensitive man overwhelmed with guilt. "I love Katrina," he told me, "but I don't think we're right for each other, and I don't think Katrina is ready to have a relationship with anyone right now. When we first got together, I felt very protective of her, and probably took care of her more than I should have. In the past six months I realized that those roles had to change, but the more I try to let go and encourage her to stand on her own two feet, the more she accuses me of abandoning her. At this point I feel like leaving for good. I'm not sure she even wants to grow up."

Simon's assessment of Katrina was accurate: **She didn't want to grow up, and she used her relationships with men as a way**

to avoid it, finding partners who would play a caretaking role with her. Katrina was falling in love to fulfill needs left over from childhood and to avoid taking responsibility for her own life.

As I'll discuss later, all really good relationships have an element of healing within their dynamics, and there are times when the woman plays Mommy for her partner and he plays Daddy for her. *However, when you live out these roles the majority of the time, you are using the relationship to remain in a childlike, or irresponsible, state.*

WRONG REASON

▼   ▼   ▼   ▼   **6**   ▼   ▼   ▼   ▼

Guilt

► Have you ever ended up in a relationship *because you didn't want to hurt the other person's feelings by rejecting him?*

► Have you ever stayed in a relationship much longer than you should have *because you were afraid to hurt your partner by leaving?*

► Have you ever been with someone you knew cared more about you than you did about them, *but you felt too guilty to break it off?*

If you answered yes to any of these questions, you understand the sixth wrong reason to fall in love: guilt. Guilt might seem like a strange motivation for getting into or staying in a relationship, but it happens all the time. You tell yourself it's love, but it's really sympathy, or in extreme cases, pity. **You remain in romantic situations not because you want to stay, but because you are afraid of what might happen if you left.** You are a prisoner of guilt.

▼
Is Your Love Life Run by Guilt?

Read the following statements, and notice how many apply to you, either now or in the past.

▶ You have a difficult time saying no to people, especially those you care about.

▶ You came from a dysfunctional family in which your feelings didn't count (e.g., alcoholic, critical, or controlling parents).

▶ You grew up feeling responsible for making others happy (a parent with problems who needed rescuing, a single parent who leaned heavily on you for affection, etc.).

▶ You have a hard time knowing what your needs are, and an even harder time asking those you love for what you need.

▶ You pride yourself on being a sensitive and giving person and would feel very hurt if someone labeled you "selfish."

▶ You dread hurting other's feelings, and go out of your way to make sure nothing you say or do offends those you care for.

▶ You have a much easier time spending time and money on someone other than yourself.

▶ You have a difficult time hearing someone you care for talk about their problems without feeling compelled to help them find a solution.

▶ You find yourself backing down from expressing an opinion or a feeling you have if you notice that it upsets the person to whom it is directed.

▶ You feel uncomfortable being happier, wealthier, or more successful than those with whom you are close.

If you can relate to only a few of these statements, you're probably affected by the same amount of guilt as most people. If more than four of these statements apply to you, you may have a tendency to allow guilt to influence your love choices. If you can relate to almost all of them, you are definitely falling in love for the wrong reasons!

HOW DANIEL'S GUILT GOT HIM INTO A ROMANTIC NIGHTMARE

I can't think of a better example of falling in love for the wrong reasons than Daniel. He was handsome, in his early thirties, and a successful television director, but Daniel's love life was a mess.

Daniel was the only son of a very dramatic mother and an invisible father. Daniel's mother was extremely demanding of his time, attention, and love. If she didn't receive it, she would pout, cry, and even become physically ill. Daniel's father had obviously been treated the same when he first married his wife, and wisely spent as much time as he could working. "My mother was an expert at making me feel guilty," Daniel recounted. "In high school she would conveniently become sick on weekends when she knew I had a date. She'd lie on the couch with smelling salts in one hand and a cold washcloth in the other, saying, 'Don't worry about me, honey, go out and enjoy yourself. If things get really bad, I'll just call an ambulance'."

When Daniel went away to college, he thought he'd left his unhealthy relationship with his mother behind. As we saw in Chapter Two, however, our emotional programming stays with us even after we are physically separated from our parents. So when Daniel told me about his relationship with Elsa, I wasn't surprised.

Elsa was a very pretty, feminine-looking twenty-six-year-old photographer's assistant whom Daniel met at a party. "The first thing that struck me about Elsa was how fragile she looked—like a china doll," he remembered. "We struck up a conversation, and she told me she had just ended a terribly abusive relationship. Her eyes filled with tears as she described what she'd been through, and I felt so sorry for her."

Daniel and Elsa began dating. He knew Elsa's self-esteem was low, so he would call her several times a day to reassure her how special she was. Soon Elsa began to look to Daniel as her savior.

TRAPPED BY GUILT

At first, Daniel felt good about the relationship. But after a few months he began to feel restless. "I was feeling emotionally stifled by Elsa's intense neediness," he explained, "but when I'd mention to her that I needed some space, she would totally freak out—sob, scream, beg me not to abandon her. It would shake me up so much that I'd promise her whatever she wanted, and for a while, things would calm down. Then I'd feel uncomfortable again, and the cycle continued.

"Don't even ask me how we ended up engaged," Daniel continued. "It had something to do with Elsa's birthday and my inability to break her heart. **I felt trapped—if I did what would make me**

happy—leave—it would kill her. If I went through with the marriage, it would destroy me. I walked around for weeks in a depression, and that's when I met Josie. She was content, independent, and strong, and I was desperate to be with a woman who didn't make me feel obligated and so damn guilty. Four days later, we ended up sleeping together.

"Dr. Barbara," Daniel said with a moan, "Elsa and I are supposed to get married next month. I know I can't go through with it, but I feel so terrible about the way I've hurt her—I can't bear to think about what will happen if I tell her the truth."

My heart hurt for Daniel as I saw the genuine anguish in his eyes. Here was a man who had started out with what he thought were good intentions—to help a woman who had been badly hurt—and he was going to end up hurting her even more. **How did Daniel get into this painful situation? He allowed himself to be motivated by *guilt* rather than by *real love*.**

If you've been a prisoner of guilt in the past, or are in a relationship now only because you feel guilty about leaving, think about this:

▼

WHEN YOU DECIDE TO BE WITH SOMEONE OUT OF GUILT AND NOT LOVE, YOU ARE RIPPING THEM AND YOURSELF OFF.

▲

WRONG REASON

▼ ▼ ▼ ▼ *7* ▼ ▼ ▼ ▼

To Fill Up Your Emotional or Spiritual Emptiness

I believe that each of us is here, in this lifetime, struggling to understand our relationship with the whole, and longing to feel part of, and not separate from, the universe we inhabit. This is our *spiritual hunger*, the urge to connect in some way with a Higher Power or meaning. And we are also here as children in grown-up bodies, yearning to feel loved, accepted, and whole. This is our *human hunger*, the urge to connect with those around us.

The wonderful thing about love is that it can fill you with a sense of joy and belonging unlike anything else in the world, and in this way satisfy those hungers. *Love gives meaning to your existence and heightened purpose to everything you do. Yet these same gifts can be dangerous when they are used to try to fill an emotional or spiritual void you carry into a relationship, a void you should be learning to fill yourself.*

A truly healthy relationship will give both people a heightened appreciation of the magic and mystery of the universe and will open the doors for their spiritual growth. It will also help each person heal the wounds of childhood, and gain a stronger sense of themselves through feeling so loved and accepted by their partner. But **when you enter a relationship with a tremendous amount of emotional and spiritual emptiness, you risk creating pain for yourself and your partner.**

There are two problems that arise when you are emotionally or spiritually empty:

1. You get involved in relationships to fill yourself up, rather than because you have found someone who is right for you.

If you walk around with a big emotional or spiritual void, you are constantly feeling empty. That emptiness can be experienced as discomfort or tension in its mild stages, becoming pain, depression, and hopelessness in its more acute stages. Just as a starving animal will eat anything to get rid of its hunger pangs, so you may seek any kind of relationship to get rid of the pain of your aloneness. *Whether the relationship is healthy or unhealthy, loving or abusive, fulfilling or draining will be unimportant to you, at least in the beginning. Just the thought "I am in a relationship" will temporarily take the edge off of your "appetite."* Lying in bed with someone, anyone, will feel wonderful for a while, because you won't have to feel yourself. Spending time with someone, anyone, will feel satisfying because you won't have to be alone with yourself.

You can see how vulnerable a person in this situation would be to getting involved in the wrong relationships with the wrong partners for the wrong reasons. Only after the high of being with someone has worn off are you left to face the person you've chosen to love. And how painful to discover that you are not filled up after all and, even worse, that being in this person's presence makes you feel even emptier and more alone than you did before.

You might find yourself going from relationship to relationship, never satisfied, always wondering when you will find the "perfect partner." **Your liberation will come when you realize that you need to feed your own heart and soul first before you are ready to have a healthy relationship.** Just as diet experts will tell you never to go shopping on an empty stomach because you'll pick all the junky, unhealthy foods, my advice is not to shop for a partner until you have filled yourself up, at least enough so you aren't "starving for love."

2. You get involved in relationships that *could* be right for you, but look to them to fill you up in ways you should be filling yourself.

How often do I hear someone complain that their partner doesn't make them feel whole and complete and that the relationship isn't worth staying in! So often this is a person who is lacking wholeness and completion in himself or herself, and is expecting their lover to fill the emotional and spiritual voids they've been carrying around long before the couple even met.

▼

If you have deep places of emptiness within you, no partner, regardless of how much they love you, will be able to fill that emptiness.

▲

You can ruin a perfectly good relationship by looking to your mate as your emotional and spiritual savior. Only you can fill those empty places; only you can save yourself. It *is* reasonable to expect your mate not to add to your emptiness, and to love you in a way that supports you in your healing process and teaches you how to love yourself again. *But in the end, you must be your own hero.*

Are You Emotionally and Spiritually Empty?

Here is a quiz to help you determine if you are suffering from emotional or spiritual emptiness. Think about each statement carefully. **If it describes how you feel:**

Very frequently . . . . **Give yourself 0 point**
Often . . . . **Give yourself 4 points**

Occasionally .... **Give yourself 8 points**
Rarely or never .... **Give yourself 10 points**

1. I have a difficult time being alone and doing "nothing." I need to have the radio or TV on, have someone with me, or keep myself busy.
2. I have no strong sense of purpose in my life and feel I don't really know what I'm doing here.
3. I'm not sure what my basic values and beliefs are, and I feel confused about what is right and what is wrong.
4. I don't do loving things just for myself, like making a fancy meal, going on a trip, dressing up, or otherwise pampering myself. I do these things when I have a partner, but not alone.
5. I don't feel comfortable thinking or talking about my feelings regarding the meaning of life, death, religion, God, my childhood, etc.
6. I like things to be predictable and under control. When I am faced with sudden change, I feel a sense of panic.
7. I compare myself and my life unfavorably with the success and happiness of others. There are many people with whom I would like to trade places.
8. I feel best when my time is scheduled and my activities are planned. I prefer structure to spontaneity.
9. I have a difficult time acknowledging good things about myself, giving myself credit for a job well done, receiving compliments or gifts, or trusting that others really love me.
10. Even when I am being loved, or good things are happening to me, I have a difficult time really feeling it and letting it in.

Now total up your points:

▶ **80–100 points: You have a healthy spiritual and emotional relationship with yourself.** Your appreciation of your inner world is as deep as your enjoyment of your outer world. *You have a strong sense of who you are and your purpose in life, and should be able to bring a lot of fullness and love into a relationship.* Take some time to think about those statements that received lower scores, and work on those areas of yourself.

▶ **60–79 points: Your spiritual and emotional relationship with yourself isn't bad, but it could be much better.** You've made great progress in some areas, but in others you still need some work to feel the peace and happiness you deserve. *Stop being so* *hard on yourself—you are "enough" just the way you are.* Work on trusting more and controlling less. You are ready to have a healthy relationship, just be careful not to sabotage it by expecting your partner to love you more than you love yourself.

▶ **40–59 points: Warning! You are living with a great deal of emotional and spiritual emptiness, and it's keeping you from having a healthy relationship.** You've been focusing too much on your external world. Now it's time for you to turn inward to find out who you really are. You can't keep running away from yourself. *The reason your love life has been so painful is that you don't even have a good relationship with yourself.* If you're single, go on a "Relationship Fast" for at least three to six months— no dating, no flirting, no sex. Instead, spend time getting to know yourself. Read, take classes, go to seminars, meditate, spend time outdoors in nature, keep a journal. If you're in a relationship and want to continue it, do these same things and create a little more space between you and your partner. *No one is going to make you happy until you are happy with yourself.*

▶ **0–39 points: Emergency! You are in an emotional and spiritual state of starvation.** Your life needs immediate attention. Stop expecting someone to come along and rescue you. Only you can rescue yourself. Wake up and remind yourself that you are on this planet for a reason—to learn and grow, *not* to avoid yourself. Stop blaming others for causing you so much pain. Stand up and fight back against your hopelessness. *You need time to discover who you are and how to love yourself before you even think of having a good relationship with a partner.* Find a support system, and follow the guidelines for the category above. You deserve to feel better than this.

Understanding and Healing Your Emptiness

In Chapter Two I talked about the decisions you make in childhood about yourself and about life based on what you experienced in your family. **The less you were loved and the more pain you were exposed to, the more emotional and spiritual emptiness you inherit.** If you received a low score on the quiz, or know you have made poor love choices because of your emptiness, make a commitment to begin deepening your relationship with yourself.

Things you can do:

▶ **Keep a journal.** This will help you get in touch with your inner self and become familiar with your thoughts and feelings. It will also give you an opportunity to access your own inner wisdom.

▶ **Learn to meditate.** I've been practicing meditation for over twenty-three years. I began Transcendental Meditation at eighteen, when I realized I had a lot of emptiness inside me. Along with helping reduce stress so you can enjoy life more, meditation can open up subtler forms of awareness and give you a spiritual anchor. There are many forms of meditation to choose from. Find one that feels right for you. It will add a powerful sense of peace to your life.

▶ **Spend time outdoors in nature.** It is impossible to walk through a forest, sit and watch the ocean, or stand on the top of a mountain and not be affected by the serenity and simple grace that nature reveals to us. In our fast-paced everyday lives, we are bombarded with electronic stimuli, and it is easy to lose touch with the beauty and balance of our home called Earth. Spending time outdoors is an easy way for you to restore yourself spiritually, whether it's just taking a walk, sitting in a park, or planning a day trip to the mountains, a lake, or the ocean. Don't forget to leave those boom boxes at home and keep talking to a minimum so you can enjoy the silence of nature and allow it to fill your soul with tranquillity.

▶ **Read books that make you think.** We often only choose to read a book when we think we will get specific advice from it. Reading can be a form of meditation, and books that make you think about life's meaning are especially helpful in beginning the process of restoring you to spiritual wholeness. Here are some of my favorites:

Chop Wood, Carry Water: A Guide to Finding Spiritual Fulfillment in Everyday Life by Rick Fields, with Peggy Taylor, Rex Weyler, and Rick Ingrasci. Published by Jeremy P. Tarcher, Inc.

Choose to Live Peacefully by Susan Smith Jones, Ph.D. Published by Celestial Arts.

Emmanuel's Book compiled by Pat Rodegast and Judith Stanton. Published by Bantam Books.

The Autobiography of a Yogi by Parmahansa Yogananda. Published by Self-Realization Fellowship.

As Above, So Below: Paths to Spiritual Renewal in Daily Life by Ronald S. Miller and the editors of *New Age Journal*.

Any books by Alan Cohen.

Falling in Love for the Right Reasons

Now that you know some of the wrong reasons for getting involved in a relationship, you're probably thinking, "What are the right reasons to fall in love?" I feel there are two conditions that should exist in your life before you are ready to participate in a healthy relationship (or be more committed to the one you are already in):

1. You feel full of love and want to share it.

When you feel full of good things in your own life, you come into a relationship truly ready to share, because you have something to share. Like a person whose arms are overflowing with gifts, you can't wait to offer some of your abundance to others. Your relationship becomes focused on what you can give rather than what you can get. This is not the same as the person who gives in order to get. Rather, you give simply because you are so full. *When you are truly in touch with your own goodness you will find it naturally overflows, just as a full river overflows onto the riverbank.*

▼

IT IS FULLNESS THAT MAKES A RELATIONSHIP WORK, NOT EMPTINESS.

▲
---

2. You are willing to learn more about yourself by looking in the mirror of your beloved.

A relationship is not a possession, it is a process. You don't acquire a relationship, you enter into one, and it affects you twenty-four hours a day. I always tell people, "A relationship is the best seminar in town," and I believe this with all my heart. When you are in love, you are faced with a mirror that reflects everything about you back for you to see. You confront your fears, your weaknesses, your selfishness, your insensitivity, your limitations, your emotional programming, and your pride. You get to look at all those parts of yourself that you dislike. *Relationships can be your greatest source of pain, or your greatest teacher.*

If you are not prepared for the intensity of the powerful learning experience love provides, you will resist your relationship and resent your partner. You will become angry at the mirror for the reflection it is showing you. The more open you are to surrendering to your relationship as a gift and a guide, the more you will grow and the easier it will be to make it work. You are ready to have a truly fulfilling relationship when you can say, *"I commit myself to learning everything I can from this person and this experience, even if it makes me uncomfortable."*

If you've read this chapter and realized that you have fallen in love for the wrong reasons in one or more of your relationships, don't despair! A wonderful quote by metaphysical philosophers P. D. Ouspensky and G. I. Gurdjieff reminds us:

"When one realizes one is asleep, at that moment one is already half awake."

Each realization you have about mistakes you've made in the past opens the door for you to make more enlightened choices in the future. Instead of being *hopelessly* romantic, you can be *hopefully* romantic.

4

▼▼▼

THE SIX BIGGEST MISTAKES
WE MAKE IN THE
BEGINNING OF A
RELATIONSHIP

▼▼▼

*When the most important things in our life happen, we quite often do not
know, at the moment, what is going on.*
C. S. LEWIS

▼▼▼

In the movie *Defending Your Life*, Albert Brooks plays a man who dies in a car accident and suddenly finds himself in Judgment City, a cosmic pit stop between Earth and the Hereafter. In Judgment City, the departed must convince a judge that he learned enough about love and happiness in his previous lifetime not to be sent back to Earth, and thereby is free to move on to a higher plane of existence. During each soul's "appointment" with the judge, he is made to review his life by watching a film of it projected onto a huge screen. Because Albert's character is no longer living that life, but observing it objectively, he can see many things about himself and his choices that were mistakes. Situations he failed to take notice of, warning signs he didn't pay attention to, feelings he ignored, chances he passed up—all of these become painfully clear to Albert sitting in his viewing room in the afterlife.

I remember watching this film and thinking that it would be wonderful if, from time to time, we could all stop, sit back, and "watch" the movie of our own life to gain a perspective that's difficult to obtain while we are busy living it! This would be especially helpful in our relationships, where *it's easy for us to see what the problems were once the love affair has ended, but not so easy to figure out what's wrong while we're still involved.*

In working with thousands of men and women over the years and in analyzing my own love life, I've learned that **so much of the hurt, heartache, and disappointment we experience in love could be avoided if we just *paid more attention* at the beginning of the relationship.** I've watched all the movies of my past love affairs, and have helped my friends and clients watch theirs, and I've concluded that there are six big mistakes many of us make when we first get involved with a partner. This chapter will introduce you to each of these mistakes and will then help you go back and evaluate your own past so you can learn from it.

▼

THE SIX BIGGEST MISTAKES WE MAKE IN THE BEGINNING OF A RELATIONSHIP:

1. **We don't ask enough questions.**
2. **We ignore warning signs of potential problems.**
3. **We make premature compromises.**
4. **We give in to Lust Blindness.**
5. **We give in to material seduction.**
6. **We put commitment before compatibility.**

▲

MISTAKE

▼   ▼   ▼   ▼   **1**   ▼   ▼   ▼   ▼

We Don't Ask Enough Questions

Imagine, for a moment, that you have decided to buy a new car. You drive up and down Main Street, where all the car dealerships are located, searching for a car that's right for you. Suddenly you spot it—a cute, sporty little model on the lot up ahead. You park and walk over to the car you are "attracted" to. "I love the way it looks!" you think. You open the door and sit in the car for a moment. "I love how it smells, and the way the seat feels against my body—this is the car for me."

As you get out of the car, a salesperson approaches you. "Can I help you?" he asks.

"I want this car," you exclaim.

"Do you have any questions about it?"

"No," you respond emphatically, "I just want this car."

"Well, would you like to know how it compares to other models, or what kind of warranty it comes with, or the kind of gas mileage it gets?"

"No, talking about all those things would ruin the excitement I'm feeling now."

"What about the price? Don't you want to know that?" the salesperson asks you in a bewildered voice.

"Oh, don't be so logical. The price doesn't matter to me—all that matters is that I love this car, I need this car, and I know it's meant for me."

This is obviously an absurd fantasy. No one in their right mind would make an important purchase such as buying an automobile without asking questions to be sure they were making the right choice. For that matter, you probably wouldn't buy a refrigerator, stereo, VCR, or even a new iron without grilling the salesperson until you felt absolutely sure you weren't making a mistake. **Yet many of us ask less questions before we start a relationship than we do before we buy a pair of shoes!** In doing this, we miss the opportunity to discover things about our potential lover that could be crucial to the success or failure of our relationship.

Why We Don't Ask Questions Before We Fall in Love

Here are some of the reasons why we don't ask questions in the beginning of a relationship:

▶ **It's not romantic:** Falling in love is romantic. *Interviewing someone is not.* So we allow ourselves to be seduced by going out to dinner, dancing, flirting, complimenting, and all the behaviors that usually manifest themselves when we first meet a potential partner and get *swept away,* so to speak. That's how the movies we saw and the books we read said it was supposed to be. You shouldn't need to ask your date lots of questions about himself. You'd look at your partner and just know he was the one.

But as we discussed in Chapter One, these love myths can get you into lots of trouble. **Asking your partner questions to find out more about them may not seem romantic, but it's the only intelligent way to really get to know someone.**

Brandy, thirty-one, told me a sad story about how she broke off her engagement to Warren, thirty-six, when she found out he had a history of physically abusing women in his life. She'd been seeing Warren for almost a year, and during that time he lost his temper quite often, but he never actually hit her until three weeks after they became engaged. Only after she left did Warren confess that he'd had a problem with violence before. I asked Brandy how much she'd known about Warren's past relationships when she got involved with him: "I'm ashamed to admit that I didn't really know anything about his past," Brandy confessed. "It's not that I didn't think about it—I did. But each time I meant to bring it up, we'd be out having fun, or about to make love, and it just seemed like it would ruin the mood. Now that I look back, I realize I never pressed him to talk about the things he avoided discussing."

I hear these same excuses when people try to explain why they don't discuss birth control or sexual protection with prospective partners.

My answer to this is: **If you want to talk about what's really not romantic, unwanted pregnancy is not romantic; herpes is not romantic; and AIDS is certainly not romantic.** Aside from finding out if you're with the right person or not, *asking a potential partner questions about himself has, in the 1990s, unfortunately become a matter of life and death.*

► **You don't want to know the answers.** Another reason we don't ask questions is simply that we don't want to know the answers, because we may not like what we hear. We don't want to hear anything bad. *If you are desperate to get into a relationship, or to make one work, you will avoid discussing anything that might sabotage your "fantasy" that you are with the right partner.*

▼

WE'RE TOO BUSY LOOKING FOR REASONS WHY WE *SHOULD* LOVE SOMEONE TO TAKE THE TIME TO LOOK FOR REASONS WHY WE *SHOULDN'T.*

▲

You finally find a partner after a long period of loneliness, or you finally meet someone who is ready to make a commitment, or you're tired of dating and just want to settle down, so you avoid asking the questions you know might "ruin" this great new relationship. As the saying goes, *"Don't destroy my fantasy by forcing me to face reality."*

▶ **You don't want your partner to ask you questions about yourself.** The third reason you might avoid asking your partner questions is to prevent them from asking questions of you. This will be especially true if:

▶ You aren't happy with yourself or your life.
▶ You are ashamed of or haven't come to terms with your past.
▶ You feel guilty about things you are presently doing.
▶ You don't have a good self-image.

When you aren't comfortable with who you are or who you have been, you will unconsciously protect yourself by not probing too deeply into your partner's life, as if to say, "I'll leave you alone, and you leave me alone. Okay?" It's obvious that two people playing this game are going to have a very unhealthy and dysfunctional relationship.

Erica, twenty-seven, spent years becoming a master of emotional hide-and-seek. She'd get into intense relationships with men she didn't know that much about. "I know why I don't get into heavy discussions with these guys," she told me. "It's because I don't want them asking me a lot of questions about me and my past." Erica was an incest victim. She'd been molested by her father from the time she was twelve until she was sixteen, when she finally escaped by running away. But Erica never really left her past behind. Like many incest victims, she tried to erase the memories because dealing with them was too terrifying. She chose men who didn't want to get too intimate with her, so she didn't have to get too intimate with them. Her worst fear was that if she found a man who was willing to share the truth about himself, she would have to reveal her terrible secret, and he'd judge her and reject her for having been part of something she felt was dirty and shameful.

Ignorance Is Not Bliss

In spite of the three reasons just discussed, the truth remains that in love, and in fact all of life,

WHAT YOU DON'T KNOW *WILL* HURT YOU.

The more information you have about someone, the better you'll be able to judge whether or not this person will make a good mate. The less information you have about someone, the more likely you will end up angry, disappointed, or heartbroken.

Here are some of the areas you should ask your partner questions about:

▶ family background and quality of family relationships
▶ past love relationships and reasons for breakups
▶ lessons learned from life experiences
▶ ethics, values, and morals
▶ attitudes about love, commitment, communication
▶ spiritual or religious philosophy
▶ personal and professional goals

MISTAKE

▾　　▾　　▾　　▾　　**2**　　▾　　▾　　▾　　▾

We Ignore Warning Signs of Potential Problems

▶ Do you ever feel stupid for not having paid enough attention to something a partner said or did that was a sign of worse things to come?

▶ Do you think of yourself as a positive person who looks for the good in people and situations?

▶ Do you look back on some of your relationships and see things now you didn't see then?

If you answered yes to any of these questions, then you've probably made mistake number two: *You notice something about your partner that should signal you to be cautious, but you choose, consciously or unconsciously, to ignore it.* You may do this by:

Minimizing its importance. "He really doesn't drink that much, mostly on weekends, and besides, it's just beer."

Making excuses for the other person. "I know she seems

overly jealous and possessive, but her ex-husband cheated on her and made her really insecure. She doesn't mean to act this way."

Rationalizing. "It would be stupid for him to get a job now, just when he's about to sell his script. This way, he has time to polish the final version and visit agents and producers."

Denying it. "What do you mean, you think he doesn't treat me well? He's wonderful to me. No one's ever loved me the way he does. You're just jealous that I'm happy and you're not."

Ironically, the more positive and loving a person you are, the more prone you may be to ignoring the warning signs in your relationships. If you have the habit of looking for the good and seeing the potential in people, you might overlook disturbing characteristics or behaviors in your partner, only to find later that you should have paid attention.

This tendency is probably one of the most dangerous mistakes we make in our love life. *We don't see what we don't want to see; thus we set ourselves up for eventual feelings of disappointment, betrayal, and anger.* "You weren't like this when I met you." "If I'd known you had this problem, I would have never gotten involved with you in the first place." "You've changed—you used to be different." These are the things we end up saying when we inevitably face the truth about our partner. And although there are cases in which a person is deliberately deceived by a partner, **most of the time we are deceiving ourselves!**

HOW MARGUERITE SET HERSELF UP TO BE BETRAYED

Marguerite is a thirty-four-year-old graphic artist who came to me to try to heal a broken heart. She'd just ended a two-year relationship with Kenneth, forty-one, because she found out he was sleeping with his ex-girlfriend. "I'm so depressed, I can't function," she told me, sobbing. "I was so sure everything was fine between us. I really believed that he was the one for me and that we would make it work. I can't believe this is happening to me."

Whenever anyone tells me they are shocked about the negative outcome of a relationship, I assume they must have ignored some warning signs along the way.

RELATIONSHIPS DON'T JUST FALL APART OVERNIGHT. IT TAKES MONTHS AND YEARS OF DETERIORATION BEFORE THE LOVE IS FINALLY DESTROYED.

When a person discovers he has cancer, it feels like the disease came upon him suddenly, but the tragic reality is that the cancer has been growing inside his body for a long time. In the same way, you may notice the effects of the deterioration of a love relationship all of a sudden, but in reality the problems have been developing all along. Although modern science may not yet know how to detect diseases such as cancer in their initial stages of growth, you *can* detect potential problems in your relationships as early as the first few weeks.

MARGUERITE'S MOVIE

To help Marguerite gain some insight into her relationship, I suggested that she participate in an exercise I'll teach you later in this chapter. I asked her to close her eyes and to imagine she was sitting in an empty movie theater. In front of her was a huge blank screen. Suddenly the screen lights up and a movie comes on. It is a love story—the movie of her relationship with Kenneth. "I want you to imagine that the movie starts from the very first moment you met Kenneth," I said. "Picture your first encounter, your first date, the conversation you had. Remember it in detail. And **as you are watching your movie, I want you to look for any warning signs, any clues you did not see or did not pay attention to at the time, that are disturbing. When you find one, freeze the scene in the movie, keep your eyes closed, and describe it to me.**"

Marguerite sat quietly for a few moments and then spoke. "Okay, I'm at the party where I met Kenneth. We are talking about ourselves, and when I ask him if he is with anyone, he answers, *'I came with someone, but our relationship is pretty much over.'* I remember feeling relieved hearing that because I was so attracted to him. Now, as I watch the movie, I realize what a strange answer that was: If his relationship was over, what was he doing taking her to a party?"

"Good," I responded. "Now let the movie start again."

"Oh, I can't believe what I just saw!" Marguerite exclaimed. "I'm at Kenneth's apartment. We've been dating for almost a month, and this is the first night we slept together. He goes in the kitchen to get us a drink, and I'm taking a tour of his place. *On his desk I notice a picture of him and a really pretty woman with their arms around each other on the beach in a tropical setting.* I wonder if it's his past girlfriend, but I'm afraid to ask about it and ruin the evening, so I ignore it. Later I find out that it is she, and over the next year we had many fights about his keeping her pictures out. I didn't even stop to ask myself why he would have his ex's picture on his desk when he's bringing me home.

"Next I see Kenneth and me sitting in a restaurant having a conversation about Julie, his ex. He's explaining to me that she is like family to him, and even though they aren't together, he is all she has, and he's helping her financially until she can get back on her feet again. I can hear him saying, *'I'm just a loyal kind of guy, Marguerite. It's hard for me to close the door on someone who's been part of my life for four years.'* I remember feeling a tight nervous sensation in my stomach, but what he was telling me sounded very loving, so I didn't confront him. I feel sick just looking back at this.

"Now it's a few weeks later. Kenneth calls me up to tell me he can't see me on Saturday night because it's Julie's birthday. It seems she called him crying and said she had no one else to be with and started getting nostalgic about this place they went to on her birthday for four years, so he is going to be a 'friend' and take her out to eat. He reassures me that it will only be for an hour or two, and he'll call me when he gets home. I see myself sitting at home waiting for the phone to ring. It's ten o'clock, eleven, midnight. Finally, at one-thirty, the phone rings. *It's Kenneth, apologizing profusely and explaining that after dinner, Julie fell apart and they went back to her place to talk. 'I couldn't leave her when she was like that, honey,'* he told me. I can see myself feeling furious, and yet loving him so much."

At this point, Marguerite began to cry. "It's so obvious, isn't it?" she said in a trembling voice. "I can see it all there in this movie. **I ignored every sign Kenneth gave me that he hadn't really let go of Julie.** I guess I wanted to believe that he had, and maybe he wanted to believe that, too. Toward the end of our relationship, we finally began to fight openly about it. She was calling him a lot, he hadn't stopped giving her money, and I thought that was wrong. He told me I didn't understand, that my jealousy was just because I was insecure."

"Now that you've seen the whole movie, when you watch the end, where Kenneth sleeps with Julie, is it still a shock?" I asked.

Marguerite looked at me with tears in her eyes. "No," she answered resolutely. "It still hurts, but it isn't a shock. I should have seen it coming. I just wasn't paying attention."

I was proud of Marguerite for not remaining a victim and for taking her power back by recognizing how *she* had made the choice to ignore information that would have forewarned her that Kenneth wasn't emotionally available. It didn't eliminate her pain, but it did give her confidence that next time, by paying more attention, she would be able to make a healthier love choice.

WHAT SOME WARNING SIGNS MEAN

Here are some examples of warning signs and possible problems they might develop into.

WARNING SIGNS	EVENTUAL PROBLEM
Avoids discussing his past, dodges direct questions, or makes light of it.	*Could be hiding something serious;* won't want to work on relationship.
Won't reveal details of family background; doesn't see or speak to family much.	*Difficult time being intimate;* hidden anger and rage at family members that will be projected onto you.
Still in frequent contact with one or more ex's; talks with them on phone a lot; doesn't include you in the friendship or introduce you.	*Won't be able to make a commitment to you;* may get back with ex. May never make you number one.
Very enmeshed with family members. Seems to talk to them too much. Doesn't stand up to them. Let's them tell him or her what to do. No boundaries.	*Won't be able to include you in family.* You will always feel like an outsider. Won't side with you if they attack.
Use of alcohol or drugs. Can't have sex or fun without them. Can't be around people without "partying."	*Could be alcoholic or drug addict.* Will deny it. Expect mood swings, emotional distance.
Extremely attentive and intense person. Showers you with love, constant affection, gifts. Seems to think about you twenty-four hours a day.	*Could be highly possessive and jealous.* Will live their life through you. Won't give you space. You will feel smothered.

Frequent flirting, staring at others. Needs lots of attention from people. Attracts sexual interest like flies.	*Watch out for possible cheater.* Will never make you feel secure. You'll feel like it's your problem.
Angry at past lovers. Feels like a victim. Blames ex's for problems in relationships.	*You're next!* Won't take responsibility for their part in things. Will end up angry at you.
Credit problems, debts, unpaid parking tickets, shaky finances, "temporary bad times."	*Get out your checkbook!* You'll hear lots of excuses but see very little action. You'll play Mommy or Daddy.
Likes to be in charge in and out of the bedroom. Always seems to be strong and to know what he wants. Never shows fear or vulnerability.	*Control freak!* It starts out feeling like you're being taken care of and ends up like you're living with a dictator.

These are just a few samples of warning signs and their possible consequences. In Chapter Six I'll talk about Fatal Flaws and in Chapter Seven we'll look at Compatibility Time Bombs so you can get a much better idea of the kinds of problems to watch out for in relationships.

Watching the Movie of Your Love Life

Now it's time for you to look at some of the warning signs you've received and ignored in past or present relationships, and to gain some understanding of how you could have predicted the problems you'd have with that partner if you had paid more attention in the beginning. You'll need some paper, a pen, and a quiet place where you won't be disturbed.

▼
Watching Your Love Movies

STEP 1 Write down the name of a partner and the dates of your relationship at the top of a page.

STEP 2 Write down the heading "Warning Signs" under the name.

STEP 3 Read these instructions. Then close your eyes and imagine that you are sitting alone in a movie theater. It is dark, and as you look up at the screen, the film suddenly begins. The title flashes on the screen and says (*Your Name*)'s *Relationship with* (*Your Partner's Name*)—*A Love Story* Example: *Barbara's Relationship with Jeffrey—A Love Story.* The first scene is the very first encounter you had. Visualize your whole relationship with that person unfolding. See yourselves talking, spending time together, having sex, etc., in chronological order, as if you were watching a movie of your relationship.

As you watch each scene of the movie, starting from the very first moment you met, watch for any behaviors, comments, discussions or experiences that don't feel right to you. *You can tell which these are by how tense your body becomes when you think about or visualize them in your mind. These are warning signs. As you notice each one, gently open your eyes and write it down under Warning Signs. Then close your eyes again and continue watching the movie where you left off. Do this until the movie is over—that is until the relationship ends or you are in the present.*

STEP 4 When you are done watching the movie, open your eyes, look over the warning signs you wrote down, and based on the problems that developed in your relationship with that partner, write a few sentences describing the outcome of that relationship.

STEP 5 Repeat this same exercise for every person you've been involved with.

▲

JUNE'S LOVE MOVIES

Here's an example of the love movie exercise by a woman named June, who took my seminar.

Name
David, 1974–77

Warning Signs
- ► Acted very mysterious about himself on first few dates.
- ► Told me he wasn't interested in settling down.
- ► Didn't call me when he left town on business.
- ► Answered questions about his attitudes toward love and relationships by quoting philosophers.
- ► Wouldn't talk much about his past lovers.
- ► Told me to not get too emotionally attached to him whenever I'd say I loved him.
- ► Always acted like my superior or teacher.
- ► Didn't like when people thought we were a couple.

Conclusion

I was madly in love with David, but it's obvious watching my movie that he wasn't in love with me. *David was petrified of commitment and had a difficult time with intimacy.* He was actually pretty honest about it—I just didn't get the hint, and kept hoping he would love me more in time. Maybe it was the fact that he was unobtainable that I found so attractive. David kept me hanging for several years in an off-again, on-again relationship (it was always on from my side) until he moved to another city and I found out he and my best friend were having an affair. I shouldn't have been surprised, but I was.

Name

Peter, 1979–80

Warning Signs
- ► Had four drinks on our first date and got smashed.
- ► Seemed passionate but impersonal in bed from the start.
- ► Bragged about how bad he'd been in high school and how he almost flunked out (I thought he was "colorful").
- ► Drove really fast, ignoring speed limits, and talked about how he could get traffic tickets fixed.
- ► Couldn't actually tell me what his job was, but said he had lots of deals in the works that involved finance.
- ► His apartment was a pig.
- ► Tried to impress my friends when he first met them and told jokes all night.
- ► Described all his ex-girlfriends as weak and helpless victims.

Conclusion

I must have been blind not to see from the first night that Peter was a rebel who had never grown up. I saw his behavior as exciting, obviously lying to myself. *I had enough warning signs in the first two weeks to know he would never be a stable, responsible partner, but I ignored them.* The year we were together was turbulent and dramatic. He was like a tornado smashing through the serenity in my life with his bravado and bad attitude toward everything "conventional." The longer we were together, the more it became apparent that he was a "weekend alcoholic," didn't have any real career direction, and desperately needed to be the center of attention at all times. Looking back, I don't even think Peter knew who I really was—he was too busy cleaning up the constant messes in his own life, with my help, of course! I finally left, and he accused me of not being able to "handle his high energy." Give me a break.

Name

Gerald, 1986–present (my husband)

Warning Signs

- ► Told me when we first met he had a bad relationship with his mother.
- ► Got angry at me for telling our friends we were seeing each other before we had a chance to discuss it together.
- ► Had immature, unenlightened friends.
- ► Very hard on himself and had difficult time acknowledging his accomplishments.
- ► Tendency to get annoyed with people and situations easily.

Conclusion

It was interesting to watch my movie with Gerald since we are married, happily, in my opinion. First of all, it was different from the others in that I wasn't chasing Gerald or trying to get him to love me. Thank God. I finally learned from the past and broke that pattern.

I could see right away that the problems we do have in our relationship could all be spotted in seed form in the beginning. Gerald's mother was never really a good mother to him, so he gets reactive when I try to mother him at all. And because he is so hard on himself, he is hard on other people as well. I'd say impatience and intolerance are his most difficult qualities. He really needs to be included in what's going on—I found that out when we had our first fight about announcing our relationship, and I've remembered that since, and always made sure to communicate with him before I rush ahead. **I think the difference between this movie and the others, aside from the fact that it's still going on, is that *Gerald is just as aware of his warning signs, or potential problem areas, as I am.* We still work through them, along with mine,** of course, but I feel like we are working as a team, and not against each other.

June learned a lot from her love movie exercise. She was able to see clearly that the outcomes of her earlier relationships weren't accidents—she didn't pay attention to the warning signs. And she can trace the trouble spots in her relationship with her husband back to the beginning.

What to Do with the Warning Signs You Discover

The point of this section is *not* to make you so paranoid the moment you see a flaw in a potential partner that you run the other way. As we saw in Chapter Two, all of us bring emotional baggage into a relationship. You won't meet anyone who, if you're really paying attention, doesn't give off some warning signs. The key questions you need to ask yourself are:

▶ Is this warning me about *something reasonable that I am willing to deal with* (partner too serious, not spontaneous enough, needs to trust love more), or is this warning me about *something unreasonable that I am not willing to deal with* (partner has no integrity, cheats, can't feel, makes you feel unloved, has addictions, emotionally screwed up, etc.)?

▶ If I decide I am willing to deal with this, *is my partner also aware of this problem or pattern and willing to work on it as well?*

I believe that with enough love and determination, a couple can overcome many obstacles. But it's almost impossible to make a relationship work when one person knows there is problem and the other is in denial.

MISTAKE

3

▼   ▼   ▼   ▼   ▼   ▼   ▼   ▼

We Make Premature Compromises

The third common mistake we make in the beginning of our relationships I call **premature compromise**—*changing or editing* *your own values, behaviors, and habits in hopes that you and your new partner will appear to get along more harmoniously.*

I'm not suggesting that you walk into a relationship thinking, "I'll do anything to get him to like me, even if it means compromising my own values." The process is a lot more subtle than this. It's an adjustment you make in what is important to you as you get to know someone. *When you discover that beliefs you've had, or interests that were important to you, or friends you care for are not acceptable to your partner, you may tend to make these less important in order to create the illusion that the two of you are much more compatible than you actually are.*

THE DANGER IN PREMATURE COMPROMISE IS THAT YOU LOSE YOUR SENSE OF SELF EARLY IN THE RELATIONSHIP AND CREATE A FALSE SENSE OF HARMONY BETWEEN YOU AND YOUR MATE.

Let's look at some common ways in which we make premature compromises:

Compromising Your Beliefs and Values

When you first meet someone, you share your beliefs and values with them and try to discover more about theirs so you can decide how well suited you are for one another. But once you come across a conflict in those values, you have two choices:

---

1. **You can stand by your beliefs and risk tension between you and your partner,**

   or

2. **You can compromise your beliefs to "keep the peace."**

You might compromise your beliefs or values by:

▶ allowing yourself to be pressured into having sex with someone before you are ready or feel it is appropriate

▶ not speaking up about something your partner is doing in his life that you feel is wrong

▶ not disclosing your beliefs on a controversial issue (abortion, politics, homosexuality, the environment, religion), or softening or denying those beliefs

▶ participating in activities you would normally avoid (gossiping, drinking, taking drugs, watching pornographic movies, etc.)

▶ not expressing an opinion if it strongly disagrees with your partner's

▶ going off your diet and eating junk food you'd ordinarily avoid

JUDY TELLS HOW SHE COMPROMISED HER BELIEFS

"I met Daryl through a coworker and was immediately attracted to him. I was twenty-seven, and had dated a lot of men, but no one I really wanted to get serious with. But Daryl seemed like he had a lot going for him, and I found myself interested in pursuing the relationship.

"I guess I was so eager to impress him that I went into our first date thinking more about trying to be who he wanted me to be than the person I really was.

"Looking back at that night, I see the beginning of a pattern. We went out to dinner, and he ordered wine. I don't drink—at least I didn't before Daryl, but I decided to have some wine. A few glasses later, I was getting pretty tipsy. But it didn't stop there. We went to a bar to meet some of his friends and dance, and drank some more. A little voice kept saying, 'Judy, this is totally unlike you. This is everything you disapprove of.' But Daryl was being so sweet to me and I felt so appreciated that I didn't pay attention. By the end of the evening, I was totally bombed. I can't say I didn't have fun, because I did, but not the way I want to have fun.

"Daryl and I dated for five months, and the story didn't change. He'd call me up and say, Let's party, babe, and I'd come running. His whole crowd drank too much and played too much, and I became just like them. I used to go to church at least a few times a month, but I gave that up. I mean, I couldn't really show up with a hangover. Sometimes I'd try to talk to Daryl about my spiritual beliefs, or suggest we calm things down a bit and just stay home together. But he'd always laugh and call me his "little Sunday school teacher," and I'd drop it.

"I broke up with him last year. It was one of the hardest things I've ever done, because I did love him, and he said he loved me. **But** it wasn't me he really loved, it was the woman I turned into when I was with him. The real me went into hibernation when I met him, and I didn't get her back again until I left. It was a painful lesson."

Compromising Your Interests and Activities

Sometimes to make a relationship work:

---

1. **You will give up your own interests or activities, especially if you suspect they aren't important to your new partner or that they might interfere with your future together,**

   or

2. **You will become very involved in interests or activities you really don't care about at the expense of your own, in order to bond with your partner.**

Some ways by which you might do this are:

▶ Stop reading as many books because your partner would rather watch TV in the evenings.

▶ Give up a sport such as cycling, tennis, or weight training because your partner doesn't want to participate.

▶ Stop attending personal growth seminars, classes, Twelve Step meetings, or support groups because your partner isn't interested in or doesn't support these activities.

STEVE TELLS HOW HE COMPROMISED HIS INTERESTS

"When I first met Valerie, she was dating someone else, and I remember telling a friend of ours to let me know if they ever broke up. Six months later I was really surprised when he called. 'Valerie is available,' he announced, and I called her that night. Our relationship started out hot and heavy, and from the first week, I was really anxious to make it work. Saturday morning arrived, and I told her I was going to meet a friend for racquetball, as I did each weekend. "Oh, you can play racquetball anytime," she practically cooed. "What am I going to do all day until you come over?" It took me about ten seconds to decide to skip racquetball and spend the afternoon with her.

"I think I played racquetball twice the whole year we dated. And that wasn't the only interest I gave up. **I stopped watching football because she thought it was "gross." I stopped running every morning before work because she'd coax me to stay in bed with her. I stopped doing anything Valerie didn't like doing.** I never thought that I was sacrificing—I guess I was just trying to avoid arguments. When I finally began reintroducing those things I'd given up into my life, Valerie went crazy. 'You never used to be like this!' she'd scream. 'You've become so selfish!' It took me all that time to figure out that Valerie needed much more attention than I could give her. **I would have seen this in the first few weeks of our relationship if only I hadn't compromised who I was so much.**"

Compromising Your Friends and Family

Other ways in which you may compromise too much in relationships is:

▼
---

1. **You stop spending time with the friends, family, and people you love if your partner is not comfortable with them**

or

2. **You start spending time with people you don't care for in order to please your partner.**

▲

Judy talked about this in the earlier example. She not only compromised her beliefs and values by drinking and partying with Daryl, but she also compromised her friends by spending less time with them and more time with Daryl's friends, whom she disliked and had little in common with. "The truth is," Judy commented, "if I had stayed in closer contact with my own friends, I probably wouldn't have gotten so far off-track, and the relationship would have ended a lot sooner and with much less pain."

Why We Make Premature Compromises

There are two reasons why you may compromise prematurely in the beginning of your relationships:

1. You must compromise to create some kind of compatibility. Your partner is so different from you in important ways that unless you start editing away parts of yourself, the relationship will be very short-lived. Perhaps your partner even expects you to compromise, and, like Daryl, ridicules or rejects you if you don't.

2. You compromise because you are desperate to be loved and accepted by your new partner and to make the relationship work. Your partner may have no desire for you to give up who you are and what you believe in, but you may walk into the relationship frightened of discovering that this is not the right person for you. So you try to make it look like you are perfect for one another by becoming a "clone" of your mate.

All good relationships contain some degree of compromise. You can't live your life exactly as you did when you were single once you make a commitment to a mate. But:

▼

WHEN YOU MAKE COMPROMISES OUT OF A DESIRE TO AVOID CONFLICT, YOU ARE COMPROMISING FOR THE WRONG REASONS.

▲

What's the solution? *Enter into a relationship knowing what your values, interests, and loyalties are, and be committed first to yourself and second to your partner.*

MISTAKE

▼   ▼   ▼   ▼   **4**   ▼   ▼   ▼   ▼

___

We Give In to Lust Blindness

As a seminar leader, I'm always attempting to create new ways of helping people learn through *experience* rather than *information*.

If I have a principle I want to teach, I try to find the most creative way possible to illustrate that principle with an exercise. One of my favorites is designed to show people how prone they are to making Mistake #4. Lust Blindness: Here's how it works when I do this exercise with single people:

Each course participant puts on a blindfold. Then, with the help of my staff, they pair up with a member of the opposite sex. Their instructions are to spend five to ten minutes together getting to know one another as if they were shopping for a prospective partner. I tell them to be as flirtatious or bold as they want to. They can hold hands or be affectionate if they wish. After the time elapses, they make notes to themselves about their reactions, and we place them together with another partner. By the time we are finished, they've had six or seven "minirelationships."

Next, I ask them to rate their partners based on how attracted they felt to each one, placing them in order (number one, number two, etc.), and to write down why they felt that way about each person.

Then the fun begins. We introduce each person to all of their partners. **You can imagine the shock on people's faces when they realize that, with their blindfold on, they felt attracted to *totally different people* than they normally would without a blindfold.** A young, athletic guy whose taste in women is blonde, buxom, and beautiful finds his number one choice was a women who is a little plump and on the plain side and with whom he had one of the most stimulating and erotic conversations of his life. A career woman who has made a habit of getting involved with the most successful guys she can find discovers that her number one choice is a schoolteacher whose voice and sensitivity she fell in love with. I love watching people stand around getting their minds blown and their boundaries broken as they begin to understand how much visual chemistry, or Lust Blindness, has limited their ability to choose partners with whom they are compatible.

I'm not suggesting that you put a bag over your head the next time you go to a party or a bar (although it is an interesting idea— *"Barbara's Bag Bar!"*). As we'll discuss in Chapter Ten, sexual chemistry and attraction is one important element of compatibility. But this exercise always reminds me of how affected we are by Lust Blindness.

How to Cure Lust Blindness

In Chapter One I talked a lot about the "Lust into Love Formula" and how it seduces you into believing you are compatible with people when you really just have the hots for them! **You are in love with the passion, not necessarily the person.** But I wanted to remind you about Lust Blindness again since we are discussing mistakes we make at the beginning of relationships, and to encourage you, if you are single, to **try to wear a psychic blindfold when you meet people so you can see who they really are beyond the physical.**

WHEN YOU LEARN TO FEEL PEOPLE WITH YOUR HEART AND NOT JUST SEE THEM WITH YOUR EYES, YOU WILL ATTRACT MUCH MORE COMPATIBLE PARTNERS INTO YOUR LIFE.

If you have a history of Lust Blindness, I suggest that you **postpone having sex with a new partner until you can't stand it any longer.**

Each of you has your own moral beliefs, and you must follow your own conscience when it comes to sexual activity. I can only share my personal views and what I've found works for people I've helped. If you do plan to be sexually active before marriage, try waiting for as long as you can with a new partner, and I'm not talking about a week, either!

Get to know everything you can about this person, using the information I'll give you in the rest of this book, before you sleep with him or her.

Here are my guidelines for deciding when it's right to become sexual with someone:

When Is It Time To Become Sexually Intimate?

▶ You should be *intellectually and emotionally intimate* before you are sexually intimate.

▶ You should spend at least *twice as much time* talking and learning about one another as you do necking or fooling around.

▶ You should *like* the person. I have a saying:
DON'T SLEEP WITH SOMEONE YOU DON'T WANT TO
BECOME LIKE.

▶ You should *respect* the person and his or her values.

▶ You should have gone through some difficult times together (one of you was sick, family crisis, job stress) and
seen how your partner operates under stress and how he
or she treats you when you are under stress.

▶ You should have *discussed birth control, sexually trans-
mitted diseases such as herpes and AIDS,* and know as
much as possible about your partner's sexual history. If
you haven't been tested for the AIDS virus, I suggest you
do so, and ask your partner to do the same. Why take
chances?

▶ You should have agreed on *what form of birth control
you are going to use,* and if it's different from a condom,
that you will *use a condom in order to practice safe sex.*

▶ If you are a woman, you should ask yourself:
WOULD I WANT TO HAVE THIS MAN'S CHILDREN?
WOULD I WANT A SON JUST LIKE THIS MAN?

These questions serve two purposes: First, they remind
you that pregnancy is always a possibility and will ensure
that you are careful about birth control; and second, they
will help you be sure that you are ready to become sexually
intimate with this man. Whether you actually want children
or not, *if you don't like this man enough to want children
that carry his genes, characteristics, and personality, then
what are you doing sleeping with this guy?*

▶ If you are a man, you should ask yourself:
WOULD I WANT THIS WOMAN TO BE THE MOTHER OF
MY CHILDREN? WOULD I WANT A DAUGHTER JUST LIKE
THIS WOMAN?

I showed this list to a friend of mine as I was writing this book,
and her response was, "My gosh, Barbara, you've taken all the fun
out of sex. Who could possibly pass this kind of test?" My answer to
her and to you is:

▶ What's fun about getting your heart broken because it turns out the person you slept with is seeing someone else?

▶ What's fun about lying in bed at night next to someone you just made love with and feeling alone?

▶ What's fun about having been sexually vulnerable with someone only to find out that he lost interest after he got you in bed?

▶ What's fun about an unwanted pregnancy?

▶ What's fun about finding out your partner gave you herpes?

▶ What's fun about testing positive for the HIV virus?

Making love can be one of the most beautiful and healing experiences in the world, but I've seen it cause tremendous pain, humiliation, and heartache for people when they enter into it blindly.

MISTAKE

▾ ▾ ▾ ▾ **5** ▾ ▾ ▾ ▾

We Give In to Material Seduction

I stood before a group of women during one of my seminars and told them I was about to describe two men, and I wanted them to judge how eligible they felt these guys were. "If you're single," I explained, "judge them on the basis of whether you'd be interested in going out with them; if you're married, judge them on the basis of whether you'd advise your girlfriend or your daughter to go out with them."

"Okay," I began, "let me describe the first man. He's very warm, caring, and open, and interested in having a serious, committed relationship. He has a dynamic personality and loves being around people. He is emotionally healthy and capable of being totally intimate with the person he loves. He is happy with his life and has an adventurous spirit with a great sense of humor. He loves to talk about his feelings and is committed to personal growth."

I looked around the room and noticed that all of the women were nodding their heads and giggling. "All right, how many of you would be interested in this guy?" I asked. All the women cheered and whistled, letting me know Candidate #1 was a hit.

"Okay, next, Mystery Guy #2. He's a very controlling person and likes to have everything his way. He can have a terrible temper and is known for being highly critical. As for sex, well, he's pretty inhibited, but that doesn't matter much, since he's afraid of commitment and has a difficult time being intimate in relationships. Besides, he's a workaholic, so that doesn't leave much time for love."

The women were crinkling up their noses and making strange faces as they listened to my description of Candidate #2. "Well, ladies, how many of you would be interested in this guy?" I asked, and the response of boos and hisses gave me my answer.

"Well, ladies, I'm glad you've made your decisions. But there is something I neglected to tell you about each candidate. **The first man, the one you all wanted to be with, is a trash collector. And the second man, the one you all booed, is a multimillionaire with homes and yachts around the world and who hangs around with royal figures and celebrities.**"

The women looked at me with shock and embarrassment on their faces. I'd fooled each one of them into facing their own attitudes about material wealth and prestige. As wonderful as Mystery Man #1 sounded at first, these ladies had a hard time with the thought of going out with a trash collector. And as bizarre as Mystery Man #2 sounded at first, it would be difficult to turn down a date with a multimillionaire.

How We Become Materially Seduced

In our society, where such an emphasis is placed on outer rather than inner wealth and accomplishment, we often fall prey to material seduction in choosing our partners. We do this by allowing ourselves to be influenced by a person's:

▶ money
▶ life-style
▶ appearance
▶ power
▶ career
▶ reputation

As much as we would like to believe that our values are so lofty that these things wouldn't have an effect on us, it is difficult to be completely immune to them.

It makes me sad that, as women, we have been so disempowered throughout history that we look for sex with famous or rich men, or for a husband with an important job and standing in the community, or a boyfriend with a nice car and a condo to make us feel worthwhile *rather than finding our own worth within ourselves.* Although times are changing and millions of women are helping support their families while others are the sole breadwinners, **we still place exaggerated value on the money and prestige a man can offer us and, in the process, neglect to discover what kind of heart and soul our prospective partner possesses.**

When a woman tells a female friend that she's involved with a new man, the friend's first response will most likely be:

"What does he do for a living?"

And when a woman meets another woman, and finds out that she has a boyfriend, or is married, she will probably ask:

"What does your husband do?"

I've heard women respond to this question apologetically, if they don't feel their partner's profession is prestigious enough. "Oh, he's just a salesman," or, "Well, right now he works in a clothing store, but he's taking classes to get into real estate." And how many of us have heard our parents or grandparents discussing a woman who *"married well,"* not meaning that she had found a caring, loving man but that she'd married a man with a good career, a prestigious job, or lots of money.

From the other point of view, although there are some guys who might attempt to marry a woman for her money, *most men care more about a woman's appearance than her bank balance.* When a man tells a male friend that he's involved with a new woman, the friend's first response will most likely be:

"What does she look like?"

Each time I lecture to men's groups I remind them that just as they hate being judged for what kind of car they drive or the size of their wallet, so women hate being accepted or rejected based on what we look like in a skirt and the size of our breasts!

The Dangers of Material Seduction

I have a thirty-four-year-old friend I'll call Robin who has had a string of unhappy and unfulfilling relationships, all because she makes the mistake of falling for material seduction. Robin is sweet and attractive, and I could never understand why she'd always end up with men with whom she wasn't compatible. Then I began to pay closer attention to the kinds of guys she chose, and I saw the problem. Robin *never* went out with a man who wasn't well off and living a flashy life-style. She looked for guys with fancy cars, high-profile jobs, and expensive habits. When I'd ask her how things were going with her latest date, her answer would always include what restaurant he'd taken her to or which lavish resort they were visiting that weekend. *In her mind, she was in a good relationship if she was spending time sunning in Palm Springs, skiing in Aspen, and playing in Mexico!*

Robin's material thrill would last for a month or two, and then the excitement would wear off and she would have to face her partner, who, in many cases, was incapable of making a commitment, or expressing real feelings, or caring about anything but how he looked and who he was seen with. She'd break off the relationship and go into a depression, wondering why she couldn't meet a wonderful man and fall in love. But a few weeks later, a friend would invite her to a fancy party in Beverly Hills and she'd start the cycle all over again.

Even if you are successful at finding a "good catch," the experience can backfire. I remember a call on my radio show from a woman who was falling apart. "I married my husband when he was a successful builder," she explained. "We didn't know each other for very long, just six months, but he really seemed to love me and swept me off my feet with exciting trips, expensive gifts, and romance. We had a huge wedding and a month-long honeymoon in Europe. But last year the bottom fell out of the building industry because of the recession, and my husband's business went bankrupt. *Barbara, I've lost my attraction to him.* I feel so guilty, because I know he loves me, *but I don't think I ever really loved him. I was in love with the life-style and the perks.* What do I do now?"

This woman learned about Mistake #5 the hard way.

▼

WHEN YOU CHOOSE A PARTNER BASED ON WHAT HE CAN OFFER YOU MATERIALLY RATHER THAN WHAT HE CAN OFFER YOU EMOTIONALLY, YOU WILL END UP IN THE WRONG RELATIONSHIP.

▲

I often meet single men who complain that although they are honest, loving, loyal, and looking for a committed relationship, women regularly pass them over because they don't have a lot of money or a prestigious job. "I'm a supermarket clerk (or shoe salesman or bank teller)," a man will explain, "and women are attracted to me until they find out what I do for a living. Then they run in the opposite direction. **These same women would rather go out with a guy who drives a Mercedes and is a doctor or a lawyer, even if he treats them like dirt, than have me pick them up in my nine-year-old VW and treat them like a princess.**"

I agree with these frustrated men: There are millions of potentially wonderful partners out there just waiting to share their love, but they may not fit your picture of what we've been programmed to believe is a "good catch." The same applies to men who complain they can't find women who are intelligent and caring, yet judge potential candidates solely on the basis of their physical attractiveness. **If you've been frustrated in your search for the right partner, consider getting to know people you would normally judge "not for you."** You may be pleasantly surprised.

MISTAKE

▼   ▼   ▼   ▼   **6**   ▼   ▼   ▼   ▼

We Put Commitment Before Compatibility

The year is 1963. I'm sitting in my sixth-grade class, staring across the aisle at Robert Smith, the boy I'm madly in love with. He doesn't really know it, and if he did, I'm sure he wouldn't want anything to do with me—I'm skinny with pigtails and the ugliest glasses in the world. But it doesn't matter, because I'm committed to loving him. I'm not paying much attention to what the teacher is saying because I'm busy with something much more important. In my looseleaf notebook I am practicing writing:

> Barbara Smith
> Barbara Ann Smith
> Robert and Barbara Smith
> Mrs. Robert Smith
> Mr. and Mrs. Robert Smith

Here I was, only twelve years old, but I was already trying out my name with his, writing it over and over again until my hand got cramped. I'm certain Robert Smith never knew the extent of the plans I had for us. I guess he will now!

If you are a woman, you're probably laughing as you read this, because most likely you did the same thing. At a young age we learned to imagine ourselves happily married to—well, to someone. It was the married part of the fantasy that was most important. Whom we were married to was secondary.

This was my first experience of commitment before compatibility, and sadly, it was far from my last. I became an expert at *"falling in love with love,"* and like many men and women, **became seriously involved in relationships before giving much thought to whether this person was really right for me or not.**

How can you tell you are making this mistake? Here are some possible warning signs:

1. **You have sex with your partner within the first month of your relationship. (We'll talk about this in Chapter Ten.)**
2. **You and your partner begin living together within the first three or four months of the relationship.**
3. **You feel sure that this person is the one for you a few weeks into the relationship.**
4. **The intensity of your feeling for your new partner is proportionately much greater than the amount of time you have spent together.**
5. **Within the first weeks or month, you find yourself saying and doing things you have done before in relationships you thought would last forever.**
6. **Within the first weeks or month, you begin fantasizing, or even planning, the rest of your year or life and how you will spend it with your new partner.**

If you are in a new relationship and have experienced one or more of these warning signs, don't panic. It doesn't *necessarily* mean that you are going too fast, or that your relationship isn't meant to last forever. But there is a good chance that you are making an emotional commitment to your partner before you know him or her very well, and need to *slow down and take your time.*

▼

You may be prone to making Mistake #6—Commitment before Compatibility—if you:

▶ like being part of a couple much more than you like being single

▶ are tired of dating and trying out new partners, and long to settle down

▶ felt unloved or abandoned as a child

▶ feel lost when you are not in a relationship

▶ feel pressured by others to find a partner

▶ are a woman and feel your biological clock is running out

▶ are the only one of your group of friends who still isn't married

▶ have a lonely inner child who desperately wants to feel loved and belonging to someone

▶ are very idealistic and find it easy to see what is lovable in people

---
▲

BARBARA'S STORY

When I was a little girl, I watched my mother feel abandoned and alone because my father was out with other women instead of being home with his wife and family. I loved my father very much, and like most children caught in the middle of a bad marriage, I didn't understand why Daddy wasn't there when we needed him. When I was eleven, my mother called me and my brother downstairs to the kitchen and told us that she and my father were getting a divorce. My worst nightmare had come true. At that point, little Barbara made an unconscious decision: *When I grew up, I would love a man so much that he would never think of leaving me.*

Ten years passed. I was twenty-one years old, when I met a young man who told me he loved me and wanted to marry me. I'd only known him a few months and knew little about him, but no one had ever asked me to marry him before. So I blindly threw myself into this relationship and made the commitment. **I wasn't in love with this man. I was in love with loving.**

I spent the next few months crying my eyes out. I never stopped to ask myself why I was so miserable, because I was too busy planning the perfect wedding and the perfect honeymoon. I was on a mission. I was going to have the best marriage in the world and be the most loving wife anyone had ever seen.

I'll never forget my wedding day. I'd been trying to go without my glasses for the past year, and being severely nearsighted, I'd been walking around virtually blind. Now, as I stood wearing the perfect dress, I looked down toward the altar where I knew my fiancé was waiting, and all I could see was a blur. This was who I was marrying. The perfect music began, and I walked down the aisle toward the blur who would become my husband.

Within a year of my marriage, I was divorced. **Needless to say, I discovered that my husband was not the man I thought he was, or, more accurately, the man I wanted him to be.** I had been blind in more ways than one.

For the next fifteen years of my life I repeated this pattern in increasingly painful ways. I'd meet a man, make an instant commitment, and stay in that relationship for many years. The relationship would end suddenly when I'd wake up and realize my partner and I were wrong for each other. **I made a commitment to my partners unconditionally, without questioning whether they were the right mate for me.** That's why I kept getting involved—I wanted so desperately to make a relationship work with someone, just like the little girl I used to be so desperately wanted to help make her mommy and daddy's marriage work.

Five years ago, the last of these relationships ended, and my heart was broken worse than it had ever been in my life. And suddenly, through the darkness of my sorrow, all at once everything became clear:

► I saw that sad little girl within me who just wanted someone to love, whether or not they loved her back.
► I saw the woman with so much to give others who could not give to herself.
► I saw the teacher who encouraged everyone else to get the love they deserved, yet constantly settled for less than she deserved in her own relationships.

And in finally seeing the truth, I saw the way out of my pattern to freedom. For the past four years I've been in the most wonderful, healthy relationship of my life. My partner and I took a long time to make a commitment to each other, and during that time I made sure I was asking for what I wanted and getting it. *I've never been so careful, asked so many questions, or talked about so much before, but my patience and effort have paid off. I'm being loved more now than I could have ever imagined.*

I wanted to share my story with you so you would understand why writing this book has been so important to me. Everything I'm talking about, I've done. Every solution I'm offering you I use in my life every day. I am finding my way out of the darkness, and I hope that by sharing my journey, I'm helping you find your own path to freedom.

AVOIDING
▼
WHO'S
▼
WRONG

▼▼▼

This section of the book will teach you everything you need to know about *what doesn't work in relationships*. Chapter Five discusses ten types of love affairs that will end in pain and disappointment. Chapter Six presents some important "Fatal Flaws" to watch out for in your partner, since they lead to serious problems. Chapter Seven will educate you about "Compatibility Time Bombs," circumstances that exist in your relationship that can suddenly blow up and cause it to self-destruct. Once you read these chapters, I'm confident that you will be able to evaluate your past, present, and future relationships with much more clarity and honesty. Have fun!

▼

5

▼▼▼

THE TEN TYPES OF
RELATIONSHIPS
THAT WON'T WORK

▼▼▼

If I tried to count the number of relationships I've heard about in all my years of counseling, teaching seminars, and hosting radio and TV talk shows, the figure would be astronomical. I've listened to every story you can imagine about every kind of problem you could invent. As I've worked with people to help them understand why their relationships turned out as they did, I noticed certain *patterns or types of love affairs that were destined to fail from the start*—So here they are, *the ten types of relationships that won't work.* As you read each one, think about your past love choices and your present relationships, as well as the relationships your family and friends have been involved in. The ten are:

▼

THE TEN TYPES OF RELATIONSHIPS THAT WON'T WORK

1. **You care more about your partner than he does about you.**
2. **Your partner cares more about you than you do about him.**
3. **You are in love with your partner's potential.**

4. **You are on a rescue mission.**
5. **You look up to your partner as a role model.**
6. **You are infatuated with your partner for external reasons.**
7. **You have partial compatibility.**
8. **You choose a partner in order to be rebellious.**
9. **You choose a partner as a reaction to your previous partner.**
10. **Your partner is unavailable.**

Important: If, after reading this chapter, you suspect that you are in one of these ten types of love affairs right now, reach out for some help: Talk with family or close friends, or seek professional counseling to help you decide whether it is wise for you to continue in this relationship, or whether you should end it.

RELATIONSHIP TYPE

▼   ▼   ▼   ▼   **1**   ▼   ▼   ▼   ▼

You Care More About Your Partner Than He Does About You

You know the feeling: You're in love, but you're not sure how he or she feels; you think the two of you could be perfect together, but he doesn't seem to be that excited about the relationship; you can't stop thinking about him when you're apart, but he seems to be just fine without you. What does all of this mean? *It means you are in a relationship that is not going to work.*

In any love affair there are going to be moments, days, or even longer periods of time when one person is more focused on their feelings for their mate and seems to be more "in love." In a good relationship this polarity will periodically switch back and forth so that both partners "take turns" pursuing and being pursued. *When a relationship is healthy, this "emotional dance" takes place in a very subtle way,* like the tide slowly creeps up onto the shore and then gradually retreats back into the ocean. **However, a relation-**

ship is not healthy when one person is the emotional pursuer most or all of the time. *This is a relationship that is out of balance and therefore will not work.*

▼

HOW TO TELL IF YOU'RE NOT BEING LOVED ENOUGH

Here are some warning signs that you may be in a relationship in which you are loving your partner more than you are being loved. *For each statement that describes how you feel or behave* **most of the time,** *give yourself one point.* **Be 100 percent honest with yourself, even if it hurts.**

1. You are usually the one who reaches out first to be affectionate physically, (reaching for your partner's hand, offering a hug, giving a kiss, etc.).
2. You want to make love, to be intimate and loving when you are in bed, but your partner is into just having sex.
3. You go out of your way to be with him or do things for him, but your partner rarely goes out of his way for you.
4. In the beginning of the relationship you told your family about your partner before he told his family about you.
5. You are the one who makes most of the plans to do things together—restaurant reservations, weekend outings, romantic evenings—and your partner seems just to go along without showing a lot of enthusiasm.
6. You seem much more excited about being in the relationship than your partner, who doesn't show you how much it means to him.
7. On special occasions your gifts to your partner are well-thought-out and personal, while his seem last-minute and impersonal.
8. You initiate most of the contact in the relationship— phone calls, discussions, etc.
9. When you talk about your relationship, your future together, or your feelings for one another, your partner becomes very uncomfortable and unresponsive, or changes the subject.
10. You seem to be fitting yourself into your partner's life, habits, and schedule, and he doesn't make efforts to fit into your life and schedule.

▲

Now total your points:

▶ **0–2 points: Your relationship with your partner is fairly well balanced,** and you're probably getting back as much love as you give out. *Pay attention to those areas in which you scored a point, and make sure you are asking for what you need and want.*

▶ **3–5 points: You may try to convince yourself you are being well loved, but you aren't.** You are working too hard to get your partner's love, and he or she isn't working hard enough to get yours. *He's either emotionally lazy, or doesn't love you enough.* Stop rowing the boat so hard and see if your partner picks up the oars and does his share. If he doesn't, you know the relationship is not for you.

▶ **5–7 points: What are you doing in such an awful relationship?** Stop kidding yourself and face the fact that you aren't getting the love you deserve. Your self-esteem is so low that you are settling for crumbs and pretending it's enough. It's not! You are in a very unhealthy situation, and the longer you stay in it, the more emotional damage you will incur. *Give your partner an ultimatum immediately about the way you deserve to be treated, or get out.* Then do some work on learning to love yourself.

▶ **8–10 points: What relationship? You aren't in a relationship, you are in a fantasy.** You are giving everything and getting nothing in return. This isn't love, it's self-mutilation. *You aren't ready to have a relationship with anyone.* **Get out now before it's too late,** *and seek some professional counseling to help you reclaim yourself.*

Why You Would Settle for Loving Your Partner More Than You Are Loved

Here are several reasons why you would attract a relationship in which you were loving more:

▶ **You're repeating a childhood pattern.** If one or more of your parents didn't give you the love and attention you needed as a child, you probably made an unconscious decision that *"I have to work hard to get people to love me."* By attracting someone whom you love more, you are "going home" and repeating the pattern.

▶ **You're punishing yourself.** If your self-esteem is low, you will attract a partner who will validate your critical opinion of yourself by not loving you enough.

▶ **You're acting out one of your parents' role with the other.** If you watched your mother always pursuing your father, or vice versa, you may have concluded as a child that this is what relationships are like *and that it's "normal" for one person to love the other more.*

No matter what the reason for being involved with someone you are loving much more than they are loving you, the results will be the same:

▶ You will end up feeling controlled by your partner.
▶ You will end up feeling hungry for love.
▶ You will end up feeling angry.
▶ You will end up feeling cheated.
▶ You will end up feeling miserable.

Solution: When you first get involved in a relationship, watch for the warning signs we discussed. *Don't fall into the trap of making excuses for your partner about why he or she can't love you the way you want to be* loved. The sooner you're honest with yourself, the less likely you are to get your heart broken. If you are presently in a relationship and realize you aren't getting the love you want, read the remainder of this book to determine whether this relationship is worth saving.

RELATIONSHIP TYPE

▼　　▼　　▼　　▼　　**2**　　▼　　▼　　▼　　▼

Your Partner Cares More About You Than You Do About Him

This is the opposite of type #1: Your partner is the one who loves you more than you love him or her. If you are in this kind of relationship, you are probably feeling guilty just reading these few sentences. You may deny it to your lover when he asks you about your feelings; you may try to convince yourself that you feel more strongly than you do. **But deep in your heart, you know you aren't loving your partner as much as he or she loves you. As in type #1, you are in a relationship that is out of balance and will not work.**

You can look at the quiz at the beginning of this chapter and reverse the questions to determine whether you are in this kind of relationship. For example, your partner calls you more; your partner initiates more of the physical contact, your partner says "I love you" more often. If you are in this type of relationship, you will probably also feel:

► defensive when accused of not loving your partner enough
► pressured or controlled by your partner's demands to be loved
► claustrophobic in a relationship, feeling you need "space" from your partner
► annoyed because your partner is too clingy and needy
► frustrated because your partner wants more than you can give

Here are several reasons why you might attract this type of relationship:

► **You're protecting yourself emotionally.** If you have ever been deeply hurt in a relationship by someone you really loved, you might make an unconscious decision that says *"I'm never going to get hurt like that again."* Then you find partners you don't love that much, so if they decide to leave you, you won't care anyway.

► **You're punishing one of your parents.** If you were not loved enough by one or both of your parents, or felt criticized or rejected by them, *you might attract a partner into your life whom you treat as your parents treated you.* You get to play the unloving one or parent, and your partner gets to play you, begging for love and not getting it. This role reversal is an unconscious way you punish your parent, even though it ends up hurting an innocent person in the process. It's as if part of you is saying, *"That's right—keep begging for my love, but you aren't going to get it, just like you didn't give it to me when I was little."* **Note: this is a very toxic pattern that you need to face and change if you ever want to have a healthy relationship.**

► **You need to be in control.** Whether you felt loved by your parents or not, if you felt very controlled as a child by one or both of your parents, you might choose to have a relationship with someone who loves you more than you love them as a way to always feel in control. When your partner is always wanting more from you and feeling more vulnerable than you feel, you have emotional power over them. *This false sense of power at someone's else's expense covers up your own deep sense of powerlessness,* which you must face if you want to have a truly meaningful relationship.

▶ **You're acting out one of your parents' roles with the other.** As I mentioned earlier, if you saw one of your parents being more aloof and distant than the other, you may think that this is what is "normal" in relationships. When you grow up and unconsciously choose which "role" you are going to play, *you choose to be the one who loves less rather than the one who loves more, since that partner doesn't get hurt as much.*

When you are in a relationship like this, you will never be truly satisfied, since you are not giving your heart completely. You may avoid getting hurt, you may convince yourself that you are in control, but you won't be happy. In addition, you will be hurting your partner by continuing to be with them when you cannot give them the love they deserve.

HOW MICHAEL LET GO OF CONTROL AND FOUND HIS TRUE LOVE

Last night as I was working on this chapter of the book, my friend Michael called me. Michael is thirty-five years old and a very talented film producer. We've known each other for many years and seen each other go through all kinds of personal and professional changes. Recently Michael ended a relationship with a twenty-five-year-old woman he'd been living with for several years, a relationship in which she definitely loved him more than he loved her. I had watched Michael agonize over his feelings for Nancy for the past nine months as she pressed him to set a date for their wedding, and he hesitated, so I wasn't surprised when he broke up with her.

Within a few months of leaving Nancy, Michael fell head over heels in love with Terri, a woman he'd known professionally for three years. I wondered if Michael would repeat the pattern he'd lived out with Nancy by holding back in this relationship and loving Terri less than she loved him, but I was happy that he had found someone new.

"Barbara," Michael said on the phone, "I have something to tell you: I've asked Terri to marry me." My mouth hung open in shock: Michael had only been seeing Terri romantically for four months. How could he be so sure that she was right for him?

"Michael," I began, "I'm sitting here at my computer working on the book, and all I think about day and night is what makes relationships work and what makes them fail. Tell me: What made you so sure about Terri after a few months when you lived with Nancy for two years and still couldn't make a commitment?"

Michael was quiet for a moment, and then he began to talk: "Barbara, I've been thinking about the same thing for the past few months. When I look at the women I've chosen in my life, I see a common theme in that **I became involved with women whom I could control.** I didn't see it this way, of course, but I've been attracted to women I would describe as 'soft and vulnerable,' when in truth they were women with low self-esteem who let me control them. Each of them loved me more than I loved them, and I guess part of me liked that—it made me feel powerful and safe. Even though I cared about Nancy, something inside me knew I could never marry her, but I couldn't put my finger on it until I left and met Terri.

"Terri is the only woman I've ever been with whom I could not control. She is powerful and confident, and I think the reason I was never attracted to her, although I've known her for a long time, is that she isn't weak and wimpy inside. Some part of me knew she'd never let me control her, and **I've always been afraid of what I can't control in my life.**

"I've always been afraid of being hurt, so I chose women who didn't have much power over me. But being with Nancy, I learned that when you know you can control someone, it doesn't work in the long run, because you're not happy.

"For the first time in my life I feel completely sure about loving someone. It's scary, because I'm not in control anymore. But I'm in love, and that's much more important."

Solution: When you first get involved with someone, be honest with yourself about whether you are taking more love than you are giving.

Important: Don't delude yourself into believing that your partner would rather have a little of your love than none at all, and use this as an excuse to stay in a relationship you do not belong in.

RELATIONSHIP TYPE

▼ ▼ ▼ ▼ 3 ▼ ▼ ▼ ▼

You Are in Love with Your Partner's Potential

"I know Fred has been out of work for a while, but he really is talented, and I know someone will come along and give him the chance he needs."

"I know Brad cares about me—it's just that he has a hard time showing his feelings. I think he needs a few more months with me to believe that I really care before he can open up."

"Sally's mood swings can be really difficult, but no one's ever taken the time to understand what a scared little girl she is inside. I just know that if I give her enough love and support, she'll get out of the depression she is in."

If these statements sound painfully familiar, you probably already know how it feels to be in love with someone's potential. **You aren't in love with who they actually are—you are in love with who you hope they could become.** Until several years ago this was my favorite type of relationship with which to frustrate and hurt myself. I'd find a man who had wonderful potential and then proceed to "help" him develop that potential, whether he asked me to or not. *These weren't really relationships—they were projects.* Was it any wonder that I didn't respect these men? Was it any wonder that after a while I'd find myself "falling out of love" with them? I didn't choose partners because we were compatible; I chose them for their "investment quality"!

These kinds of relationships are highly addictive, because you get hooked into what you wish would happen, and *then it becomes hard to break away.* After all, you never know when that miraculous change in your partner will occur. It's really not that much different from gambling.

------------------------▼------------------------

ARE YOU IN LOVE WITH YOUR PARTNER'S POTENTIAL?

Here are some symptoms that may indicate you are in relationship type #3:

▶ You tell yourself that your partner just needs a little more time to get himself and his life together.

▶ You tell yourself that no one has ever really loved your partner enough, that only you can love him enough to change him.

▶ You feel that everyone else misunderstands and underestimates your partner and that only you know the "real" person inside him or her.

▶ You make excuses to your family and friends for your partner's problems or the problems in your relationship.

▶ You feel you can't give up on your partner because it will just validate his feelings of worthlessness, and then he'll never change.

▶ You believe in your partner more than he believes in himself.

▶ You know you aren't getting the love you deserve, but you talk yourself out of your pain about it by telling yourself, "He's trying."

Why You Would Fall in Love with Your Partner's Potential

Here are several reasons why you may be prone to making this relationship mistake:

▶ **You need to be in control.** When you are in a relationship to "improve" your partner, you get to feel superior, and feel some control or power over your partner. *Even if you don't behave in a controlling way, your **thought** that your partner isn't enough as he or she is puts you in a controlling position.* If you felt very controlled by people or circumstances as a child, you may attract partners as an adult to whom you are virtually saying, "You're not quite enough as you are—perhaps with a little work . . ."

▶ **You get to avoid your own life and your own dreams by focusing on what your partner needs to do and how your partner needs to change.** When you're busy looking at how someone else could improve, you don't have much time left over to face your own inadequacies. *Falling in love with someone's potential can be a highly effective method of procrastination.*

▶ **You made a decision as a child that you couldn't get what you wanted.** If you felt rejected or unloved as a child, you may have unconsciously decided that you can't get what you want from the people you love. *Thus you unconsciously seek out people who don't give you what you want—who aren't enough as they are—and you get to feel frustrated and deprived all over again.* This was my motivation in continually finding men whom I tried to fix and improve but who were never fixed enough to give me what I wanted—I got to replay my childhood experience of hoping my father would change and be there for me, and then getting disappointed when he didn't.

Obviously, every relationship between two people involves some hopes and dreams of how you'd like to see your partner grow and improve. The key is feeling satisfied with how your partner is today, not living for the future. As I said in my book *Secrets About Men Every Woman Should Know:*

HAVING A HEALTHY RELATIONSHIP WITH A PERSON MEANS LOVING HIM FOR WHO HE IS NOW, NOT LOVING HIM IN SPITE OF WHO HE IS TODAY, OR IN HOPES OF WHO HE WILL BE TOMORROW.

If you fall in love with someone's potential, you will probably end up feeling:

▶ angry at them for not becoming who you expected them to be
▶ turned off to them sexually since you are acting like their parent, not their lover
▶ bitter that you wasted so much time in the relationship
▶ hurt and let down because your dream of how it was supposed to turn out didn't come true

Solution: If you begin a relationship with someone, make sure you love, respect, and enjoy that person as he or she is *today*. It's okay to have preferences of how you'd like to see him grow, but he should be enough for you as he is now. **If you keep hoping to change your partner so that you'll be happy with him, you aren't loving, you're gambling.**

RELATIONSHIP TYPE

▼   ▼   ▼   ▼   *4*   ▼   ▼   ▼   ▼

You Are on a Rescue Mission

▶ Do you find yourself feeling sorry for your partner more often than you'd like?

▶ Do you feel responsible for helping your partner get his or her life together?

▶ Do you feel afraid that, if you left, your partner would fall apart emotionally?

If you answered "yes" to any of these questions, you may be a "rescueholic" and not know it. **Rescueholics manage to get into relationships with partners whom they feel compelled to help, rather than partners with whom they feel compatible.** You find someone who seems wounded, fragile, unloved, and feel irresistibly drawn to caring for that person. They feel so grateful, and you feel so noble. Before you know it, you're in a relationship that looks more like a rescue mission than a healthy, balanced love affair. And once you're in it, it's *really* hard to get out.

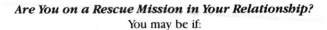

Are You on a Rescue Mission in Your Relationship?
You may be if:

▶ You are with someone who has *serious emotional, physical, or financial problems*.

▶ Your partner frequently feels *confused, overwhelmed, helpless, or victimized,* and you console, calm down, and encourage.

▶ You often take a *parental role with your partner*—giving advice, warning him or her about possible problems, feeling frustrated when your advice isn't taken, etc.

▶ Your partner has been *mistreated or badly hurt in the past,* and you feel obligated to "make it up" to him or her.

► Your partner very *rarely acts as a support system or source of strength for you* as you do for him or her.

► You feel you have to *tiptoe around your partner to avoid upsetting him or her,* and consequently you avoid asking for what you want or confronting your partner with things that bother you.

► You *tolerate and excuse behavior in your partner* that you would never put up with from a friend or an employee.

► When friends and family question why you are involved with your partner, you feel they are picking on him or her, and you *become very protective,* as you would with a child.

► You feel like *no one else would understand or love your partner like you do,* and therefore you can't leave.

► You secretly wonder whether, if you ended this relationship, your partner would find anyone else or, as you suspect, *would end up unloved and alone.*

If you can relate to even a few of these statements, you are prone to going on Emotional Rescue Missions. This kind of relationship is similar to type #3, falling in love with your partner's potential, because you hope that in time your partner will improve and change. And as with type #3, it is easy to get hooked into a rescue-type relationship because the *payoff is delayed—you don't know when your partner will get better, and you want to stick around to see it happen, especially after all your hard work!*

This type of relationship is also very different to end, since you will most likely feel you are abandoning your partner and hurting him or her terribly. *The same guilt that got you into the relationship in the first place can keep you in the relationship long after you know you should leave.*

Why You Might Go On Emotional Rescue Missions

► **You are completing unfinished business from childhood.** Remember in Chapter Two, when we discussed how we accumulate unfinished emotional business in our childhood that we then play out in our adult lives? If you are an "emotional Robin Hood," always finding partners in need of your help, you may in fact be attempting to rescue Mom, Dad, or another family member. **If you** saw one of your parents or siblings ignored, unloved, or mistreated when you were a child, you will find that person in the form of a partner in need, and will work hard to give him the love, support, and strength you feel you failed to give your family member.

▶ **You need to feel important and superior.** When you choose someone who is a mess, it automatically makes you look better, wiser, and more together. *By playing the hero in a relationship, you get to avoid your own feelings of inadequacy and powerlessness.*

▶ **You need to be in control.** When you are in a relationship with the agenda to "rescue" your partner, you feel some power over your partner. *Sometimes we forget that "helping" can be a very controlling way of relating to others.*

▼

PEOPLE WHO GO ON EMOTIONAL RESCUE MISSIONS OFTEN MISTAKE SYMPATHY FOR LOVE.

▲

HOW MARGO RESCUED HER HUSBAND AS AN EGO BOOST

When I first met Margo, twenty-nine, at one of my seminars, and heard her story, I felt sorry for her. "I'm married to an alcoholic who is in total denial," she stood and shared. "He can't keep a job; I'm the one who has been supporting us the last few years; and on top of that, he is a rageaholic. I don't know what to do."

I knew what Margo should do—leave her husband—and I told her so on the spot. "I know you're right," she said with her face all screwed up, "but if I left him, he'd think I was saying he wasn't good enough."

"Guess what, Margo: He's not good enough for you," I responded firmly.

"Well, he's trying, he really is," she replied with a weak smile.

Over the next few months as I worked with Margo, the situation deteriorated: Her husband spent the money she had saved for rent on an expensive stereo system; he would only talk about their problems if she threatened to leave him; and he would fly into rages. Finally Margo got the courage to ask him to move out to get his life together, and he left. "At last," I thought, "Margo will have a chance to blossom now that she is not taking care of her husband's mess."

That is just what happened. Margo became tremendously empowered living on her own. She looked and felt better than she had in a long time. So I was shocked when she called me one day and told me her husband was moving back in. "What happened?" I asked. "I thought you were going to give him a chance to take care of himself and become responsible." Margo hemmed and hawed and mentioned that her husband had been staying with a friend for a month, and now that the time was up, had no place to go. "We're really going to work on it this time," she insisted.

Margo's husband moved back in, and within days Margo's energy went from passionate and bubbly to tense and protected. I thought long and hard about Margo until I figured out what was going on: **Margo was a control freak. Feeling unloved, inadequate, and frightened of rejection, her method of feeling safe was to be in control. She needed to live with a man who chronically required rescuing because it made her feel competent, in command, and superior. Margo was using him as much as he was using her.**

Like many rescueholics, Margo kept herself busy trying to rehabilitate her husband to avoid her own pain and terror. The only way she will ever leave is if she finds the courage to face the emptiness she carries inside her.

Solution: If you find yourself attracted to someone who has big problems, *ask yourself if you are mistaking sympathy for love.* The key word to remember is **"RESPECT"**—you should feel respect as well as love for your partner, and be proud of who he or she is. Take time to get clear on what your needs are.

RELATIONSHIP TYPE

▼　　▼　　▼　　▼　　**5**　　▼　　▼　　▼　　▼

You Look Up to Your Partner as a Role Model

► The young actress who falls in love with her director . . .
► The student in graduate school who falls in love with his professor . . .

▶ The new salesperson who falls in love with the Marketing Director . . .

▶ The paralegal who falls in love with the well-known trial lawyer . . .

All of these people may be making the same mistake: **They are putting their partner on a pedestal.** Theirs is not an equal relationship. *The balance of power is inequitable before the relationship even starts because of the lofty status their new partner has in their eyes.*

When you fall in love with someone who is your role model, it is difficult to have a normal relationship. You can act like you are equals; you talk as if you are equals. But if, in your mind, you have given your partner a heightened status, it will prevent you from ever feeling really empowered in the relationship.

▼

Have You Put Your Partner on a Pedestal?

You have when the following occurs:

▶ You feel he or she is more intelligent than you are.

▶ You quote him or her a lot: "Joe says . . ." or "Joe believes . . ." or "Joe told me . . ."

▶ You don't challenge your partner on his opinions, beliefs, etc., because you just assume he knows more than you do.

▶ You go out of your way to let people know whom you are involved with in order to impress them.

▶ You feel there is no way you could ever achieve as much or become as wonderful as your partner.

▶ You often do things not because you feel they are right but because your partner thinks you should.

▶ You often say "I am so lucky to be with (name)," not just because you love him but because you feel it's some sort of fluke that he chose you!

▶ You would give anything to be more like your partner.

▲

It's important to emphasize here that it's not the difference in the status of the two partners that makes the relationship fail, but *the **attitudes** of the two partners, one who looks to the other as the role model, and the second who willingly steps up onto the pedestal. It's okay to be with someone who's smarter, more accomplished, or whatever, as long as both of you maintain your own sense of self.*

Why You Might Fall in Love with Role Models

▶ **You're falling in love with Mom or Dad.** If you never got the kind of attention or love you wanted from one of your parents, *you might attract an authority figure for a partner when you grow older, to finally get the sense of protection and guidance you missed out on as a child.* The opposite can be true as well: If you got a tremendous amount of attention from parents and *were perhaps too emotionally enmeshed with them, you might find it difficult to break away from the parent/child role, especially* **if you felt controlled by them,** and thus attract a powerful figure who treats you as less competent than he or she is and keeps you in a childlike role.

▶ **You are emotionally or spiritually empty.** We talked in Chapter Three about the dangers of choosing love partners when you are feeling empty yourself. *When you have a weak sense of self, you might be attracted to individuals with a particularly powerful sense of self and make them your role models.* But you aren't in love with the persons, and you are in love with their power and self-confidence.

Solution: If you realize you have put your partner on a pedestal, don't expect him or her to step down. You're the one who keeps your partner up there by not respecting your own opinion, not asking for what you want, and not loving yourself enough. **The only way your relationship can work is if you love and admire yourself as much as you love and admire him, and your partner is willing to relinquish his role as your mentor.**

RELATIONSHIP TYPE

▼　　▼　　▼　　▼ **6** ▼　　▼　　▼　　▼

You Are Infatuated with Your Partner for
External Reasons

▶ "It was his blue eyes—they just pierced my soul, and I knew I had to have him."

▶ "When I first heard Sam play the guitar, I felt like he knew me inside and out, and our relationship started that night. I've always wanted to fall in love with a musician."

▶ "Ginger's hair was magic—it was long and blond and silky, and when I was with her, it made me feel like I was really a man. That's what made me fall in love with her."

▶ "Jennifer danced like I always imagined my soulmate would, slinky and sexy. When I watched her at that party, I knew we were meant for each other."

▶ "I've always had this fantasy about flight attendants, so when I met Christine, I felt like it was destiny that we got together."

Hair, eyes, dancing ability, musical talent—are these reasons to start a relationship with someone? The answer is obviously no, yet many of us become infatuated with partners because of something about them that has little to do with their true character, and more to do with their external qualities. These relationships usually don't last long. After all, how many hours can you spend staring at your girlfriend's hair, or listening to your boyfriend play the guitar before you want more? *But I've met many people who have gotten into this type of relationship for a night, a week, even a few months, only to discover that they were really kidding themselves.* Then they are stuck with someone they really don't want to be with and are faced with the unpleasant task of breaking this news to their partner. How do you tell someone you were infatuated with them without sounding like an idiot?

"Ginger, you are a really sweet person, but as much as I'm madly in love with your hair, it's just not enough to keep me interested in you for the next forty years."

THE SPELL OF THE JUGGLER

Here is a story from my own life I think you'll enjoy:

In 1974 I was living in Mill Valley, just outside San Francisco, finishing up my bachelor's degree. I was twenty-three and very excited to be living in a part of the country where there was so much artistic and psychological experimentation. One of my favorite yearly events was the Renaissance Faire, in which a forest is transformed into an Elizabethan village and everyone roams the grounds in costume. **It was on one such "faire" day that I came under the spell of the juggler.**

I was walking by a grove of trees when I saw a crowd forming around a young man who began to juggle balls, clubs, lit torches, and anything else he had with him. I stood spellbound as I watched his graceful sensuality, dancing and laughing as he entertained the crowd. He had long, dark hair and an earring in his ear—I was in love!

I spent the rest of that day following him around, mesmerized by his personal magic. I left the fair that night determined to find out who he was and to get to know him. I begged some of my friends who worked at the fair to introduce me to him, and the next day, they did. I felt like I was walking on air. We spent the afternoon together, and promised to meet again the next day.

For the rest of the summer and throughout the fall, I was his number one groupie. I went everywhere he went—I couldn't believe I was with this incredible artist, this sensitive soul who would understand me as I did him.

HOW THE SPELL WAS BROKEN

I won't go into the embarrassing details of my disastrous attempts to consummate my relationship with him except to say that *after spending one night with him I came back to reality really fast.* Driving home, I wept tears of anger and disappointment. How could my knight in shining armor, my sensitive artistic muse have been so cold, so uncaring? In my heart, I knew the answer: **I wasn't in love with him, I was in love with his juggling, his presence, when he performed. I took one special quality he had and *projected other qualities onto him* that I thought someone like him should have.** *He wasn't any of the things I'd imagined. I had been under a spell of my own making.*

Let me pass on this warning from one who's made this relationship mistake:

If you ever find yourself infatuated with one element of a new partner's personality, ask yourself: "if this person didn't have [blue eyes, gorgeous hair, a great voice] *or wasn't* [a juggler, a basketball player, a flight attendant, etc.], *would I still want to be with him* [or her]? Be honest with yourself. It could save you a lot of heartache and disappointment.

RELATIONSHIP TYPE

▼　　▼　　▼　　▼　　7　　▼　　▼　　▼　　▼

You Have Partial Compatibility

Have you ever met someone with whom you didn't have much in common—except for one area in which you really connected? This kind of relationship can be very deceptive, **especially when the way in which you are compatible is so important to you that you mistake what is simply a powerful bond for love.**

Here are some examples of partial compatibility:

▶ **You meet your partner through a cycling club. You love cycling,** and are excited at first to share this hobby with a partner who feels the same way. You spend every weekend biking for hours on end. *But after two months of cycling and sex, you realize you don't have much else in common, and it's causing the relationship to be very rocky.*

▶ **You and your partner are thrown together on a project at work. The project requires long hours and teamwork, and in the middle of it you feel like you're falling in love.** For four months you have a passionate affair and spend most of your time talking about the project, sharing your ideas. Then the project is complete, and within a few weeks you begin to feel uncomfortable with one another. *Your common bond has been removed, and you are left alone with the fact that, outside of work, you don't share any of the same values or beliefs.*

▶ **You spend part of your summer renting a house with some friends by the beach in a resort town, and a few weeks into your vacation, you meet someone there.** For the next month you have a blast, taking long bike rides in the mornings and making barbecues on the grill at night. You've never felt so relaxed with anyone before, and when the vacation is over, you have no doubt that your relationship will continue back in the city. But you are wrong. Your first weekend away from the beach is a disaster. You can't agree on anything; you are getting on each other's nerves, and within a week you end the relationship. *Looking back you realize you'd never seen your partner under stress, and that once you did, he wasn't the same person you knew over the summer.*

You are susceptible to getting involved with this type of relationship when:

► You meet your partner under unusual circumstances that are different from those in your daily life or routine (stuck in an elevator, in physical therapy, etc.).

► You and your partner are thrown together with an activity or focus that is somewhat out of the ordinary (working on a special project, attending a seminar, serving on a committee).

► You meet your partner in an unusual environment (vacation, jury duty, etc.).

► You meet your partner during a time when you are both focused on an activity you don't participate in on a daily or frequent basis (skiing, ballroom dance classes, etc.).

You don't need a grasp of any great psychological secrets to understand the phenomenon of partial compatibility. *Like attracts like,* and it's natural for you to feel drawn to individuals with whom you have something significant in common, even if you share that bond for only a week or two. And often that initial connection *can* be the basis for what turns into a lasting and fulfilling relationship. Two cyclists won't necessarily lose interest after a few months— they may find out they are compatible in many other areas as well. Someone you meet on a ski trip or at the beach may not be just a vacation romance but also could turn out to have all of the qualities you are looking for.

The danger, however, is in becoming so infatuated with that area of partial compatibility that you don't pay attention to the rest of the relationship. This sets you up to get involved with people you normally wouldn't end up with at all, only to feel let down and disappointed when the relationship doesn't work out.

MY FRENCH FANTASY THAT FLOPPED

You may have figured out by now that the reason I know so much about these relationship mistakes is that I've made most of them myself. Here's another story from my past that is a perfect example of the problems that come with partial compatibility:

· In 1975 I was still living in Mill Valley but was enrolled in a six-week meditation course in Avoriaz, France, in the French Alps. There, with about a hundred other men and women, I spent eight to ten hours a day meditating, doing Yoga and breathing exercises, all designed to purify my nervous system and expand my consciousness.

I was living in a hotel that had been turned into our meditation academy for the summer, and was run by a young Frenchman, Jean-Pierre. Three weeks into the course, I noticed Jean-Pierre for the first time—**he was handsome, friendly, drove a Jeep, and, most important of all, *he was French!*** What more evidence did I need to have the fantasy love affair with a Frenchman that I'd always dreamed about?

Jean-Pierre spoke some English, and I spoke fairly fluent French, so our communication was pretty good, though limited. It didn't really matter, because most of our time together was spent riding through the mountains in his Jeep or French kissing in the true sense of the phrase. We spent three glorious weeks together, and were both so sad when it was time for me to go back to the States. Jean-Pierre promised me he would come to visit the first chance he got, and I could hardly wait.

About a month after I returned to San Francisco, I received a letter from Jean-Pierre saying he had three weeks off and was coming to see me. I was so excited—the thought of my French boyfriend in California seemed too good to be true. It was.

I'll never forget what happened when I was at the airport gate, watching the passengers get off, and I spotted Jean-Pierre wearing the same green rubber raincoat he wore in the mountains. As he waved and started toward me, I thought, "That is the dumbest-looking coat I've ever seen." And as Jean-Pierre reached out to give me a kiss he'd traveled seven thousand miles to get, I had a sinking feeling that things weren't going to turn out the way I'd planned.

The closer we got to my apartment, the more panicky I felt. And as we sat on my couch and drank some tea, it hit me: *Jean-Pierre was here, but France wasn't. There were no mountains, no Jeep, no French shops and French culture.* **When Jean-Pierre was removed from his environment, my interest in him all but disappeared.**

I hardly knew Jean-Pierre. I wasn't in love with him; I was in love with France. I was horrified at my reaction, but try as I might, I couldn't get the feeling back. I'd left in Avoriaz along with the croissants and Camembert.

Poor Jean-Pierre! I tried explaining my feelings to him, but I'm sure I did a terrible job. Only years later, when I began to do some serious work on myself, did I realize that my relationship with Jean-Pierre was a perfect example of partial compatibility. Jean-Pierre was a really nice guy, but not what I'd imagined him to be. *The magic of my feelings came not from the person himself but from the circumstances surrounding our meeting.*

Solution: If you meet someone in one of the circumstances I described earlier, try to step back from the relationship and ask yourself the following questions:

▶ **"How much do I really know about this person aside from our area of partial compatibility?"**

▶ **"What are my needs and requirements for a partner? Does this person meet them?"**

▶ **"What possible problems could occur if my partner and I no longer shared this area of partial compatibility?"**

If you take the time to answer these questions, you'll be less likely to get hurt yourself, or unintentionally hurt your partner.

What if you are just looking for a summer romance, or a French fling? If that's your goal, then enjoy yourself, but be careful. And remember, in the end, there's nothing as magical or exciting as love that lasts.

RELATIONSHIP TYPE

▼　　▼　　▼　　▼　　**8**　　▼　　▼　　▼　　▼

You Choose a Partner in Order to Be Rebellious

Here's an exercise for you: *Make a list of all of the qualities your parents or family would want you to find in a mate. Then, next to that, make a list of all of the qualities in your partner.* **If the two lists are diametrically opposed, you may be in a relationship as a way of rebelling against your parents, not because you are with the right person.**

This relationship type isn't as common as the others, but it can create tremendous drama in your life. Here's what I'm talking about:

▶ Your parents are *conservative white people* and you've had three *black boyfriends.*

▶ Your parents are Jewish and have always *insisted you marry a Jewish girl,* and you only go out with *Catholic women, or vice versa.*

▶ Your parents always emphasized the importance of *money and prestige,* and your partners are always *broke and anti-establishment types.*

▶ Your parents always insisted on order and discipline in your house, and all of the women you get involved with are total slobs.

▶ Your father brought you up believing that the family lineage was everything, and you continue to fall in love with women who do not want or cannot have children.

▶ Your father is in the military, and all your boyfriends have been peace and environmental activists.

▶ You were brought up with strict religious discipline, and all your partners tend to be wild, immoral, and irreverent.

By now, you get the picture. **Some people choose partners based not on who is right for them, but on who is wrong for their family.** This will be especially true if:

You have a lot of resentment and bitterness toward one or more of your parents, or felt very controlled as a child.

You tend to choose the same types of "unacceptable" partners over and over again.

You stay in relationships that aren't particularly fulfilling rather than break them off and have your parents point out that they were right all along.

The point here is *not* that relationships between people of different backgrounds can't work. (Chapter Seven will talk more about some of the problems you might face in that situation.) **But if you have a pattern of choosing partners who not only don't fulfill you but also upset your family, you are probably acting out of rebellion.**

HOW BRENDA USED THE MEN IN HER LIFE TO GET BACK AT HER PARENTS

Brenda's story is a classic case of this type of relationship. Brenda is a thirty-three-year-old art historian who comes from a conservative Jewish background. From the time Brenda was a small girl, her parents told her that she was "expected" to grow up and marry a nice Jewish boy. Along with this, Brenda's father was very strict and old-fashioned in his ways. Brenda loved her parents, though she feared her father's disapproval, and didn't date much in high school.

All that changed when Brenda left New York to go to college. Suddenly she found she was interested in men, and within two months had her first love affair—with a black law student. Brenda never even considered telling her parents about him, and when the relationship ended shortly, she felt tremendous relief. Her relief was short-lived. Three weeks later, she met a man at a fraternity party and ended up spending the night with him—another black man.

In four years of college, Brenda had several relationships, all with black men, none of whom was Jewish, and none of whom her parents knew about. After she graduated, Brenda moved back to New York to pursue her master's, and that's where she met Edward—a black art history major enrolled in the same program she was. This time it was serious, and soon Edward and Brenda moved in together. For two years, Brenda tried to hide the relationship from her parents, but finally gave up and blurted it out during a phone call. *Her parents reacted as she had expected them to—they stopped talking to her for three months, and when they finally restored contact, they refused to discuss "what's-his-name."*

A year later, Edward and Brenda broke up. Brenda threw herself into her work, landing a prestigious job at one of New York's finest museums. Her friends would try to fix her up with men, some Jewish, some not, but she'd lose interest after a few dates. On Brenda's thirty-first birthday, her coworkers from the museum threw her a party, and that's where she met Robert, an art professor who was *black, Baptist, and married.*

I met Brenda when she attended my Making Love Work Seminar. She'd read my books and desperately needed help. She was still in love with Robert; he still hadn't left his wife. And she'd written her parents a letter about him, which they responded to by pretending she hadn't mentioned it. "I'm so confused," she confessed. "I know I'm stuck in some kind of pattern, but I don't understand anything about it."

I asked Brenda to make a list like the one I mentioned earlier. This is what she came up with:

WHAT MY PARENTS WANT FOR ME	WHAT I END UP WITH
White	Black
Jewish	Catholic, Baptist, other Christian
Single	Unable to commit or married
Successful	Successful sometimes

"It's pretty transparent, isn't it?" she said with a wry smile.

"Yes, it is," I answered.

"You know, I've never thought about it this way, but if I'm honest with myself, I have to admit that I secretly like knowing that what I'm doing in my life drives my parents crazy. But I love them. So why am I trying to hurt them?"

"You're not trying to hurt your parents as much as you're trying to define yourself as separate and distinct from them. It may not even be a conscious decision to rebel. *If fulfilling your own desires would, in any way, make it appear that you had conformed to your parents' wishes, then, in your unconscious mind, you would have "lost" the power struggle. By unconsciously rebelling against them, you're declaring your autonomy (but in an unhealthy way)."*

Solution: If you suspect you have a pattern of choosing partners in order to be rebellious, you need to get to a place where you can reconcile your need to be independent from your desire to find a relationship that may be just what your parents want for you. Once you're free from your need to rebel, you may fall in love with whomever—black, white, Jewish, etc.—**but you'll be doing it out of choice, not out of compulsion.** I suggest you seek professional counseling to help you understand and release the deep childhood programming that is running your love life.

RELATIONSHIP TYPE

▼ ▼ ▼ ▼ **9** ▼ ▼ ▼ ▼

You Choose a Partner as a Reaction to Your Previous Partner

I think we've all made this mistake at one time or another: **You end a relationship with someone and, for your next partner, you don't just choose someone different, but someone who is the complete opposite of your previous partner.** For instance:

▶ Your ex-husband was boring and predictable; your new boyfriend is wild and irresponsible.

▶ Your ex-boyfriend was unambitious and professionally passive; your new boyfriend is a workaholic who cares more about money than he does about you.

▶ Your ex-girlfriend was needy, clingy, and overly dependent; your new girlfriend has a hard time opening up and keeps you guessing.

▶ Your ex-wife was loyal, loving, but prudish and uncomfortable with her sexuality; your new girlfriend is an uninhibited, raunchy sex maniac.

This tendency to swing from one extreme to the other is the result of a sort of primitive way in which we communicate with our unconscious mind. It's as if you say to your brain, *"Boy, was I miserable with him. He never made any money; he never even worked hard. What a wimp! I never want to go through that again."* Your mind, like a faithful servant, takes in that information and reprograms itself:

"Old choice had no money, no drive, no aggression. New choice must have money, drive, aggression. Reprogramming complete."

Then you go out and find yourself wildly attracted to someone who is successful and materialistic, works twelve hours a day and is highly aggressive. For a while, you're in heaven. "My new boyfriend is so wonderful," you brag to your friends. "He's everything my ex wasn't." But one day you'll realize that your new love is too aggressive, too materialistic, and too work-addicted, and that you're not happy. That's when you feel like giving up on relationships and buying a dog.

There's nothing wrong with looking for qualities your last relationship was lacking. It's only natural that the most important things on your mind when selecting a new partner will be those areas you were most dissatisfied with in the old partner. **The mistake you make is in looking *only* for those missing qualities, rather than making them an important but incomplete part of an entire wish list of characteristics you want in a mate.**

FROM SWEETNESS TO SLEAZE: MARVIN'S STORY

Marvin, a forty-six-year-old salesman, epitomizes this relationship pattern. He met Shirley, his first wife, when he had just graduated from high school. Marvin was eighteen, Shirley seventeen. "My family loved Shirley," Marvin told me. 'She was perfect wife material—kind, loving, polite. I didn't have much experience with girls, and to tell you the truth, I felt flattered that Shirley seemed to care for me so much. Two years later we were married, and on my wedding day I was sure I'd made a great choice.

"The problems started on our honeymoon. Shirley was a virgin and didn't seem to enjoy sex that much. I didn't know much more than she did, and I figured with practice, she'd warm up. But she didn't. It's not that she refused to have sex with me—I don't think Shirley ever said no in her life. She was a devoted wife and a terrific mother, but as a lover, Shirley didn't satisfy me at all. *She even told me once that if we never had sex again, she wouldn't miss it!"*

"I hung in there for fifteen years and three kids, but finally I couldn't take it anymore. For years I'd fantasized about other women. I never cheated, but I came real close. Right after my fortieth birthday, something snapped, and I packed my bags and left. Oh, I felt sad, all right. *But I also felt like I could breathe again.*

"Four nights later I went out to a bar and met Darla. I couldn't take my eyes off her. She was the sexiest thing I'd ever seen. We talked and danced for a few hours, and then she invited me over to her place. We made love all night long. I felt like I'd died and gone to heaven.

"I was the happiest man alive. I felt bad for Shirley and the kids, but I was having such a damn good time. Darla was wild—she wanted me morning, noon, and night. Then one day Darla asked me what my intentions were. I figured she was kidding, so I grabbed her and said she could guess, but she pulled away and said she wanted to get married. I hadn't thought about it, but it made sense. We were happy, we had fun. What else was there? The next weekend, we flew to Vegas and got married.

"After that, everything started to unravel. It began the night I invited my daughters out to dinner to meet Darla. She'd picked an outfit I thought was a little provocative. 'You always loved this dress!' she yelled. And she was right. *But somehow because I was seeing her through my daughters' eyes, Darla suddenly looked cheap and trampy.* **I felt like I'd woken up from a dream.** Her party attitude and fun personality suddenly irritated me, and she seemed loud and disrespectful. Believe it or not, I started comparing her unfavorably to Shirley. That's when I knew I was in trouble. Two months later, I left.

"I've been alone since. I feel so confused. I don't know what I want. I even wonder if I was wrong to leave Shirley." *Marvin rebounded from Shirley, an asexual mother stereotype, to Darla, a whorish bad-girl stereotype.* **He was so intent on getting what he didn't get from Shirley that he looked only for that quality and no others.** His healing will come in learning to get in touch with what he really needs and wants, and looking for a partner who is balanced in what she can offer him.

Solution: *If you've come out of a particularly unsatisfying or frustrating relationship,* **be extra cautious about rebounding to a partner who is the opposite of the one you just left.** Discover *all* of the qualities you need in a mate, and look for a relationship that is balanced.

RELATIONSHIP TYPE

▾ ▾ ▾ ▾ **10** ▾ ▾ ▾ ▾

Your Partner Is Unavailable

I've saved this type of relationship for last because in many ways, by definition, it's not a relationship at all.

The first requirement you should have for a partner is that _he is available._ For those of us who like to pretend we don't know what available means, here's a definition:

Available: _Free to be in a relationship with you; not involved with anyone else; not married; not engaged; not going steady; not sleeping with another person; alone; single; all yours._

The following are _not_ definitions of available:

▶ With someone, but promises to leave soon
▶ With someone, but he doesn't really love her
▶ With someone, but they're not having sex anymore
▶ With someone, but says he's just staying for the kids
▶ With someone, but she knows about you and it's all right
▶ With someone and isn't leaving, but wants you to stick around anyway
▶ Just left someone, but might be going back

In other words,

STAY AWAY FROM PEOPLE WHO ARE MARRIED OR IN OTHER RELATIONSHIPS!

I don't care what the circumstances or excuses are, the result will be the same: _You are going to get your heart broken._

You may be prone to choosing unavailable partners if:

▶ **You felt abandoned by a parent as a child.** You repeat this pattern as an adult by _finding partners who can't be there for you either._

▶ **You have low self-esteem.** If you came from a very dysfunctional home that left you with little self-esteem, _you may feel you don't deserve to have a mate all to yourself, so you'll take whatever you can get._

▶ **You're afraid of intimacy.** Being in a relationship with a partner who is unavailable is a great way to avoid true intimacy. _If you were sexually of physically abused as a child and had your boundaries violated, or made a decision when you were young that you would never let anyone get close enough to hurt you again, you may find it "convenient" to choose partners with whom you can never have a truly committed relationship as an unconscious method of protecting yourself from pain._

Solution: If you meet someone and feel strongly toward him, but he is married or involved, it doesn't mean you will never be together. It does mean you should say:

"I care about you very much, but I have a rule—I never get involved with someone who is with another person. If you leave the relationship, please let me know."

If you are involved with someone who is married or in a relationship, you should find the courage to say:

"I love you very much, but what we are doing is not healthy for anyone, and I love myself too much to let myself be treated this way. I can't see you anymore. If you leave your partner, call me and let me know."

Don't forget:

▼

WHEN YOU GET INVOLVED WITH SOMEONE WHO IS IN A RELATIONSHIP WITH ANOTHER PERSON, YOU ARE ACCEPTING THAT PERSON'S LEFTOVERS.

▲

You deserve better than that!

After reading about these ten types of relationships that don't work, you may be wondering if there are any kinds of relationships left! Take it from me, there are—healthy, loving relationships in which you love your partner not because you feel sorry for him, or want him to take care of you, or are in love with his potential, *but because he is fulfilling your emotional needs.* We'll talk more about how to tell it you're with the right person in Chapters Eight through Twelve, so you can create the kind of relationship that does work!

6

▼▼▼

FATAL FLAWS

▼▼▼

If you want to learn a great lesson in making sure you are with the right partner, spend a few hours in the produce section of your local supermarket watching the shoppers choose fruits and vegetables. A woman carefully examines the bananas: First she looks at their color—she wants to make sure they aren't too ripe, but they can't be too green, either. Then she turns them around to see if she can spot any bruises. Finally she holds the bunch in her hand and compares it to others, making sure she gets the right amount of bananas. Only then does she place it in her basket.

This shopper is taking her time buying her groceries because **she is trying to avoid buying flawed produce. She wants the best, and she's trained herself to notice the flaws so she can purchase better merchandise.**

This chapter is about flaws, not the kinds you'll find in fruits or vegetables, but the kinds you will encounter in people you choose for partners in a relationship. *I call these* **"Fatal Flaws,"** *those characteristics in a person that can make a relationship anything from challenging all the way up to a nightmare.*

IMPORTANT: If someone you love has one or more of these traits, it does not necessarily mean he is incapable of having a relationship. It does mean that those "character flaws" will cause problems in your relationship that could be fatal to its longevity.

None of us is perfect, and it's obvious that we each have flaws or imperfections that affect our love life. But some of these characteristics are much more dangerous and destructive to our relationships than others, and those are the Fatal Flaws I'll talk about in this chapter.

FATAL FLAWS TO WATCH OUT FOR IN A PARTNER

1. **Addictions**
2. **Anger**
3. **Victim consciousness**
4. **Control freak**
5. **Sexual dysfunction**
6. **Hasn't grown up**
7. **Emotionally unavailable**
8. **Hasn't recovered from past relationships**
9. **Emotional damage from childhood**

FATAL FLAW

▼　　▼　　▼　　▼　　**1**　　▼　　▼　　▼　　▼

Addictions

Don't lie to yourself: When you get involved with a person who has an addiction, you are playing with fire, and you will probably get burned. Pretty strong way to start off a chapter, hmm? Well, let me explain. I have spent years listening to horror stories from people who loved someone with an addiction. I have watched them get their hearts broken and their families destroyed, and after a while I feel like saying, "I told you so: If you put your hand into a fire, you will get burned. If you walk in front of a moving car, you will get hit. *If you love an alcoholic or a drug addict or any other sort of user, you will get hurt.* It is inevitable." There's no polite or sensitive way to say it, and if you are an addict (we'll talk about what that is soon), I offer you no apologies for this section. **You need to hear it, because you are hurting the people you love.**

How Addictions Can Hurt Your Relationships

The physiological harm that addictive substances cause is well documented, but you need to understand the emotional harm as well. The first problem is:

▼

WHEN YOU LOVE SOMEONE WITH AN ADDICTION, YOU ARE IN A LOVE TRIANGLE—YOU, YOUR PARTNER, AND WHATEVER HE IS ADDICTED TO.

▲

If your partner has an addiction, he is in love with something other than you—the alcohol, the drugs, etc. **He is, in effect, cheating on you.** *That substance is your rival—it will take his time, his attention, and his spirit away from you.* You will end up hating it as much as you would hate another woman, or if you're male, another man.

Here's the second point: **Loving an addict also means loving someone who is a slave**—he is enslaved to drugs, alcohol, sexual addictions, gambling, or some activity that has become his master. Technically there are dozens of things one can get addicted to, from gambling to shopping to caffeine to cigarettes, which affect the individuals who use them but don't usually have as devastating an effect on relationships as drugs and alcohol, so I've chosen to focus on those two.

▼

WHEN YOU LOVE SOMEONE WITH AN ADDICTION, YOU ARE LOVING SOMEONE WHO IS NOT A FREE PERSON.

▲

You will have a hard time getting an addict to admit he is a slave, because he is controlled by the activity or substance that is his master, and he *will cover up that sense of impotence with **denial**.* To admit he is addicted would mean admitting he has been powerless, a frightening and humbling experience. This is what is so horrifying about addictions—they remove your desire to be addiction-free.

The third negative effect addictions have on your relationship is that they interfere with your partner's ability to be intimate with you. Addictive substances numb one's ability to feel. That's one of the reasons people drink the alcohol or smoke the joint—they don't like how they feel and want to feel better, only "better" means more numb. When one gets drunk or high, he's oblivious to much of what is happening outside and inside himself. This habit of emotional numbness will make it difficult for your partner to feel as much as you'd like him to.

THE REGULAR USE OF AN ADDICTIVE SUBSTANCE ROBS A PERSON OF THE ABILITY TO FEEL FULLY.

Loving Someone Who Loves Alcohol

Alcoholics are not just people who stumble along the street with their liquor hidden in a paper bag. Alcoholics are not just people who get so drunk that it's obvious they have been drinking. *Alcoholics are people who need alcohol to function, and to whom alcohol is a consistent part of their life.*

An alcoholic may use alcohol all day long, but an alcoholic is also the person who has a few drinks after work every night. *Just because you don't drink during the day doesn't mean you are not an alcoholic.* And just because you don't drink hard liquor doesn't mean you aren't an alcoholic, either. Wine and beer count, too.

Then there are the **weekend alcoholics,** the most insidious group, because their behavior fits into what is socially acceptable. They don't drink during the week, but when they go out on weekends, consuming alcohol is a large part of their activity—the person who has several drinks every time she goes on a date or to a party; the guy who shares a few six-packs with his buddies watching sports on TV; the couple who shares a bottle of wine or champagne every Saturday night before they make love.

One beer on the weekend doesn't make someone an alcoholic. A few beers after work every night does. One glass of wine with dinner once or twice a week doesn't make someone an alcoholic. A few glasses of wine each evening does.

The problem with noticing that someone is an alcoholic is that *we live in a society where substance abuse is normal, even chic, and controlled alcoholism, in particular, is acceptable.* I cringe each time I get on an airplane and watch the flight attendants offer liquor to passengers along with soft drinks, as if they are the same thing. I watched part of a football game on TV with my boyfriend this past Sunday and counted dozens of beer commercials. At first it was hard to tell they were beer commercials at all—I saw shots of healthy places like the beach, the mountains, national parks, and good-looking young people engaged in athletic activities. Then they show the beer. And what do we bring friends when we visit their home? A bottle of wine or champagne. We even celebrate our friends when they reach the legal drinking age, as if they have achieved some wonderful feat!

You may be thinking, "Oh, come on, it's not that bad," but I couldn't disagree more. *I can't tell you how many thousands of letters I receive every year and how many phone calls I got on my radio talk show from people whose relationships were destroyed by their partner's drinking.* The majority of these people who drink are in such complete denial that **they don't even think they have a problem.** That's the scariest part.

▼

If you love someone who drinks, be prepared to deal with the possibility of:

- ▶ inconsistent and unpredictable behavior
- ▶ outbursts of anger and violence
- ▶ consistent depression
- ▶ irresponsibility
- ▶ emotional deadness
- ▶ emotional unavailability
- ▶ lack of sexual desire or inability to perform properly
- ▶ fighting and bickering
- ▶ frequent "bad moods"
- ▶ lots of ups and downs in the relationship

▲

GAIL'S BATTLE WITH HER BOYFRIEND'S BOTTLE

Gail, thirty-two, called me on my radio talk show seeking advice about her relationship with Danny, thirty-six. "Help me, Barbara," Gail cried on the phone. "I don't know what to do. I love Danny very much, but our relationship has gotten to be so painful, and I feel trapped." Gail explained that when she met Danny, "He was funny and warm and sensitive, and I felt like he was 'the one.' We fell in love right away. I couldn't believe how much we had in common. Everything seemed great until about six months into the relationship. Danny never drank that much, mostly on weekends, and it didn't really bother me. But all of a sudden he started drinking more on weeknights when we'd be together, and he'd get really irritable, and soon we'd be fighting. I've tried everything—walking out of the room; trying to reason with him; agreeing with him; fighting back. But in the end, he blows up and leaves. The next day he'll call and apologize and say he's under pressure at work, or worried about his bills, and he's so sweet I forgive him. But it's been going on for months now, and I can't take the verbal abuse anymore."

"Gail, do you realize that Danny is an alcoholic?" I asked.

"Well, I wouldn't say that. He doesn't ever really get drunk or anything," she responded sheepishly.

"Gail, I want you to listen closely. Danny is an alcoholic. *Unless he stops drinking, he'll continue to act this way. Nothing you can do will make a difference. You are not the problem. His drinking is the problem."*

Gail began to weep. "I've tried to talk to him about drinking less, but he tells me to stop policing his behavior, and says it's not the problem."

"That's called DENIAL, Gail," I answered. **"If you love him, you will insist that he get some help; if he doesn't, and you love yourself, you will leave."**

My heart ached for Gail. *Like many codependents who love someone with an addiction, she felt responsible for Danny's behavior and believed if she changed, he would stop drinking.* The only hope for their relationship was Danny going into recovery and facing his addiction. The saddest part was that **Gail could have avoided her pain if she had paid attention to Danny's drinking in the beginning of the relationship, instead of making excuses for it.** By not talking about it until it became a big problem, she missed an opportunity to prevent it from becoming worse.

What You Can Do

If you are single: When you meet someone, *determine his or her values and habits regarding alcohol from the very first date.* Watch his behavior carefully, and don't delude yourself or make excuses for him. *Don't compromise your beliefs or values to accommodate to your partner's addiction.*

If you are in a relationship and suspect your partner has a drinking problem: If, after reading this section, you suspect your partner is an alcoholic and realize you've been avoiding facing it, **deal with it *now*. Give your partner an ultimatum: Either he**

or she gets help and deals with the alcoholism, or the relationship is over. That may seem harsh, but any professional will tell you that patience, understanding, and love will not help someone stop drinking. No one is ever "ready" to stop. It is never "easy." There is no "right time." These are all *excuses; it's DENIAL talking.*

Think of it this way: If your partner had a sudden heart attack, you'd insist he get help. You wouldn't let him talk you out of it, because you love him. Well, your partner *is* sick. He needs help. **Love him enough to insist that he get it, and if he won't, love yourself enough to leave, because it is only going to get worse.**

Al-Anon, a twelve-step recovery group for families and friends of alcoholics, is a good place for you to get support for yourself as you go through this process.

If you are the one with the drinking problem: If, after reading this section, you feel ready to admit that *you* may have a problem, **your first step is to get some help.** Reach out to your friends and family and tell them you will need their support in your recovery. **Don't forget,** *facing the pain that caused the behavior is where your real healing begins.*

Loving Someone Who Uses Illegal Drugs

Everything I said about alcohol is also true about drugs, but even more so, for several reasons: **Drugs are illegal, and drugs are expensive.** Loving someone who uses drugs means you may have to face additional problems. I've seen a family's entire savings drained by a cocaine-using husband. I've seen a woman steal from her boyfriend to support her crack habit. I've seen a wife's dream shattered when the police came to the house to arrest her husband for using and selling amphetamines.

In many ways, drugs are more dangerous than alcohol because they affect your nervous system more powerfully. Alcohol disappears from your bloodstream within twenty-four hours. However, blood tests can detect traces of drugs in your system for up to three months. *That means, for three months after using a drug, it is still altering your body chemistry and therefore affecting your ability to think, behave, and feel.*

The one drug I want to single out is marijuana. **Don't kid yourself about pot: Consistent use will render you emotionally and intellectually dull and devoid of passion.** The problem with marijuana is it appears to be relatively harmless, and its proponents claim it is no different from having a drink. They are wrong. The long-term effects of smoking marijuana are subtle but powerful. *It can diminish memory, create lethargy, and interfere with communication from one part of the brain to another, which hinders clear thinking. Emotionally, long-term marijuana smokers have a sort of permanent "What, me worry?" attitude, which they may describe as being "laid back" but on closer inspection is actually emotional numbness.*

I'm not talking about someone who smoked pot a few times a month during college (although that will still create the other problems mentioned earlier). I'm talking about people for whom smoking pot is part of their life, something they do every day, or every weekend, for years.

HOW POT KEPT KARA'S HUSBAND FROM GROWING UP

Kara called me on the radio to get some guidance for her failing marriage. She was thirty-eight, and her husband, Nick, was thirty-nine. Nick was lazy and irresponsible, couldn't remember to pay the bills, hated working, continually lost his jobs, and was emotionally distant and detached. "I feel like Nick's mother," Kara complained. "I can't count on him for anything."

"Do you have any idea why Nick behaves this way?" I asked.

"Yes," Kara answered quietly. "I just haven't wanted to face it. *It's his pot smoking.* He smokes all the time. When we first met, in our twenties, we both smoked at parties and on weekends. I stopped when I enrolled in nursing school, but Nick never did. He says it relaxes him at the end of the day and that he does it for a treat on the weekends. *The truth is, it numbs him out completely.* I don't think he feels much of anything. And when he's high, I feel like he's far away. Our sex life is just about nonexistent. He doesn't care about sex anymore, or about anything else, for that matter. When I try to talk to him about our problems, he tells me to stop being obsessive and chill out. Well, I can't! For years I've tried to ignore it, but it's gotten to the point where I am so angry I could scream!"

Nick's addiction to marijuana had made him emotionally dysfunctional and kept him in a state of permanent lethargy, preventing him from growing up. I have seen this pattern many times. Some people, like Kara, are aware that chronic pot smoking is the source of the problem. Others are surprised when I make the connection, having believed, as many do, that marijuana is harmless.

Kara and Nick's story had a happy ending. Months later I

received a letter from Kara, telling me she had confronted Nick that night and threatened to leave unless he faced his addiction and got some help. He agreed, more out of fear than a desire to change, at first. But with professional help, he stopped smoking pot.

"I didn't notice a big change at first," Kara wrote. "Then slowly, Nick began to come alive. He was sleeping less, working harder, and his sex drive was returning. That's when he realized how addicted he'd been, and after that he was like a changed man. Thank you, Barbara, for the kick in the pants I needed."

UNFIT FOR LOVE

I feel fortunate that I have never had a relationship with someone addicted to drugs, but I've experienced the pain that comes from knowing drugs have stolen your partner's ability to feel and be present with you. Years ago I ended a very intense and difficult relationship, partially because I didn't feel my partner loved me the way I deserved to be loved. Months after we broke up, we met at a restaurant to talk about what happened between us and do some more healing. I remember sitting across the table from him, putting a forkful of pasta into my mouth, when he said, **"You know, Barbara, I smoked dope when we were together."** I went into complete shock. How could that be? I had lived with this man; he knew how I felt about regular drug use. How could he have been smoking dope without my knowing it?

He proceeded to tell me about the times we'd been away on vacation, and he'd procured marijuana from someone and been stoned, or the times he would smoke it for three straight days at home. *"You always knew something was wrong," he confessed. "You'd accuse me of being distant and detached, and whenever I'd smoke I'd always pick fights with you and my sex drive would disappear."* All of a sudden, it made sense—the times when we'd be away at some beautiful beachside resort and he would be in a lousy mood for days on end; the sudden mood changes when he would become argumentative and difficult for no apparent reason; the feeling I had so often that he just wasn't there. I was relieved to know the cause of his behavior.

When I look back on this, I feel very angry. I'm angry that someone I loved was choosing to alter his consciousness without informing me. I'm angry that he used drugs to numb himself when I was begging him to feel more. I'm angry that I kept trying to understand his moodiness, his irresponsibility, and his temper—to get through to him—never dreaming he was stoned and unreachable.

Don't delude yourself: **Drugs make you unfit for love.** They interfere with your ability to be intimate on a consistent basis. And if you and your partner rely on doing drugs together as the way to create intimacy, you're fooling yourselves.

Loving Someone Who Is Addicted to Prescription Drugs

One day a few years ago, I was counseling a friend of mine I'll call Gordon, who was having a difficult time in his marriage. "Harriet is a mess," he told me. "She's always freaked out about something. She can't seem to handle any stress at all. She blows up at the slightest provocation. I feel like if this continues, I'll have to think about leaving."

I thought for a moment and said, "Gordon, what's your biggest complaint about Harriet?"

"Well, I guess it's those damn pills she takes all the time."

"What pills?" I asked. I knew Harriet well but didn't know she was on medication.

"I don't know—painkillers, Valium, a whole bunch of stuff."

I sat there in shock. *Harriet, a pill junkie? Hard to believe, but it explained all the symptoms Gordon described.* I urged him to confront his wife and beg her to get help immediately.

Several days passed, and I received a call from Harriet. "Barbara, I went to the doctor yesterday, and I'm on a three-week detoxification program. You were right: **I was addicted to prescription drugs, but I didn't even know it.** I've been taking so many pills for years—uppers, downers, painkillers, tranquilizers. I told myself I needed them, but before I knew it, it was *Valley of the Dolls* revisited! I have to tell you, I hated you when Gordon came home. I guess I was so embarrassed for you or anyone to know how I've been living. It's going to be hard, but I have to do it to save my marriage."

Harriet went through a very rough three weeks. All of the emotions she'd been trying to numb herself to with the pills came up at once, and her body went through an enormous purification once she gave it a chance to rid itself of the poisons she'd been putting into it. I saw her a month later and hardly recognized her. **She looked ten years younger!** "I feel like I just woke up from a long dream," she exclaimed. Two years later, Harriet is as beautiful and drug-free as she was then, and she and Gordon are a very happily married couple.

In our pill-pushing society, where we're told that the cures for

headaches, stomach aches, acid indigestion, constipation, sleepless-
ness, and fatigue can all be found in pills, it's no wonder that millions
of men and women are addicted to prescription drugs and don't
know it.

If you are single and meet someone who takes a lot of pills, ask
questions and get thorough information to make sure you aren't
getting involved with a **"legal drug addict."** If you, like Gordon, are
in a relationship with someone whom you suspect is abusing prescription drugs, insist they get help immediately, *and not from the
doctor who is prescribing all that medication.* And if you are like
Harriet, a slave to your tablets and capsules, *do yourself a favor and
find a physician to help you determine what you really need and
what is making you an addict.*

What to Do if Your Partner Has an Addiction

*Relationships are difficult enough without knowingly getting
involved with someone still enslaved by an addiction.* Does that
mean I don't think addicted people deserve to be loved? Of course
not. It means that they need to get into recovery and free themselves
of the addiction as well as understand the pain beneath it before
they're capable of having a healthy relationship with anyone.

**I guess what I'm saying is, if you're looking for a partner,
don't get involved with someone who is still addicted, or
freshly into recovery.** That person needs to give himself 100
percent of his love and energy to heal. He won't be able to give you
what you need right now. And if *you're* the addicted person, please
love yourself enough to get the help you need, so you can be whole
one day soon and have the relationship you deserve.

If you are already seriously involved with someone who has an
addiction, and this chapter is helping you face facts, here is what I
suggest:

▼

IF YOUR PARTNER IS AN ADDICT:

1. Tell your partner that *you refuse to live with an addict
   any longer.*
2. Tell him you will stay with him *only if he agrees to get
   some help and takes action IMMEDIATELY.*
3. Tell him that if he does not get help immediately, *you are
   leaving and not coming back.*

4. Stick to your word, and if your partner does not get immediate help, do not give him another chance. *LEAVE.*
5. DO NOT RETURN *unless your partner is clean and sober,* involved in a recovery program, and shows significant behavioral and attitudinal changes.

▲

FATAL FLAW

▾ ▾ ▾ ▾ 2 ▾ ▾ ▾ ▾

Anger

▶ "My partner is a rageaholic. I live in fear every day."
▶ "The slightest thing sets him off. I have to tiptoe around the house."
▶ "She's wonderful and warm until she doesn't get her way. Then she turns into a screaming, raving bitch."

Living with an angry person is like living with a time bomb: You never know when it's going to go off, so you live in constant tension and fear. **When you love someone who has outbursts of rage, you feel controlled by his anger** and it keeps you from ever truly relaxing, since you don't want to be caught off guard.

Anger is a terrorist—it holds the people it comes in contact with hostage. If your partner has a problem with anger, you adapt your behavior to the situation, editing yourself so as not to upset your partner.

I'm not talking about normal, healthy expressions of anger: Your partner comes home an hour late and doesn't call, and you raise your voice to tell him you're angry; your wife neglects to tell you about an important phone call, and you bark at her in an annoyed tone of voice; your child spills nail polish all over the carpet, and you scold her with angry words.

The kind of anger that is a Fatal Flaw is anger that is out of the ordinary and inappropriate.

IS YOUR PARTNER A RAGEAHOLIC?

Here are some warning signs that your partner may have a serious problem with anger:

► Your partner gets very angry when little things don't go his way, and takes it out on the people around him.

► When you disagree with your partner, he responds with shouting, name-calling, threats, or other overreactive behavior.

► Your partner has very little patience, and becomes extremely annoyed if he has to wait for service, drive behind a slow vehicle, get put on hold on the phone, listen to you explain things, etc.

► When you ask your partner to do a simple task, he becomes defensive and rebellious.

► When you give your partner any feedback whatsoever about how his behavior affects you, he interprets it as an attack and viciously attacks back.

► Your partner acts out his anger by slamming doors, hanging up on you on the phone, storming out of rooms, leaving the house, sleeping on the couch at night, etc.

► Your partner can switch from a seemingly loving and warm mood to an angry mood within seconds.

► Your partner is quick to yell at you or put you down if you aren't doing what he wants you to do, or if he feels you made a mistake.

► Your partner often raises his voice or becomes angry in public places—restaurants, shopping malls, friends' homes, etc.

► Your partner expresses his anger physically, hitting or throwing objects, or shoving or striking you or your children.

Spotting someone who has potential problems with anger is one of the easier Fatal Flaws to detect. No one turns into a rageaholic overnight. You'll see signs of difficulty similar to the ones on this list in the beginning of the relationship—they're like sparks that tell you the fire is sure to follow. The most important point for you to remember is: **Don't ignore the warning signs that indicate your partner has an anger problem. Trust your gut instinct, and don't let yourself be intimidated or talked out of your feelings.**

If a few of these statements fit your partner, you need to take action immediately to confront the problem and insist your partner get help.

If many of these statements fit your partner, you are in a very dysfunctional relationship and should give your partner an ultimatum to *stop the abusive behavior immediately, or you will leave.* You need to face the fact that you've been playing the victim in the relationship, and need to get counseling for yourself as well.

If most of these statements fit your partner, get out of this relationship now! Even if your partner is willing to get help, it's going to take him a long time to work through his rage, and you shouldn't have to be mistreated one day longer. *Take care of yourself first, and work with a professional on recovering your self-esteem and self-respect.*

"Why Is My Partner So Angry?"

There are many reasons people grow up to become rageaholics:

▶ *They were physically, verbally, or sexually abused as a child* and stored up the rage inside, letting it out as an adult when they finally feel "safe."

▶ *They felt unloved or abandoned as a child,* either through divorce, an absent parent, or the death of a parent, and act out that childhood rage as adults when they meet people who love them (potential "leavers").

▶ *They felt powerless as a child*—they had alcoholic parents they couldn't save; they watched helplessly as one parent abused the other; they never had permission to express their feelings, and, as adults, they compensate for that powerlessness by controlling others with their anger.

We've already talked about how many of us were not given permission as children to put words to our feelings. If a child experiences any of the situations I just mentioned, he will naturally feel enormous sadness and grief. If he is unable to feel that grief at that time, it will surface years later as anger and rage.

REPRESSED GRIEF FROM CHILDHOOD GETS ACTED OUT AS RAGE IN ADULTS.

This is why trying to "control" one's angry behavior is a useless form of therapy. The anger is a symptom, albeit a totally unacceptable symptom, of the rageaholic's deep hurt and sadness. **Treating the anger without understanding the cause is a temporary and dangerous solution. Traditional talk or psychotherapy will not be an adequate form of help for someone suffering from chronic anger.** Experiential emotional work such as psychodrama, physical forms of release such as hitting punching bags, screaming into pillows, and using batakas to strike out, and innerchild work will all be essential ingredients in helping a person transform his anger into grief and finally into healing.

When I had my radio talk show, I heard questions such as, "Why is my partner so angry?" every day. "Why does my husband hit me? Why does my wife lose control and fly into uncontrollable rages?" And I would always answer my listeners with the same comment:

"You're asking yourself the wrong question. The right question is: 'Why am I putting up with this behavior?' Then ask yourself: 'What am I going to do about it?' "

Trying to understand your partner's anger is fine if:

1. Your partner has made a **commitment** to get serious help in healing his rage
   and
2. Your partner has taken **action** toward getting that help
   and
3. Your partner has made visible and significant **progress** in changing his behavior

But often, partners of rageaholics focus more on helping their angry mate than they do on dealing with their own feelings about being treated so badly.

Why You Might Attract an Angry Partner

No one consciously looks for a mate with a violent temper. As we discussed in Chapter Two, your unconscious emotional programming drives you to choose someone who is angry for several reasons:

▶ **You had one or more angry parents as a child, and you have anger and love closely associated in your mind.** If you grew up with a rageaholic and were accustomed to many of the symptoms I just listed, you may have an extremely high tolerance for angry behavior, since it was "normal" in your household. Your emotional programming may say: *"People who love me get angry with me."* So you meet a partner who yells a lot, or loses control, and although you may not like his behavior, you don't think he has a big problem. **Sadly, people who were physically or verbally abused as children often grow up to become battered spouses.** They can also become batterers, which we'll talk about later.

▶ **You have very low self-esteem and are an easy "victim" for an abusive partner.** If your self-esteem is low and you live with a high degree of powerlessness, you'll be a perfect partner for a rageaholic, since you're probably *easily intimidated and upset.*

▶ **You have a difficult time expressing your own anger.** *I believe that we often unconsciously attract our opposites as partners in order to heal the imbalances in our own personality.* The man who is emotionally shut down may attract a highly emotional woman who cries on a regular basis; the woman who can't express any anger or negativity may attract a man who is overly angry. In addition, as I explained in my first book, *How to Make Love All the Time,* **the emotions you suppress, your partner may express.** When you repress or deny your angry emotions, your partner picks those up, and they augment his own stored-up anger.

A LETTER FROM CLAUDIA

I know of no better way to sum up this fatal flaw than to share a letter with you that I received from one of my radio listeners:

Dear Dr. Barbara,

Let me tell you my story. I'm twenty-eight years old and have two small children, four and one and a half. I'm presently on public assistance due to the circumstances I'll explain, and I'm working as a housekeeper for two friends to try to support myself and my children. If you had ever told me I would end up living like this, I would have thought you were crazy.

My childhood was very lonely. My mother died when I was four, and my father remarried a year later. **My stepmother resented me from the start and her verbal abuse was constant, except when they were both ignoring me.** I felt very lost and hopeless.

I dated a little in high school but didn't have a lot of self-confidence. When I was twenty, I was working and going to school part time, and that's when I met Hank. He was a few years older, and the first guy who ever really paid attention to me. Hank and I started going out, and he really seemed to care. I started fantasizing about spending my life with him, and we began seeing more and more of each other.

I'll never forget the first night I saw another side of Hank. Driving home from the movies, Hank missed a turn, and I teased him about being forgetful and spacing out. **Hank slammed on the brakes, got out of the car, and pulled me out onto the road. "Don't you ever correct me like that, do you hear?" he screamed.** I was in such shock, I didn't know what to say or do. We got back in the car, and I cried the whole way home.

The next day, Hank called and apologized. He'd been tired and cranky and had "lost his temper." He was so sweet, and I was so stupid, I forgot the whole thing. Things were fine until a few weeks later, when he flew into a rage again. **I was so in love that I told myself he had a "fiery personality."** In a way I got used to the outbursts—scenes in restaurants, screaming arguments late at night in bed; and, Hank's favorite, the car fights. I hated this part of him, so I tried not to do anything that would get him upset.

When Hank asked me to marry him, I didn't even stop to think about the anger. I was so happy that someone wanted to be my husband! We got married a few months later, after a terrible fight the night before the wedding during which Hank pushed me up against the wall of our apartment and screamed in my face for ten minutes about how I didn't appreciate how much he sacrificed for me. I still didn't get it!

We had our first little girl a year later, and that's when I started to wake up. **It was one thing for Hank to take his rage out on me, but when I saw him do it to my daughter, I got scared.** I won't bore you with the gory details, but things got worse. **I couldn't wait for Hank to go to work each morning so I could at least have eight hours of peace. When I'd hear his car pull**

up, my stomach would get tied in knots. But as I've heard you say on your program so many times, part of me was in total denial, and blamed myself for the problem rather than facing the truth about Hank. **What made it even harder was that when Hank wasn't being angry, he was wonderful.**

Eight months ago, my daughter told me she had started praying that Daddy would die so we could all be happy. That night I told Hank I wanted him to leave, and he totally lost it. I grabbed the kids and ran to a neighbor's house, where we stayed until I found an attorney. Hank refused to leave the house, refused to give me any money, claimed I was an unfit mother, and we are still battling it out legally.

I'm on welfare and cleaning houses because I ignored all the warning signs in the beginning. That's why my children are afraid to go to sleep at night. That's why I am twenty-eight and feel fifty-eight. **Because I didn't pay attention, and now I am paying the price.**

I don't want you to get the idea that I'm a lost cause. I feel good that I have broken the chain of anger and abuse that began with my stepmother. I feel good that I get a chance to start over. And I feel good knowing I'll never let anyone treat me or my kids that way again.

—Claudia

FATAL FLAW

▼   ▼   ▼   ▼   **3**   ▼   ▼   ▼   ▼

Victim Consciousness

Victim consciousness is an attitude some men and women adopt toward the events in their life, an attitude that blames others for their problems. It's often difficult to spot a victim because none of us really mind hearing our partner complain to us about his or her past relationships. If you meet a man, for instance, and he often tells you horror stories about his ex-girlfriend, you're secretly glad he's not missing her or comparing you to her unfavorably. After all, you certainly don't want to hear how wonderful she was. *But if your partner has a habit of blaming others for his* *circumstances and not taking responsibility for his part in problems,* **watch out: You will be the next person whose fault everything is.**

The tricky thing about victims is, in spite of their complaints about not having been loved or understood in the past, **they'll have a hard time receiving your love and support.** *Victims enjoy suffering: Holding on to their pain gives them the illusion that they have power over those who've hurt them.*

Therefore, when you love a victim, you may feel:

No matter how much you give, it is never enough.

No matter how much you try to console them, they refuse to be cheered up.

▼

ARE YOU IN LOVE WITH A VICTIM?

Here are common traits your partner will display if he or she is a victim. See how many could apply to your mate (or yourself):

1. My partner rarely gets directly angry with me or others; instead, he complains or pouts about the situation.

2. When I make a suggestion or offer to help my partner with something he's upset about, he always seems to find a reason why my ideas won't work, and has an *"it's just no use"* attitude.

3. My partner won't come right out and tell me what's bothering him, but walks around looking miserable and makes me pull the information out of him.

4. Even when I try to love and comfort my partner, I feel like it doesn't help, and isn't even making a dent in his unhappiness, as if he is inconsolable.

5. My partner always seems to find something to be upset about in his life, and rarely has days or weeks go by without an event that puts him in a bad mood.

6. My partner often feels sorry for himself, and doesn't understand why unpleasant things happen to him.

7. My partner has a difficult time making decisions and often spends more time complaining about what might happen than taking action.

8. My partner still blames people in his past (parents, ex-mates, friends) for his misfortunes and the way his life has turned out.

9. My partner often feels trapped in circumstances that he feels are the causes of his unhappiness and can see no way out.

10. My partner is jealous of the success and happiness of others and frequently compares himself to them, resulting in either his feeling bitter or depressed.

▬▬▬▬▬▬▬▬▬▬▬▬▲▬▬▬▬▬▬▬▬▬▬▬▬

If you can relate to **one or two** *of these statements,* **your partner has a small victim streak** that you should talk about together. If you ignore these characteristics, you'll end up feeling angry and resentful.

If you can relate to **three to five** *of these statements,* **your partner has a serious problem with victim consciousness.** Make sure you aren't enjoying playing "rescuer," or setting yourself up to feel your efforts don't make a difference. This won't be an equal and healthy relationship until your partner gets some help and faces the victim inside himself.

If you can relate to **six or more** *of these statements,* **you are in love with a professional victim.** Good luck trying to discuss this with your partner: He will definitely feel attacked, become upset, and accuse you of not understanding or loving him—in other words, he will handle it just like a victim would! *This is not a healthy relationship, and if you don't already feel controlled, resentful, and turned off, you will soon. Your partner needs help now, and so do you.*

Here are the *symptoms* of victim consciousness:

▶ **Victims don't take responsibility for the events or circumstances in their life.** They feel sorry for themselves, they complain, eat, sleep, become depressed; they do everything but take action to improve the situation. Try suggesting to a victim what he or she should do to feel better or solve a problem and you will get a list of reasons why none of those things will work. Some victims will expect you to rescue them and solve their problems for them; *others don't expect anything but sympathy, since the only way they know how to get attention is to have someone feel sorry for them.* So, naturally, becoming responsible and autonomous wouldn't be practical. Who would pay attention to them if they didn't need help?

▼

VICTIMS SPEND THEIR TIME COMPLAINING ABOUT WHAT'S WRONG RATHER THAN DOING SOMETHING TO CHANGE IT.

▲

▶ **Victims are experts at blaming others for their problems.** From a victim's point of view, it's always someone else's fault that things are the way they are. Victims blame their parents, ex-spouses, children, friends, health, the economy, or whatever for the fact that they're not happy and fulfilled in their lives today. Some victims blame *overtly,* and are honest about their resentment. Some blame *covertly,* never actually expressing anything negative but simply not taking responsibility for fixing their own life. If this rationale doesn't make sense to you, and you say so, you'll be blamed for not understanding your partner.

▶ **Victims see life as an adversarial situation.** "It's the world against me," the victim thinks. *A victim perceives others as existing for the purpose of making him miserable, ruining his chances, interfering with his happiness, and disappointing him.* For many victims, this was true as a child, but when he projects that perception onto his adult relationships, he inevitably sets others up to fail him. Some victims go so far as to choose unsuitable partners who victimize them, only proving to themselves that they are, indeed, victims. Often victims will have only other victims as friends, since only they can truly understand.

▶ **Victims express their anger covertly.** Victims are rarely direct with their anger. *They would rather make you feel guilty by looking upset and hurt than lose your sympathy by confronting you with their true hostility.* **They may make statements that don't sound angry or hostile, but indirectly communicate their hostility while still allowing them to maintain the appearance that they're not angry.**

For instance, a woman is upset with her partner for not making her birthday more special. She says, "I guess we were just brought up differently. Some families teach their children to care about other people's feelings and some don't." When her boyfriend accuses her of calling him insensitive, she responds with disbelief: "Sweetheart, I didn't say you were insensitive, did I? I'm just making a point about how people are different." She would be a lot more honest if she said, "I'm pissed off at you for giving me one lousy card for my birthday and making me feel like I'm not special to you."

▶ **Victims think of themselves as powerless and helpless.** They're experts in negativity thinking. "I can't," "It won't," "I'll never" are common phrases you'll often hear from a victim. *Victims often procrastinate because they don't trust themselves enough to take action.* They may appear to be leaning on you for support until you realize it's not support they want, it's rescuing. **Adult victims may have been victimized as children, either sexually, physically, or emotionally. The powerlessness they experienced then prompted them to make an unconscious decision about themselves: "I am powerless. Others have power over me."**

▶ **Victims repeat the same negative patterns in relationships and in life because they don't attempt to find the source of the patterns.** When faced with a problem, the powerful person asks:

"Why is this happening, and how can I change it?"

The victim asks:

"Why is this happening to ME?"

When a victim focuses on the persecution aspect of a crisis rather than understanding how this crisis occurred and what can be done to avoid creating it next time, he robs himself of the opportunity to learn from his mistakes.

What to Do If You Are in Love with a Victim

All of us have a secret victim inside us. But when this pattern dominates someone's personality, it becomes toxic to their own mental health and their relationships. **If you become involved with someone who possesses this Fatal Flaw, it's essential that you confront this issue with him or her, even though it will undoubtedly make your partner very uncomfortable.** As with all of these Fatal Flaws, victim consciousness can be successfully combated with commitment and perseverance if your partner is willing to change. But don't kid yourself: If you ignore this pattern, it won't go away. *People involved with victims learn the hard way that, in time, your sympathy for them turns into apathy.*

FATAL FLAW

▼　　▼　　▼　　▼　　4　　▼　　▼　　▼　　▼

Control Freak

▶ Does your partner always have to have things his way, and if he doesn't, becomes very upset?

▶ Do you live in fear of displeasing your partner by doing things the "wrong way"?

▶ Do you feel criticized, judged, and constantly scrutinized by your partner?

If you answered yes to any of these questions, you might be in love with a control freak. I've chosen this name for the fourth Fatal Flaw since I have heard it used so often over the years by clients and friends to describe *someone who is addicted to being in control.* A control freak is virtually the opposite of a victim. While a victim often avoids making any decisions, **a control freak must make all the decisions himself.** A victim looks to others for help and rescuing; a **control freak almost never asks for help, since he tells himself he can handle it.** A victim often wants you to tell him what to do; **a control freak tells you what to do.**

Most human beings like to feel in control of their lives and feel uncomfortable being out of control. The difference is that **control freaks must be in control of their lives, and they** *will do anything to avoid feeling out of control.* This presents serious problems in relationships:

▶ *Control freaks have a difficult time opening up* and showing you their vulnerable and emotional side.

▶ *Control freaks don't like to admit that they need you,* or . . .

▶ Control freaks need you so much they *want to control all your time, becoming highly possessive and jealous.*

▶ *Control freaks can become easily upset,* expressing either anger or hurt when they don't get their way or feel out of control.

▶ *Control freaks can be compulsive* about their living habits, routine, work, etc., and therefore be very difficult to live with.

► *Control freaks can attempt to control the choices and habits of those around them*—coworkers, friends, children, and *you!*

► *Control freaks don't like being told what to do*—it makes them feel out of control.

► *Control freaks may have sexual problems*—either a difficult time letting go in bed, an attachment to a particular idea of how sex "should" be, a need to control you but a resistance to losing control himself.

► *Control freaks have a hard time relaxing*, whether after work, on weekends, or on vacations; they may be workaholics.

► *Control freaks can be very impatient and irritable.*

► *Control freaks may become very domineering and critical parents*, since by definition, babies and young children are beyond their control.

Partners who as children felt controlled by adults or by circumstances that rendered them powerless may make an unconscious decision that, when they grow up, they'll never be out of control.

▼

Why You Might Be Attracted to a Control Freak

Here are some reasons why you might find yourself attracting control freaks into your life:

► You had a very controlling mother or father, and therefore *you associate LOVE with CONTROL.*

► You feel somewhat powerless yourself and *mistake your partner's addiction to control for power and purpose.*

► *You are a victim,* looking for someone to tell you what to do and take charge of your life for you.

► *Your last partner was passive, weak, and wimpy,* and you've made the mistake I talked about in Chapter Five, choosing a partner in reaction to a previous partner.

► *You were physically, sexually, or verbally abused as a child* and only see yourself relating to others when they're in control and you're afraid of them.

► *You are a control freak yourself* and have attracted your own mirror image.

▲

This Fatal Flaw is one of the most difficult to cure, since by definition a control freak hates being out of control, and that includes admitting he has a problem, and especially being given an ultimatum by a partner.

If you're in love with a control freak, don't kid yourself: If left untreated, the situation will only get worse with time. Your partner must acknowledge the problem and take action to improve it, or you should reconsider the relationship.

FATAL FLAW

▼   ▼   ▼   ▼   **5**   ▼   ▼   ▼   ▼

Sexual Dysfunction

▶ *"My husband is addicted to pornographic magazines and X-rated movies, and it's ruining our relationship. What should I do?"*

▶ *"My wife couldn't care less about sex. I have to practically beg her to do it. Now I'm feeling like having an affair. How can I help her?"*

▶ *"My boyfriend has always been a terrible flirt, making comments about women's bodies, coming on to my friends. Now I just found out he's been sleeping with this girl he knows from work. Is there any hope for our relationship?"*

Every day on my radio talk show, I heard questions like these from people in love with partners who exhibited Fatal Flaw #5: sexual dysfunction. Despite what you might think, sexual dysfunction does not simply mean problems with sexual performance, such as impotence, or inability to have an orgasm. For the purpose of our study of fatal flaws, I've divided sexual dysfunction into the following categories:

1. **Sexual addiction and obsession**
2. **Lack of sexual integrity**
3. **Sexual performance problems**

Sexual Addiction and Obsession

Here are some warning signs to look for that indicate your partner might have a problem with sexual addiction or obsession:

▶ When you and your partner have sex, he almost always includes some form of fantasy (pornographic materials, verbal play-acting, films, etc.).

▶ Your partner is an avid reader of pornographic magazines.

▶ Your partner rents pornographic videotapes and watches them alone.

▶ Your partner needs you to dress up in sexual costumes on a regular basis in order to get turned on.

▶ Your partner calls 900 sex numbers for phone sex.

▶ Your partner frequently goes to topless bars, strip clubs, or other types of sex-related facilities, alone or with friends.

▶ Your partner is addicted to masturbation, and engages in it many times a week or even daily, in spite of your active sex life.

▶ Your partner is compulsive about a particular sexual fantasy (being tied up, having pain inflicted upon him, being raped, raping, etc.), which he uses to become aroused.

▶ Your partner needs to have sex one or more times a day, every day, regardless of whether you're in the mood or not.

▶ Your partner enjoys seeing you engage in sex acts you find humiliating (anal sex, sadomasochism, etc.).

▶ Your partner has sexual feelings for children that he acts on or fantasizes about.

If you know that one or more of these statements describes your partner, don't hide from the truth any longer: **your partner has a problem with sexual addiction.** These are not healthy behaviors, and they will definitely affect your relationship in a negative way.

There are several problems you might face when identifying and confronting someone with this Fatal Flaw:

1. **You mistake your partner's sexual addiction for sexual interest in you.** It's easy, especially in the beginning of a relationship, to get seduced and flattered by a partner's excessive sexual interest, rather than seeing it for what it is: obsession with sex.

Cindy, twenty-eight, described it this way: "Charlie wanted to have sex every day, which I thought was great at first, and he seemed so turned on to me that I didn't mind when he wanted to watch films together or have me act out his fantasies. But after about three months, I began to get uncomfortable when I realized *it wasn't me he couldn't live without, it was sex,* and kinky sex to boot."

2. **Your partner makes you feel that your discomfort with his habits is "your problem" and that you have sexual hang-ups.** I've had so many women ask me if I thought there was something wrong with them because they minded the fact that their partner wanted sex three times a day, or watched porno films whenever the wife left the house, or masturbated every morning in the shower while refusing to have sex with her. In each case, I would reassure these women that, no, there was nothing wrong with them, but there was something wrong with their mate. The sighs of relief I heard were unbelievable, because *each of these women had been told by their partners that they were too conservative, too frigid, or too sexually boring and that their concerns were un-founded.* **Women who are used to being victims or to giving up their power often find themselves being talked out of their feelings in this way.**

3. **You're embarrassed or frightened to confront the problem because you don't want to rock the boat.** It's not easy to say to your husband, "Honey, I think you're a masturbation addict," or "Sweetheart, the fact that you have to watch porno films to get turned on really frightens me and I won't put up with it anymore." However:

IF YOU DON'T FACE THE TRUTH ABOUT YOUR PARTNER'S SEXUAL ADDICTIONS, YOU'LL DESTROY YOUR RELATIONSHIP.

It's not that people with sexual addictions are "wrong" or "bad," but their behavior is disruptive to the intimacy and safety in the relationship:

▶ You'll feel "cheated on" by your partner because he needs something other than you to become aroused.

▶ You'll feel insecure about your body, your sexuality, and your ability to satisfy your partner.

▶ You'll feel emotionally distant from your partner during sex, as if he's not completely "there" with you.

▶ You'll feel sexually used and manipulated rather than loved.

▶ You'll feel angry and resentful toward your partner for not respecting your feelings.

▶ You'll eventually feel turned off to sex, since for you it's associated with humiliation, control, and a feeling of inadequacy.

WHY PORNOGRAPHY DESTROYS INTIMACY

Recently I was asked to be a guest on a national TV show. When the producer called me to talk about the show, I told him that I had very strong views on fantasy and pornography, and he responded by telling me that's why they wanted me as an expert. The evening of the taping arrived, and I met the other guest, a man who believed sexual fantasy was harmless and should be enjoyed by everyone. I sat there listening to him and the host of the show talk about how "normal" it was to be in bed with your partner and fantasize about making love to someone else, or what "innocent fun" it was to leave your wife at home and go to a topless bar and become aroused by the waitresses.

As I watched the faces of the audience members, I noticed something very interesting: When the host would ask, "Come on, don't you all fantasize about making love to other people while you're in bed with your partner?" there would be applause and nervous laughter. But the women, in particular, looked very uncomfortable. I knew what was going on in their minds. *They were feeling pressured to be sexually open and "hip" by pretending they weren't bothered by their partner's interest in fantasy or pornography, when the reality was that it upset them.*

Finally the host turned to me and asked my opinion, and I let loose. **"If you're making love with your partner and fantasizing about having sex with someone else, you're cheating on your partner!"** I wasn't surprised when all the women began applauding wildly. **"Indulging in sexual fantasy about other people, in your mind, through reading magazines or watching films, is a form of infidelity,"** I continued. **"You've made a commitment to be sexually monogamous with your partner, and you're breaking it by deliberately focusing your sexual attention on someone else."**

The guest next to me responded with a smirk on his face: "How can you make such a broad statement?" he asked. "There's nothing wrong with fantasizing or looking at naked women as long as you don't do anything about it. It's harmless."

"Harmless?" I responded. "Tell that to the thousands of women who've called me in tears because they found out their husband watches porno movies each night after their wives go to bed alone. Tell that to the woman making love to her boyfriend, not knowing he's imagining that she's his secretary. Tell her it shouldn't bother her. Tell that to the man who feels sexually inadequate because his girlfriend can get turned on only when she fantasizes about her ex-husband. And while you're at it, try convincing the woman whose husband looks at pornographic magazines while lying in bed with her that she shouldn't feel upset because it's harmless."

My response pretty much shut this guy up for the rest of the program. I wasn't coming on strong because I wanted to be right but because I feel so passionately about this subject. *As someone who works with couples in crisis, I have heard thousands of stories, mostly from women, about how their partner's obsession with pornography and sex is ruining their relationship.* I have seen women burst into tears during my women's seminars when they finally give themselves permission to express the rage and humiliation they feel because of their partner's sexual addiction. It's a problem often overlooked and minimized because of the sexist attitude in our society that supports milder forms of pornography such as the *Sports Illustrated* Swimsuit Edition or commercials selling beer by using bikini-clad women and claiming to disapprove of so-called hard-core pornography.

Intimacy is the shared experience of closeness and connection by two people. Sexual compulsion and addiction destroy intimacy because, by definition, they introduce a third element into your relationship: the thought or picture or video of another person or sexual situation. Although some couples claim they both enjoy sharing pornography together, I strongly doubt that it creates more intimacy. **What it does create is more eroticism, which many couples mistake for intimacy.**

HOW TO PROTECT YOURSELF

It's not as easy to spot this Fatal Flaw on the first few dates as it is with other problems we're talking about. But it's important for you to find out as much as you can about your partner's sexual history, habits, and taste to make sure you're not getting yourself into something you'll regret later. Obviously, each person must define for herself what she's comfortable with sexually and what she finds unacceptable. My advice would be: **Trust your instincts.** If something bothers you, don't let yourself be talked out of your feelings about it. It's not a question of what's normal and what's not. It's a question of what's healthy or unhealthy for *your* relationship.

If your partner has a problem with sexual addiction, encourage him to get professional help. Sexaholics Anonymous has support groups throughout the country that are helpful, and for a serious "sexaholic," psychological counseling is essential in understanding and breaking free from the addiction. *If your partner is willing to work on the problem, there is hope for your relationship. If not, get out while you still have some self-esteem left.*

Lack of Sexual Integrity

This is the second of the sexual Fatal Flaws, and it's related to the first in that *your partner doesn't honor the sanctity of your monogamous relationship—in this case, by "leaking" his sexual energy in someone else's direction.* This includes:

- ► flirting with other people
- ► constant staring at other people's bodies
- ► making sexual comments about your friends, strangers, etc., to you
- ► making sexual comments to your friends, strangers, etc.
- ► inappropriate touching of other people
- ► actual sexual infidelity

Here are some of the ways in which you might be in denial about this Fatal Flaw:

1. **You dismiss your reactions by telling yourself, "I'm just being paranoid."** None of us likes to appear overly possessive, so often, if you notice your partner behaving in a way that makes you uncomfortable, you might ignore it rather than confront your mate. This may especially be true if, based on your emotional programming, you don't trust your own feelings or perceptions. *Your partner may even minimize your feelings by calling you jealous and insecure.*

2. **You rationalize your feelings by telling yourself your partner's behavior isn't that bad.** "He never really does anything but look." "She doesn't ever cheat—she just flirts with guys." These are comments from people attempting to talk themselves out of their discomfort. If you're afraid to confront your partner about his lack of sexual integrity, you might convince yourself that what he's doing really doesn't bother you that much. This may be especially true if you dislike conflict and have a difficult time expressing anger.

3. **You tell yourself your partner will grow out of this behavior in time.** "He's probably just acting this way because we've only been together for a little while—if we're married, I'm sure he'll change." Don't kid yourself—**if your partner doesn't treat you with respect in the beginning of the relationship, he won't suddenly learn respect later.**

All of these reactions are dangerous when it comes to lack of sexual integrity, because:

▼

WHAT STARTS OUT AS A PARTNER WHO FLIRTS AND OGLES MAY VERY WELL END UP AS A PARTNER WHO CHEATS.

▲

HOW JODY CHEATED HERSELF OUT OF HER OWN HAPPINESS

Jody was a thirty-five-year-old mother going through a marital crisis with her husband, Ned. "Ned's flirting ruined our marriage and destroyed my family. I met him eight years ago through work, and we clicked right from the start. Ned was very outgoing, and he told me he'd never really had a long-term relationship before because commitment scared him. Like most women, my first thought was, 'I'll fix that,' and I decided he was the man I wanted to spend my life with. My only real complaint about him was his flirting. *He looked at every woman within twenty feet,* and not just looked, mind you, but stared. I used to hate it! We'd be out to eat, and I'd be talking to him, and suddenly I'd see his eyes shift to the left and I'd know he was staring at some girl. *Whenever he met any female, even my friends, he would have to get them to pay attention to him, joking, telling them they looked nice, or something.*

"**Every time he did things I felt awful, but when I'd try to talk to him about it, he'd accuse me of being insecure and controlling. I didn't want to be a controlling bitch**—that's how my mom treated my dad—so I tried to ignore it. Looking back, I realize I just didn't want to face the truth. Ned and I got married a year and a half later, and even at our wedding he was flirting with one of my bridesmaids. I kept looking at the ring on my finger, telling myself he was mine now.

"Once we got married, Ned's behavior seemed to get worse. We started fighting more, and I became increasingly insecure. Then, I got pregnant. I thought having a baby would force Ned to grow up a little, but I was wrong.

"One night last year while Ned was supposedly out with his friends at a hockey game, the phone rang and a woman's voice said, 'Ned?' When I asked who was calling, she hung up. My heart started pounding a mile a minute. When Ned came home, I confronted him and we had a terrible fight. He told me I was crazy, and he denied everything. I was desperate, and the next time he went out, I put the baby in the car and followed him. *When his car pulled into a cheap motel, I felt like my world had collapsed.* **And I'm having a hard time forgiving myself for being so blind. If I'd paid attention in the beginning, maybe I wouldn't have to be feeling this pain.**"

Jody cheated herself by ignoring the Fatal Flaw she noticed when she first met Ned. *By overlooking the problem in Ned's personality, Jody set herself up for much bigger problems later.*

A person who exhibits a lack of sexual integrity almost always had a childhood in which he didn't feel he received enough love and affection. This individual has a voracious appetite for attention from the opposite sex, almost like an addiction. With some good counseling, this Fatal Flaw can be healed, but only if you spot it and deal with it. **IF YOU IGNORE IT, IT WON'T GO AWAY.**

Sexual Performance Problems

I've saved this until last because it's often the least "fatal." Sexual performance problems can be resolved with some honest communication and hard work by both you and your partner, but the first step is admitting you have a problem. Although none of us has a perfect sex life, some sexual problems can be serious enough to create tremendous tension and unhappiness in a relationship. They are:

1. Impotence: Many men experience periods of less sexual potency at certain times in their lives. *However, if you're just beginning a relationship and encounter this problem from the start,* **don't ignore it, no matter how embarrassed you feel discussing it with your mate.** Impotence, or the inability to achieve and maintain an erection, can be caused by the following:

▶ *Suppressed anger and resentment:* If your partner is carrying around a lot of unexpressed rage toward women, his mother, or an ex-lover, he may have difficult performing sexually. I think of it as if his penis is "on strike"—*"I refuse to get excited or satisfy you."* Your partner may be totally unaware of this unconscious anger, but I've found this to be the case with most impotent men. The impotence may also be a form of "getting even," or retaliation, if your partner feels you've hurt him deeply (i.e., you cheated on him, etc).

▶ *Feeling controlled or overly mothered:* If your partner feels "emotionally impotent" in your relationship, or felt this way in the past, his body might reflect that powerlessness by not being able to get an erection. This will also occur if he has set you up as his mother or if you treat him like a child—a man can't sleep with his mother, so his body unconsciously refuses to perform.

▶ *Extreme fear of intimacy:* Most of us battle with fear of intimacy, but in extreme cases a man might be unable to perform sexually. It's as if his penis is saying, *"I don't want to be engulfed by her. It's too frightening for me to be that close to someone else."*

▶ *Physical causes:* Anyone experiencing regular sexual impotence should immediately see a physician. There are many physical causes for impotence, including complications from medication, a diet extremely high in fat, etc. However, if no physical source is found, your partner should investigate the emotional sources I've mentioned.

2. Premature ejaculation: As I mention in my book *How to Make Love All the Time* most men experience difficulty with premature or "early" ejaculation at some point in their lives. If the problem is chronic, it can be a source of frustration to both partners. Here are some common causes of early ejaculation:

▶ *Improper lovemaking techniques:* Early ejaculation occurs when a man is too tense physically, mentally, or emotionally. This can be due to poor lovemaking habits, such as trying to get turned on much too quickly, tensing the buttocks to intensify the pleasure, or rushing to get to orgasm. There are many excellent books that discuss techniques for handling the sexual tension during lovemaking so it doesn't release too soon. I would also suggest you read *How to Make Love All the Time* and learn about "gourmet sex" verses "greedy sex." It'll help both partners enjoy their sexual experience much more.

▶ *Withholding emotions from a partner:* If your partner is holding back feelings of anger, guilt, or fear when he's making love to you, or has a secret he hasn't told you, he'll have more of a tendency to ejaculate quickly. The holding back creates tension that makes lasting longer difficult. Men who have a hard time communicating or sharing their emotions often have problems with premature ejaculation.

▶ *Fear of or dislike for sex:* If your partner was ever sexually molested, or taught that sex was dirty, he may "rush" through lovemaking to get it over with. It's as if his penis says, *"Let's come and get out of here in a hurry."*

▶ *History of having sex with women he didn't love:* If your partner has a history of sleeping with women he didn't care for, or visiting prostitutes, he may find it difficult to take his time making love to you. His penis is in the habit of making "quick departures."

▶ *Fear of intimacy:* As in the reasons for impotence, premature ejaculation can be a way your partner's body responds to fear of getting too close during sex. Coming quickly ensures that he won't spend too much time loving you.

3. Difficulty experiencing orgasm for women: When I teach women's seminars, this topic comes up all the time. Statistics tell us that over half of all women have difficulty achieving orgasm, and a smaller percentage of women have never experienced it. Aside from having an unskilled man make love to you, the reasons for "female impotence" are similar to those I mentioned earlier regarding male impotence and premature ejaculation.

► *Anger:* I would say that suppressed anger and rage is the main cause for a woman's inability to achieve orgasm. Anger doesn't allow us to feel pleasure. Women who've been molested or raped, abandoned, unloved, or cheated on may have anger locked inside them that prevents them from feeling joy and passion.

► *Fear of being controlled and going out of control:* Being in control is the opposite of orgasm, which is a total letting go. If a woman has a problem with control, is feeling controlled by her partner, or has felt victimized by men in the past, she may have a difficult time "losing control" enough to have an orgasm. Like impotence, withholding orgasm from your partner is an unconscious way of saying, *"See, you can't even turn me on. You don't have any power over me."*

► *Dietary causes:* The same link between a high-fat diet and male impotence applies to nonorgasmic women. Sexual excitement is caused by blood flow, and if your diet is too high in fat, you may have a sluggish circulatory system, making it difficult for you to experience sexual arousal and orgasm.

4. **Lack of interest in sex:** The fourth kind of sexual performance problem is no performance at all! If you meet a partner who seems to have a very low sexual desire and who tells you he or she could easily live without sexual contact, don't convince yourself this won't create conflict in your relationship. Asexuality is more complex than it appears. *While it may look like a disinterest in sex, it usually covers up an aversion to sex.* I've heard so many sad stories from men or women who've complained that their partner never really enjoyed sex, and after they were married, lost all desire for it so that, much to the dismay of their mate, the marriage was celibate. Disinterest in sex can stem from the same problems mentioned earlier, such as fear of intimacy, anger, etc., **but more often it can be traced to serious trauma such as sexual molestation, incest, rape, or other violent forms of abuse.**

Whether your partner is addicted to pornography, flirts too much, can't perform sexually, or isn't sexually interested, DON'T IGNORE THESE SEXUAL FATAL FLAWS! I know they aren't fun to talk about or deal with, but avoiding them won't make them disappear. As I mentioned at the beginning of this section, sexual disorders can be easily treated with some professional counseling and good communication between you and your partner.

SEXUAL PROBLEMS DON'T HAVE TO BE FATAL TO YOUR RELATIONSHIP, BUT THEY WILL BE IF YOU AVOID DEALING WITH THEM.

FATAL FLAW

▼ ▼ ▼ ▼ 6 ▼ ▼ ▼ ▼

Your Partner Hasn't Grown Up

▶ *"He never remembers where he puts things; he's always losing his wallet or car keys; he constantly forgets appointments—honestly, I feel more like his mother than his wife."*

▶ *"I think my girlfriend wants a sugar daddy more than a boyfriend. She promised me she'd get a job over nine months ago, but she really doesn't make an effort to look. All she does is shop, watch TV, and eat. I wish she'd wake up and start acting like a grown-up."*

▶ *"My boyfriend is very sweet, but his finances are a mess. He owes money to people all over town; his credit is awful; he never balances his checkbook; and he doesn't pay his bills on time. When I ask him why he lets things get this bad, he just laughs and tells me he 'lives in the moment.'"*

All of these comments are from people in love with partners who possess fatal Flaw Flaw #6—they haven't grown up. I'm not talking about a person who has a healthy relationship with his own inner child, allowing him to be playful, joyful, and adventurous. **The men and women with this Fatal Flaw have an adult side that refuses to behave in a responsible, mature manner, forcing you, as the partner, to take on the role of parent.**

Here are some of the warning signs to look for in determining whether your partner hasn't fully grown up:

1. Financial irresponsibility. I hate to admit it, but I've been in several relationships with men who were financially irresponsible, and like a typical rescuer, I didn't see it as a Fatal Flaw, but convinced myself my partner just wasn't a "practical" person. Practically infantile was more like it!! *Financial irresponsibility is a strong indicator that your partner has some deep Emotional Programming that needs to be changed in order for you to have a healthy relationship.*

▼
Is your partner financially irresponsible?

Here are some specific signs that indicate your partner might have Fatal Flaw #6. Watch for someone who:

- ► bounces checks
- ► never balances his checkbook
- ► frequently needs to borrow money from you or from others
- ► doesn't pay bills on time and waits until he receives collection notices
- ► doesn't plan ahead financially and spends all his money on luxury items (clothing, stereo equipment, jewelry, etc.) rather than saving for expenses
- ► has a poor credit record
- ► can't seem to keep a job for any length of time
- ► waits until all of his money runs out to make more
- ► counts on you to bail him out of financial trouble
- ► has owed people money for quite some time without paying it back

▲

If any of these sound familiar, don't ignore them. Your partner's financial irresponsibility not only affects him or her but you as well, since you usually end up footing the bill or feeling responsible to "help." And don't make the mistake I did, of convincing yourself your partner is just "not good with money." The truth is, he neglects the financial portion of his life because he doesn't want to grow up and take responsibility for himself. **Your mate's carelessness with his finances will be reflected in his carelessness toward how he treats you, and his unreliability will prevent your relationship from growing into a healthy, mature partnership.**

2. Undependable. We don't expect a small child always to be on time, keep all his promises, remember all the rules, or do everything he says he will. A patient parent knows that her child is learning what it means to be responsible and that at three or four the concept is still sinking in. *But you should expect your adult partner to be dependable, and if he isn't, you're in love with someone who hasn't grown up.*

Lack of dependability means:

▶ Your partner constantly *makes promises to you and then breaks them.*
▶ Your partner is frequently *late* for dates, events, etc.
▶ Your partner is *forgetful* of important information you've told him.
▶ Your partner agrees to do things for you (pick up some food for dinner, make reservations at a restaurant, etc.) and often *forgets.*
▶ Your partner is a *procrastinator,* putting off doing things for as long as possible.
▶ You are hesitant to count on your partner, since *he's let you down* so often in the past.

When you're in relationships with someone who's undependable, you begin to act like a parent, reminding them of things they should remember themselves, doing things for them they should be doing for themselves, and making excuses for their lack of dependability to your friends and family. You don't have much trust in or respect for your partner and will inevitably store up a great deal of anger and resentment.

3. Unmotivated.

▶ Does your partner seem to have no direction or purpose in his life?
▶ Is your partner waiting for something outside himself to motivate him to take action?
▶ Does your partner have a difficult time making plans for the future?
▶ Does your partner put off making decisions of any kind?
▶ Is your partner still trying to figure out what he wants to do when he grows up, but he's over thirty years old?
▶ Does your partner have significant problems he's unwilling to face?
▶ Is your partner waiting for someone to give him his "big break"?

If you answered yes to any of these questions, you're involved with someone who isn't taking responsibility for the quality of his life, but, like a child, is waiting for someone to figure it out and do everything for him. We all go through stages in our life when we examine how we're living and question whether or not we should continue doing what we're doing. But when this stage lasts for years, it's not a stage—it's an immature state of mind.

Why People Resist Growing Up

If you're in love with someone who hasn't grown up, you're in love with a complex person. The resistance to responsibility isn't simply a bad habit, like reading pornographic magazines, that can be put aside. Rather, **it's an unconscious response to circumstances that left your partner feeling robbed of his childhood.** Your partner might exhibit this Fatal Flaw if:

▶ **He had to grow up too fast.** Sometimes children are thrust into adult roles too soon by tragic events: A mother dies, and the oldest daughter takes on her role in the household; a father abandons the family, and the only son assumes the responsibility for his mother; a parent is unreliable due to alcoholism, and a child becomes like a parent to his or her siblings. These people may grow up feeling unconsciously resentful that they missed out on childhood, and resistant to acting as responsible adults now. It's as if their mind is saying, *"I had to be grown up when I was little. I'm tired of it, and now I want to play."*

▶ **He felt very controlled as a child.** *If your partner grew up in a family with lots of rules and strict discipline, he may rebel as an adult by ignoring the rules.* For instance, a little boy always told exactly how to behave and punished for acting like a "kid" might grow up into a rebellious man who doesn't pay his bills on time, forgets to do things you ask him to do, etc.

CHILDREN WHO ARE ANGRY AT THEIR CONTROLLING PARENTS OFTEN GROW UP INTO ADULTS WHO REBEL AGAINST ALL AUTHORITY FIGURES, RULES, PROTOCOL, LEGAL SYSTEMS, ETC.

▶ **He felt neglected as a child.** If your partner didn't get enough caretaking when he was small, *he might act out irresponsible and*

*childish behaviors as an adult as an unconscious way to say,
"Take care of me."* If you're always reminding him to remember
his appointments, helping him find his keys, or motivating him to
do well, you're "mothering" (or "fathering") him in a way he was
never parented as a child.

Parenting Your Partner Kills the Passion in Your Relationship

No matter how helpful you tell yourself you're being, parenting
your partner will create an unhealthy relationship. You'll end up
feeling:

▶ angry
▶ taken advantage of
▶ manipulated
▶ disrespectful toward your partner
  and
▶ sexually turned off.

As I said in my book *Secrets About Men Every Woman Should
Know,* how turned on can you get to a man when you just spent
fifteen minutes looking for his wallet, or when he acts like an
irresponsible six-year-old? How attracted can you be to a woman
who can't make simple decisions, or spends money without keeping
track of it like a thirteen-year-old? **The more your partner behaves like a child, the worse your sex life will be.**

Of course, if you've attracted someone like this into your life,
it's important that you look at your role in the relationship. You're
playing rescuer; you get to feel superior and avoid your own life by
constantly helping your partner. You need to stop the role-playing
and let your partner confront the consequences of his irresponsibility.

FATAL FLAW

▼   ▼   ▼   ▼   *7*   ▼   ▼   ▼   ▼

Your Partner Is Emotionally Unavailable

I could write an entire book on this Fatal Flaw, defining what it means, how to spot it, and what causes it. All you really need to know is:

STAY AWAY FROM PARTNERS
WHO ARE EMOTIONALLY SHUT DOWN!

There are so many people in the world eager to love you and receive your love in return. Why choose someone who has a hard time opening up and spend your time trying to pry open that person's heart?

Naturally, there are varying degrees of emotional unavailability. We all have emotional walls that hide parts of us we're afraid of showing others, and part of the purpose of a healthy relationship is to learn to become increasingly open and trusting. **But some people aren't ready to have a relationship because they're too emotionally blocked.** They need to do some serious healing before they are capable of giving and receiving love.

I've talked a lot in this chapter about symptoms of emotional damage, but let me sum up by listing some warning signs to watch for in spotting an emotionally unavailable partner:

1. Your partner cannot show emotions.

"I know John is a very sensitive person inside—it's just hard for him to show any feelings because he's been so hurt in the past."

What's the point of being in a relationship with someone if he can't show you how he feels? Why not just be alone? The very definition of relationship means interaction between two people, not one person trying to interact and the other doing nothing. If your partner can't share his feelings with you, your relationship will be shallow and frustrating. You'll become a "human can opener," trying to get your partner to open up all the time. **THAT'S NOT YOUR JOB—IT'S HIS.** You should expect your partner to be *capable of demonstrating basic emotions* such as happiness, sadness, disappointment, excitement, desire, and love. If he or she can't, they're not ready to be in a relationship with anyone.

Remember: There's no such thing as someone who "just isn't an emotional person." We were all emotional infants. Have you ever seen a baby who couldn't express his feelings? There's such a thing as someone who's emotionally damaged from childhood and has lost his ability to feel and show emotions.

2. Your partner cannot or will not talk about feelings.

"I know Lawrence loves me. He just isn't the kind of person who can talk about feelings."

Once again, the purpose of a relationship is not just to keep each other company, but also to *relate.* That means to share feelings, ideas, and insights with your partner, and in order to do that, you have to speak. Nothing saddens me more than hearing someone say, "My husband can't talk about his feelings." I feel like saying, "Then why do you pretend you're even in a relationship? You're living in the same house, but you aren't relating."

▼

IF YOU'RE MARRIED TO SOMEONE WHO WON'T COM-MUNICATE WITH YOU ABOUT EMOTIONS, YOU AREN'T IN A RELATIONSHIP—YOU HAVE A LIVING ARRANGE-MENT.

▲

We've seen that, for many people, talking about feelings is difficult, especially if they were taught not to express their emotions as children. But if your partner refuses to even try learning to express himself, or is just noncommunicative, your relationship is going to be awful. *Communication is one area where couples can really make a difference in their relationship if they are willing to learn how.* Reading books, taking workshops or classes, and going to marriage counseling are all effective methods of learning to talk with one another. **But both partners need to work on this problem.**

3. Your partner can't open up or trust.

"Andy says he doesn't want to lose me, but he refuses to let me in emotionally."

As I said earlier, there are some people who are not capable of having a healthy relationship because they are too emotionally shut down. They may want to open up but not know how, or need to do some intense healing before they're willing to relinquish their emotional armor enough to let you in. **When it comes to having a**

lasting relationship, good intentions don't count for much—you need to find someone willing to do what it takes to knock down their own protective walls. Otherwise you'll get into an emotional tug-of-war, you pushing your partner to open up and him pushing you away.

If any of these descriptions sounds familiar to you, go back and read the beginning of Chapter Five, where I talk about why you'd choose someone who doesn't love you as much as you love him. You need to understand your own emotional pattern that got you involved in a relationship with someone emotionally unavailable.

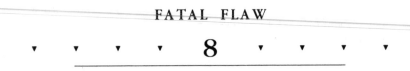

FATAL FLAW

▼　　▼　　▼　　▼　　**8**　　▼　　▼　　▼　　▼

Your Partner Hasn't Recovered from Past Relationship(s)

We all carry emotional baggage from our past relationships into each new one. But sometimes that baggage can be so overwhelming that it's fatal to your love affair. If you meet someone who hasn't recovered from a past relationship, you're in for heartache and disappointment. Here are some specifics to watch out for:

1. Your partner still carries tremendous anger and resentment toward his previous mate.

One of the questions I always advise singles to ask prospective partners on a first date is: *"How do you feel about your ex-lovers?"* If your date launches into a tirade about what a bitch his ex-wife is, or bitterly denounces his ex-girlfriend as a slut who cheated on him, I would think long and hard before going out on a second date. As we saw earlier, that unresolved anger and blame will eventually be projected onto you. Your partner may not have recovered from his previous relationship enough to have a healthy relationship with you. He may need time to evaluate the events of the past and to take responsibility for his part in what occurred.

▼

THE MORE ANGER TOWARD THE PAST YOU CARRY IN YOUR HEART, THE LESS CAPABLE YOU ARE OF LOVING IN THE PRESENT.

▲

This flaw isn't permanently fatal. The passage of time combined with some good therapy can eradicate this problem. **Note:** It's *possible* to work on this while you're in a relationship, but it's much more difficult and *can backfire by creating anger in you if your partner's healing takes longer than you feel it should.*

2. Your partner still feels guilty and responsible for his previous mate.

▶ Does your partner call or receive calls from his ex, claiming it's only because he's worried about her?

▶ Is your partner continually talking about his ex and allowing his concern for her to interfere with his being happy in his new relationship?

▶ Do you feel your partner hasn't set up proper boundaries to his ex about appropriate and inappropriate behaviors?

▶ Do you feel your partner is "leading his ex on" by not making it crystal clear that there's no hope of reconciliation in their relationship?

▶ Does your partner try to "protect" his ex from being hurt by lying about his relationship with you, hiding it from her and his children, or procrastinating about confronting her with the truth?

If you answered yes to any of these questions, you're involved with someone who hasn't completely let go of his past relationship. This behavior is acceptable only if you and your partner got together very close to the time of his breakup and it's been only a few weeks or months since then and your partner is still adjusting to the sudden change. *Even under these unusual circumstances, this behavior shouldn't continue for longer than a month or two at the most.* But if it's been a while since your partner ended his relationship, and one or more of these warning signs is still present, you've got a problem.

If your partner is feeling guilty or sorry for his ex-mate, it will interfere with his ability to surrender to the new relationship. It also creates a triangle even if he has no direct contact with his ex, so there are three people in the relationship, not two. **If you meet someone who fits this description, give him your phone number and tell him to call you when he has resolved his feelings about this ex.** Otherwise you'll be in competition with her, and it's impossible to compete with a memory, especially a sympathetic one.

3. Your partner is still traumatized from being hurt or abused in his or her past relationship.

▶ Does your partner seem emotionally fragile?

▶ Is your partner afraid to trust you?

▶ Does your partner frequently cry on your shoulder about how terribly her previous partner hurt her?

▶ Does it seem that no matter what you do or say, you can't make your partner happy?

If these sound familiar, be careful. You may be with someone whose heart is not healed enough to love yet.

Rescuers, beware! You'll be tempted to become involved with people who've just come out of a painful or unloving relationship, and to act as the healer who repairs their broken heart. Go back and read the part of Chapter Five where I talk about Rescue Missions as one of the wrong reasons to get involved in a relationship. **If someone is that damaged, give them time to heal themselves.** If you step in too soon, you'll be setting up a negative pattern in your relationship from the start.

Remember what I said in Chapter Five about getting involved with people who are not emotionally available: It can be a way for you to avoid intimacy, or to deprive yourself of love by choosing someone who can't love you in return. **If you always seem to find partners who haven't let go of the past, get some help in looking at your own fear of commitment.**

FATAL FLAW

▼　　▼　　▼　　▼　　*9*　　▼　　▼　　▼　　▼

Emotional Damage from Childhood

All of us carry emotional baggage from our childhood into our adult relationships. We are formed, to a large extent, by our past. If you want to meet someone who doesn't have some emotional damage from childhood, good luck! We all do. When looking for Fatal Flaws, however, we need to ask ourselves three questions:

1. How *severe* was the emotional damage incurred by my potential partner when he was young?
2. Is my partner *aware* of this emotional damage and how it affects his ability to function in a relationship?
3. Is my partner *actively working* on himself to repair this emotional damage (reading, therapy, seminars, etc.)?

The answers to these questions will determine whether your partner's past will be "fatal." The truth is, you could meet someone who had a relatively happy childhood but was totally spoiled by his mother, and because he is unaware of this pattern, always insists on having his way to the point where he is incapable of having a good relationship. And you could meet someone who was sexually molested and beaten as a child but is totally aware of the emotional trauma and working on healing it and is therefore capable of having an excellent relationship.

▼

YOUR PARTNER'S WILLINGNESS TO FACE HIS EMO-TIONAL PROGRAMMING AND TAKE ACTION TO HEAL IT WILL GREATLY DIMINISH THE EFFECT ANY FATAL FLAWS MIGHT HAVE ON YOUR RELATIONSHIP.

▲

All of the Fatal Flaws discussed in this chapter can be symptoms of painful events from childhood. But it's important to look for a history of certain more serious childhood traumas in your partner so you can better understand him, or if the traumas are so severe and his recovery from them is insufficient, so you can avoid getting involved in a very painful and disappointing relationship. I've broken down emotional damage from childhood into the following categories:

1. **Sexual abuse and sexual trauma**
2. **Physical or verbal abuse**
3. **Parental abandonment: divorce, death, adoption, suicide, emotional distance**
4. **Eating disorders**
5. **Parental addiction to alcohol, drugs, pills, etc.**
6. **Religious fanaticism**

Because we're talking about things that happened in the past, emotional damage may be more difficult to spot than a present problem with addiction or some of the other Fatal Flaws. For each category I've included some questions about your partner; it's important to know the answers to these questions to determine whether there may be severe emotional damage. **Obviously I'm not suggesting you discover the answers to all these questions in your first few months. And I'm not advising you to make a psychological diagnosis of your mate, since you're probably not a mental health professional, and aren't qualified to do so.** But within the first few weeks of your relationship, and *before you become sexually involved,* it's important to get some idea of whom you're dealing with.

IMPORTANT: **DON'T FORGET ALSO TO ANSWER THESE QUESTIONS ABOUT *YOURSELF,* TO GAIN INSIGHT INTO YOUR OWN PERSONALITY.**

Sexual Abuse and Sexual Trauma

1. Does your partner remember being sexually molested or abused as a child? Was it by a family member, friend, authority figure such as a priest or teacher, or stranger? Has your partner been in recovery or therapy? Has she told family members or confronted the abuser?

2. Is your partner aware of other family members who were sexually abused? Have they been in recovery?

3. Was your partner ever caught masturbating or having sex and punished for it?

4. What attitudes and values was your partner taught about sexuality?

5. Was your partner aware of a parent having inappropriate sex (affairs, multiple partners, prostitution)?

6. Has your partner ever been raped? Has she worked with a rape crisis center or support group, or received individual counseling to help heal the trauma?

Possible Problems

▶ **Sexual addictions or dysfunction.** Victims of sexual abuse often develop either an obsession with their sexuality, which we'll discuss later, or an aversion to it, losing sexual desire and becoming dysfunctional. I've received hundreds of calls over the years from frustrated husbands, telling me they've just discovered their wife, who dislikes sex, was molested as a child but has never received any help. **It's very difficult to have a normal sex life and love life if you've been sexually abused and haven't received professional counseling to help you deal with the powerlessness and rage. Recovery work is essential.**

Even if there was no physical molestation, but your partner grew up with inappropriate sexual behaviors going on around her, similar problems can develop.

▶ **Difficulty being intimate.** Victims of sexual abuse may have a difficult time with emotional boundaries, either becoming too passive with no boundaries, or very protected and closed with rigid boundaries. Often partners who were sexually violated will not let you in emotionally.

Adults who were taught to feel shame about sex as children, either through religious teachings, parental discipline, or having been caught in sexual activity and punished, can also have a hard time opening up emotionally and sexually.

▶ **Weight problems.** One of the first questions I ask people who seek my help and are very overweight is whether they were abused as a child. Over two thirds of them answer yes. Violated individuals often unconsciously protect themselves by building a physical shell around their damaged inner child, insulating themselves from further pain.

▶ **Deviant sexual behavior.** We'll discuss this more later in this chapter. It's important to note that adult survivors of childhood sexual abuse may often turn to fantasy, pornography, and promiscuity to act out their confusion about sex.

Physical or Verbal Abuse

1. Was your partner or one of his family members ever physically hit or beaten as a child? How often and how severe was the abuse?
2. Was your partner physically terrorized in other ways (locked in the basement, starved for a day, had hands put in burning hot water, etc.)?
3. Did your partner grow up in a home where there was a lot of expressed rage in the form of constant fighting, shouting, name-calling, etc.?
4. Did your partner have a parent he was afraid of or hated?
5. Was your partner verbally abused as a child (told he was no good, screamed at, constantly criticized and humiliated, or simply made to feel nothing he did was ever quite good enough)?
6. Did your partner feel there were an unusual and unreasonable amount of "rules of behavior," either expressed or unexpressed, in his home, and that if he broke any of those rules he would be severely criticized, rejected, or punished?
7. Did your partner witness one of his parents verbally abuse the other?
8. Has your partner ever physically hit any of the people he's been in relationships with as an adult?

Possible Problems

▶ **Acting out stored-up anger and rage.** Children who grow up being physically or verbally abused usually carry tremendous rage inside them. *Without professional help they'll act out that rage by becoming rageaholics, just like their parents, abusing you in the process. **This acting out may take the form of being highly critical, difficult to please, and moody, or may manifest itself in actual physical abuse of you or your children.***

▶ **Addiction (Substance Abuse).** If people who were physically abused decide to repress their rage, *they may be susceptible to taking on an addiction that will help them "numb" themselves to their suppressed feelings.*

▶ **Controlling behavior.** When a person feels out of control as a child, he may grow up to be very controlling in his relationships.

▶ **Inability to handle conflict or problems.** Some children from homes with tremendous anger and turmoil grow up with an intense aversion to conflict. *In their adult relationships they hate discussing problems, avoid conflict at all costs, and refuse to tell you what's bothering them.*

▶ **Addiction to drama.** When a child lives in a home in which there's constant drama, he grows up associating love with drama. *If your partner lived in a chaotic, unpredictable environment, he may unconsciously create drama in his adult life because that's the way "home" is supposed to feel.*

Parental Abandonment: Divorce, Death, Adoption, Suicide, Emotional Distance

1. Were your partner's parents divorced? Did your partner remain in contact with both parents afterward? Was it a friendly or a nasty divorce?
2. Did your partner's parents fight for custody of the children?
3. Did your partner's parents bad-mouth one another after the divorce, or use him as a go-between to manipulate each other?
4. Did your partner's parents remarry? What were his relationships to his stepparents, if any, or his parents' dates?
5. Did one or both of your partner's parents die when he was a child? What were the circumstances (illness, sudden death, suicide, etc.)?
6. Was your partner adopted? Does he know anything about his birth parents?
7. Were your partner's parents emotionally cold and distant? Is it hard for him to remember being told "I love you" as a child? Did his parents have a difficult time showing love and affection?

Possible Problems

► **Fear of commitment.** If your partner felt abandoned as a child due to divorce or death in the family, or lack of love, he may find it difficult to make emotional commitments. *Not committing is a way he unconsciously protects himself from getting abandoned again.* (See Chapter Eleven for more on commitment.)

► **Premature commitment.** We talked about this earlier in the book. *Often adults who felt cheated out of a "normal" family as a child may rush into relationships and commitments, hoping to create what they never had.* They are in love with the "idea" of being committed vs. being ready to commit.

► **Insecurity, possessiveness, and mistrust.** The more abandoned and rejected your partner felt as a child, the more likely he is to have a problem with *insecurity, possessiveness, jealousy, and mistrust.* It may be hard for you to convince him that you really love him, won't cheat on him, or betray him in some way.

► **No picture of a healthy relationship.** When a child grows up in a home where the parents' marriage did not stay intact, he doesn't have a healthy role model of what a lasting relationship should look like. *He may have a difficult time with romance and affection if he never saw his parents demonstrating love and affection toward him or one another.*

Eating Disorders

1. Did your partner have a weight problem as a child? Was he too thin or too heavy? Was he teased about his weight? Was food used as a reward or withheld as a punishment?
2. Has your partner ever had an eating disorder—anorexia, bulimia? Did she receive professional treatment?
3. Does your partner use food to cover up feelings? Does he have food addictions to sugar, or salty foods, that he can't control?

Possible Problems

► **Suppressed anger:** Eating disorders often cover up anger and resentment a person doesn't feel safe expressing. This person could be a time bomb waiting to go off.

▶ **Self-esteem problem:** People with food issues very often have a low sense of self-esteem due to childhood events, and the food problems make the self-esteem even lower, creating a vicious circle.

▶ **Control issues:** Your partner is probably a control freak. *Eating is about control and power,* and anorexics and bulimics are especially addicted to control.

▶ **Hidden sexual abuse:** As I mentioned earlier, an eating problem might be covering up sexual abuse from childhood.

Parents Were Addicted to Alcohol, Drugs (Prescription or Nonprescription), Pills, Etc.

1. Did one or both of your partner's parents drink or do drugs excessively? Did your partner see them drunk or high? Did they become abusive when under the influence? Did they ever get clean and sober?
2. Did their addiction cause financial, marital, or legal problems?
3. Is your partner in denial about his parents addiction? Was he in denial as a child?
4. Did your partner feel responsible to take care of his parents or the family because of their addiction?
5. Did your partner feel deprived because his parents couldn't be there for him due to their addiction (sleeping, hangovers, spacing out, etc.)?

Possible Problems

▶ **Codependency:** The biggest problem all adult children of addicts have is the tendency toward codependent behavior. Much has been written on this subject, but in simple terms, *the codependent person has learned to make someone's else's reality more important than his due to traumatic events in childhood. Your partner may be codependent if he:*
    1. has difficulty setting boundaries with you and others (can't say no, etc.)
    2. has a hard time knowing what he wants and asking for it, and is more concerned with your needs

3. doesn't trust his own instincts, perceptions, and feelings and often gives his power away to others

4. is dependent on others to make him feel good about himself

▶ **Tendency toward addictive behavior:** Children of addicts learn how *not* to cope with feelings by watching their parents numb themselves with drugs, alcohol, food, etc. Your partner may have a tendency to become easily addicted in order to numb himself to unpleasant emotions.

▶ **Difficulty communicating:** Children of addicted parents often didn't have permission to communicate at home, and *become adults who have a hard time expressing their feelings or talking about problems.*

▶ **Difficulty trusting:** If your partner grew up in a home where a parent was addicted, he most likely didn't have a stable, safe environment in which to grow. *He may have difficulty trusting you and your love, and letting you in emotionally.*

Religious Fanaticism

1. Did your partner grow up in a home with extremely strict religious values and no room for questioning those beliefs?

2. Was your partner told he was "evil," "bad," or "a sinner" as a child and that if he didn't obey, would go to hell? Was your partner afraid of God as a child?

3. Did your partner's parents profess to be godly people, yet were cold, unaffectionate, and physically or verbally abusive?

4. Was your partner taught that sex was dirty and sinful?

5. Was any expression of "unholy" thoughts or feelings such as anger, hurt, or disappointment prohibited in your partner's home?

Possible Problems

▶ **Sexual dysfunction or obsession:** When a child makes early associations with sex as evil and sinful, he'll either have to make sex dirty as an adult to participate in it, or will have a strong aversion to sex.

▶ **Inability to communicate emotions:** If your partner wasn't given permission to feel or express "unholy" emotions, *he'll grow into an adult who has a hard time recognizing, let alone verbalizing, all but the most loving feelings.*

▶ **Low self-esteem:** If a child is told God thinks he's bad, *he'll grow up as an adult who has a difficult time loving and accepting himself just the way he is.*

WHAT'S NORMAL AND WHAT'S NOT?

I hope you've learned a lot from this list. *My purpose in pointing these patterns out to you is NOT to scare you away from having relationships with anyone with a flaw. **All of us have emotional baggage we carry with us.*** My intention is to make you aware that **it's important for you to learn about the emotional background of your partner, as well as your own, so you can know what to expect in the relationship.**

So if you meet someone whose parents were divorced, you shouldn't say, "Sorry, you have a Fatal Flaw. I can't go out with you." However, you should discuss your partner's life with him, and if, a month or two into the relationship, you notice he has difficulty expressing his feelings or making a commitment, be extra cautious before getting more deeply involved.

Remember those three questions I presented earlier?:

1. **How *severe* was the emotional damage incurred by my potential partner when he was young?**
2. **Is my partner *aware* of this emotional damage and how it affects his ability to function in a relationship?**
3. **Is my partner *actively working* on himself to repair this emotional damage (reading, therapy, seminars, etc.)?**

The bottom line is: There is no such thing as a normal person, or normal problems. *None of us is normal—we are all unique.* And understanding our uniqueness and its history is the key to emotional freedom. **Out of the greatest pain can come the most powerful lessons, and with some hard work, you and your partner can turn your emotional baggage into emotional building blocks, helping to create a foundation for a loving and healing relationship.**

When I finished this chapter on Fatal Flaws, I gave it to a single friend of mine, who'd been begging me to show her this information as soon as I could. The next day she left a message on my answering machine that she needed to talk to me right away. When I returned her call, she said, "Barbara, I stayed up all night reading your chapter, and I learned things I wish I'd known years ago. But I'm worried about something: I met this guy last week who I really like, but he had a bad marriage, and he told me he's working on learning to express his feelings more. Does that mean he has Fatal Flaws? Should I tell him I can't see him anymore?"

She was relieved when I reassured her that, yes, she could keep dating her new man. But, listening to her, I realized that I needed to add something to the end of my chapter. So let me repeat something I said when I first started my discussion of Fatal Flaws:

IMPORTANT: If someone you love has one or more of these traits, it does not necessarily mean he is incapable of having a relationship. It does mean that those "character flaws" will cause problems in your relationship that *could* be fatal to its longevity.

Human beings are capable of tremendous personal transformation. Flaws are fatal only when we refuse to face them and run away from the exciting challenge of healing ourselves.

7

▼▼▼

COMPATIBILITY
TIME BOMBS

▼▼▼

Two households, both alike in dignity,
In fair Verona, where we lay our scene,
From ancient grudge break new mutiny,
Where civil blood makes civil hands unclean.

From forth the fatal loins of these two foes,
A pair of star-crossed lovers take their life;
Whose misadventured piteous overthrows,
Doth with their death bury their parents' strife.

FROM THE INTRODUCTION TO *ROMEO AND JULIET*
BY WILLIAM SHAKESPEARE

▼▼▼

$\mathbf{I}$n the late 1960s, the famous Italian filmmaker Franco Zefferelli brought the most famous star-crossed lovers in history to life in his beautiful movie *Romeo and Juliet.* I'm sure you won't be surprised to discover that I saw the film at least ten times, weeping just as much with each viewing for the tragic romance the innocent couple endured, and moved, as millions of other people have been, by the ill-fated love William Shakespeare so compellingly created when he wrote *Romeo and Juliet* almost four hundred years ago.

The tragic relationship may be wonderful entertainment as an artistic fantasy, but when it becomes a reality in your own life, you're sure to get your heart broken. Sadly, too many people end up having love affairs that are doomed to fail because of what I call *Compatibility Time Bombs* (CTB).

Unlike Fatal Flaws or Emotional Programming, Compatibility Time Bombs have very little to do with obstacles in your *inner world,* but rather are obstacles in your *outer world* that make having a lasting relationship with a particular partner difficult.

For this reason, Compatibility Time Bombs may often be impossible to change, whereas Emotional Programming or Fatal Flaws can be worked on. For instance, if you meet someone who has a hard time expressing his feelings, you'll have problems in that relationship. These problems can disappear, however, if your partner gets some counseling, or if you work on learning to communicate together. On the other hand, if you fall in love with someone who's a devout Catholic and you're Jewish, your problems are more serious: You can't change or improve the situation as if it's a bad habit or an unhealthy emotional pattern. *You may be able to compromise or adjust, but the situation itself will always remain.*

Remember in Chapter One where I talked about the Love Myths that give us a low Love IQ? One of myths was "True love will conquer all," and the reality was that love alone isn't enough to make a relationship work. This truth is never more sadly apparent than with a couple who love one another but have been hit with a compatibility time bomb. **In spite of their strong feelings, circumstances, mostly beyond their control, turn them, like Romeo and Juliet, into star-crossed lovers. Their love isn't enough to overcome the obstacles in their path and make their relationship last.**

Here are seven Compatibility Time Bombs that can destroy a relationship:

1. **Significant age difference**
2. **Different religious background**
3. **Different social, ethnic, or educational background**
4. **Toxic in-laws**
5. **Toxic ex-spouse**
6. **Toxic stepchildren**
7. **Long-distance relationships**

I call these obstacles Compatibility Time Bombs because *the problems they present to a relationship usually emerge over time rather than in the beginning of a love affair.* When you first meet someone with whom you share a CTB, you're too busy falling in love to pay attention to what's probably an uncomfortable issue for both of you. *"It doesn't bother me." "We'll deal with it when it comes up." "We'll love each other so much that it won't matter."* These are the kinds of things you tell yourself to avoid facing what you suspect could potentially be an insoluble problem. But one day the realities you've been ignoring explode in front of you, and you're forced to deal with them.

As you read about these Compatibility Time Bombs, I hope you'll learn about what to watch for in your present or future relationships, and gain an understanding of what may have contributed to the failure of your past relationships.

IMPORTANT: DON'T FORGET WHAT I'VE EMPHASIZED THROUGHOUT THIS SECTION OF THE BOOK: IF YOU RECOGNIZE A POTENTIAL PROBLEM IN YOUR RELATIONSHIP, WHETHER A FATAL FLAW OR COMPATIBILITY TIME BOMB, **IT DOES NOT MEAN YOUR RELATIONSHIP IS DOOMED.** IT DOES MEAN YOU NEED TO PAY CLOSE ATTENTION TO THE PROBLEM RATHER THAN IGNORING IT AND HOPING IT JUST GOES AWAY.

COMPATIBILITY TIME BOMB

▼   ▼   ▼   ▼   **1**   ▼   ▼   ▼   ▼

Significant Age Difference

► Eric, fifty-eight, and his wife, Janelle, thirty-two, are having the same fight they've had for the past nine months. Eric wants to spend the weekend relaxing at home, and Janelle wants to go out to a friend's party and dancing. "You used to like going out," Janelle says accusingly. "But since we've gotten married, every time I want to go out, you make excuses about being too tired or just wanting to stay home."

"We've gone over this before," Eric answers bitterly. "My idea of a good time isn't being around a bunch of people in a room with music so loud I can't hear myself think. What's wrong with wanting to stay home with my wife?"

"What's wrong is that it's boring," Janelle complains. "After working all week, I like a little fun on the weekend."

"Well, after working all week, I like a little peace and quiet. I'm sorry I'm not exciting enough for you anymore. Maybe I'm too old for you after all."

"Oh, don't start again, Eric," Janelle pleads. "And don't lecture me as if I'm your daughter."

▶ Andrea, thirty-nine, is arguing with her boyfriend, Don, twenty-six, about the same issue they always argue about—his fear of making a commitment. "We've been together for almost a year, Don, and I feel like we need to take things to a deeper level. But every time I bring it up, you react like a rebellious teenager."

"Don't start pulling that age thing on me again," Don retorts angrily. "I've told you over and over again that I'm just not ready to tie myself down and start a family right now—I don't feel financially stable enough in my business yet, and I just need more time."

"Well, if you worked a little harder, you'd be ready by now. Maybe you've got all the time in the world, but I haven't."

"Stop telling me how to run my life, Andrea, you sound like my goddamn mother. Just let me do things in my own time, okay? I'm only twenty-six, and I'm just not ready yet. If you want to marry me, you're just going to have to wait."

Significant age differences between partners can cause serious problems in relationships. The word "significant" is important here: If your partner is four or five years older or younger, it won't make much of a difference. **However, if your partner is ten or more years older or younger than you, it can cause difficulties depending on your ages and other aspects of your personalities.**

Eric and Janelle love each other very much, but there's a twenty-six-year difference between them, and after less than a year of marriage, they're discovering that this age gap is posing a lot more problems than they ever expected it to. Janelle, in her early thirties, has different social needs and interests than Eric, who is almost sixty. Eric has been married before and has three grown children. He's worked very hard for most of his life in a fast-paced profession, and while he was dating Janelle, was willing to endure the fast times and whirlwind social life she loved. Now that he's married again, he wants to slow down and enjoy life in a simpler way. Janelle has never been married before and has a fantasy picture of what the social life of a married couple should look like—dinner parties with other couples, dancing, etc. Neither of them is right or wrong; they just have some incompatible needs. *Like many couples with Compatibility Time Bombs, Janelle and Eric weren't aware of their conflicts in the beginning of the relationship. Dating didn't give them an accurate picture of what their partnership would feel like once it settled into a routine.*

Andrea is thirteen years older than her lover, Don, and insisted when she got involved with him that their age difference wouldn't have an effect on their relationship. In the beginning, it didn't. Andrea and Don started off with a very passionate sexual affair filled with excitement and romance. Nothing seemed to be lacking, and Andrea had never felt more loved in her life. But six months into the partnership, when the initial sizzle began to quiet down, the problems emerged. *Andrea began feeling impatient with the way Don was handling his life, and in spite of herself, had a hard time not pressuring him to "catch up" to where she was, and began offering advice, judging him and feeling resentful that he wasn't more prepared to make a commitment. And although Don's crazy about Andrea, at his age he's just not ready to give her the things she wants: marriage, children, stability.*

I've found that age differences mean less as both partners get older. For instance, a fifteen-year age difference between a thirty-five-year-old man and a twenty-year-old woman will probably create more potential hazards than that same fifteen-year span between a sixty-five-year-old man and a 50-year-old women. The age difference will affect the first couple more, since their maturity and experience levels are usually much more dissimilar than the second couple's. There are common life experiences that mold us that most people pass through from ages twenty to forty-five, a softening and mellowing-out process. A forty-year-old woman and a fifty-five-year-old man will have more of these life experiences in common than a twenty-year-old woman and a thirty-five-year-old man.

I'm obviously making generalizations about age here. There are, after all, fifty-year-olds who have never grown up and are totally irresponsible, as well as twenty-four-year-olds who are mature and wise way beyond their years. Nevertheless, significant age differences between partners are too important to be dismissed as inconsequential.

Although you may recognize some of these characteristics in other types of relationships, here are some potential problems to watch out for with this Compatibility Time Bomb:

IF YOU'RE THE OLDER PERSON IN THE RELATIONSHIP

1. You can become impatient with your partner.

If you are significantly older than your mate, *you may begin to lose patience with his level of immaturity, lack of life experience, and learning process.* This will be especially true if your mate is twenty to thirty years of age. After all, you've already gone through a lot of what he's dealing with: You've learned how to ask for what you want and take charge of your life; you've realized it's not the end of the world when you go through a crisis; you've made mistakes and figured out how to do things the right way. So it's not easy watching your younger partner stumble through these same life experiences. In fact, it can be quite exasperating watching someone you love go through life lessons you're glad to have left behind.

One of the reasons that Andrea and Don fight so much is because she's becoming impatient watching Don "grow up." She's been a successful marketing consultant for over ten years, but Don is just beginning to do well as a writer. He doesn't make that much money yet, and is still learning a lot about selling himself and his work. Don's self-doubts are normal for a twenty-six-year-old guy just starting out, but they drive Andrea crazy, and she feels like he's taking too long to make a lifelong commitment to their relationship. **What Andrea forgets is that the confidence and easy expertise that come so naturally to her now took years to develop.** And her impatience is only making it more difficult for Don to feel good about himself and move confidently forward. *She's not wrong, and Don isn't right—they're just in very different life phases.*

2. You have a tendency to act like a parent to your mate.

When you have ten, twenty, or thirty more years of life experience than your partner has, you'll find it next to impossible not to offer advice, correct, and direct him or her. After all, you've been through this before—you know the best way to do it. Your intentions are loving; you're only trying to help. But the effect can be very destructive to your relationship. **YOU BEGIN ACTING LIKE A PARENT AND TREATING YOUR PARTNER LIKE A CHILD.** Naturally, your mate feels as if you don't trust or respect him, and responds just like a rebellious teenager would—he becomes resentful and pulls away. And this parent-child game will quickly destroy the passion in your sex life.

Sometimes if your partner has been looking for a parental figure, you will unwillingly find yourself playing this role, desperately longing to get out of it but unable to as long as your mate continues to be irresponsible and overly dependent on you. These relationships can be very toxic and usually end up with the older person feeling let down and disappointed, and the younger person feeling abandoned.

3. You may be much more financially successful than your partner.

Most older partners have more financial stability, and therefore more power in the relationship. You've had many more years to build up your income, purchase property and other possessions, etc. This financial superiority can create tension between you and your partner in numerous ways: You may feel resentful about being the one who provides more, especially if you're a woman: You may feel like you should make the important decisions (what to spend, where to live, what kind of vacation to take) because it's your money, and your partner might not feel this is fair. You may have difficulty lowering your standards of living to accommodate to your mate's.

When Leslee, a thirty-eight-year-old film editor, met Martin, a twenty-seven-year-old fitness trainer, they fell head over heels in love. Three months into the relationship, their troubles began when they started planning a vacation together. Leslee wanted to go to a resort in Mexico for a week, and Martin, knowing he could barely afford to leave town at all, suggested they go on a camping trip. "I don't mind paying for the vacation," Leslee insisted. "I've gone to Mexico for the past five years, and look forward to it for months."

"I know you'll pay," Martin responded angrily, "But that makes me feel really humiliated. If we go somewhere, it has to be a place I can afford to split with you."

"Why should I stop taking the kinds of trips I'm used to just because you don't have the money to go? I've worked hard for the past fifteen years to be able to afford these vacations. It's stupid for me to pretend I'm having a great time camping just so you don't have to feel bad," Leslee complained.

4. You may be tempted to control your partner because you hold more of the power in the relationship.

All of the warning signs above add up to this one—it's easy when you're much older than your partner to get into a power trip and become controlling. You have more money, success, and experience, and therefore it's tempting to "pull rank" on your mate.

5. You may be tempted to compromise or sacrifice your interests, friends, and activities to appear more compatible with your partner.

· If your mate is much younger, you may give up interests he or she doesn't appreciate and take on habits that make you appear younger. I knew a man once who met a young actress when he was in his fifties. This guy loved to play bridge, listen to classical music, and watch old movies on television. I bumped into him at a restaurant with his new girlfriend and was shocked at what I saw. He was dressed in leather from head to toe, had pierced one of his ears, and told me he was on his way to a Madonna concert. Now, I'm not saying that leather and rock music are not for people over thirty, but this man was trying so hard to bridge the age gap between himself and his lover that he looked ridiculous.

If you're involved with a much younger person, here are some questions to ask yourself to avoid Compatibility Time Bomb #1:

▶ "Do I respect my partner?"
▶ "Am I proud of my partner?"
▶ "Do I trust my partner?"
▶ "What am I learning from my partner?"

IF YOU'RE THE YOUNGER PERSON IN THE RELATIONSHIP

1. You may put your partner on a pedestal and give up your power because of his or her age.

If your mate is much older than you, he or she is probably more successful, experienced, and financially secure. This may influence you into unconsciously feeling your partner is "better" than you are, and tempt you to idealize him rather than see him for who he really is. **When you allow yourself to feel less important because of your mate's chronological advantage, you give up your power. You take his advice rather than trusting your own; you blindly believe his criticisms rather than questioning whether he's correct; you invalidate your own needs and feelings out of deference to your partner.** You tell yourself:

▶ "He's the one who's paying for it, so we'll do it his way."
▶ "I'm sure he knows what he's doing. After all, look how successful he is."

► "He knows much more about these things than I do because he's older."

Even if your partner doesn't want to play this role with you, you may be tempted to fall into this pattern simply because of the age difference. And if your partner happens to enjoy his role as the older, wiser one, or actually uses it to control you, watch out: Your relationship won't be very healthy.

2. You may set your partner up to be like a parent.

Another consequence of being the less experienced, less worldly one in a relationship is that you may be tempted to re-create a parent/child dynamic with your partner. **If you're always asking his advice, counting on him to help you, depending on him for money, using his connections to your advantage, or allowing him to make decisions for you, you are, in essence, behaving like a child** and giving him the authority to be your father (or if you're the younger man, your mother). This prevents you from truly growing up and opens the door for all kinds of emotional programming to run itself out.

Even when your partner doesn't control you, you may *feel* controlled and intimidated just by virtue of the fact that he or she is that much older. You may react by becoming rebellious, withdrawn, or difficult. Perhaps this is the relationship you had with your own parents, or you may be acting out the anger you never had the courage to express to them when you were growing up.

3. You may be tempted to compromise or sacrifice your interests, friends, and activities to appear more compatible with your partner.

If you are involved with a much older person, here are some questions to ask yourself:

► "Does my partner respect me?"
► "Does my partner treat me as an equal?"
► "Do I feel like an equal with my partner?"

When It Can Work

A relationship between two people of very different ages can work if both partners avoid falling into the patterns we've just talked about.

The more you have in common and the more committed

you are to working on the relationship, the better your chances for survival.

If you use the challenge of your situation to grow as individuals, your age difference can actually serve as a great teacher to you both.

Remember Andrea and Don? Their relationship ended up working despite the thirteen-year age difference. Andrea realized that she was trying to control Don by wanting him to run his life according to her plan, and that she needed to give him a chance to follow his dreams. Don saw that he was avoiding taking responsibility for their relationship by putting Andrea off. They agreed to give things another chance, and within six months their relationship radically changed for the better. Don's career started to take off, and he was able to give Andrea more of what she wanted because she wasn't breathing down his neck all the time. And Andrea learned that Don could be trusted to be responsible and committed to their relationship. **From Andrea, Don learned more about commitment, and from Don, Andrea learned more about trust and letting go of control.**

When It Can't Work

Some couples never recover from the Compatibility Time Bomb of their age difference. Eric and Janelle, twenty-six years apart, didn't make it, **because their ages created too much incompatibility in their relationship.** The longer they lived together, the more unhappy they became. Eric realized that although he loved Janelle, he'd been so physically attracted to her that he'd neglected to ask himself what kind of life she expected. Once the sexual intensity calmed down, Eric found himself feeling that Janelle just didn't fit into his life as he'd hoped she would. She expected him to keep up the active social pace they'd set when dating, whereas he wanted a more mellow life-style. Eric didn't like Janelle's friends, and she wasn't crazy about his, either. To make matters worse, Eric was very close with his grown children and enjoyed spending time with them, but Janelle couldn't get used to the fact that Eric had a family whom he loved—her picture of a marriage was more traditional, and although she tried, she couldn't ever quite accept the reality that Eric had had a life before her. As their dissatisfaction with one another grew, their fighting escalated until they split up.

A significant age difference between partners can be a wonderful inspiration for growth, stretching each person's ability to love and understand the other, or it can be the cause of consistent tension and unhappiness that ultimately make staying together impossible.

COMPATIBILITY TIME BOMB

▼ ▼ ▼ ▼ **2** ▼ ▼ ▼ ▼

Different Religious Background

One of the most painful types of telephone calls I used to take on the radio came from the people who wanted my advice on the religious conflicts they were facing in their relationship: The Jewish man whose fiancée was a practicing Catholic; the born-again Christian who'd fallen in love with an agnostic; the Unitarian girl whose boyfriend was a Mormon. Many of these couples were discovering the hard way that differing religious backgrounds is one of the most difficult and deadly Compatibility Time Bombs. At least when there is an age difference, you know that your age and the characteristics that go with it will change over time, but for most people, religious preference stays the same. Many time all I could offer these broken-hearted lovers was a shoulder to cry on.

Compatibility Time Bomb #2 often makes a surprise attack on the relationship, simply because, for most of us, our spiritual beliefs and values aren't topics of discussion in the early days of a relationship. You don't need to share the same religious philosophy to enjoy a date with someone; you don't need to know his feelings about God to have a good time at the movies. Even if you do know you come from different backgrounds, you're tempted to put the information aside and focus instead on what you have in common. *Unfortunately, you only begin to notice the problems when your relationship has matured and become more serious, but by then your feelings for one another are so strong that it's very difficult to separate, even if you know it's inevitable.*

Here are the areas where different religious backgrounds create conflict in a relationship. *Remember, as in all Compatibility Time Bombs, the more extreme the differences, the worse the explosion!*

Customs and holidays.

This is usually the first place where religious differences become uncomfortable. Everything is fine until the Christmas season rolls around, or Passover comes, and suddenly the issues you've been unconsciously ignoring are thrust into the limelight. Holidays and special occasions reveal much about our religious and spiritual beliefs, and accentuate differences two people might be telling themselves aren't that great.

Beth, twenty-nine, and John, thirty-one, are a couple in a compatibility crisis. Beth and John have been in a serious, committed relationship for eight months, and are very much in love, but there's one problem: *Beth is Jewish, and John is Protestant.* Although neither consider themselves devoutly religious, they both enjoy the customs and teachings of their respective faiths. They've spoken about their backgrounds before, but never really had to face the effect it would have on their life until their first holiday season together.

Beth frequently spent the night at John's apartment, and often stayed the whole weekend. Even though she had no immediate plans to move in with John, she considered his place like a second home. Three weeks before Christmas, John picked Beth up after work and asked her to help him pick out his Christmas tree. He noticed that Beth seemed unusually quiet as they walked through the lot and on the ride home. When he finished setting up the tree in his living room, he asked Beth if there was anything wrong. "I feel strange telling you this," Beth confessed, *"but I don't feel comfortable having a tree in the house.* We never had one growing up—my parents felt very strongly about keeping our Judaism pure. I didn't think it would bother me that much, but it does."

John didn't really know how to respond to Beth. "I can understand how you feel, honey, but I've always had a tree. Christmas is my favorite holiday, and I love everything that goes with it. *I can't just give up what I believe in, even though I hate making you uncomfortable."*

"I'm not asking you to give anything up," Beth answered defensively. "I just don't know if I feel right staying here during the holidays. How can I light my menorah and celebrate my heritage with a Christmas tree staring me in the face?"

Beth and John are arguing over more than holiday traditions: They're confronting a major difference in their spiritual belief systems. **If they discover that their belief systems are too dissimi-**

lar and that those conflicts in customs and attitude interfere with their happiness together, they'll have to end their relationship.

Children.

If you want to flush out any hidden religious incompatibility with a partner, just ask him what religious or spiritual background he'd like to pass on to his children; then tell him your preferences and watch the sparks fly! **Nothing forces us to examine our values and beliefs more honestly than thinking about raising our children.** We all know someone claiming to be quite liberal and nonreligious who, upon having a child, suddenly becomes ultraconservative and rushes to sign his son or daughter up for Sunday school. Unfortunately, this pattern can cause tremendous pain to couples in love. When they discuss marriage, becoming pregnant, or having a child, they suddenly discover that they have very different and rigid religious views after all.

What to Do if You're in This Situation

If you and your partner have very different religious backgrounds, here are some suggestions:

1. Be honest about your feelings in the beginning of the relationship.

It's very tempting to downplay your religious convictions or spiritual beliefs when you suspect that standing by them might alienate your partner. Don't give in to the temptation to be dishonest. If you have strong religious affiliations, share these with your mate when you first begin dating, rather than waiting until you're closer or more serious. The longer you wait, the more painful a possible realization of incompatibility will be.

2. Don't avoid talking about the future.

Make a point of discussing how you want to bring up your children, celebrate holidays, and integrate spirituality into your life with your partner *early in the relationship.* Don't use the excuse that discussing these topics will put pressure on your mate, or make the person feel you're asking him or her to marry you, etc. You can have a philosophical exchange of ideas that'll help you discover whether you and your partner may be sitting on a Compatibility Time Bomb without promising to spend your lives together. **If you** aren't sure of your feelings about this, take some time to explore your own religious and spiritual beliefs. Don't wait until it's too late.

3. **If you're serious about pursuing your relationship, seek advice from clergy or other interdenominational couples.**

Don't attempt to explore the hazardous waters of interdenominational relationships by yourself. There are support groups available for couples in this situation, and clergy of all faiths are available to give you advice and guidance.

When It Can Work

The more flexible you and your partner's religious beliefs are, the greater your chances of avoiding this Compatibility Time Bomb. Even if your differences aren't extreme, it'll still take a lot of compromise and commitment for your relationship to adapt.

Maybe you have a strong relationship with God but not a strong connection to organized religion. You rarely attended church services and are more attracted to a loose interpretation of your faith, emphasizing loving values rather than doctrine. Maybe you don't even care about bringing up your children in a particular faith; you just want them to understand and hopefully experience a relationship with a Higher Power.

In this case you may discover that you would be comfortable sharing in the traditions of your partner's religion while acknowledging your mutual belief in God. *If you're not a strict adherent to your faith, it's quite possible you'll be able to find enough religious compatibility to make a relationship of differing faiths work.*

When It Can't Work

The stronger your own religious beliefs, the more difficult it will be to avoid this Compatibility Time Bomb.

It's not easy to walk away from someone you love because of differing religious beliefs, but the longer you wait, the harder it becomes. I know a woman who believes in God but doesn't follow any particular religion, and who fell in love with a wonderful man who was everything she wanted in a partner except for one thing: He was a born-again Christian. They dated for three months, and even though he didn't try to push his beliefs onto her, she knew how strongly he felt. They weren't even talking about a future together, but she realized that one day they would, and she would have to tell him she was unwilling to embrace the life-style he wanted for himself. *She decided to stop seeing him, and as hard as it was for her, it was a lot easier than it would have been if she'd waited six months or a year.*

DON'T LET THIS COMPATIBILITY TIME BOMB BLOW UP IN YOUR FACE—CONFRONT THIS ISSUE BEFORE YOU BECOME SERIOUSLY INVOLVED WITH SOMEONE.

COMPATIBILITY TIME BOMB

▾　　▾　　▾　　▾　　**3**　　▾　　▾　　▾　　▾

Different Social, Ethnic, or Educational Background

In 1990, one of the most popular films of the year was *Pretty Woman,* in which Julia Roberts played a hooker who fell in love with millionaire Richard Gere and got him to marry her. For three quarters of the movie the audience sees the extreme differences between the backgrounds of the two characters. Richard Gere's character is well educated and well bred, highly intellectual, and an expert on everything from opera to wine. The hooker never graduated from high school, comes from the seedy side of town, and has probably never even seen a copy of *The Wall Street Journal.* Toward the end of the film they both decide their relationship would be impossible, only to realize in the movie's last few minutes that they can't live without one another, and they reunite in a wonderfully romantic scene and supposedly live happily ever after.

Pretty Woman is certainly not the first film, play, or book to depict lovers from different sides of the tracks. Who can forget Tony and Maria in the Broadway musical *West Side Story* singing "There's a Place for Us," dreaming of a time when it wouldn't matter if one of them was white and one Puerto Rican, as long as they loved one another, or Professor Henry Higgins in *My Fair Lady* falling in love, in spite of himself, with Eliza Doolittle, the flower seller he'd plucked from the ghettos of London? I think one of the reasons we enjoy seeing these fictional lovers survive against all odds is because, in our everyday reality, different social and educational backgrounds can be a very painful Compatibility Time Bomb.

In many countries around the world this problem doesn't even exist, because marrying out of one's social class is unacceptable. America, however, is the melting pot of the world, and especially in large urban areas, each of us is exposed to people from all financial, social, and ethnic backgrounds as part of our daily existence. *And as much as, in principle, we'd like to believe we accept all people regardless of how they were brought up or who their ancestors were, those beliefs get challenged when we or one of our children falls in love with someone "different."*

A healthy relationship is based in part on the commonality you share with your partner—mutual interests, beliefs, tastes in style, and reference points. All of these serve to make living together comfortable rather than full of friction. **It's not that you and your partner have to agree on everything and have gone through all the same experiences. But there's a point beyond which *too many differences will create too much tension, and make a harmonious relationship next to impossible.***

This Compatibility Time Bomb is one of the most difficult to detect until you're actually living with someone, because you may be unfamiliar with their habits or life-style unless you make a point of finding out what their values are. This sounds easier than it is, because many people are hesitant to talk honestly about these sensitive issues. For instance, it's hard to admit to yourself, *"I'm embarrassed by my partner's lack of education and poor habits,"* or *"I love my girlfriend, but when I think of having racially mixed children with her, I become upset."* It's even harder to tell your mate, "You're not sophisticated enough for me, and I don't feel comfortable introducing you to my friends," or the reverse, *"I feel like your family makes me feel inferior because of my background, and I don't think they'll ever accept me."*

I believe that in a perfect world, we all would be able to love enough to transcend these differences. What's important for you to know is this: **If you suspect that you have strong feelings and preferences regarding background in a partner, don't deny them, even if you don't approve of your own judgments.** I've seen so many couples get into trouble by telling themselves their differences *shouldn't* matter, when in reality, right or wrong, *they did.*

▼

Trying to accept something you aren't comfortable with in your partner will only hurt that person more in the end, when your true feelings emerge.

▲

As usual, I'll remind you that the *more extreme the differences, the more likely they'll be to cause problems.* And depending on what those differences are, in some cases even small ones will be big problems, while in others, major differences can be accepted.

Possible Problems Different Backgrounds Will Create

1. You may not have enough in common.

Olivia, a forty-six-year-old physician, met Ted, a forty-eight-year-old gardener, at an Alcoholics Anonymous meeting. Both were in recovery, and immediately hit it off. "You're dating a gardener?" Olivia's friends at the hospital would remark. "What do you talk about?" Olivia would laugh and tell them how happy she was to be in a healthy, sober relationship for a change. In the back of her mind, she wondered about the differences between her and Ted. Olivia was very involved with the arts, and most of her friends and activities revolved around concerts, theater, and creative pursuits. Ted was the complete opposite. He'd never gone to college, and had worked all his life outdoors. *"I don't think I've worn anything but blue jeans for twenty years,"* he'd boast proudly. It was part of what Olivia loved about him—he was so unlike many of the pretentious men she'd dated.

For the first few months of their relationship, Ted and Olivia got along wonderfully. They spent most of their time alone together, or going to AA meetings. The problems began when Olivia asked Ted to attend a benefit gala she'd helped to organize for the hospital.

"I'll only go if I don't have to wear a tuxedo," Ted insisted.

"Look, it's only for one night," Olivia pleaded. "And you'll love my friends. I've told them all about you." Ted reluctantly agreed.

The evening was a disaster. Ted was bored to death by Olivia's friends and their talk about this artist and that opening, and hardly said a word all night. Olivia felt torn in half—one part of her wanted to enjoy the gala she'd worked so hard to put on, and the other wanted to make Ted comfortable. By the end of the evening, she was in tears.

Over the next few months, the problems between Ted and Olivia escalated. Ted tried introducing her to his friends at a bowling party, and she felt just as out of place as he had at the gala. "Your friends are very warm and good people," she explained at the end of the evening, "but I had a hard time finding anything to talk to them about." That night, as she lay in bed, Olivia knew she couldn't run from the truth anymore: It would never work out with Ted. They were too different. *She thought about the gentle, sleeping man she loved, and she wept for what could never be, and for the love that wasn't big enough to bridge the gap between them.*

Some couples make their differences work for them. They learn from each other, and each becomes more well rounded. But if the differences are too extreme, they'll only produce conflict and alienation.

2. You may have very different values.

Each of us forms our value system based on our upbringing, our ethnic background, and our educational and life experiences. *If your background is radically different from your partner's, you'll probably find your values greatly differ as well.*

▼

COUPLES WHO SHARE SIMILAR VALUES HAVE A MUCH GREATER CHANCE OF CREATING A HAPPY, HARMONIOUS, AND LASTING RELATIONSHIP.

▲

Your values determine many aspects of your personality, including:

- ► how you treat other people
- ► how you treat yourself
- ► how you spend money
- ► how you raise your children
- ► what kinds of goals you set and how you go about achieving them
- ► your political opinions
- ► your attitude toward those less fortunate than you
- ► your health habits

Your values effect you every day of your life. **When your values and your partner's are very different, you'll experience tremendous tension in the relationship on a consistent basis.** This can turn your relationship into a battleground.

Mark, thirty-six, and Juliana, twenty-nine, were newlyweds when they came to me for help in their relationship. "All we ever do is fight about money," Mark complained. "Juliana acts like we're living on welfare, and I'm tired of her telling me how to spend the money I make."

"Well, if you wouldn't be so extravagant, we wouldn't fight so much," Juliana insisted with tears in her eyes. "All I'm trying to do is get you to save for our future, but you're so used to doing whatever you want that it's impossible to talk to you about it. I'm tired of you blaming me for doing what any good wife would do."

You can understand how this Compatibility Time Bomb hit Mark and Juliana if I tell you about their backgrounds. Mark came from a fairly wealthy family. His father was a self-made man who owned a chain of clothing stores and prided himself on giving his children everything he didn't have himself as a child. Mark spent each Christmas skiing in Colorado, and went to Europe every summer. He attended a very expensive private college and came back home to work for his father. *He didn't consider himself financially reckless—he simply liked to enjoy the good things in life.*

Juliana's past was quite different. She was the oldest of four children raised by a single mother—her Dad left when the kids were small and only sent money sporadically. There was a lot of love in Juliana's house, but not much of anything else. Her mom worked in two jobs to support the kids, and as soon as Juliana was old enough, she went to work after school to help pay the bills. "Thrift" was the motto she lived with. *Money was something you worked hard to get, then spent on practical things such as food, rent, and doctors' bills.*

When Mark met Juliana, he was instantly attracted to her down-to-earth practicality. "She wasn't like all the other girls out husband-hunting," he told me. He knew about her upbringing, but he couldn't understand why she wouldn't buy herself new clothes, or why she'd become upset when Mark gave her expensive jewelry for special occasions. "I spent weeks looking for the right bracelet for our first anniversary," he said angrily, "and all she could say when she opened the box was, 'Mark, you shouldn't have spent so much money on this. I won't feel right wearing it.' "

Juliana shook her head. "He doesn't even ask me when he makes big purchases. I feel so left out, like he's hiding something from me."

When It Can Work

When both partners are willing to compromise their values and find a common ground together, they can overcome this Compatibility Time Bomb. Mark and Juliana are a couple who had enough in common to give them a foundation for working through their area of incompatibility. They were successful in saving their relationship because *compromising didn't mean sacrificing, but rather enhancing their needs.*

Many of Juliana's values were due to emotional programming, and not simply preferences. She'd learned to be financially conservative as a child out of necessity. In going through counseling, she realized that she was still operating out of "poverty consciousness" and wasn't giving Mark a chance to prove that he could spend money without putting them into financial jeopardy. Mark saw that he was still spending money as if he were single and not consulting Juliana about big purchases or including her in his decision-making. He promised to be more sensitive to her feelings, and she committed herself to trusting him more. **By working together, Mark and Juliana created new, healthier values for themselves as individuals and grew even closer in the process.**

CAUTION: I do not suggest that you even consider compromising values you feel are part of you. Sacrificing what you believe in to keep the peace in a relationship will only backfire later. For instance, if you're committed to taking good care of yourself, and your boyfriend eats junk food, smokes, and isn't interested in changing, you should not start abusing your body to become more like him. Reexamining your values is always a good idea, and if you find room for change, great. *But do it for yourself, not to make your partner happy or keep the relationship going.*

When It Can't Work

Some couples are just too far apart in their thinking and background to live together compatibly. This was the case for Shelly and Ali. Shelly was a soft-spoken, beautiful woman from Arkansas farm country who moved to Texas and met Ali, a handsome and successful Persian. At first he was everything Shelly imagined a lover should be—charming, well educated, and very polite. He courted Shelly with fervor, showered her with gifts and exciting trips, and when he proposed, she was ecstatic.

From the moment they got married, though, everything changed. Ali seemed to become much more conservative and demanding, expecting Shelly to work full-time, do all the housework, and shop and cook, too. And *as she became familiar with Ali's family traditions, she became truly uncomfortable.* They began to see his family several times a week, segregating the men and women in separate rooms.

Shelly didn't understand what had happened to Ali, but Ali really hadn't changed that much. Now that they were married and living together, his values about marriage and family had begun to emerge, and she just hadn't realized how different their backgrounds were. She tried talking about it with Ali, and they ended up having an enormous argument during which he told her that *he was the man of the house and his desires were more important.*

Shelly tried to ignore her increasing discomfort but became more and more unhappy in the process. Desperate to save their marriage, Shelly went to a counselor by herself. After a few sessions she began to face the painful truth that she and Ali had very different value systems and came to understand more about his cultural background. "All this time I've been blaming him," she told me on the phone, "making him the bad guy. Ali is just being who he is. **This is the way he lives; this is how his family is. Women have a very different role in his culture, and it's not wrong—it's just very different from how I was brought up.** I never took the time to talk about these things before we got married because I was too swept up in all the romance."

Shelly had to come to terms with the fact that not only was Ali not going to change, he didn't want to change. He had the right to live as he wished. It just wasn't how Shelly wanted to live.

Shelly learned an important if painful lesson from Ali: She needed to find out more about the values of a prospective partner *in the beginning of a relationship.*

COMPATIBILITY TIME BOMB

▼ ▼ ▼ ▼ **4** ▼ ▼ ▼ ▼

Toxic In-laws

▶ "My mother-in-law is driving me crazy. She calls my husband ten times a day and criticizes me every time we are together."

▶ "My wife's family decided I wasn't good enough for their daughter when we first met, and have never accepted me. My wife won't confront them, and I'm starting to resent her for it. What should I do?"

▶ "Why won't my husband stop rescuing his mother? He runs over to her house the minute she calls him to change a light bulb, or if she has a headache. We fight about her all the time. I'm at the end of my rope."

These are the kinds of phone calls I got on the radio and letters I've received from frustrated men and women who'd been hit with Compatibility Time Bomb #4, **Toxic in-laws.** If you're fortunate enough to be unfamiliar with this phenomenon, you're probably laughing at the phrase. But for the thousands of people who've come to me for help, there's nothing amusing about having in-laws who are ruining your relationship.

Before I talk more about this CTB, I want to emphasize the following point:

IF YOUR PARTNER HAS TAKEN A STAND WITH HIS PARENT OR PARENTS, COMMUNICATED HIS FEELINGS, AND SET CLEAR BOUNDARIES AS TO WHAT BEHAVIOR HE WILL ACCEPT, YOU WILL NOT HAVE A PROBLEM REGARDLESS OF HOW TOXIC YOUR IN-LAWS MAY TRY TO BE.

You may not particularly like your in-laws. But if your mate refuses to tolerate any unloving or disruptive behavior from them, your relationship won't be in jeopardy. **You *will* experience a Compatibility Time Bomb when your partner refuses to ac-**

knowledge or confront his parents on behavior or attitudes that are negatively affecting your relationship (of course, the same applies to you if you're the one with the toxic parents driving your mate crazy).

The term "toxic" comes from the Greek word *toxicon,* meaning "poison." Poison is something that harms whatever comes in contact with it. And that's what a toxic in-law is—**a parent of your spouse whose contact with you is harmful to your happiness.**

Toxic in-laws make great CTB's because of their delay factor in striking:

► **You may not know much about them until you're part of the family, and then it's too late.** If your partner is in denial about his parents, or tries to avoid the problem, you may have been presented with a very different picture of your in-laws until you got to know them personally.

► **You may not have been a threat before you were married.** I have a male friend whose mother adores all his girlfriends—that is, until he tells her he's thinking of marrying them. Suddenly she turns into Attila the Hun and makes life so miserable for the prospective brides that they get out of the relationship as quickly as possible. If you aren't this lucky, your in-law will wait until you're already married to reveal his or her true vicious self.

► **You may not experience the full impact of the problem until you become pregnant or have children.** Some women in couples report that only after they have a child do the in-laws start to meddle heavily in their lives and cause all sorts of tension.

▼

DO YOU HAVE TOXIC IN-LAWS?

Here's a brief quiz to help you determine whether you have toxic in-laws.

► If the statement applies to you **almost always,** give yourself **2 points.**

► If the statement applies to you **frequently,** give yourself **1 point.**

► If the statement applies to you **rarely or never,** give yourself **0 point.**

NOTE: If you suspect that your parents are Toxic in-laws for your mate, answer the questions as he would, or better yet, ask him to take this quiz!

1. Sometimes I feel like I'm sharing my partner with his mother (her father).
2. My in-law calls our house more than anyone else in our lives.
3. My partner and I argue about his parent(s) at least once a week.
4. I dread visits to or from my in-laws.
5. When we are around my in-laws, my partner and I almost always fight.
6. I have never felt totally accepted by my in-law(s).
7. I often feel nothing I do will ever be good enough for my in-law(s).
8. I sometimes fantasize about my in-law(s) dying, and how much easier our life would be.
9. I don't feel like my partner takes a strong enough stand with his parent(s).
10. When I try to talk about my in-laws to my partner, he becomes defensive, or tells me it's my problem.

▲

Now total your points:

▶ **0–4 points: You're safe for now!** You have some of the normal problems people have with their in-laws. Try working on those areas in which you scored highest.

▶ **5–9 points: Your in-laws are causing too much tension in your relationship.** Does your mate know how hard it is on you? What may seem tolerable now will get worse over time. Start asking for what you want and insist on some action.

▶ **10–14 points: Warning! You have a full-blown case of Toxic in-laws.** Are you really willing to live this way for the rest of your life? Either your partner needs to grow up and stand up to his parents, or you need to get out.

▶ **15–20 points: EMERGENCY! TOXIC IN-LAW FATALITY WARNING!** I'm surprised you are even alive to read this. Stop fantasizing about their funeral and face reality: Your partner isn't married to you, he's married to his parents. When you finish reading this section, put the book down and talk to your partner immediately. If he won't listen, call your attorney.

Some of the Problems Toxic In-laws Can Cause

Toxic in-laws do not respect the boundaries of your marriage and the boundaries between them and your spouse. Here are some of the ways this can manifest:

1. They become "time and energy vampires."

Toxic in-laws think the purpose of your life is to be there for them. *They'll call your house incessantly, making feeble excuses or none at all. They'll feel offended if you don't have time to talk with them.* "Dan's mother must call him several times each day at the office and call the house four or five times, often after ten o'clock at night," complained Susie. "She very rarely has anything to say, but she talks nonetheless! If I tell her I'm busy, or have to put the kids to bed, she'll sound dejected, and Dan will hear about it the next day when she calls him at work. 'Your wife isn't being very nice to me,' she'll begin. Not Susie, but 'your wife.' Then he comes home and gives me the 'Be nice to my mother lecture.' It's at the point where I dread answering the phone."

Toxic in-laws drain your time by insisting that you see them constantly. Naturally, an ill or very aged parent will demand a lot of time and energy from the children. **But Toxic in-laws simply haven't let go of their kids and don't respect the autonomous life they're trying to lead.**

2. They attempt to interfere in your life.

You can spot a Toxic in-law by how much *unsolicited advice* they give you on raising your children, decorating your house, investing your money, choosing your wardrobe, and everything else under the sun. Toxic in-laws don't know the meaning of the phrase "mind your own business." They'll pull you into arguments, get you to lose your temper, force you to become rude, and raise your blood pressure, all by interfering in what you thought was your private, personal life.

3. They may refuse to acknowledge you or your relationship.

A favorite pastime of Toxic in-laws is to punish you for taking their child away from them either by acting as if you don't exist or treating you like dirt. There are many ways in which they do this:

▶ addressing cards or letters to your spouse and not to both of you
▶ calling and asking for your spouse without speaking to you
▶ asking you to wait on them when they visit as if you're the maid

▶ forgetting your name, or, better yet, calling you by the name of your spouse's ex

▶ talking about you in the third person when you're present: "If your wife would cook more, maybe you wouldn't be so thin"

▶ fawning over your spouse when they see him and ignoring you completely

▶ treating the children as if they belong solely to your spouse and his side of the family

▶ inviting your partner to family events without you

▶ criticizing you in front of your spouse or your children

Even when these tactics are used in a seemingly unconscious manner, as if your in-law made a simple mistake or oversight, the results are the same: *you feel rejected.* Sometimes in-laws will behave this way to express their disapproval of their child's choice of you as a partner—if you are of a different religion, for instance. *But often they do it because they can't accept the presence of someone their child loves. Perhaps they've made their child into a "pseudospouse," looking for the love they aren't getting from their own partner.*

4. They may attempt to drive a wedge between you and your partner.

If you and your mate seem to fight all the time about his parents, and you suspect it's harming your relationship, your Toxic in-law has succeeded in creating dissension in your relationship and driving a wedge between you. It works like this: Your mate's parent does something to upset you. You naturally react with anger or annoyance. Your in-law then goes to your spouse and complains about the way you've treated him or her. Your spouse comes to you and says things like:

▶ *"Why can't you learn to get along with my mother?"*

▶ *"All I ask is that you be nice to her."*

▶ *"I refuse to get involved. You two work it out together."*

▶ *"Look, she's old, she may not be here soon. If she wants to be this way, why upset her by getting angry?"*

You feel unsupported and misunderstood by your partner and even more furious at your in-law who is manipulating your spouse to see you as the bad guy.

When It Can Work

If you have a Toxic in-law, you only have one choice if you want your relationship to survive: **YOU MUST INSIST THAT YOUR PART- NER CONFRONT HIS PARENT AND SET BOUNDARIES IN THEIR RELATIONSHIP.** *As long as your spouse thinks it's your problem and refuses to get involved, you'll continue to grow farther and farther apart.*

I believe that when you marry someone, you make that person number one in your life. They're now your family, your priority. That doesn't mean you ignore everyone else, but it does mean that the demands on your time and energy change. If your partner is allowing his parent to interfere with your happiness, he doesn't have his priorities straight. And the same goes for you if you're allowing your parent to be a Toxic in-law to your spouse.

Sons and daughters who tolerate hurtful and harmful behavior from their parents toward themselves and their spouse are children who've never grown up and taken their power back from their parents. They're still being controlled by their need for approval from Mom or Dad.

The child of a Toxic in-law needs to communicate the following information to their parents if they want to save their marriage:

1. **I have chosen my spouse to be my lifelong mate, and I expect you to treat her (him) with total respect, cour- tesy, and warmth. We're a couple, and when you criti- cize or hurt my partner, it's the same as hurting me.**

2. **If you can't bring yourself to behave with respect around my spouse, then I do not wish to see you. You'll either see us together and treat us with love, or not see us at all.**

3. **My home is mine, not yours. When you come over, you'll call first, and if we want to see you, we'll tell you. When you do come over, you will not tell me or my wife how to run our lives, raise our children, arrange our furniture, etc.**

4. **You need to respect our time and privacy. That means**

> **I do not wish you to call my house five times a day. Give us the space to want to call you. Naturally, I will be here for you if there's a real emergency.**
>
> **5. I know this may be difficult for you to understand, but that's the way it is. I want you in my life, but not if you can't accept my marriage and respect our relationship.**

I'm not suggesting you use these exact words or this tone. At first, try sitting down and having a serious talk with the parent. **However, if you've done that over and over again and the problem persists, your spouse needs to give your parent an ultimatum.** I've found that the in-law is often upset, and may even refuse to talk to you for a while, but often they come back and comply with your requests without actually admitting they're doing so.

There really is no alternative. Your partner (or if it's your parent, you) needs to grow up and take a stand. You won't believe the positive difference this will make in your relationship. I used to give this advice on the radio at least once a week to sufferers of Toxic in-laws, and I still get letters thanking me for giving them the push to confront their husband or wife, and sharing the wonderful change it made in their marriage.

When It Can't Work

If you discuss this with your partner and he repeatedly refuses to confront his parent, you can try suggesting marriage counseling so he can get a third opinion. If he refuses that, you need to ask yourself why you're staying in this relationship. It isn't going to get any better, and you know it's already tearing you apart. **You are married to someone who has some heavy-duty emotional baggage about his parents and isn't ready to have a grown-up relationship, because he hasn't ever emotionally left home.** You deserve better than this.

COMPATIBILITY TIME BOMB

▼   ▼   ▼   ▼   **5**   ▼   ▼   ▼   ▼

Toxic Ex-Spouse

Jerri, a thirty-eight-year-old photographer, is dating Herb, a forty-five-year-old recently divorced real-estate appraiser. "I've never been in such a wonderful relationship," she gloats. "Herb is sensitive, faithful, and caring. I think this may be it. We've been talking about marriage, and I'm secretly hoping Herb asks me on my birthday next month. Well, there is one small problem: Herb's ex-wife, Marlena. *I don't think she's let go of Herb yet.* She still calls him all the time, sometimes after midnight when we're asleep, and she's usually crying and depressed. Twice she showed up at his apartment without calling and threw herself at him. Herb says she's unstable. *I'm hoping that when we get engaged, she'll finally realize it's over between them.*"

Boy, is Jerri in for a surprise. Not only will Marlena not get better when she hears they're engaged, she'll get worse. She'll barrage Herb with hysterical phone calls, make him feel guilty for abandoning her, and find all kinds of problems with their children that she needs his advice on. Why? **Because Marlena is a Toxic ex-spouse.** Like Toxic in-laws, Toxic ex-spouses don't respect the boundaries of their relationship with their ex. They exhibit all of the same behaviors we discussed in the last section:

► **They don't respect your privacy.**
► **They use guilt to try to drive a wedge between you and your mate.**
► **They become "time and energy vampires."**
► **They don't acknowledge your relationship.**

In addition, they can:

► **Financially blackmail your mate by threatening to ask for more money as a way of punishing him for being with you.**
► **Emotionally blackmail your mate by threatening to ask for total custody of the children if your relationship becomes serious.**
► **Turn the children against you.**
► **Continually come on to your mate sexually as a way to interfere.**

I hope none of these sounds familiar to you, but if any does, you're probably already feeling the painful effects of this Compatibility Time Bomb. Toxic ex-spouses are less common than Toxic in-laws but no less deadly. I'm not talking about an ex-wife who's upset that your partner isn't paying his child support on time, or an ex-husband who's angry that your partner is saying bad things about him to the kids. **Toxic ex-spouses are partners who've never really let go of their mates and will hang on for dear life, all the while destroying your relationship.**

If your partner has a Toxic ex-spouse, **you're in an emotional triangle, a threesome.** And don't blame it on on the ex. Unless he or she is really mentally ill, your mate is just as guilty because he hasn't made his boundaries clear. What I said for children of Toxic in-laws applies to mates of Toxic ex-spouses:

▼

IF YOUR PARTNER HAS TAKEN A STAND WITH HIS EX-SPOUSE, COMMUNICATED HIS FEELINGS, AND SET CLEAR BOUNDARIES AS TO WHAT BEHAVIOR HE'LL ACCEPT, YOU WON'T HAVE A PROBLEM REGARDLESS OF HOW TOXIC HIS EX-SPOUSE MAY TRY TO BE.

▲

People with Toxic ex-spouses have often never really broken off those relationships. They're still emotionally married to their ex, and have a difficult time doing anything that would hurt them. It's also possible that your mate *has* let go, but his ex really is disturbed, and becomes obsessed with getting him back, as depicted in the frightening film *Fatal Attraction,* starring Glenn Close and Michael Douglas. If this is the case, make sure your partner isn't in denial about his ex's mental problem, and don't accept excuses such as:

▶ *"Give her time. She'll get used to it."*
▶ *"Oh, I know he can be dramatic, but he'd never really do anything to hurt you."*
▶ *"If we just ignore her, I'm sure she'll stop bothering us."*

How You Tell if Your Partner Has a Toxic Ex-Spouse

If you suspect your partner has a Toxic ex-spouse, take the quiz in the previous section, and instead of asking the questions about in-laws, ask about his ex-spouse. Except for questions 4–7, the others all apply.

Just like Toxic in-laws, Toxic ex-spouses may not emerge as a problem in the beginning of your relationship. The ex may not start the disturbing behavior until he or she realizes your partner is serious about you. You may also not see how much of a problem it is until you move in with your partner. Perhaps he never told you about the phone calls and visits because he didn't want to upset you. But once you live together, it may become apparent that his ex is much more in the picture than you believed her to be. **It's important to pay close attention and asks lots of questions *when you first meet someone* whom you suspect may have a Toxic ex-spouse.**

If you're in love with someone who has a Toxic ex-spouse, it is normal to feel:

▶ **angry that your partner seems to be more concerned about his ex's feelings than about yours**

▶ **angry when he accuses you of being jealous instead of understanding how you feel**

▶ **frightened that the problem won't get better with time (it won't)**

▶ **impatient with his excuses about feeling sorry for his ex**

▶ **suspicious that your mate is using his ex as a way to avoid becoming more intimate with you and going forward in his life (quite possible)**

▶ **resentful that your partner never brings you along when he sees his ex, picks up the kids, etc., because he "doesn't want to upset her"**

People with Toxic ex-spouses often have emotional programming that makes letting go of the past very difficult. Your mate might feel guilty abandoning his ex if one of his own parents left the other, or *he may feel guilty for leaving if he was left by one of his own parents, and be punishing himself by unconsciously sabotaging his new relationship with you.*

When It Can Work

If your partner has a Toxic ex-spouse, you must insist that he honor his commitment to you by letting go of his ex and relinquishing his responsibility for her. He needs to set boundaries for their relationship and stick by them. If the problem has been chronic, a period of no contact whatsoever will be necessary. If there are children involved, this still needs to be enforced. That means the kids run out to the car when he picks them up, and not that he comes in for ten minutes and lets his ex do her number. *It's up to your partner to break the pattern. Don't wait for the Toxic ex to do it.*

IMPORTANT: If your mate has a friendly relationship with his ex that is *not* toxic, and you have a real problem with jealousy, don't give your partner this ultimatum and say you read it in my book! Get some help on your jealousy, or better yet, attend some counseling sessions together.

Sometimes your mate might need you to give him a bottom line to realize what he's been doing and to change his behavior. In these cases your relationship will become even closer after you confront your partner.

When It Can't Work

If you discuss this with your partner and he repeatedly refuses to confront his ex, you can try suggesting counseling so he can get input from a professional. If he refuses that, you need to ask yourself why you're letting yourself be treated in this way. **Until he makes a complete commitment to you, you're going to be miserable. Your partner isn't emotionally available because he's still involved with his ex.** Tell him you're leaving, and to call you when he's finished with his other relationship.

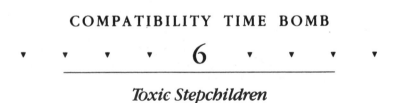

COMPATIBILITY TIME BOMB

▼　　▼　　▼　　▼　　**6**　　▼　　▼　　▼　　▼

Toxic Stepchildren

You meet a wonderful man at a party, and spend the evening getting to know one another. He seems to be everything you're looking for, and you're thrilled when he asks you out for Saturday night. "By the way," he says, "I forgot to mention that I have two children from a previous marriage. They'll be staying with me this weekend, so you'll get to meet them." "Great," you think. "He's a devoted father, too. I love children. I bet his are terrific."

Saturday evening finally arrives and you drive over to his house. He greets you at the door enthusiastically and explains that he needs to make a quick phone call. "Kids, come meet my new friend and talk to her while I make a phone call," he says. Suddenly two boys, ages nine and eleven, tear into the room, punching and kicking each other.

"Are you Dad's new girlfriend?" the older one asks in a sarcastic voice, looking you up and down.

"No, I'm just a friend," you answer.

"Are you and my Dad going to have sex?" the younger one says, shrieking with laughter.

"Shut up, Brian." Punch.

"Ouch. DAAADDD, Larry hit me."

"You little asshole, I'm going to get you."

"DAADDD!!!"

Suddenly your fantasies of romantic evenings by the fire and quiet mornings in bed change into scenes of "STEPCHIL-DREN FROM HELL."

This story describe the first glimpse of Compatibility Time Bomb #6: Toxic stepchildren. Now, before I upset anyone, let me make myself clear: I'm not saying children are toxic, and I'm not saying stepchildren are toxic. **I *am* saying that some stepchildren can make their new stepparent's life so miserable that they can actually threaten the future of your relationship with your mate.** If you don't know how to handle these kids, you'll be in for a rocky ride.

Why am I so sure of this? *Because I was a "Stepchild from Hell."* Just ask my stepfather, Dan. Although I didn't bite his leg or ask him embarrassing questions, I did treat him so terribly that I made my mother miserable and, no doubt, caused him to question whether he wanted to move in with a thirteen-year-old brat. Looking back, I realize that he must have loved my mother even more than I knew in order to put up with me.

What was I trying to accomplish by my obnoxious behavior? The same thing any potential stepchild is hoping to achieve—**I wanted to scare him off so I could have my mother all to myself, and maybe preserve the slim chance that my parents would get back together.** Of course, now I'm thrilled that my nasty plan didn't work. He and my mom have been married for twenty-seven years, and we are all very close.

Toxic stepchildren are really kids in a lot of pain. They feel let down by their parents, possibly rejected by the one who left, and frightened of being hurt again. Many times they are also misunderstood children whose emotional turmoil was underestimated or overshadowed by the drama their parents were going through. Suddenly they're expected to welcome a stranger into their lives to take the place of the missing parent, and everyone gets angry at them when they don't feel like being nice to this stranger. Out of this explosive mix of emotions comes the rebellious behavior that can make stepchildren a compatibility time bomb.

The problem, however, is not the stepkids, but the parents and stepparents who don't want to deal with the situation. I have a saying,

"Guilty parents make bad parents."

When a parent feels guilty about divorcing (and who doesn't?), they may have a tendency to overlook a problem with their children, hoping it will go away, or be too lenient in dealing with a problem, frightened that setting boundaries for the children will traumatize them even further.

This guilt interferes with their ability to see their children realistically. Josh, the father of Larry and Brian, is an example of a lenient dad. He sees his kids once every other weekend, so when they're visiting, he tends to let them do whatever they want. Josh knows his children are behaving terribly, but is afraid to punish them out of the fear of alienating them even more. In the case of a single mom whose kids live with her, this guilt may take the form of allowing the children to interfere with her ability to start a new relationship by manipulating her in some way (sleeping in her bed, criticizing her new mate, etc.).

When a parent of a Toxic stepchild gets into serious relationships or remarries, the new spouse will have to deal with these Compatibility Time Bombs and will probably go through problems similar to those caused by all Toxic stepchildren:

▶ **You and your partner argue about the kids.**
▶ **You feel your partner takes the kids' side and not yours.**

► You feel like the kids are ruining your relationship.
► You feel your partner is too lenient with the kids.
► You feel like you can't talk to your partner about the kids without her becoming defensive.

When It Can Work

With over half of all American children growing up in families different from their one of origin, it's essential that we all find ways to make stepfamilies work. Here are some steps you can take if you fall in love with someone who has children:

1. Work on your relationship with the kids as much as you work on your relationship with your new spouse.
Talk honestly about your feelings, acknowledge theirs, and don't pretend everything is fine when it's not. Kids will respect and accept you more if they feel you're being real with them.

2. Discuss all potential problems with your new partner while the relationship is developing.
Don't tiptoe around the issue of your potential stepchildren. If you're dating someone and feel there are some issues they aren't facing about their kids, talk about it. If your partner refuses to discuss it with you, or remains in denial, you may want to reconsider going further with this relationship. *Don't wait until you move in together or get married to deal with it—it'll be too late, and the time bomb will explode!*

3. Agree with your partner about how you'll treat the children and how they'll treat you.
Consistency and solidarity are two important keys in dealing with children, especially stepchildren. *You and your partner must present a united front to the kids.* If they suspect they can create a crack in your relationship, they'll be relentless. Have family meetings in which you can discuss the guidelines and air grievances.

4. Get outside support.
The Stepfamily Association of America is a wonderful network of specially trained counselors and support groups designed to aid stepfamilies in the challenging process of blending together. They can be contacted c/o *STEP FAMILY ASSOCIATION, 215 Centennial Mall South, Suite 212, Lincoln, NE 68508; tel. (402) 477-STEP.* Another good organization is the *The Stepfamily Foundation;* tel. *1-800-759-7837.* Remember, you're not alone! Reach out to other

families in your situation. (Experts estimate that it takes five to seven years for a stepfamily to come together harmoniously! Hang in there!)

When It Can't Work

Stepfamilies will only be as healthy as the parents who create them. **If you're in a relationship with someone who doesn't seem to know how to parent his or her kids, and refuses to get help or face the issues even when you give them an ultimatum, I suggest you end the relationship.**

COMPATIBILITY TIME BOMB

▼   ▼   ▼   ▼   7   ▼   ▼   ▼   ▼

Long-Distance Relationships

Have you ever examined your face closely in the mirror? You start seeing all kinds of things you didn't know were there—tiny scars, discolored areas, pores that suddenly look gigantic. Yet if you stand back a few feet, you can't see any of the imperfections, just a smooth face. The point I'm trying to make is that *things look different close up than they do from a distance—faces, paintings, and even relationships.*

This brings us to our final Compatibility Time Bomb, long-distance relationships. There's nothing wrong with the long-distance relationship—in fact, many happy marriages began as commuter romances. However, there are hazards in this arrangement that many unsuspecting people overlook until they get hit with the Compatibility Time Bomb months or even years later.

A LONG-DISTANCE ROMANCE MAKES IT EASY FOR YOU TO THINK THE RELATIONSHIP IS MUCH BETTER THAN IT IS BECAUSE YOU DON'T SPEND CONSISTENT QUALITY TIME TOGETHER.

The very same factors that make a long-distance relationship romantic also make it hazardous:

- ► the distance that separates you
- ► the fantasizing about seeing your partner
- ► the brief, intense moments of intimacy during phone calls
- ► the erotic thrill of knowing you only have a few days together
- ► the emotional good-byes

It's easy to get caught up in the ongoing drama of your love affair rather than looking at the relationship as it really is.

THE GOAL OF TWO LOVERS IN A "NORMAL" RELATIONSHIP SHOULD BE *TO BECOME MORE LOVING AND INTIMATE WITH ONE ANOTHER.*

THE GOAL OF TWO LONG-DISTANCE LOVERS BECOMES *TO SEE ONE ANOTHER AGAIN.*

Here are some of the ways in which this Compatibility Time Bomb can affect you:

1. You don't get to see what your partner is really like.

If you know you have three days to spend with your long-distance lover, you put your best self forward—you make sure you look great, and you try to be as loving and affable as you can. *It's easy to hide the difficult parts of your personality for seventy-two hours so that your partner only gets to see the wonderful parts of you, just as you see only the terrific parts of him.* The problem is that you never really get to know one another. You don't get to see your mate under pressure, in a crisis, when he is tired and cranky, when he is faced with fear, when he is ill. All of these situations reveal a lot about someone's *character.* **There are dimensions of people you experience only when you're with them on a consistent basis.**

2. You avoid dealing with problem areas.

Let's imagine that you haven't seen your long-distance lover in two months, and he's flown in to spend the weekend with you. Over dinner that night, he says something that annoys you. Now you have to make a decision: Do you confront him with what's upsetting you, and risk ruining your weekend, or do you forget about it? Most people choose to avoid the confrontation, fearful that by the time they get through the argument and hurt feelings, half of the weekend will already be over. **The problem with this habit is that you and** your partner never learn to problem-solve together, or advance the relationship to deeper levels of communication and harmony. **The unresolved issues and the unexpressed resentments just sit there like emotional time bombs, waiting to explode.** It may look like you have a great relationship on the surface, but you haven't allowed it to move through the transition stage every healthy love affair must experience.

3. <u>You have an unrealistic view of your compatibility.</u>

Long-distance lovers often don't even know how little they have in common because they are too busy entertaining themselves. *If you only have three days with your partner, you will treat it like a minivacation*—you'll spend all your time together; you'll go out to restaurants, movies, shows, etc., you'll have lots of sex; and you'll avoid friends and family. This gives you a very unrealistic picture of your relationship. You may actually enjoy the excitement of the fun weekend more than you enjoy your partner and not even know it. Many couples find themselves extremely disappointed when they finally move to the same city or decide to live together. *"It doesn't feel like it used to,"* they often complain. Of course it doesn't. **It's not a twenty-four-hour-a-day party anymore. It's a full-time relationship, and if you and your partner aren't truly compatible, you'll find out really fast.**

If you and your partner do move to the same town, you are likely to experience:

▶ an increase in arguments and disagreements
▶ a decrease in your sexual activity
▶ a discovery of things about your partner that annoy you

None of these time bombs will necessarily destroy your relationship unless you are unprepared for them or unwilling to deal with them.

When It Can Work

For a long-distance romance to evolve into a healthy, lasting relationship, *both partners will eventually have to live in the same place.* That's the only way you can truly know if you're compatible, and develop the level of intimacy you need to sustain your love. **But while you're still apart, the most successful long-distance affairs are those in which the couple treats the relationship like it is a full-time romance:**

► They don't try to make every moment together special, but do normal things together.

► They don't try to hide difficult parts of their personality, but are themselves.

► They don't edit how they feel, but allow themselves to communicate honestly and deal with conflicts as they come up.

If you follow these guidelines you'll have a much better chance of avoiding this Compatibility Time Bomb.

When It Can't Work

If your partner wants to keep things "light," avoid intimacy and commitment, and isn't interested in working with you to create deeper levels of communication and love, save your airfare and long-distance-phone bills and find a new relationship!

AVOIDING WHO'S WRONG

I have a single friend who recently ended a very frustrating and painful six-year relationship. When I told her the topic of this book, she begged me to let her read each chapter as soon as I'd finished it. "I'm desperate," she explained tearfully. "I can't go on making the same mistakes. I need to understand what I'm doing wrong." I agreed to have her be my first reader.

Late last night the phone rang, and when I answered, it was my friend. "Barbara," she exclaimed in a trembling voice, "I just finished reading the section on avoiding who's wrong. I can't believe how accurate it was. You've described every mistake I've ever made in my relationships. But I feel so angry at you."

"Angry at me?" I answered in shock. "What for?"

"For not writing this book ten years ago, so I could have avoided all this pain," she responded with a chuckle.

She wasn't alone in her desire. I, too, wish I would have understood about Fatal Flaws, Compatibility Time Bombs, and the Ten Types of Relationships That Won't Work. I could have saved myself a lot of heartache. But making many of my own poor love choices, along with helping thousands of people recover from theirs, have helped me to get to the place where I knew enough to write this section.

I hope that this section, on avoiding who's wrong, has helped you understand more about why some of your past relationships didn't work, and has given you a lot to think about in evaluating your present or future relationships. The most uncomfortable part is over. Now that we've looked at everything that can cause a relationship to fail, we'll spend the rest of the book learning about what makes a relationship work!

KNOWING
▼
WHO'S
▼
RIGHT

▼▼▼

The last three chapters were designed to help you avoid partners who are wrong for you, and understand more about obstacles that can prevent your relationships from working. Now it's time to learn about what you should look for when choosing a partner, and how to tell if your mate is right for you.

▼

8

▼▼▼

SIX QUALITIES TO
LOOK FOR IN A MATE

▼▼▼

I frequently travel around the country giving lectures and seminars, and whenever I make a presentation, I always leave room at the end to take questions from the audience. Since many of these people have read my books or seen me on television, they feel they know me, so I'm not surprised when someone asks me something personal. No matter what city I'm in, sometime during my "Ask Barbara Anything" segment, a man or a woman will step up to the microphone and say: *"Barbara, I'm single now, but I've had terrible relationships in the last few years. Can you tell me what kinds of qualities I should look for in my next partner so I don't get hurt again?"*

At this point I usually turn the tables and ask the questioner what kinds of chacteristics have attracted her to mates in the past. I'll hear answers such as *"someone with a good sense of humor,"* *"a person who loves the outdoors,"* *"men who enjoy traveling and eating good food."*

"That's your problem," I respond. **"You're looking for *personality traits* when instead you should be looking for *character*."**

It's taken me years to understand how to answer the question **"What should I look for in a partner?"** because I, like many of you, made most of the mistakes we've talked about in the earlier chapters of this book: falling in love for all the wrong reasons, choosing partners based on one or two appealing things rather than looking at the whole person, ignoring Fatal Flaws. But the most important lesson I've learned about compatibility is one that has changed my life:

▼

THE KEY TO CHOOSING THE RIGHT PARTNER IS TO LOOK FOR A PERSON WITH GOOD CHARACTER, NOT SIMPLY A GOOD PERSONALITY.

▲

Most of us become initially attracted to a mate because of something about their personality—his ability to make you laugh; her softness; his interest in cycling, etc. While these traits might be enjoyable, they aren't what's going to determine whether this relationship truly makes you happy. For that, you have to look for character. **Character determines how a person will treat himself; you; and, one day, your children. It's the foundation of any healthy partnership.** If you think of a relationship as a cake, personality is like the icing, but character is the substance.

This chapter presents six qualities to look for in a partner. Remember, these are different from a list of specific qualities you want in a mate. **Rather, these are the building blocks of good character in a person.** Whether you're single, married, or in between, *learning about these characteristics will help you determine how successful your relationship can be by determining how ready your partner is to be in a loving relationship.* Instead of only asking yourself the question

"Does my partner love me?"

you need to ask

"How capable is my partner of loving, period?"

At the end of each section I've included some questions you can ask your partner that will reveal a lot about his character. If you've been involved with your mate for some time, you may already know the answers to some of the questions, but don't skip them. It's important to think about these in your own mind.

IMPORTANT: **Don't forget to apply everything you read to evaluating yourself and your own qualities as well!**

▼

SIX QUALITIES TO LOOK FOR IN A PARTNER:

1. **Commitment to personal growth**
2. **Emotional openness**
3. **Integrity**
4. **Maturity and responsibility**
5. **High self-esteem**
6. **Positive attitude toward life**

▲

QUALITY

▼ ▼ ▼ ▼ **1** ▼ ▼ ▼ ▼
_____

Commitment to Personal Growth

I've listed this quality first because I feel it's one of the most important traits to seek in a partner. If you find someone who's committed to his or her personal growth, you'll have already avoided many of the problems couples face: One person wants to work on the relationship and the other doesn't; one partner tries to talk about the issues and the other refuses; one person sees areas that need improvement and the other is in denial.

Commitment to personal growth means:

▶ **Your partner is *committed to learning* everything he can about how to be a better person and a better spouse.** When you love someone who places a high value on personal transformation, your relationship is guaranteed to be much easier. Whether it's a small fight or a big crisis, your partner should be willing to use everything in your relationship to learn more about becoming more loving and compassionate. *Only when he's committed to learning (along with you, of course!) will your relationship truly become an adventure in personal growth, rather than a power struggle between two people, each trying to be right and make the other wrong.*

▶ He is *willing to receive help and guidance* in the form of books, tapes, lectures, seminars, and counseling if necessary. So many relationships experience crisis when one partner recognizes the need for improvement and the other refuses to participate.

▼

There is no way a relationship can work if one partner refuses to seek help when necessary.

▲

This is something to find out in the beginning of a relationship. Don't avoid this issue only to discover when you're in a family crisis that your mate "doesn't believe in counseling" or is too stubborn to pick up a book and learn how to make a relationship work.

▶ He is *conscious of his blind spots and childhood programming,* and is aware of what emotional baggage he has brought into your relationship. We've already seen that *it's not our childhood programming or emotional baggage that destroy our relationships, but our denial of them.* **It's dangerous to become involved with someone who's oblivious to his weaknesses and problem areas.** I'm not saying he has to be an expert on them, but he must at least be open to understanding more about why he's the way he is, and acknowledge that he, like you, is coming into the relationship with some emotional handicaps. You will find that this quality of *humility and lack of pride* really helps to keep your partnership from turning into a battleground.

▶ He has *personal goals for his own self-improvement,* and you can see specific, positive changes in him over time. It's important to find someone who is not only interested in growing but also is doing something about it! Lots of people give lip service to the concept of improving themselves, but when it comes to taking action, they wimp out. *When you see your partner motivating himself by setting goals and achieving them, whether it's to stop smoking, to become more patient with you, or to be more assertive, you'll respect him and have confidence that he won't depend on you to constantly push him or nag him into growing.*

QUESTIONS TO ASK YOUR PARTNER ABOUT COMMITMENT TO PERSONAL GROWTH:

1. **What have you learned about yourself emotionally in the past ten years, and how has it changed you?**

2. **What have you learned from your past relationships, and what do you do differently now?**

3. **What are your greatest weaknesses, and where do you think they come from?**

4. **If I asked your past partners to list their biggest complaints about you, what would they be? Do you agree or disagree?**

5. **What sources of help have you used in the past when you or your relationships were in crisis (books, counseling, etc.)? Did these help?**

6. **How would you like to change in the next five years? What parts of yourself would you like to get rid of? What qualities would you like to acquire more of?**

QUALITY

▼   ▼   ▼   ▼   2   ▼   ▼   ▼   ▼

Emotional Openness

An intimate relationship is not based on sharing a home, a bed, or a bathroom. It's based on sharing *feelings.* That's why the second quality you should look for in a partner is emotional openness. This means your mate:

▶ has feelings
▶ knows *what* he is feeling
▶ chooses to *share* those feelings with you
▶ knows *how* to express those feelings to you

I can't tell you how many excuses I've heard from men and women in unhappy relationships about why their partner can't express feelings:

► *"His father never told him he loved him, so he can't tell me."*

► *"She was really hurt by her ex-husband, so she has a hard time showing me that she cares."*

► *"He never shows me what's going on inside him. I think growing up in an alcoholic family made it scary for him to have feelings."*

All these evaluations are very accurate, but they miss the point.

IF YOUR PARTNER CAN'T IDENTIFY AND SHARE HIS FEELINGS WITH YOU, HE'S NOT READY TO BE IN AN INTIMATE RELATIONSHIP.

What's the purpose of being with someone who is emotionally shut down? **Staying in a relationship with a person who cannot share feelings is a form of self-punishment.**

Another way to describe emotional openness is "emotional generosity." We think of people as being generous with their money, or their time, but it's so important to find a mate who is generous with his love. Generosity means to give freely, abundantly, and without restriction. This means a partner who tells you how much he loves you and shows you how much he appreciates you. I don't mean once a year, on your anniversary, or when he's had a few drinks, or only when you threaten to leave. **You deserve to have someone in your life who shows you his love and appreciation on a consistent basis.**

The opposite of emotional generosity is emotional stinginess—hoarding love and emotions as if they were in limited quantity and offering you tiny pieces of one's heart. Emotionally stingy people will make you practically beg for love; they'll make you pull their feelings out of them, and then they'll expect you to make a big deal about the tiny scrap you received. These people probably never learned how to love, but that's not your problem. *Unless you want a full-time job as a teacher, avoid relationships with emotionally stingy partners!*

Emotional openness in a partner gives you access to his inner world. It is his way of offering you the key to his heart. It's the true fulfillment of the promise you make when you decide to be together. Don't put up with anything less.

---▼---

QUESTIONS TO ASK YOUR PARTNER ABOUT EMOTIONAL OPENNESS:

1. **Do you feel comfortable expressing your feelings to the people you love? To whom in your life right now do you often say "I love you?"**

2. **What feelings are difficult for you to talk about? What feelings are easy? Has this changed over time?**

3. **Are there parts of yourself you don't feel comfortable sharing? Why do you think that is?**

4. **When you do open up and share your emotions, how do you feel afterward?**

5. **Do you think your inability to express yourself has ever caused problems in your relationships?**

6. **If I asked your past partners whether you were emotionally open, what would they say?**

---▲---

QUALITY

▼ ▼ ▼ ▼ **3** ▼ ▼ ▼ ▼

Integrity

I'll never forget the time I was counseling a couple with marital problems, and the wife complained that she couldn't trust her husband. When I asked him if her accusation was correct, he defended himself by answering, "I only lie when I'm not comfortable telling the truth." What a bargain! The scary part was that he seriously believed there was nothing wrong with his dishonesty.

I couldn't disagree more. **Honesty, integrity, and trustworthiness are essential ingredients for a healthy relationship.** Knowing that you can count on your partner to be truthful with you at all times will give you a tremendous sense of security. On the other hand, if you live in constant fear that your partner is somehow lying to you, it'll be next to impossible to relax in the relationship. You'll be tense, doubting, and resentful. The long-term effects of loving someone you don't trust are devastating both to your self-esteem and to your love affair. As I emphasized in my book *How to Make Love All the Time,* **not telling the truth is the most significant way couples kill passion and destroy their intimacy.**

People who frequently bend the truth may have a "life isn't fair" attitude, and they consider dishonesty a strategy for getting an advantage. In other words, something is inherently wrong with their value system. And I can tell you from painful experience that *when you live with a liar, you end up covering up for him and eventually becoming a liar yourself.*

Finding a partner who has integrity means seeking:

▶ **Someone who is honest with himself:** There are many people who don't lie to you but lie to themselves. Honesty begins at home, so to speak. *That means you should avoid mates who are masters of self-deception.* You may tell yourself your boyfriend is an honest person, but then you remember that he avoids facing his dependence on alcohol, or that he claims it's over between him and his ex-girlfriend even though they talk almost every day. It's not that he's a liar—he's just not very good at being honest with himself.

▶ **Someone who is honest with others.** Does your partner lie to his clients or associates, all in the name of "business"? Does your girlfriend hide the truth about her life from her family? Does your mate often justify doing things at work you feel are dishonest? *If you doubt your partner's integrity, you'll lose respect for him,* and it'll be difficult for you to trust his behavior toward you.

▶ **Someone who is honest with you.** Whenever I meet friends I haven't seen in several years, they always remark how calm and serene I appear. I know that this can be attributed in part to how secure I feel in my relationship and how deeply I trust Jeffrey. What a fabulous feeling to love someone who, time and time again, proves to me that I can count on him always to be truthful. I contrast this with my last very painful relationship, in which I didn't ever completely trust my partner. I never quite knew where he was when he went out, or how he handled his finances, or whether he actually did what he had promised to do.

A partner who is honest:

1. will not hide parts of his life or personality from you
2. will not tell you only what you want to hear in order to protect himself
3. will share the truth with you without your having to trick him into admitting it, or pry it out of him

▶ **Someone who doesn't play games.** Games belong on the playground, not in relationships. Yet many adults can't have relationships without playing emotional games: "I won't tell you how I feel and you have to guess," or "I'll tell you things I know will make you jealous, and then I'll feel in control." All of these games involve dishonesty. **Look for a partner who is up front about how he feels and what he wants, and someone whose actions match his or her words.**

When your partner is consistently honest with you, you will naturally trust him.

QUESTIONS TO ASK YOUR PARTNER ABOUT INTEGRITY:

(Obviously, if your partner is an incurable liar, he'll answer these questions dishonestly, but trust your gut instincts and watch his actions to see if they reflect trustworthiness.)

1. **Do you think partners should be honest about everything in a relationship, or do you think some things should be kept private? For instance . . . ?**

2. **Have you ever been lied to or betrayed in a relationship? What happened? How did it make you feel?**

3. **Have you ever lied to or betrayed someone in a relationship? What happened? Would you do it again?**

4. **What things, if any, would you lie about in a relationship? An affair? Unhappiness with your partner's appearance? Etc.**

5. **If I asked your past partners if you were honest and trustworthy, how would they answer? Why?**

6. **What kinds of things do you feel are inherently wrong, and what wouldn't bother you (cheating on income tax, taking office supplies home from work, littering, not returning money you found, etc.)?**

7. **Are you telling me the truth right now?** (Watch eyes closely for reaction!)

QUALITY

▾ ▾ ▾ ▾ 4 ▾ ▾ ▾ ▾

Maturity and Responsibility

There are people who just aren't ready to be in a committed relationship. They may be very lovable; they may even love you very much. *But if they haven't reached a certain level of maturity, you'll feel like you've adopted a child rather than found a lover.*

For those of us who enjoy rescuing others, this is a quality to be especially adamant about finding in a partner. Otherwise you'll probably end up feeling, **"I LOVE MY MATE SO MUCH—I JUST WISH HE'D GROW UP!"**

Here are some signs that your partner is mature enough to have a relationship:

<u>He (or she) can take care of himself</u>. If your partner has grown up sufficiently, he'll be able to:

▶ earn enough money to support himself
▶ know how to keep his living space relatively clean
▶ know how to feed himself

You may think I'm joking, but I'm very serious! I've heard countless stories from women and men who've fallen in love with someone who couldn't take care of themselves. These weren't twenty-one-year-olds, either! These people were always out of work, borrowing money from family and friends, or living in chaos.

I remember a woman who called my radio show to ask my advice about her boyfriend. She was forty-four and he was forty-seven. They'd dated for six months and she really liked him, but was suspicious because he never invited her back to his apartment. In fact, in the time they'd been together, she'd never even seen where he lived. One night she insisted that he show her his place.

"Barbara," she told me conspiratorially, *"I've never seen a dwelling this filthy in all my life. There were dusty piles of magazines three and four feet high on the floor. There were clothes strewn everywhere; not just a few items, but hundreds of things! I don't think this man ever put his clothes away! And the kitchen! It looked like it hadn't been cleaned in decades! There was old food crusted over everything, and of course pots and dishes in more piles. I was sick to my stomach. Now, what I want to know is this: Do you think I should keep dating him?"*

I had to control myself to keep from laughing. Since I'm a firm believer in the principle *that our outer world is a reflection of our inner world,* I was sure that, from her description, this guy she was dating was a real mess! It was obvious that part of him had never grown up enough to take care of himself, so I doubted that he could emotionally take care of her.

I've worked with a lot of young people (late teens, early twenties) through my seminars, and I always feel concerned when I see a couple this age planning to get married, or deciding to have a child. Many of them can hardly take care of themselves, or are just learning how, and aren't really ready for the responsibility of a partnership, let alone a family.

He's responsible. Responsibility means doing what you say you're going to do. It means remembering to pay the bills, keeping your promises, showing up on time, and not letting people down. Responsibility isn't saying you're responsible but acting irresponsible. **It isn't a concept—it's an action.**

Part of maturity is being responsible and being accountable. We don't give children a lot of responsibility because we know they're not mature enough to handle it. *When you find a partner who's irresponsible, you have, in a sense, stumbled upon a child in an adult's body. Lovable, perhaps even sympathetic, but certainly not ready for an adult relationship*—that is, unless you don't mind being disappointed all the time.

Everyone deserves to be loved, but not everyone's ready for the responsibility that goes along with an adult relationship. Trust me—it's easier to make your love affair work when your partner is a grown-up!

He's respectful. One of the ways in which we note the maturation of children is by their increased respect for the world around them and the people in it. A child who didn't respect any boundaries and took his brother's toys learns not to touch what is not his. Instead of leaving out the milk and cookies after having a snack, he learns to respect his mother's time by putting them back in the refrigerator. Rather than shouting and banging on the table when he's in a restaurant, he learns to respect the environment he's in and moderate his behavior.

In this same way, look for maturation in a partner by noticing how respectful he is of:

▶ your feelings
▶ your boundaries
▶ your time
▶ your possessions
▶ his possessions
▶ our environment
▶ his employees, employer, or coworkers
▶ other people's feelings

▼

QUESTIONS TO ASK YOUR PARTNER ABOUT MATURITY AND RESPONSIBILITY:

1. **Are you usually on time or late for appointments, etc., in your life?**

2. **In what area of your life would you say you are the most irresponsible (finances, health, returning phone calls, etc.)?**

3. **Have you been fired from your jobs, or have you quit? If you were fired, what were the reasons?**

4. **Do you feel you act more as the caretaker in your relationships, or as the one who's taken care of?**

5. **If I asked your past partners, would they say you were very responsible, very irresponsible, or somewhere in between? On what would they base these conclusions?**

6. **Do you consider yourself sensitive to other people's feelings?**

7. **Do you usually return things when you borrow them from people?**

8. **How do you feel about littering?**

Note: Aside from just asking questions, pay attention to how your partner lives his life. That will tell you everything you need to know about this quality.

▲

QUALITY

▼　　▼　　▼　　▼　　**5**　　▼　　▼　　▼　　▼

High Self-Esteem

You've probably heard it said before, but it's true:
YOUR PARTNER CAN ONLY LOVE YOU AS MUCH AS HE LOVES HIMSELF.

One of the biggest mistakes we make in choosing partners is focusing on how much our mate loves and treats us, not how he treats himself. I know a man who was sure he'd met the woman of his dreams. "She'll do anything for me," he boasted. "She's so giving and so loving. She makes me feel like the greatest guy in the world." He neglected to notice that this woman had no self-esteem. She was afraid to make a move without him; she constantly criticized her appearance and insisted she was fat, even though she was bulimic; she interpreted any suggestions he gave her as condemnations. **She loved him, but not herself, and soon he realized that the love she lavished on him was really *hungry love,* not full love.**

▼

A PERSON WITH LOW SELF-ESTEEM LOVES *IN ORDER* TO FEEL GOOD ABOUT HERSELF. A PERSON WITH HIGH SELF-ESTEEM LOVES *BECAUSE* SHE FEELS GOOD ABOUT HERSELF.

▲

The healthier your partner's sense of self-esteem, the stronger your relationship will be. That's why it's important to look for these signs of self-esteem:

► **Your partner takes pride in himself.** If your mate walks around apologizing for his life and seems embarrassed by who he is, or is constantly putting himself down, then he has no pride in himself. You need a partner who has some satisfaction with who he is now and who he's becoming. I'm not talking about arrogance, or false bravado masquerading as self-confidence. True pride gives someone a sense of solidity and inner strength. *Another good way to tell is to ask yourself if you're proud of who he is.*

► **Your partner doesn't abuse himself, but takes good care of himself.** I know a man who grew up with a tremendous amount of shame. He drank, he smoked, he abused drugs and sex. Then somehow he found his way to my seminars in Los Angeles. Two weeks later he stopped drinking. He came back for another seminar, and a week later he stopped smoking. He did four more seminars in a row and gave up every vice he had. When a friend asked him why, after years of attempting to get clean, he finally did it, he answered: **"I loved myself too much to do that stuff anymore."**

▼

THE MORE YOU LOVE YOURSELF, THE HARDER IT WILL BE FOR YOU TO ABUSE YOURSELF PHYSICALLY OR EMOTIONALLY.

▲

You can tell how someone feels about himself by observing how he treats himself: the food he eats, the environment he lives in, the way he takes care of his body, his car, his possessions. All of these are reflections of self-esteem. Someone who mistreats himself and doesn't mind it won't mind mistreating you, either.

► **He doesn't allow others to abuse him.** "I'm married to a wimp," a middle-aged woman complained to me once while I was signing autographs. "He lets everyone push him around. His boss doesn't respect him. His own brother takes advantage of him all the time, and my husband won't stand up to him. The worst part is, he says he doesn't love me anymore!"

"How could he?" I answered. "He doesn't love himself."

One very clear symptom of low self-esteem is the way you let other people treat you.

THE MORE YOU LOVE YOURSELF, THE LESS YOU'LL ALLOW OTHERS TO MISTREAT YOU.

This is why victims are poor choices for partners, even though loving them might make you feel needed. **All the terrible things they complain that others have done to them are merely reflections of their own low self-esteem.**

▶ **He expresses his self-confidence by taking action in his life.** *True self-esteem manifests itself in action.* It inspires us to take chances, go after our dreams, and reach out beyond our comfort zone. You can always spot someone with self-esteem because he's *doing* something. In contrast to this is **the procrastinator, a person with low self-esteem, who avoids action because he's scared to death of failing and feeling even worse about himself.** Look for partners who do something about their goals instead of just talking about them.

QUESTIONS TO ASK YOUR PARTNER ABOUT SELF-ESTEEM:

1. **What are you the most proud of about yourself and your life?** (Notice whether he has a very difficult time finding anything to say.)

2. **What kind of emotional abuse or mistreatment have you tolerated in the past? Why did you put up with it? Would you tolerate it now?**

3. **What do you do to show your love for *yourself* (bubble baths, massages, special vacations, etc.)?**

4. **What are your worst health or living habits?**

5. **Do you procrastinate a lot of the time, much of the time, or not much at all?**

6. **What risks have you taken in your life? What was the most recent risk? Are there any risks you've been avoiding taking?**

QUALITY

▼   ▼   ▼   ▼   **6**   ▼   ▼   ▼   ▼

Positive Attitude Toward Life

There's an old saying, *"There are two kinds of people in the world: positive people and negative people."* If you had to spend the rest of your life with one of these two, which would you choose? Tough decision, right?! Unfortunately, we often fall in love with someone without discovering whether he has an essentially positive view of the world, or an essentially negative one, and it really makes a difference.

Negative people:

- ▶ always focus on the problems, and resist solutions
- ▶ always find something or someone to complain about
- ▶ allow fear and worry to rule them
- ▶ are cynical and pessimistic about the future
- ▶ don't trust easily

Positive people:

- ▶ always focus on finding the solution
- ▶ turn obstacles into opportunities and adversity into lessons
- ▶ trust in their ability to make a difference
- ▶ believe that things can always get better
- ▶ use their vision to change their reality

Naturally, it follows that negative people create similarly negative relationships, and positive people create equally positive relationships. No surprise, then, that having a love affair with a negative person is about as much fun as listening to someone slowly drag chalk across an old blackboard.

Love is a positive force: It thrives in an atmosphere of positivity and starves in an atmosphere of negativity. That's why it's so important to find a partner who has a positive attitude. You'll be able to tell by spending a little time with someone whether he's positive or negative. Look for the symptoms I just listed.

Relationships are much easier when you're with a positive person. You work through conflict faster; there's less blame and more cooperation. Most of all, there's more love.

QUESTIONS TO ASK YOUR PARTNER ABOUT A POSITIVE ATTITUDE TOWARD LIFE:

1. **Do you feel people are essentially good or essentially bad?**

2. **When lots of things go wrong at once, how do you react? What goes on in your mind? Give an example from your recent past.**

3. **What are some of the most important lessons you've learned about pain in your life?**

4. **If you could sum up your philosophy of life in a few sentences, what would it be? Has it changed since you were younger?**

5. **If you had to explain why the world is the way it is to your children, what would you say?**

6. **Do you believe things always turn out for the best? Whether your answer is yes or no, explain why.**

Taking the time to discuss these six categories of questions with a new partner will reveal much about his character and will help you determine whether he can be the kind of person you want to spend your life with. And talking about these with your longtime mate may surprise you! You might learn things about your partner you didn't know, and the quizzes will help you focus more clearly on problem areas in your relationship.

If you've finished this chapter but didn't answer all the questions about YOURSELF, you avoided a wonderful opportunity for your own personal growth! **Go back and read the chapter again, this time concentrating on evaluating your character.**

9
▼▼▼

SEXUAL CHEMISTRY: WHAT TURNS YOU ON AND WHAT DOESN'T

▼▼▼

▶ Are you in a relationship but sometimes wonder if you'd be sexually happier with another partner?

▶ Are you single and find the partners you're sexually attracted to are the ones who aren't good for you?

▶ Do you know someone who would make a great spouse except for the fact that you feel no chemistry between the two of you?

▶ Do you ever worry that your partner's not attracted enough to you, or that you're not attracted enough to him?

Life was so much simpler before we discovered sex. Remember when you were seven or eight and had buddies of the opposite sex? It was so easy to hang out together riding bikes or playing games. You knew that grown-ups did things like holding hands and getting married, but it didn't interest you one bit, and besides, it seemed really gross. "I'm never kissing a boy!" you vowed to your friends. "I'm never going to act goofy around girls!" you promised your pals.

And then, sometime between ages ten and thirteen, you were struck by a plague that ravages all adolescents: *hormones!* And all of a sudden, the other sex looked very different to you, especially certain people. Now, if you were a girl, all boys weren't the same anymore—a few of them looked *really good.* When you saw them in the hallway at school, you got a funny feeling in your stomach. When you stood near them, your heart started beating rapidly. Just the thought of that one special guy gave you goose bumps! **You didn't know it then, but you were having your first experience of SEXUAL CHEMISTRY.**

Sexual chemistry turned a boy you thought of as a friend into someone who made you melt. It took a girl you wouldn't have been caught dead with a year before and transformed her into the star of a fantasy that kept you up each night. *It divided everyone you knew into two very distinct categories: the ones you were "attracted to" and the ones you weren't.*

WHAT IS SEXUAL CHEMISTRY?

Many years have passed for all of us since our first crush, and yet sexual attraction is as mysterious a process now as it was then. For one thing, it's hard to define. **You either feel it, or you don't.** Have you ever had a friend describe a fabulous man to you, assuring you that this guy had everything a woman could want, and you became very excited to meet him, only to find when you're finally face to face that there's "no chemistry"? Or have you ever found yourself powerfully attracted to someone you had nothing in common with, didn't respect or approve of, and with whom you would never want to spend your life? This is what's so exasperating about understanding sexual attraction. **It seems we often feel it too much under the wrong circumstances and not enough under the right ones.**

Over the course of a relationship, sexual chemistry will naturally fluctuate: It can grow as you become closer; it can diminish as you build emotional walls between you; it can even be lost and reignited. But one thing is for sure:

▼

SEXUAL CHEMISTRY NEEDS TO EXIST BETWEEN YOU AND YOUR PARTNER *IN SOME FORM* IN ORDER TO DISTINGUISH YOUR RELATIONSHIP FROM A FRIEND-SHIP.

▲

After all, what's the difference between how you feel toward your friends and how you feel toward your partner? *What makes your partner more than just a best friend?* The answer is: the sexual, erotic connection between you. **It binds you together in a very primal, very physical way that's difficult to experience with someone unless you have sex with that person.**

One way to define "sexual chemistry" is as a kind of **resonance.** You and your partner resonate together. The dictionary defines resonance as:

> *"energetic vibrations of a body produced by application of a periodic force of nearly the same frequency as that of the free vibration of the affected body."*

Even though this term is used most frequently to describe a certain quality of sound, the principle of how sound waves resonate can be applied to people as well. In simple terms, **when something of one frequency comes into contact with a "body" (or in this case, a person) with a similar frequency, the energetic vibration between the two is called resonance.** We experience this resonance in different ways, one of which is sexual attraction. It certainly feels like an energetic vibration! And that's really what sexual energy is.

WHY YOU'RE TURNED ON BY SOME PEOPLE AND NOT BY OTHERS

If sexual chemistry occurs when there's resonance between two people, then what causes that resonance in the first place? Scientists and sociologists have only just begun to study this psychic, invisible dimension of our lives. Whether you're a skeptic or a believer, you've probably experienced picking up "vibrations" without realizing it. I'm sure you've met people and either really liked or disliked them before they even opened their mouth to say anything. You're picking up their energy. If they're full of love, compassion, and forgiveness, and you are, too, you'll probably feel "good vibes." If they're they holding a lot of negativity inside them, such as anger and bitterness, and you aren't, you'll probably feel "bad vibes." **But if you have the same kinds of emotions inside you, you will resonate.**

To understand why some people's "vibrations" turn you on, let's go back to our analogy of sound. Sound is also a vibration, but a very manifest one that we can actually hear. Every piece of music vibrates at a different frequency. A piece of classical music, for instance, produces a different vibrational quality than a piece of heavy metal rock music. Or there might be a very explosive symphony by Beethoven that has an even more intense vibrational effect on you than a rock love song. Your body feels different when you listen to each of these types of music, and each produces a very different effect on your nervous system. *You enjoy listening to sounds (or music) with which your nervous system resonates.* Just as sounds give off certain energies, so do people. We each have several different "categories" of energy or vibrations in our lives:

▶ Your *physical vibration* is the sum of everything you do to your body with food, cigarettes, drugs or alcohol, exercise, or sex, and can also be affected by strong mental or emotional vibrations.   .

▶ Your *mental vibration* is the sum of all your thoughts, judgments, and beliefs.

▶ Your *emotional vibration* is the sum of all your feelings, past and present, including all your emotional programming.

▶ Your *spiritual vibration* is the sum of your sense of peace with yourself and your world, your spiritual philosophy, as well as a reflection of all your other vibrations combined.

YOU RESONATE WITH (OR ARE TURNED ON BY) PEOPLE WHOSE VIBRATIONAL ENERGY IS SIMILAR TO YOURS.

So when you find yourself sexually attracted to someone, it probably means the two of you have very similar vibrations in one or more areas—physical, mental, emotional, or spiritual. This doesn't necessarily mean you will be compatible partners, however:

PHYSICAL ATTRACTION AND COMPATIBILITY ARE NOT THE SAME THING.

Physical attraction is one element of a compatible relationship, but it alone will not be enough to make you and your partner compatible. For total compatibility you'll also need mental

attraction, emotional attraction, and spiritual attraction (see Chapter Ten). Otherwise your relationship will be a case of Lust Blindness, based purely on your sexual resonance.

INSTANT ATTRACTION VS. GRADUAL ATTRACTION

One of the biggest mistakes many of us make in looking for the right partner is judging that person too hastily. *If you meet someone and aren't instantly attracted to them, it doesn't necessarily mean that you won't **become** attracted to them as you get to know them better.* Sharing your thoughts and feelings with one another may create strong mental and emotional resonance that will spark sexual resonance. ***The attraction should not just be based on how your partner looks, but also who he is and how you feel about yourself when you're with him.*** For this reason, gradual attraction may actually be more genuine than "lust at first sight." **You're attracted to the whole person.**

In Chapter One I told you the story of how I almost missed the chance to have the most wonderful relationship of my life with my partner Jeffrey because of my habit of looking for instant attraction. I knew Jeffrey for two years and never would have considered myself attracted to him. It had nothing to do with his looks—he's incredibly handsome. He was just so different from the types of men I'd chosen in the past (he was healthy!) that I didn't even consider the possibility that I could fall in love with him. It was only after getting to know what he was like on the inside and developing a powerful emotional, mental, and spiritual resonance that the feelings of sexual attraction began to emerge.

Looking back, it's hard to believe I ever wasn't wildly attracted to Jeffrey, because that's the way I feel now. But we needed time to create enough resonance between us before we could recognize and appreciate the wonderful symphony our separate energies create when they come together. How grateful I am that I gave the relationship time to develop instead of judging it before it even had a chance to blossom!

Falling in love with your best friend can be the most fulfilling emotional experience of your life. **Studies report that couples who were friends before they became romantically involved have more successful and satisfying marriages.** From my own experience, I believe this is because they build a solid foundation of communication and compatibility upon which the relationship can truly grow. *If you become involved with someone based only on chemistry and attraction, you may wake up one morning and find out that you don't even like the person!!*

If you're trying to break the habit of "Lust-At-First-Sight," you'll need to be more patient in your new relationships and give the true attraction a chance to reveal itself. **It's important to remember, however, that giving sexual chemistry some time to develop does not mean staying in a passionless relationship for months and years with the hope that you'll wake up one day and suddenly and miraculously find yourself attracted to your partner.** Although there are instances when two people have known one another for five or ten years as friends and all at once they realize they've been in love all along, it's more common for us to linger in unsatisfying partnerships because we're afraid to face the truth.

When You Love Someone You're Not Attracted To

One of the most painful questions I'm frequently asked is about the importance of chemistry in love relationships:

"Is it possible to have a lasting relationship with someone I'm not really attracted to?"

People who ask me this question are usually involved in a relationship they wish were different. They feel love for their partner but don't feel sexually attracted to them. *They don't want to leave, so they try to rationalize their lack of sexual chemistry and make it "okay."*

My honest response to this question is: **"No, I don't believe it's possible to have a healthy, lasting, romantic relationship with someone whom you aren't attracted to,** *at least for anyone who wants to include sexuality as part of their life."*

Perhaps if a couple met when they were both quite elderly and no longer had an interest in sex, they wouldn't need more than a strong friendship as a foundation to live together happily. But there's no reason why people in their seventies and even older can't enjoy active and fulfilling sex lives, so I don't like to use this example. Besides, it's not sixty- or seventy-year olds who usually ask me about love without attraction—it's men and women in their twenties, thirties, and forties.

Here are some of the reasons why you might attract or stay with partners to whom you're not sexually attracted:

1. You are avoiding true intimacy. A sexual connection binds a couple together in a very special way. *There's nothing more intimate than taking someone inside your own body, if you're a woman, or putting a part of yourself into someone else, if you're a man.* When you're making love, you create tremendous intimacy between yourself and your partner. **Although it may look like you're avoiding sex, becoming involved with someone to whom you aren't attracted may actually be a way you're unconsciously avoiding intimacy in your life.** Since you know you aren't going to have a strong sexual relationship, you're naturally protected from feeling too vulnerable. This will be especially true if you have a pattern of choosing partners with whom you have no chemistry.

2. You are avoiding sex. Some people aren't just avoiding intimacy by selecting mates they aren't attracted to, they are also avoiding sex. If . . .

► you've experienced any form of sexual molestation or abuse
► you've been raped
► you've felt sexually controlled by previous partners
► you were brought up with negative sexual programming

. . . then you may consciously fall in love with people who don't turn you on sexually. In this way you get to avoid sex. You may not be aware that you have these sexual issues. You may even bemoan the fact that you keep attracting partners in whom you're not sexually interested. *But if a lack of chemistry is a recurring theme in your relationships, you may need to do some work on healing your sexuality.*

3. You are trying to maintain a position of control. When you feel sexually attracted to someone, you are, in a sense, giving that person some control over you. It's as if your mind is saying, "You affect me so strongly that you make me want to lose control around you." *If you have issues with needing to be in control, or being afraid of being controlled by others, you may choose partners toward whom you feel no or little sexual attraction in order to keep yourself "safe."* Because you don't feel a strong sexual pull toward them, you get to maintain a certain emotional distance, creating the illusion that you hold more of the power in the relationship.

How We Cover Up Our Lack of Sexual Fulfillment

I'll never forget the woman who came up to me at a seminar and, with a pained expression on her face, asked me if I thought it was important for her to be sexually attracted to her husband. When I answered that yes, I felt it was very important, an amazing thing happened. Her facial expression changed before my eyes, and she looked at me with a stiff smile. "Well, I think sex is overrated," she responded loudly. "There are many more profound ways to love someone other than just sexually." I felt sad as I watched her walk away, and even sadder when I found out from her best friend that she hadn't had sex with her husband in six years! *Like many of us, she was sexually unhappy, but was an expert at covering it up with rationalizations and excuses.*

▼

SEXUAL EXCUSE CHECKLIST

Here are some common excuses I hear from people who don't feel sexually attracted to their partners and don't want to deal with the situation. See how many of these you relate to.

1. We're not much different from other couples.

▶ *"Most couples end up not having much sex as they get older anyway, so I don't think it's such a big deal if we aren't that sexual now. I mean, the honeymoon can't last forever, right?"*

One of the ways in which we justify our lack of fulfillment is by finding other people who are unfulfilled and using them as evidence that we're not unusual. This excuse is just as ludicrous as if you told yourself, "Lots of people get cancer, so it's no big deal if I get it."

2. He's such a nice person, who cares about sex?

▶ *"I was wildly attracted to my last boyfriend, but the relationship was a nightmare. He always lied to me, and made me feel really insecure. My new partner is the opposite—so sweet and polite, and really considerate of my feelings. I feel like I've finally found a nice guy, and even though I'm not really attracted to him, the good things in the relationship make up for it."*

This person is swinging from one extreme to another. She used to choose relationships based on "lust blindness," but since that didn't work, she's taking the opposite tack by choosing a man she's not attracted to, and assuming that will make her happy. What she's failing to see is that **it wasn't the sexual attraction that caused her pain in her past relationship, but the lack of compatibility with her partner in other areas.**

3. **It's not that I don't want sex, we just never seem to find the time.**

    ▶ *"When Kevin and I first met, we were both really busy with school, so we never really had much time for sex. After the wedding, I was responsible for packing up our apartment and moving us to a new town, so that took a lot of energy. Then I got pregnant, and was sick a lot, and since our son was born, I haven't really been in the mood for sex. I love Kevin, but something always seems to get in the way of our being sexual together."*

    This woman has convinced herself that it's not her lack of attraction to her partner that's the problem, but her lack of time. If she's asked whether she enjoys sex when they rarely engage in it, she'll be forced to admit that she doesn't, and that **she uses work and children as excuses to cover up the real problem: She's not attracted to her husband. COUPLES WHO NEVER SEEM TO "FIND THE TIME" FOR SEX ARE AVOIDING THE SEXUAL PROBLEMS IN THEIR RELATIONSHIP.**

4. **I'm not that interested in sex anyway.**

    ▶ *"Lately I just haven't been feeling very sexual, period. I gained about twenty pounds and have been really stressed out about work, so sex is the last thing on my mind. That's why it doesn't bother me that my husband and I aren't having sex right now. In fact, I prefer it that way."*

    This is denial in its purest form—convincing yourself that sex isn't important to you, and therefore, feeling attracted to your partner is unnecessary. The truth is that **this woman has some deep sexual issues that she gets to avoid by having an asexual relationship with her husband.**

5. **She's such a good wife and mother/he's such a good provider.**

   ▶ *"Maureen is such a loving mother to the kids, and a great support to me. I couldn't ask for a better wife. I've accepted the fact that I'm not attracted to her in a sexual way, and I think we both can live with that."*

   ▶ *"Paul and I are like best friends. He's a fabulous provider and gives me a wonderful life-style. Our sex life is pretty nonexistent, from my side mostly, but I'd be crazy to give all of this up just to have good sex with someone else."*

   These two people are not only being unfair to themselves but are ripping off their partners as well. They've both settled for a marital arrangement that "looks good" to the world and fits their picture, even though each is unsatisfied. Instead of dealing with their issues, they talk themselves out of them. **This man and woman are in just the type of situation that makes them ripe to have an extramarital affair.**

▲

If one or more of these sexual excuses sound familiar, it's time to stop lying to yourself and give your relationship the attention it deserves.

HOW IGNORING YOUR LACK OF SEXUAL ATTRACTION FOR A PARTNER CAN DESTROY YOUR RELATIONSHIP

Ignoring the lack of chemistry between you and your partner is really another of our compatibility time bombs. It will eventually cause both you and your partner tremendous pain:

▶ *You'll miss the opportunity to bond with your partner in a way in which you do not bond with anyone else.*

▶ *You'll hurt your partner by constantly rejecting him (unless, of course, he isn't attracted to you either!).*

▶ *You'll make yourself prone to sexual infidelity.*

This third risk is by far the most destructive. I've seen so many cases where people ignored their lack of attraction to a partner, telling themselves it wasn't that important, only to wake up six months or five years or twenty years later and find themselves intensely sexually attracted to someone else, or worse, involved in a complicated affair.

WHEN YOU STAY IN A RELATIONSHIP WITH SOMEONE YOU AREN'T ATTRACTED TO, YOU'RE SETTING YOURSELF UP FOR EVENTUALLY CHEATING ON THAT PERSON.

Here is a story of a couple with this problem:

HOW CARLOS ENDED UP SLEEPING WITH HIS WIFE'S SISTER

Carlos and his wife, Wendy, attended one of my seminars in hopes of saving their ravaged marriage. Wendy stood up on Friday night and announced she wanted to forgive Carlos for cheating on her but didn't know if she could because of the circumstances. When I asked her what they were, she answered: *"My husband not only cheated on me, he cheated on me with my sister."*

The next morning Carlos pulled me aside to explain. "I'm ashamed to admit it, but what Wendy said was true. I had a six-week affair with her sister, Stacie. I just don't understand it, Barbara. How could I do anything so awful?"

I suggested he do some deep soul-searching over the weekend to figure it out, and the next morning Carlos approached me again, and I could tell by the tears in his eyes that he'd had a breakthrough.

"I think I figured it out," he explained. "I haven't wanted to admit it, but **the truth is, I've never been sexually attracted to Wendy. She's more like a best buddy.** She was the first girl who ever loved me just for me, not how much money I had or what I could offer her. She didn't care that I was a plumber and didn't have a fancy job, like other girls I'd dated. I was so happy to feel so totally accepted by a woman that I guess I didn't pay much attention to our sex life. *I knew I loved Wendy very much, but now that I look back, I see that I avoided having sex with her from the beginning.* I thought my lack of desire was a sign of maturity, but it never went away, and a physical attraction toward her never developed."

"Wasn't she suspicious?" I asked Carlos.

"Frankly, I think she was relieved at first. Wendy hadn't had a lot of sexual experience, so my lack of interest took the pressure off her. A few years into our marriage, she started asking me questions about it, and I'd blame it on work or whatever. The truth was, I felt very sexual, but not toward Wendy.

"When her sister, Stacie, moved to California, she stayed with us for a month, and the energy between us was intense. Barbara, I wanted to run away, because **I felt all the attraction for Stacie I would have given anything to feel for Wendy.** Things got better once Stacie moved out, but last year, when Wendy went to a business conference out of town, she had Stacie promise to come over and cook me dinner. I tried to tell her I'd be fine, because I didn't trust myself alone with Stacie, but Wendy insisted. I was like dry wood being lit by a match—we just ignited together. We both felt awful afterward and vowed we would never do it again, but the passion was too intense. *I know I was terribly wrong to cheat on my wife, but am I wrong to want to have a good sex life?* I've tried, but I can't live without that kind of passion anymore."

Carlos was right—although his affair had devastating effects on the whole family, it did have one positive result: **Carlos was no longer in denial. The affair forced him to face the sexual frustration he'd kept secret from himself for so long.** He and Wendy did a lot of healing together that weekend, but agreed to separate. *They were in a relationship that couldn't work because there was no sexual compatibility.*

YOU CAN'T CREATE SEXUAL CHEMISTRY

▼

IF YOU HAVEN'T FELT SEXUALLY ATTRACTED TO YOUR PARTNER FROM THE BEGINNING OF YOUR RELATIONSHIP, YOU'LL BE UNLIKELY TO DEVELOP THOSE FEELINGS OVER TIME.

▲

One of the hardest things I ever have to tell a couple is that I don't think their relationship has enough compatibility to work. They often come to me hoping that a miracle will allow them to avoid facing the fact that it's over. (We'll talk later about how to tell if your relationship can survive or not.)

If you and your partner used to, at one time, feel very attracted to one another but have lost that sexual spark

through the years, *you may be able to reignite it by doing some serious emotional healing.* I know because this is what I help people do in my seminars. BUT IF YOU'VE NEVER FELT THAT CHEMISTRY, AND GOT TOGETHER ANYWAY, AND STILL DON'T FEEL IT, YOU PROBABLY NEVER WILL. (An exception: If you've never felt sexually attracted to anyone, and suspect you have a problem with your own sexuality, it's possible that with some professional help you can slowly discover sexual feelings toward your partner as you heal yourself.)

If I had the formula to make people attracted to one another, I'd probably be a billionaire! People would pay anything for an elixir that created sexual chemistry. Through all of my books, seminars, and tapes, I feel confident that I can help a couple who has lost the sexual magic, but I can't help a couple who never had it. **That's why it's so important that you make sure *before* you become seriously involved with someone that the right kind of chemistry exists between the two of you.**

How to Tell If You Have Enough Sexual Chemistry with Your Partner

Here's a quiz to help you determine how sexually attracted you are to your partner. This is different from a quiz that would determine how happy you are with your sex life, since **it measures *how you feel about your partner's sexual attractiveness, not his ability as a lover or the frequency of your lovemaking.***

▶ You can take this quiz about your present partner.
▶ You can take the quiz about previous partners (how you *used to feel* about them).
▶ Ask your partner to take the quiz with you.

I know it's scary to be honest about this topic, but don't avoid it—*the more you understand about your relationship, the better your chances of not getting hurt. So answer honestly.*

▼

YOUR SEXUAL CHEMISTRY QUOTIENT

Read each statement and ask yourself how accurately it describes your feelings:

If you feel this way ALMOST ALWAYS   Give yourself 4 points

If you feel this way **FREQUENTLY**   **Give yourself 3 points**
If you feel this way **SOMETIMES**   **Give yourself 2 points**
If you feel this way **ONCE IN A WHILE**   **Give yourself 1 point**
If you feel this way **RARELY OR NEVER**   **Give yourself 0 point**

1. I like the way my partner looks in clothing.
2. I like the way my partner looks naked.
3. I like the way my partner's skin feels.
4. I like the way my partner smells.
5. I like the way my partner tastes.
6. I like the way my partner holds me.
7. I like the way my partner kisses me.
8. I like the way my partner touches me when we aren't having sex.
9. I like the way my partner touches me when we are having sex.
10. I look forward to having sex with my partner.
11. When I think about having sex with my partner, I feel physically aroused.
12. I feel sexually excited when my partner's body is pressed against mine.
13. When I don't have sex with my partner for a while, I miss it.
14. I like the way my partner moves his or her body.
15. I think my partner is sexy.

Now total your points:

► **50–60 points: YOUR PARTNER REALLY MAKES YOU SIZZLE SEXUALLY!** You are highly attracted to him or her, and it doesn't take much for him to turn you on. *Make sure you're compatible in other areas of your relationship—the chemistry is so strong that you could be a victim of lust blindness if your relationship isn't well balanced.* Pay attention to those questions that produced lower scores and discuss the results with your partner.

► **36–49 points: YOU FEEL NATURALLY ATTRACTED TO YOUR PARTNER, BUT THERE ARE OTHER PROBLEMS THAT ARE INTERFERING WITH YOUR ABILITY TO ENJOY HIM OR HER SEXUALLY.** Chemistry isn't the issue—there's lots of it—but *you may have emotional resentments that are affecting your sexual closeness.* It's also possible that you aren't totally happy with your partner's sexual technique, or that *you have some blocks in your* *own sexuality that are preventing you from fully enjoying your relationship.* Think about these issues and communicate honestly with your partner about problem areas.

▶ **21–35 points: YOU MAY NOT WANT TO ADMIT IT, BUT YOU ARE NOT REALLY ATTRACTED TO YOUR PARTNER.** It's possible that you never were, or perhaps the problems in your relationship have turned you off completely. *Ask yourself why you are staying in this relationship.* Is it convenient? Are you afraid you can't do better? Are you protecting your partner, or your children? *You are not sexually happy with this person. Get some professional help and either work on trying to find the passion again, or get out.*

▶ **0–20 points: YOUR PARTNER IS A TOTAL TURNOFF!** What are you doing with him or her? You must spend your time either physically disgusted, numb, or avoiding your mate as much as possible. *You may have such low self-esteem that this is what you think you deserve, or you could have some serious sexual blocks due to past trauma. You deserve to feel happier than this. Stop lying to yourself and end this relationship.*

Remember, this quiz doesn't test your overall compatibility, **it only tests how attracted you are to your partner.** So:

▶ You could score very high on this test (50–60 points) but still have a bad relationship overall.

▶ You could score in the middle of this test (36–49 points) but still have a strong relationship that happens to have some sexual and emotional problems.

If you score very low on the test (0–35 points), please think carefully about the information in this chapter. You probably don't have enough natural attraction to your partner ever to have a fulfilling sexual and romantic relationship. Stop waiting for it to happen, and focus on getting back in touch with your needs. This is *not* the way love is supposed to feel!

WHEN YOU AND YOUR PARTNER AREN'T SEXUALLY COMPATIBLE

Remember that earlier I explained sexual chemistry is *not* the same as sexual compatibility? **You may feel a lot of sexual chemistry with your partner but be sexually imcompatible** with him or her. Here are some situations that can create sexual incompatibility:

REASONS FOR SEXUAL INCOMPATIBILITY

1. **You and your partner don't physically fit together.**
2. **You and your partner have different sexual frequency requirements.**
3. **You and your partner have different Sexual Styles.**
4. **You or your partner is sexually addicted or dysfunctional.**

---

1. YOU AND YOUR PARTNER DON'T PHYSICALLY FIT TOGETHER.

This will only sound amusing if it's never happened to you, but if it has, you won't laugh reading this. Some people's bodies just fit together better than others, and some people's bodies don't fit together at all. I frequently receive heartbreaking letters from men and women complaining that their relationship isn't working because the two partners aren't physically compatible. Women write about men whose penises are too large to fit comfortably inside, or so small that they can't feel anything during intercourse. Men write about women with vaginas so tight that intercourse becomes extremely painful for the male partner, or vaginas so large that the man feels lost when he enters. **These mismatched lovers end up dreading sex because it's so physically uncomfortable, and the problem creates tremendous tension in their relationship.**

If the physical differences aren't extreme, a couple can work together to adapt their sexual behavior to alleviate the problem. **However, if the physical differences are extreme, a couple will have a difficult time finding sexual happiness together.**

This situation becomes more complicated when a couple decides to wait until after they're married to have sexual intercourse. I recently met a woman who shared a sad story with me. She and her husband had been married for thirty-two years but almost never had sex! *It seems she'd decided to stay a virgin until she got married, and on her wedding night discovered that her husband's penis was so large that it virtually couldn't fit inside her without causing horrific pain and bruising.* This woman went from doctor to doctor, but none could offer any remedy for the couple's embarrassing predicament. Since she refused to have sex with her mate, he began having affairs about five years into the marriage, affairs she knew about but tolerated because of the circumstances. They finally decided to get divorced after over three decades of sexual incompatibility.

"**I'm a Catholic, and I was taught to wait,**" she told an audience of women with tears in her eyes, "**but please don't make the same mistake I did. Find out if you and your partner will be physically good together before you get married.**"

I can't tell you how to make your sexual decisions when you're single, but like this unfortunate woman, I, too, am concerned about couples who have no sexual knowledge of one another before they make a permanent commitment. *If you're planning to remain celibate until you're married, at least take the time to have a very frank discussion with your partner about physical compatibility in order to avoid any sexual blocks on your wedding night!*

2. YOU AND YOUR PARTNER HAVE DIFFERENT SEXUAL FREQUENCY REQUIREMENTS.

▶ "I like to make love several times a week. My wife only wants sex a few times a month. We fight about it all the time, and it's poisoning our relationship. What can we do?"

▶ "My boyfriend wants sex at least once a day, and sometimes twice a day on weekends. When we first met I felt flattered that he was so turned on by me, but now I almost dread sex. It feels like a chore. Can you help us?"

▶ "My husband can go without sex for months at a time, and I walk around constantly horny. I don't want it all the time, but sometimes would be nice. When I talk to him about it, he says sex isn't important to him, but it is to me. Do you think we're just incompatible?"

All of these couples have one thing in common: Their sexual compatibility is threatened by the differences in their sexual frequency requirements. This is not about whose sexual rhythms are right and whose are wrong, but about the fact that they're *different enough to produce conflict.*

No two people are exactly alike, so naturally one partner's desire for sexual contact won't always coincide with his or her mate's. On the night you're in the mood, he's exhausted from work. The morning he's suddenly aroused, you wake up with cramps. These moments when you and your partner are sexually out of sync are normal parts of any long-term relationship. *The problem arises, however, when you're almost always out of sync because your sexual rhythms are so different from those of your lover.*

The good news is, in many cases, you and your partner can work through this crisis with professional guidance and honest communication. Perhaps the man who wants sex every day is using it as a tension reliever, not a way to make love to his wife. By developing other means of reducing stress in his life, such as exercise or meditation, and by dealing with conflicts rather than avoiding them, he may find his need for constant sex balances out. And perhaps the woman who only wants sex twice a month is avoiding intimacy with her partner. Maybe she doesn't like the way he makes love to her; maybe she has some sexual issues in her past that have turned her off to sex. Or perhaps she doesn't feel good about her body and sexuality and has numbed herself to that part of her relationship.

There are reasons why you either want or don't want sex. *Exploring these and discussing your feelings with an understanding mate can help you and your partner find a common ground of sexual frequency that makes both of you happy.* **However, if your partner insists that "This is just the way I am" and shows no interest in either compromise or communication, you must face the fact that your sexual frequency conflicts make you incompatible.**

3. YOU AND YOUR PARTNER HAVE DIFFERENT SEXUAL STYLES. Each of us has a Sexual Style that reflects the many aspects of our personality. You might be Miss Romantic or Mr. Speedy, Miss Control Freak or Mr. Sensitive, to name just a few.

Your Sexual Style will reflect:

▶ **your past sexual experiences**
▶ **any emotional programming you have about sex from childhood**
▶ **your level of comfort or discomfort with your body**
▶ **your level of self-confidence**
▶ **your level of emotional openness or fear**
▶ **your attitude toward intimacy**
▶ **how much you feel you deserve love and pleasure**
▶ **how much you know or don't know about sex**

In addition, a person's Sexual Style can and will change over time as he or she changes physically, emotionally, mentally, and spiritually.

THE CLOSER YOUR SEXUAL STYLE IS TO THAT OF YOUR PARTNER, THE MORE SEXUALLY COMPATIBLE YOU'LL BE; CONVERSELY, THE FARTHER APART YOUR SEXUAL STYLES, THE LESS SEXUALLY COMPATIBLE YOU'LL BE.

How can you figure out someone's Sexual Style? The only way I know of is to have sex with him or her. Soon you will know all there is to know! You will either love it, hate it, or like some parts but not others. And your partner will have his or her own opinions about your Sexual Style.

▶ **In a good relationship, you and your partner will create a Sexual Style that's a synthesis of the best parts of each of you.** For instance, when Alan met Victoria, his Sexual Style was very different from hers. She was a very emotional lover, and Alan was a much more physical lover. By learning more about themselves and from one another, Alan began opening up more in bed and allowing himself to feel more emotion, and Victoria started giving herself permission to be more sensual and lusty. Their Sexual Styles became increasingly compatible as their relationship blossomed.

▶ **In a bad relationship, one partner will sacrifice or modify his Sexual Style to please the other or to avoid conflict.** Susanna was attracted to Charlie when she first met him but very uncomfortable with his Sexual Style. Charlie was into a lot of sexual fantasy, X-rated movies, and role-playing in bed, whereas Susanna's Sexual Style was more grounded in intimacy and love. Because she didn't want to lose Charlie, Susanna did whatever he wanted in the bedroom, but as the weeks went by, Susanna became more and more resentful, until she stopped wanting to have sex at all. Charlie became frustrated and eventually left her. He actually did her a favor, because the relationship wasn't healthy.

If your Sexual Style and your partner's clash, examine the rest of your relationship and you'll probably find similar conflicts. After all, sex is just an expression of who you are emotionally and intellectually. So if your emotional style and mental style aren't compatible with your partner's, your Sexual Style most likely won't be, either. (See Chapter Ten for more about overall compatibility.)

What if your Sexual Style is very different from your partner's and it's causing problems between you? Some couples who start out with different Sexual Styles work together to learn more about themselves and all those elements that contribute to Sexual Style I mentioned earlier. Through constant communication, a willingness to make their relationship work, and professional guidance, if necessary, they actually improve their sex life. Other couples with very different Sexual Styles try to work on solving their problem, but fail. They are simply such different people that they're incompatible in many areas. It all depends on you and your partner, and how willing you are to use your sex life as an opportunity to learn many things about yourselves.

The truth is: **Different Sexual Styles can sometimes create sexual incompatibility, but just as often they serve as an impetus for a couple to work together as a team to grow in love, sensitivity, and maturity.**

4. YOUR PARTNER IS SEXUALLY DYSFUNCTIONAL. In Chapter Six, *Fatal Flaws*, we discussed sexual dysfunction at length and explained why it's so destructive to relationships. Just to remind you, I included three categories of behavior under sexual dysfunction:

1. **Sexual addiction and obsession**
2. **Lack of sexual integrity**
3. **Sexual performance problems**

If your partner has a problem in any of these areas, you may not be sexually compatible with one another. *It all depends on how severe the problem is and how willing your partner is to change or get help* (or if you're the one with the problem, how willing you are to change or get help).

▼

NO MATTER HOW MUCH YOU LOVE SOMEONE, YOU'LL HAVE A DIFFICULT TIME TRANSCENDING THE PAIN THAT PERSON'S SEXUAL DYSFUNCTION CAUSES YOU.

▲

If it hurts to read this, and you know this is a problem in your relationship, make sure you've read about sexual dysfunction in Chapter Six very carefully.

WHEN THE SEXUAL CHEMISTRY DISAPPEARS

One of the most frightening feelings in the world is waking up next to your partner in the morning and, as you watch him sleep, realizing that you aren't sexually attracted to him anymore. I wrote my first book, *How to Make Love All the Time,* in hopes of helping couples avoid making the common relationship mistakes that eventually destroy the passion they used to feel. **Often the chemistry isn't gone—it's just buried underneath piles of unexpressed feelings and bad habits. With hard work and emotional retraining, it's possible not only to rediscover the passion but also to experience more love and intimacy than you did before.**

Sometimes, however, the chemistry disappears because you and your partner have grown in separate directions. Remember, we defined sexual chemistry as resonance:

▼

IF YOU AND YOUR PARTNER BEGIN TO RESONATE ON VERY DIFFERENT VIBRATIONAL LEVELS, YOU WILL NOT FEEL ATTRACTED TO ONE ANOTHER ANYMORE.

▲

This is an important point to understand. *It's not that you stop feeling attracted to your partner, and therefore the relationship stops working.* **It's that you stopped feeling attracted to your partner because the relationship stopped working.** When you and your partner stop resonating physically, emotionally, intellectually, or spiritually, you will stop resonating sexually.

Yesterday I took a break from writing this chapter and had lunch with a friend I'll call Dianne. I like Dianne because she's a woman completely devoted to her personal growth. She's spent the past five years facing her addictions, her codependency, and her denial. As part of that process, she recently ended a ten-year relationship. When Dianne asked me which chapter I was working on, I told her it was this one.

"That's appropriate," she said with a laugh. "One of the reasons I finally left Spencer was because I had turned off to him sexually. It's strange, because in the beginning of our relationship I was crazy about him."

I explained my concept of sexual resonance to Dianne, and all of a sudden her eyes lit up. "I get it!" she exclaimed. "For the past five years, I was growing in so many areas of my life. I changed my diet, I changed the way I communicated, I changed from victim consciousness to empowerment consciousness. Even though Spencer was trying, he didn't change that much. **According to what you're saying, we began vibrating at very different frequencies. You know, it really felt as if suddenly we were in two different worlds. I still loved him, but I couldn't feel connected to him as I did before."**

"That's why you stopped feeling attracted to him," I continued. "There wasn't enough resonance left between you to create sexual chemistry."

I was glad to have helped Dianne understand more about sexual chemistry and her relationship. I hope, through this chapter, that I've helped you understand more, too.

Sex is really just a mirror for us—a mirror that reflects the state of our mind, our heart, and our soul. Knowing this, your sex life can transform from something mysterious and confusing to something enlightening and magical.

10

▼▼▼

COMPATIBILITY: FINDING OUT WHO'S RIGHT FOR YOU

▼▼▼

W̲e've finally arrived at the most exciting part of the book, the chapter where you get to put everything we've talked about together and use it to discover exactly what kind of partner is right for you! Whether you're looking for a relationship, recovering from one, or committed to one, I know the exercises that follow will help you focus on what you want and need from a mate.

This chapter includes sections on:

1. **HOW TO TELL IF YOU'RE READY TO HAVE A RELATIONSHIP**
2. **HOW TO MAKE A COMPATIBILITY LIST**
3. **HOW TO TELL IF YOU AND YOUR PARTNER ARE COMPATIBLE USING THE COMPATIBILITY FORMULA**

Throughout this chapter I'll be asking you to do some writing and make some lists, so have a notebook and a pen handy. I'll also be reminding you of some important points from earlier chapters so you can apply them directly to your own love life.

IMPORTANT: It's normal to feel a little nervous starting out on this chapter. If you're in a relationship, you might be thinking, *"Uh-oh, what if I find out my partner and I aren't* *compatible? Maybe I'll just skip this chapter."* If you're single, you might worry that you'll do the exercises and find out you aren't ready to be in a relationship! NO MATTER HOW YOU FEEL, DON'T AVOID THIS CHAPTER. Trust me—it'll help you create the loving relationship you deserve.

<u>STEP ONE</u>

HOW TO TELL IF YOU'RE READY TO HAVE A RELATIONSHIP

If you aren't emotionally ready to be in an intimate relationship, you'll have a difficult time determining whether you're with the right person. *The relationship won't feel right because of your own problems, **not** because you aren't compatible with your mate.*

▼

ARE YOU READY FOR LOVE?

Here are some questions to ask yourself to help determine whether you're ready to have an intimate relationship.

1. Am I still in love with an ex-partner?
2. Am I still carrying tremendous resentment and rage toward an ex-partner?
3. Do I often feel spiritually or emotionally empty within myself?
4. Do I dislike the person I am?
5. Do I feel I have very little that's valuable to offer a mate?
6. Do I have any addictions I'm not dealing with?
7. Do I feel so lonely and desperate that I'm totally miserable without a relationship?
8. Do I feel no one would want to be in a relationship with me?
9. Do I find it almost impossible to feel any emotion?
10. Am I unwilling to talk about my feelings with others?

▲

If you answered YES to even one of these questions, you may not be emotionally ready to have an intimate relationship with anyone. Either you haven't recovered sufficiently from a pervious relationship to give your heart to a new person, or your self-esteem is so low that you can't possibly love another person, or you feel so empty inside that you have nothing to offer except your extreme neediness. If you answered YES to questions nine or ten, you need to find your own emotions before you can expect someone else to be with you.

If you answered YES to some of these questions and you're already in a relationship, you are, no doubt, aware of the problems your lack of readiness is causing. *You may need some time away from your partner to find yourself, or heal whatever is preventing you from being totally available. You aren't being fair to your mate by expecting him or her to deal with what are **your** blocks to intimacy.*

There are times in our lives when we're ready to become involved with another person, and times when we need to be alone. **If you suspect you aren't ready for love, go on a "Relationship Fast" and work on improving your relationship with yourself.** When you can take this quiz and answer NO to the questions, you're ready to fall in love.

STEP TWO

HOW TO MAKE A COMPATIBILITY LIST

When I wrote my first book, *How to Make Love All the Time,* I talked a little about the importance of making a Compatibility List for both singles and couples. Over the past five years I've received countless letters from readers about their experiences making a list, and I'm excited to be able to update the process for you in this chapter.

If you are in a relationship that's working well, your Compatibility List can help you locate problem areas as well as remind you of how much you have to appreciate about your partner. If your relationship is troubled, your Compatibility List can help you understand what is and what isn't working between you and your mate, and make it easier to decide whether it's time to separate. If you're looking for a new relationship, your Compatibility List acts like a shopping list, directing you toward partners who are right for you and helping you avoid partners you don't need and who will be a waste of time.

In Chapter Nine we talked about the resonance between two people as what attracts them to one another. **Your Compatibility List will clarify and define how you "resonate" in ten different areas of your life, and therefore reveal what kind of resonance, or compatibility, you're looking for in a partner.**

The first step is making your Compatibility List. Later in this chapter I'll explain how you can use your list and my Compatibility Formula to determine how compatible you and your partner are.

Here's how to make a Compatibility List:

▶ **Find a quiet place where you won't be disturbed.**

▶ **Write down the qualities you seek in a mate in the following ten categories** (I've included a brief list of examples from each category):

---

1. Physical Style

Appearance
Eating habits
Personal fitness habits
Personal hygiene

EXAMPLES

Well built, dark hair
Eats healthfully/no meat
Exercises regularly
No drugs or alcohol
Cares about appearence
Likes clothes/dresses well
Keeps body clean

---

2. Emotional Style

**Attitude toward romance and
    affection**
How he treats you
How he expresses feelings
How he treats the relationship

EXAMPLES

Always very affectionate
**Supportive of me and my
    dreams**
Cries easily
Expresses feelings easily
Makes romantic gestures
Committed
**Sentimental about special
    occasions**
Proud of me and shows it
Faithful and devoted

---

3. Social Style

Personality traits
How he interacts with others

EXAMPLES

Warm and friendly
Very outgoing, aggressive
Likes socializing
Good sense of humor
Down to earth/practical

Sophisticated
Kind and sensitive
Likes to play and be light
Stands out in a crowd

---

4. Intellectual Style

EXAMPLES

Educational background
Attitude toward learning
Attitude toward culture
Attitude toward world affairs
Creative expressions

Well educated/college +
Creative mind
Interested in culture
Interested in world events
Likes learning new things
Enjoys philosophical
discussions

---

5. Sexual Style

EXAMPLES

Attitude
Skill
Ability to enjoy

Enjoys frequent sex
Very sensual
Sensitive, skilled lover
Seductive
Likes to cuddle
Easily aroused—no hangups

---

6. Communication Style

EXAMPLES

How he communicates
Attitude toward
communication
Other forms of expression

Loves talking
Verbally articulate
Good writer/sends cards
Takes feedback well
Willing to discuss problems
Tells me what's going on inside
him

---

7. Professional/Financial Style

EXAMPLES

Relationship with money
Attitude toward success
Work and organizational habits

Financially responsible
Hard worker
Ambitious in career
In a field that helps others
Well organized
Generous with himself and
others
Enjoys good things in life
Honest and ethical

8. Personal Growth Style

Attitude toward self-
improvement
Ability to look at self and
change
Willingness to work on
relationship

EXAMPLES

Committed to learning about
self
Reads books on growth
Attends seminars
Sees own shortcomings
Enjoys discussing growth
Makes concrete changes

9. Spiritual Style

Attitude toward Higher Power
Spiritual practices
Philosophy of life
Moral views

EXAMPLES

Believes in God
Enjoys meditation and prayer
Open to the mystical
Optimistic outlook on life
Compassionate toward less
fortunate
Respectful of all living things

10. Interests and Hobbies

EXAMPLES

Loves to travel
Enjoys music
Loves to dance
Loves dogs
Loves entertainment (movies,
theater)

You can make your Compatibility List as long as you like. I've found that *the more specific you are on your list, the more helpful it'll be to you in determining whether you're in the right relationship.* I suggest you work on your list during one session, then put it down for a day or two. During that time you'll probably remember other qualities you want to include. Then look at the list again and add your new items to it. *One way to be thorough is to remember qualities that were missing from past relationships that caused conflict or problems, and to include them.*

Making a Compatibility List will teach you a lot about yourself. When you're done with it, read it over and ask yourself:

▶ Which of these qualities do I feel I possess?
▶ Which of these qualities do I wish I possessed?

You may be surprised to find that your Compatibility List not only describes your ideal partner *but also your ideal picture of you!*

I suggested in my book *How to Make Love All the Time* that if you're single, you should carry a copy of your Compatibility List in your wallet or purse at all times. Read it often. Share it with your friends. *I believe the list can actually act like a magnet, attracting that special person into your life.* I've heard some incredible stories from people who have followed this advice and reported that soon after they wrote their list, they met their ideal partner.

Later in this chapter I'll explain how to use this list with a **Compatibility Formula** that will determine how compatible you are with a particular partner. That's when the fun begins!!

STEP THREE

HOW TO TELL IF YOU'RE COMPATIBLE WITH YOUR PARTNER

Now it's time for you to apply everything you've been reading about to your relationship. I've divided this section into several parts based on how long you've known your partner:

▶ **0 to three months**

▶ **three to six months**

▶ **six months or longer**

I've done this because there are certain things you can find out about your partner within a few weeks of knowing him, but others may take several months to discover. **Therefore, deciding whether or not you're compatible with someone should happen in stages. At each stage of involvement you should decide whether you're compatible enough to go on to the next stage of involvement.**

Stage One: 0 to Three Months—the New Relationship

Let's say you've determined that you're ready for a relationship; you've made your Compatibility List, and you've met someone you're very interested in. **How can you tell if the relationship is worth pursuing, or if it's going to be a waste of your time?**

Here is a **new relationship checklist** which will help you figure out whether to continue with someone or to stop seeing him.

You'll recognize some of the questions from earlier chapters in the book. Within the first few months of a new relationship, you should be working on this checklist.

NEW RELATIONSHIP CHECKLIST

1. I've asked my partner a lot of questions about himself in the following areas, and received answers I feel good about.

Family background and quality of relationships, past and present	☐
Past love relationships/reasons for breakups/lessons learned	☐
Attitudes about love, commitment, children	☐
Sexual attitudes and preferences (including contraception)	☐
Sexual history (including discussion of AIDS)	☐
Spiritual or religious philosophy and practices	☐
Personal and professional goals	☐
Financial habits, background, and goals	☐
Attitude about *personal growth,* counseling, books, etc.	☐
Attitudes and behaviors about *food, exercise, and health*	☐
Attitudes or history with *addictions*	☐
Ethics, morals, and values	☐

Obviously I'm not suggesting that you meet your partner for your first date, and after the waiter takes your order, you pull out a questionnaire with four hundred questions you want answers to! But over several months of dating someone **you need to have conversations about these topics to really get to know him or her.** There's nothing wrong with bringing up the topic by simply saying, *"I'd like to know more about you. Tell me about all your ex-girlfriends and why the relationships didn't work, and then I'll tell you about my love history,"* or *"How do you feel about God and religion? Are they important to you? Have your views changed over the years?"* **Remember: If you and a partner can't even talk about these things, you aren't ready to be in an intimate relationship with one another.**

2. I'm not making the Six Big Mistakes We Make in the Beginning of Relationships (see Chapter Four).

I'm asking enough questions (see above).	☐
I'm not making premature compromises.	☐
I'm not giving in to Lust Blindness.	☐
I'm not giving in to material seduction.	☐

I'm not putting commitment before compatibility. ☐
I'm not ignoring warning signs of potential problems (see
   rest of checklist). ☐

Before you become too involved, make sure you aren't making these common mistakes. Remember: It's easy to be so excited to have finally found someone you like that you fall into these six traps. Stop, take a deep breath, and check before you go forward. *If you feel confident that your relationship is on the right track, continue with it. If you aren't sure, take some space from it for a week or two, then see how you feel about your partner.* **Slowing down can't hurt, and it may help you avoid becoming more involved in a potentially painful relationship.**

Stage Two: Three to Six Months— The Developing Relationship

When you first meet someone you spend most of your time trying to figure out if you like him enough to keep seeing him. **If you make it to three or four months, your relationship will probably become "serious." You consider yourself "in love"; you're officially a couple. At this point you should consciously stop and decide whether it's in your best interests to continue deepening this relationship.**

▼

THE THREE- TO SIX-MONTH PERIOD IS A CRUCIAL STAGE OF A RELATIONSHIP, DURING WHICH YOU ARE GOING TO BECOME MORE EMOTIONALLY INVOLVED. THEREFORE YOU WANT TO BE SURE YOU'RE MAKING THE RIGHT DECISION BEFORE MAKING YOURSELF EVEN MORE VULNERABLE.

▲

This is the time to ask yourself some more serious questions about your partner's character, since you're starting to see beyond his outer shell and getting to know the real person inside. *You also need to be honest with yourself about how this relationship is making you feel.* The following checklists will help you evaluate the situation.

DEVELOPING RELATIONSHIP CHECKLIST

1. I've checked my partner for Fatal Flaws (using the criteria in Chapter Six) and found him to be clear of them:

	CLEAR
Addictions	☐
Anger	☐
Emotional damage from childhood	☐
Victim consciousness	☐
Control freak	☐
Sexual dysfunction (as far as you know at this point)	☐
Hasn't grown up	☐
Emotionally unavailable	☐
Hasn't Recovered from past relationships	☐

2. I'm not in one of the Ten Types of Relationships that Won't Work (see Chapter Five).

I do not care more about my partner than he does about me.	☐
My partner does not care more about me than I do about him.	☐
I am not in love with my partner's potential.	☐
I am not on a Rescue Mission.	☐
I do not have my partner on a pedestal as a role model.	☐
I am not infatuated with my partner for external reasons.	☐
I have more than just partial compatibility with my partner.	☐
I did not choose my partner in order to be rebellious.	☐
I did not choose my partner only as a reaction to a previous partner.	☐
My partner is available.	☐

3. I've tested my sexual chemistry with my mate (see Chapter Nine) and scored at least 36 of 60 points, indicating that there is basic sexual attraction between us. ☐

If you determine that your partner is healthy, your relationship is healthy, and the attraction is there, you'll feel a lot more confident going ahead to the next level of intimacy.

Stage Three: Six Months or Longer—a Serious Relationship

Once you've been with a partner for six months or longer, you're probably asking yourself, "Is he the one for me?" You know you love one another; you think you get along well. Now you begin to wonder if there's anything that could interfere with the happiness of this relationship. This is the time to go through the following checklist, since it will help you become clear about potential problems that could sabotage this relationship.

SERIOUS RELATIONSHIP CHECKLIST

1. I have checked my relationship for Compatibility Time Bombs (see Chapter Seven), discussed any potential problems with my partner, and, if necessary, made agreements with him about how to handle these issues.

Significant age difference ☐
Different religious background ☐
Different social, ethnic, or educational background ☐
Toxic in-laws ☐
Toxic ex-spouse ☐
Toxic stepchildren ☐
Long-distance relationship ☐

2. I've found the Six Qualities to Look For in a Mate (see Chapter Eight) in my partner.

Commitment to personal growth ☐
Emotional openness ☐
Integrity ☐
Maturity and responsibility ☐
High self-esteem ☐
Positive attitude toward life ☐

THE COMPATIBILITY FORMULA

Now you're ready to look at all the aspects of your relationship and determine how compatible you and your partner are together. I've created a Compatibility Formula that will give you an accurate analysis of how much you're getting what you need from your mate. Here's how it works:

Get out your Compatibility List. Make sure you've written down at least four or five items you want under each category. *The more complete your list is, the more accurate the Compatibility Formula will be.*

You're going to assign a point value to each item on the list based on how much of that desired quality or behavior your partner possesses. For instance, let's say that under "emotional style" you listed the following qualities you want in a partner:

Always very affectionate
Supportive of me and my dreams
Cries easily
Expresses feelings easily
Makes romantic gestures
Committed
Sentimental about special occasions
Proud of me and shows it
Faithful and devoted

You will "grade" your partner as to how much he demonstrates these qualities using this scale:

Almost always	5 points
Frequently	4 points
Sometimes	3 points
Occasionally	2 points
Rarely or never	1 point

So if your partner is **frequently** affectionate, but not always, you'd give him **4 points** next to that item.

Always very affectionate   **4 points**

Next you'd ask yourself how supportive your partner is of your dreams. Maybe he supports you in some areas but not in others, and that's been a problem. So you would give him **3 points** for **sometimes.**

Supportive of me and my dreams   **3 points**

Then you check the next item: cries easily. "My partner cries once in a while, but it's hard for him," you think. "I wish he did cry more and show more vulnerability." So you give him **2 points for occasionally.**

Cries easily   **2 points**

Step-by-step Instructions for Using the Compatibility Formula

1. **Go through your entire Compatability List and grade your partner based on how much he fulfills the items you've listed. Use the system we just described.**

2. **At the end of each section, total the possible score, then total your partner's actual score.**

To determine the *possible score,* multiply the number of items in that category by 5 points. So if you listed nine items under "emotional style," you multiply that by 5 points and come up with a possible perfect score of 45 points. To determine your partner's *actual score,* simply add up the number of points you wrote next to each item.

Sample:

Always very affectionate	4
Supportive of me and my dreams	3
Cries easily	2
Expresses feelings easily	3
Makes romantic gestures	3
Committed	5
Sentimental about special occasions	5
Proud of me and shows it	5
Faithful and devoted	5
Total:	**35**

You should have two numbers, or totals, at the end of each section.

Sample:

POSSIBLE SCORE	PARTNER'S ACTUAL SCORE
45	35

Now divide the first number (the possible score) into the second number (your partner's actual score).

▼

WHEN YOU DIVIDE YOUR PARTNER'S ACTUAL SCORE BY THE POSSIBLE SCORE, YOU'LL GET A NUMBER THAT REPRESENTS THE PERCENTAGE OF COMPATIBILITY YOUR PARTNER IS GIVING YOU IN THAT CATEGORY.

▲

So if under "emotional style" your partner's possible score was 45 and his actual score was 35, you divide 45 into 35:

$$35 \div 45 = .777 \text{ or } \textbf{77 percent compatible}$$

If in another category, your partner's possible score was 25 and his actual score was 23, you divide 25 into 23:

$$23 \div 25 = .92 \text{ or } \textbf{92 percent compatible}$$

At the end of your list, total all ten categories to arrive at a *total possible score*. Then total all the actual scores to arrive at your partner's *total actual score*.

Next, divide your partner's total actual score by the total possible score to get a total compatibility percentage:
Sample #1:

TOTAL POSSIBLE SCORE	TOTAL ACTUAL SCORE
230	197

$$197 \div 230 = .856 \text{ or about } \textbf{86 percent compatible}$$

Sample #2:

TOTAL POSSIBLE SCORE	TOTAL ACTUAL SCORE
220	134

$$134 \div 220 = .609 \text{ or about } \textbf{61 percent compatible}$$

IMPORTANT NOTE: Make sure each of your ten compatibility categories has roughly the same number of items listed, give or take a few. For instance, maybe "physical" has seven, "emotional" has eight, and "social" has six. DO NOT make a list that is much shorter or much longer than the other nine, or it can throw off the Compatibility Formula. For example; if most of your lists have six to nine items, that's fine. But if one list has only two items, or twelve, it may affect your final score. (If you're mathematically proficient you can adjust the scoring accordingly, but it could get complicated!)

A SAMPLE COMPATIBILITY EVALUATION

Roxanne and John

Roxanne, twenty-eight, has been dating John, thirty-one, for about nine months. Here's her compatibility evaluation of John:

1. Physical Style

	JOHN'S SCORE
Cares about eating well	3
Good build/works out	4
No addictions (smoking, etc.)	5
Takes care of himself	4
Dresses nicely	2
Not a lot of body hair	5
Good-looking	4

Possible score: 35   Actual score: 27
Percentage of physical compatibility: 77

2. Emotional Style

	JOHN'S SCORE
Likes touching and holding me	3
Makes the relationship important	3
Expresses feelings easily	2
Romantic	2
Not afraid of commitment	2
Sentimental about special occasions	3
Likes being a couple and tells his friends about us	2
Doesn't make me jealous	4
Sensitive to how I feel	3

Possible score: 40   Actual score: 24
Percentage of emotional compatibility: 60

3. Social Style

	JOHN'S SCORE
Likes having fun	3
Has an easy time being with people	2
Enjoys parties, groups	1
Funny	3
Reliable	3
Commands respect from others	2
Warm and friendly	3
Considerate	3
Polite and respectful	5

Possible score: 45   Actual score: 25
Percentage of social compatibility: 55

4. Intellectual Style

	JOHN'S SCORE
Good education	5
Well read	5
Knows about lots of things	5
Interested in world events	5
Smart	5
Likes teaching me what he knows	5

Possible score: 30   Actual score: 30
Percentage of intellectual compatibility: 100

5. Sexual Style

	JOHN'S SCORE
Good lover	3
Comfortable with his body	2
Likes to kiss and touch a lot	3
Appreciates me sexually	2
Makes love, not just sex	1
Wants sex a few times a week but not more	1

Possible score: 30   Actual score: 12
Percentage of sexual compatibility: 40

6. Communication Style

	JOHN'S SCORE
Talks about his feelings and thoughts	3
Enjoys discussing ideas with me	2
Tells me when he's upset instead of clamming up	1
Open to my opinions and feelings	3
Expresses himself clearly so I understand	3
Doesn't lose his temper a lot—calm	1

Possible score: 30   Actual score: 13
Percentage of communication compatibility: 43

7. Professional/Financial Style

	JOHN'S SCORE
Responsible financially	5
Cares about getting ahead	5
Organized and efficient	5
Frugal and conservative with money	5
Has good taste	3
Honest in his work	5
Plans for the future	5
Reasonably successful/owns own home or condo	5

Possible score: 40   Actual score: 38
Percentage of professional compatibility: 95

8. Personal Growth Style

	JOHN'S SCORE
Interested in growing	2
Has worked on himself through counseling or books	1
Would discuss our problems and work with me on solving them	1
Is honest with himself about his problems	1
Flexible and willing to change	2

Possible score: 30   Actual score: 7
Percentage of personal growth compatibility: 23

9. Spiritual Style

	JOHN'S SCORE
Believes in God	3
Christian	5
Goes to church sometimes	1
Positive view of the world	2
Appreciates creation and God's gifts	1
Accepts my spirituality and involvement with church	2

Possible score: 30   Actual score: 14
Percentage of spiritual compatibility: 46

10. Interests and Hobbies

	JOHN'S SCORE
Enjoys cycling	5
Likes museums and art	5
Cares about the environment	4
Likes food and dining out	5
Likes camping	4

Possible score: 25   Actual score: 23
Percentage of interest compatibility: 92

Roxanne's overall compatibility summary for John:

TOTAL POSSIBLE SCORE	TOTAL ACTUAL SCORE
335	213

Percentage of total compatibility with John: 63

What Your Total Compatibility Percentage Means

Once you have scores in each category, and a final score, you can assess your overall compatibility with your partner. When I did the research for this book, I asked dozens of people to use this Compatibility Formula to evaluate their partner. I also used the formula myself, and I not only evaluated my present partner but also scored several former partners to see what percentage of compatibility we had. After comparing the scores of the relationships, I came up with a scale that I feel is highly accurate in interpreting your compatibility percentage.

80–100 PERCENT COMPATIBILITY: You and your partner are highly compatible. There is enough overall resonance in values, habits, behavior, and goals to create consistent harmony and enjoyment between you. Naturally, there will be areas of less compatibility. *Notice in which categories your partner scored a lower percentage. These will probably be the areas of greatest conflict in your relationship, and the topics you fight about the most!*

No relationship will be 100 percent compatible, since no two people are completely alike. The closer your score is to 100 percent, however, the better you'll get along and the more fulfilled you will feel. This doesn't mean you should feel bad about your lowest area of compatibility:

▼

THE AREAS IN WHICH YOU AND YOUR PARTNER EXPERIENCE THE GREATEST CONFLICT IN YOUR RELATIONSHIP WILL BE YOUR GREATEST TEACHERS.

▲

Perhaps you and your mate have 86 percent overall compatibility, but you notice that in the social category he scored only 65 percent. You can be sure there are important lessons for both of you around the topic of personality style. Maybe your list asks for someone dynamic, outgoing, and aggressive like yourself, but your partner is quiet, introspective, and cautious. It's possible that you're together so you can learn to be more like him and balance your need to always be active, while he may need to learn to take more risks and become a little more like you. This becomes your LEARNING AREA in the relationship.

Partners with compatibility of more than 80 percent usually have one or two major LEARNING AREAS. **The rest of their strong compatibility gives the relationship a firm foundation upon which to work through the weaker areas.** *If you have three or four areas with tremendous conflict, however, you won't just be* *learning from one another—you'll be clashing constantly.* (When this is the case, your overall score would probably be much lower than 80 percent.)

It *is* possible to have an incompatible relationship even if you score 80 percent or higher. Perhaps the area of lowest compatibility is so important to you that it outweighs the good compatibility in the others. For instance, your partner scores an overall 81 percent, but in the personal growth style category he scores only 53 percent. If your growth is highly important to you and you're experiencing constant conflict every time you try to talk about problems or explore new ways of loving, you may find it impossible to stay in the relationship in spite of all the good that exists. I'll talk more about this in the next few pages.

It's also possible to score a high percentage and be incompatible because of the other factors we've examined in the book: You and your partner might be compatible in many ways but have a Toxic in-law problem that he's unwilling to deal with. Or perhaps your mate is ideal for you in all ten areas—except that she's an alcoholic and in major denial. **Remember: Even one Fatal Flaw or Compatibility Time Bomb can be powerful enough to sabotage an otherwise well-matched partnership.**

If you and your partner are committed to growing together, *you can use the results from this formula to strengthen your compatibility with one another.* Naturally, you both need to make your list and do your evaluation. Share them together, talk about what you need more from each other, and make new commitments to give your partner more of what each other needs. When I used this formula, **I scored my partner twice—once for how he was when we first met, and once for how he is now.** The results were exciting: Jeffrey scored many points higher when I graded him now versus the way he was when we first began our relationship. He had the same experience in making his list about me. We talked about this afterward and agreed that all the hard work we've done to communicate our own needs and learn to fulfill each other's needs has really paid off. **We've actually become more compatible over time, and used our LEARNING AREAS to stretch ourselves into more loving, caring partners.**

70–80 PERCENT COMPATIBILITY: This relationship is *partially compatible,* with some significant areas of incompatibility that are producing conflict and discomfort for both partners. If you score your mate at this percentage level,

you're probably feeling confused and torn about whether your relationship is right for you. Your dilemma is understandable, and I hope by using this formula you can see why: You're very compatible in some areas and very incompatible in others. **This does not necessarily mean that you need to end the relationship.** *It does mean that you need to communicate honestly with your partner about those areas in which you aren't happy, and hopefully agree on a plan of action you can both take to remedy the situation.*

Stop making excuses such as "We're a lot better off than most couples," or "Look at all the good things we share together." This may be true, but you aren't feeling fulfilled, and *time will only make the situation worse, not better.* You might consider working with a professional counselor or therapist who can help you focus on the problem areas and transform them into powerful learning experiences. **If your partner refuses to participate in improving the relationship, you may need to face the fact that you're not with the right person for you. You aren't miserable, but you aren't as happy and loved as you could be, and you're cheating yourself.**

What I said earlier about Fatal Flaws and Compatibility Time Bombs is true for the 70–80 percent group as well—especially with less than 80 percent compatibility, you may not have enough of a foundation to fight off the destructive effects of these other problems.

0–69 PERCENT COMPATIBILITY: You are most likely *not* in a relationship with the right person for you. You may feel you love your partner. You may have years of history together, but you aren't resonating in enough areas to create a consistently loving, enjoyable partnership. *You've probably developed a high tolerance for tension, conflict, struggle, loneliness, and pain because you haven't been getting what you want, and yet you're still with this person.* I know it's painful to read these words, but if you're honest with yourself, you'll realize you've been secretly feeling this way for a while. Perhaps you've dreaded facing it, and have avoided looking at your relationship until now. Perhaps you stayed for other reasons, such as children, finances, or illness. **But the fact is that this relationship is causing you more unhappiness than it is happiness.**

The lower your percentage is, the worse your relationship is. If your partner scored in the fifties or sixties, your relationship is extremely incompatible. If he scored less than 50 percent, it's a nightmare! *Even with professional help, there are probably too many areas of inherent incompatibility for the two of you ever to be right for one another. It's not that you or he is bad or wrong— you just don't belong together.*

Evaluating Your Ten Compatibility Categories

The easiest way to get an overall picture of the ***balance of compatibility*** in your relationship is to list the percentages of compatibility in all ten areas. Each area reflects many aspects of your being, but some categories reveal more about certain parts of you than others:

▶ Your ***value system*** is reflected in your personal growth, spiritual, physical, and professional categories.

▶ Your ***emotional programming*** is reflected in your emotional, sexual, communication, social, and professional/financial categories.

▶ Your ***background*** is reflected in your professional, intellectual, and interest categories.

IMPORTANT: Each of us has certain compatibility categories that are more important to us than others are. For instance, if you're a professional athlete you might care more about finding a high percentage of compatibility in your physical category than you would in your spiritual or personal growth categories. In that way, the physical category would really be worth more than one tenth of the Compatibility Formula. On the other hand, if you're a minister, the spiritual category would be more important to you than the physical, and even if you had a low percentage of physical compatibility, it might be outweighed by a high percentage of spiritual compatibility. Take this into account when evaluating your ten categories.

Let's look at some examples:

ROXANNE AND JOHN

Roxanne and John have been dating for nine months, and Roxanne has been confused about whether or not to continue the relationship. When we look at her compatibility evaluation of John, we can see why she's been having so many problems. John's overall compatibility with Roxanne is 63 percent, much lower than what would be needed to create a harmonious relationship. However, when we examine the percentage of compatibility in each category separately, we understand more about Roxanne's dilemma.

CATEGORY	COMPATIBILITY PERCENT
Physical style	77
Emotional style	60
Social style	55
Intellectual style	100
Sexual style	40
Communication style	43
Professional/financial style	95
Personal growth style	23
Spiritual style	46
Interests and hobbies	92

Roxanne and John have what in Chapter Five I called "partial compatibility." Their intellectual and professional styles are highly similar, and their interests are perfectly matched. This explains why Roxanne was attracted to John in the first place. He's intelligent, successful, and worldly. He also happens to share Roxanne's passions for cycling, camping, and dining. Naturally, Roxanne thought she'd met the man of her dreams. **The strong partial compatibility Roxanne and John share created the illusion that they were right for one another.** *It wasn't until several months into the relationship, when Roxanne started wanting more emotional connection and intimacy from John, that their inherent incompatibility began to surface, and the relationship quickly deteriorated.*

Here's a diagram of what "partial compatibility" looks like:

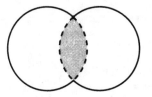

The shaded area is the area of shared compatibility. As long as Roxanne only focuses on that part of her relationship, it will appear that John is perfect for her. But as soon as she focuses on her emotional/social needs, the trouble begins. In every area that affects the dynamics of a relationship, (emotional, sexual, social, and spiritual) John is completely different from Roxanne. And look at that 23 percent compatibility in personal growth style. To John, growth means that his stock portfolio increases in value!

Using this Compatibility Formula not only helped Roxanne realize that John was not the right one for her, but also gave her a clear understanding of *why* the match was so wrong. This made it a lot easier for her to end the relationship without worrying that she was making a horrible mistake, and helped her focus on what she needed to look for in her next partner.

REMINDER: Use the Compatibility Formula to evaluate your former partners. You will have some interesting revelations about your past choices, and some fun, too. If you're presently single, you can use your Compatibility Formula right now, before you even meet a new partner.

MONICA AND CHARLES

Monica's Compatibility List for Charles was used as our prototype earlier. When Monica tallied his scores and applied the formula, she and her husband, Charles, came out 91 percent compatible, which is very high. But Monica says she's been feeling some unhappiness with the relationship, **so when she individually lists the results from all ten categories, she'll get a clear picture of the trouble spots in the relationship.**

CATEGORY	COMPATIBILITY PERCENT
Physical style	100
Emotional style	86
Social style	93
Intellectual style	83
Sexual style	73
Communication style	83
Professional/financial style	95
Personal growth style	100
Spiritual style	100
Interests and hobbies	96

What can you see about Monica and Charles's marriage from looking at this list? First of all, it's obvious why they're together:

Their value systems are almost identical, as reflected in the personal growth, physical, and spiritual categories. This means they operate on a very solid foundation of shared vision. Their personalities are also very similar, as reflected in their professional/ financial, social, and interest categories. In most of these areas they experience little or no conflict.

The problem area in their relationship is the one with the lowest percentage: their sex life.

Enjoys frequent sex	2
Very sensual	3
Sensitive, skilled lover	5
Seductive	2
Likes to cuddle	5
Easily aroused—no hangups	5

Looking at that category again, Monica sees that although she's very satisfied with Charles's ability as a lover, and his affectionate nature, she's not happy with the infrequency with which they have sex and the minimal effort Charles makes to be romantic and seductive. This is an area Monica and Charles need to work on together. Fortunately, they have so much compatibility in the personal growth area that they shouldn't have a problem improving their sex life. Monica also notices that Charles's emotional and communication styles are not quite as compatible with hers as she'd like (not uncommon between men and women, by the way). This is also something they continually need to discuss and uplevel.

A Picture of a Compatible Relationship

A truly compatible relationship will resonate in the majority of areas while still maintaining the individuality of each partner. It might look something like this:

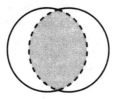

The differences add spice, challenge, and opportunities for growth, but the majority of the relationship is a strong, central core of resonance and harmony. I believe that for a relationship between two people to last a lifetime, their two spheres of individuality will, over the years, merge more and more into one. If the opposite happens, and their two spheres move apart, they'll have a difficult time living together happily and harmoniously, and they may need to separate.

Only You Know Who's Right for You

When I first began writing *Are You the One for Me?* I was very concerned about the chapter on compatibility. I knew I needed to give my readers some guidelines and formulas with which to assess their relationships, but I was adamantly opposed to presenting some brief compatibility quiz where I would profess to tell you how happy you were in your relationship based on my questions. I spent a lot of time thinking about how I could support you in evaluating your relationship *based on your own standards and needs, not mine.* Out of this concern came my idea for the Compatibility List and formula. I'm happy with the results, and I hope these tools have helped you become clearer about your love choices.

Ultimately, all that matters is your own happiness and what *you* think of your relationship, not what I think. So if your partner came out 63 percent compatible with you, and I said that's probably not good enough, but you still think your relationship can work, go with your feeling. I hope it will work, and I'll be happy to have been wrong. My categories are simply general comments on what I've found to be true much of the time. They aren't set in stone; they're not scientifically accurate. So use them if they serve you, and if they don't, go on to the next section!

For those of you who like simplicity and hate percentages, division, and math of any kind, here's a Sixty-second Compatibility Test you can use to see how well matched you are with someone. I sometimes suggest this to people who want to get an instant sense of how they feel about a particular partner. It's also fun to talk about at parties and on dates. Let me warn you, however, that these four little questions are deceptive—answering them can be a more intense experience than you expect it to be. Ready? Here goes:

THE SIXTY-SECOND COMPATIBILITY TEST

Ask yourself the following four questions about your prospective or present partner:

1. Would I want to *have a child* with this person?
2. Would I want to have a child *just like* this person?
3. Do I want to *become more like* this person?
4. Would I be willing to spend my life with this person *if he never changed from the way he is now?*

If you answered yes to all four questions, you're probably compatible with one another. If you answered no, ask yourself why not.

Have you figured out that answering these four questions could take you as long as reading this whole chapter again? I didn't promise you that they'd be easy—just that there would be no math!

The quest for understanding compatibility may not seem as compelling as the search for passionate, romantic love that, in spite of all odds, binds two people together. But as the philosopher Friedrich Nietzsche said:

> "It is not lack of love but lack of friendship
> that makes unhappy marriages."

With love *and* compatibility, I know it'll be much easier for you and your partner to live happily ever after.

11

▼▼▼

COMMITMENT:
MAKING AND KEEPING ONE
WHEN IT'S RIGHT,
AND LETTING GO
WHEN IT'S WRONG

▼▼▼

If you never want to see a man again, say,
"I love you. I want to marry you.
I want to have your children . . ."
They leave skid marks.
COMEDIENNE RITA RUDNER

▼▼▼

Here's an idea for an interesting evening: Get a bunch of single people together, bring up the topic of "commitment," and watch the intense reactions. You'll notice most of the women get a kind of hungry look of longing on their faces, while the men will act as if you're torturing them by making them even talk about it. "The C Word," as I call it, seems to have that effect on people, evoking powerful emotions of hope and happiness, resistance and fear.

During the two years when I did my radio show in Los Angeles, I must have received thousands of phone calls about commitment:

▶ **"How do I know when I've been with my boyfriend long enough to expect a commitment?"**

▶ **"My girlfriend is pushing me to ask her to marry me, but I don't feel ready. How long should I wait?"**

▶ **"I've been married for two months, but I only knew my husband for six months before the wedding. We're having problems, and I wonder if we made a commitment too soon."**

So far, this section of the book has looked at the importance of chemistry and compatibility in choosing the right partner. Now it's time to add the third component, commitment.

▼

YOU AND YOUR PARTNER NEED THREE INGREDIENTS TO MAKE YOUR RELATIONSHIP WORK:

1. **CHEMISTRY**
2. **COMPATIBILITY**
3. **COMMITMENT**

▲

Without commitment, your relationship will be superficial and directionless. You and your partner won't be able to experience the depth of love and intimacy that can come only when you've truly committed yourselves to one another.

Here are some of the values of making a commitment in your relationship:

▶ **Commitment gives your relationship purpose.** A relationship without commitment is like a boat without a rudder in the ocean—it has no power of its own to seek a particular direction. It's at the whim of every current and every breeze. Commitment gives your relationship purpose and direction and thus allows it to move forward, rather than round and round in circles.

▶ **Commitment invests you in your relationship.** *The difference between being with someone without a commitment and with a commitment is the same as the difference between renting* *or buying a house.* Most people are much less careful and conscious about their treatment of an apartment or home when it is not theirs. All of that changes when you purchase your first house. Suddenly you notice every scratch and every stain. You watch your children, friends, or pets like a hawk to make sure they aren't spilling on, chipping, or damaging your precious property.

Once you fully commit to a partner, you treat your relationship differently because more of you is invested in it. This allows your relationship to grow and thrive in ways it cannot without that commitment.

▼

WHEN YOU MAKE A COMMITMENT TO A RELATIONSHIP, YOU INVEST YOUR ATTENTION AND ENERGY IN IT MORE PROFOUNDLY BECAUSE YOU NOW EXPERIENCE *OWNERSHIP* OF THAT RELATIONSHIP.

▲

▶ **Commitment creates emotional safety.** Can you imagine renting an apartment or office space without a lease? At any moment, your landlord would have the right to throw you out on the street. Imagine the kind of tension you would live with knowing his commitment to you was so tenuous. This is the same underlying tension that exists in relationships that have no commitment as their foundation. **You experience a lack of safety that produces a constant state of unconscious anxiety.** I'm not talking about dating someone for three months without a serious commitment. *I'm talking about being sexually and emotionally involved with someone over a significant period of time without receiving a commitment from that person as to his or her hopes or plans for the relationship.*

Naturally, commitment doesn't totally protect you from pain or loss, just as a lease doesn't protect you from being evicted, or from your landlord selling the building. But it does reflect your partner's **intentions,** and that gives you a level of emotional safety that allows you to relax in the relationship.

▶ **Commitment creates freedom.** Many people have negative associations with the word "commitment." Often, men, in particular, resist commitment because they identify it with *limitation and loss of freedom.* **I believe that commitment has the opposite effect:**

It frees you from expending your emotional energy in many different directions and allows you to focus it on one person. You're free to immerse yourself in the relationship, to love and give fully with no restraints. This creates an experience of letting go, of surrendering, not to your partner, but to love itself. This only becomes true, of course, when you are with the *right person.*

MAKING A COMMITMENT TO THE *RIGHT PERSON* WILL EMOTIONALLY LIBERATE YOU. MAKING A COMMITMENT TO THE *WRONG PERSON* WILL EMOTIONALLY IMPRISON YOU.

Why We Fear Making Commitments

Whenever people tell me their partner is afraid of making a commitment, I remind them that it's not the fear of commitment that's the problem, *but rather an unconscious, underlying fear.* I've found four basic fears that keep us from feeling comfortable making commitments:

COMMITMENT FEAR

▾   ▾   ▾   ▾   **1**   ▾   ▾   ▾   ▾

Fear of the Future

I've often heard men and women who are reluctant to commit to their partner claim that making a commitment would be a dishonest act. "How can I promise my girlfriend I will always love her?" a man will ask. "What if in ten years we grow apart, or what if she cheats on me and I leave her? Then I've broken my commitment."

With one of every two marriages ending in divorce, it's natural to experience a lack of confidence and certainty when committing to a partner. We live in an unpredictiable and sometimes frightening world. None of us knows what the future holds. The more aware you become of this fact, the less comfortable you might feel making commitments *if you think that commitment means promising someone how you'll feel and behave at a future date.*

My response is this:

I believe when we make a genuine commitment, it can only be *a commitment to fully loving our partner in each moment, and for so long as the relationship allows us to also love and respect ourselves,* rather than a commitment to the amount of time our love will last.

For instance, you can commit to a marriage and later discover that your partner isn't willing to work on the relationship, or to stop drinking or abusing you or your children. If you feel strongly about keeping your commitment, you'll find yourself in a terribly painful dilemma. "I promised to stay in this marriage," you tell yourself, "but I'm miserable." **On the other hand, if you're committed to the act of loving as long as it's healthy for you, you'll be able to end that relationship** *once you've done all you could to save it,* because *you're keeping a commitment you made to yourself.*

I'm *not* suggesting that the moment you experience a little discomfort, you should break your commitment. I'm saying that if you or your partner have been resisting making a more serious commitment to one another because of your fear of the future, you may want to redefine the meaning of commitment so it feels honest.

COMMITMENT FEAR

▼ ▼ ▼ ▼ **2** ▼ ▼ ▼ ▼

Fear of Being Hurt

Most people who have ever been divorced or gone through a major breakup tend to become somewhat "commitment phobic." After all, you have evidence that giving your heart totally to someone causes you pain and sorrow. As a recently wounded friend of mine put it, "Why would I want to volunteer for combat again after what I just went through?"

I can totally sympathize with this point of view, having been married and divorced not just once, but several times. (Premature commitment was one of my favorite pastimes!) However, one of the important lessons I learned along the way was:

▼

IT'S NOT FALLING IN LOVE OR MAKING A COMMITMENT THAT EVENTUALLY CAUSES US SO MUCH PAIN—IT'S MAKING A COMMITMENT TO THE *WRONG* PERSON.

▲

I hope you can understand the distinction here, because it's one of the most important points in this book. Avoiding commitment because you've been hurt emotionally is as unnecessary as if you decided you're never going to eat out again because you got food poisoning in one bad restaurant! Just choose your restaurants more carefully. And that's been my message throughout these chapters. When you make more intelligent love choices, relationships become a source of joy, not heartache.

In many ways, those of us who have made the biggest mistakes in love are in a much better position to make better choices the next time, *if we learn from our past and choose partners with whom we're truly compatible.* We know the cost of not paying attention to the problems in our relationship, or of not asking for what we want from our mate. So if you've been feeling handicapped by your past, why not change your attitude and consider yourself *extra qualified* to create successful relationships!

COMMITMENT FEAR

▼　　▼　　▼　　▼　　**3**　　▼　　▼　　▼　　▼

Fear of Choosing the Wrong Person

If you've ever been frightened of making commitments, you've probably had this awful fantasy:

You've been in a relationship for a while with someone you love very much, but have been afraid to make a commitment, worried that one day you'll meet someone "better" or with whom you're more compatible. You've put off making any decisions for a long time, and finally you decide that your paranoia is foolish, and you agree to marry your partner. You have a perfect wedding and a glorious honeymoon. Several weeks after you return, you're standing in a store, or at a meeting, and as you look across the room, your heart stops. Your eyes stare into those of someone you instantly know is your true soulmate. You fall in love on the spot. You always knew he was out there, just as you imagined him. You've never felt like this before. And then, all of a sudden, you gasp: **"Oh, my God," you think, "I'm married!"**

Am I the only one who has ever had this nightmare? From the research I've done, I don't think I'm alone. It's natural to worry when you're committing yourself to someone, hopefully for a lifetime. You wonder, if I just waited a little bit longer, would someone even more right come along? How can I be 100 percent sure that I'm not making a mistake? It's as if we all would like God to come down and say, in my case, **"Hi, Barbara. Listen, I know you've been wondering whether you should marry Jeffrey. Let me reassure you that he is indeed the one I had in mind for you, so trust me, you're not making a mistake. Feel better now? Good. Gotta run. Lots to do in heaven. Bye-bye."** Whew! Now that God told me I'm making the right choice, I can relax.

Unfortunately, we don't get that kind of supreme reassurance about our love choices. I believe that some degree of doubt is normal when you contemplate making a permanent commitment to a mate. *However, more than a little doubt may be a warning sign from your heart that you're not making the right choice.* Ultimately, only time will tell if your choice was correct. After all, it's not as if it's totally up to fate. **It's up to you to choose a compatible partner and commit to making the relationship work.**

If you're contemplating commitment but have serious concerns about your partner, make sure you read every chapter in this book *twice* and carefully do all the exercises. I've designed all the quizzes and checklists to alleviate as many of your doubts as possible and to give you hard evidence that'll determine whether you and your partner will be compatible.

COMMITMENT FEAR

▼ ▼ ▼ ▼ **4** ▼ ▼ ▼ ▼

Fear of Turning Out Like Your Parents

"I don't want to get married to my girlfriend," a man told me once. "Right now, our relationship is great. We have a wonderful time; we have great sex; we appreciate one another. If we get married, we'll end up just like my parents and every other married couple I see. We'll start picking on each other all the time; my girlfriend will get fat and I'll get out of shape; we'll take each other for granted. **I'm sorry, but I refuse to let marriage ruin my relationship!**"

Whenever I ask audiences how many of them would like to have a relationship just like their parents had, almost no one raises their hands, and most people burst into uncomfortable laughter. It's sad but true that few of us witnessed healthy and happy marriages while we were growing up. So it's natural for us to feel reticent about "settling down" with one person, even more so for children from divorced families. That phrase "settling down" itself sums up the less than positive view of marriage—it will bring us *down* rather than raising us up! Many people I've worked with feel:

COMMITMENT = BOREDOM, LOSS OF FREEDOM,
DRUDGERY, NO FUN, NO SEX

Part of the problem is that we've inherited *our parents' definition and picture of commitment* but haven't taken the time to redefine for ourselves what we want commitment to look like. Commitment, with or without marriage, doesn't automatically produce a set of predetermined experiences. *You* have the freedom to create the experiences and give the meanings you want to your relationship. *I feel it's important for any couple, whether they're considering commitment or are already committed, to take time to discuss what they want their commitment to mean and how they want their relationship to look.* Sometimes just doing this eradicates your concerns about making a long-term commitment and turns your fear into excitement!!

Are You Commitment-Hungry?

► Do you gaze with longing at bridal magazines, dreaming of the day when you'll be qualified to buy stacks of them?

► Do you mentally marry and have kids with each new man you meet, all within the first few minutes of meeting him?

► Do you dread checking the box marked "single" on applications and other forms?

► Do you secretly hate your friends who keep meeting nice, eligible men and getting married?

► Does the term "mother-in-law" actually turn you on?

If you answered yes to any of these questions, or remember when you would have, then you understand the term "commitment-hungry" firsthand. I hate to sound sexist, but I've found that women are "commitment-hungry" to a much larger extent than men, for obvious sociological reasons. (Read my book *Secrets About Men* for more clarification.) **When you're commitment-hungry, you're looking for a commitment rather than looking for a good relationship.**

Commitment-hungry people often end up making premature commitments, one of the big mistakes we make in the beginning of relationships. *They're so anxious to get a commitment from their partner that they pay little or no attention to the quality of the relationship itself.* All too often they wake up after they've moved in together or gotten married, and find themselves in a totally incompatible relationship.

I used to receive calls on the radio from commitment-hungry women all the time. I could tell within the first few minutes of the call that they were in this category:

"Dr. De Angelis, I need your help. I've been going with my boyfriend for seven months, and I really want to get married, but he says he's not ready. I'm twenty-one and he's twenty-two, and I really love him. I want to be engaged by next Christmas. Should I give him an ultimatum?"

My answer to people like this was always the same: **"What's the rush?** Why are you in such a hurry to become engaged or get married?" The question was really rhetorical, since I already knew the answer. **Commitment-hungry people (and I used to be one, so I know) have a deep need to belong to someone.** The key is that they are more concerned with the "belonging" part than with who the "someone" is. From the moment they get into a relationship, they push for commitment, often alienating their partners and actually prolonging the process. Sadly, many women in this category are trained to be commitment-hungry by their mothers, who were probably commitment-hungry themselves. You'd be suprised at how many young women in their late teens and early twenties feel pressured to find a man and get married.

Getting married before you have created a strong, mature, loving relationship is simply irresponsible, even more so if you decide to have children right away. All the excitement of being engaged will end. All the planning and preparation for the wedding and honeymoon will be over. And you will be left with what was underneath all that glamor and activity all along: an underdeveloped, immature relationship. This is why folk wisdom says, *"The first year of marriage is hell."* **The truth is that the first year and many more years of marriage are hell if you aren't ready to be married in the first place.** When you have built a solid foundation of communication, trust, and respect, the first year of marriage is *heaven.*

If you are commitment-hungry, work with the exercises in this book to understand more about yourself and your needs. *Take the time to fill yourself up from within.* Discover who you are and what your special contribution is as a human being. Stop pushing so hard, and instead focus on building the strongest, most loving relationship you can.

The Four Levels of Commitment

I was discussing the topic of commitment in one of my women's seminars last year when one of the course participants stood up and shared this story: It seems she met a very nice man and had been dating him for about two months. Things were heating up between them, and she decided that before she went any farther, she needed to know how he felt about the future of the relationship. One night, toward the end of their date, she told him that to continue seeing him and deepening their intimacy, she needed some kind of commitment.

"My partner got very quiet," she recalled, "and made some excuse about being too tired to get into a serious conversation. I figured that I caught him off guard and that we'd discuss it the next day. But the next day he didn't call, or the day after that, or even a week later. I called him and left messages, but he seemed to be ignoring me. At first I was hurt. Then I got really angry because I couldn't understand what had happened.

"I decided I couldn't stand not knowing anymore, so one day I waited for him outside his office. When he saw me, his face turned bright red. I told him I hadn't come to try to get him back but to find out why he ran away so fast.

" 'I really liked you,' he answered, 'but I just wasn't ready for marriage, not now, anyway. I need more time to get to know you. I guess I didn't know how to tell you that. I'm really sorry.'

"Marriage?" I exclaimed in shock. "Who said anything about marriage?

" 'Well, you did,' he responded with a puzzled look on his face. 'You told me you didn't want to go any farther without a commitment.'

"I couldn't believe my ears," she told all of us in the seminar. "All I wanted from him was an agreement that we stop seeing other people and be sexually monogamus. The poor guy thought I wanted a proposal!"

Many of us make the same mistake the woman's unfortunate date did: *We equate the word "commitment" with the word "marriage."* You meet someone and like them, and at a certain point feel you need to make some kind of commitment to solidify the relationship, so you ask yourself, "Would I ever want to marry this person?" If it's too soon to be able to answer that question, which it probably is, you become confused and wonder, "What do I do now?"

I've found there are **four basic levels of commitment a relationship passes through as it grows.** Here is a description of each one. I think you'll find them helpful in understanding your own relationships and knowing when it's time to move on to the next level:

COMMITMENT LEVEL

▼   ▼   ▼   ▼   **1**   ▼   ▼   ▼   ▼

Commitment to Be Sexually and Emotionally Monogamous

If you're single and dating, you'll probably spend some time getting to know a new partner. This period corresponds to the "new relationship" category in Chapter Ten. At some point, *within weeks and certainly by a few months,* you'll need some kind of commitment in order to go forward. This should be a commitment to be sexually and emotionally monogamous.

▼

COMMITMENT LEVEL 1 AGREEMENTS:

▶ You and your partner agree that this is your **one and only intimate relationship,** and commit to putting your time and energy into sharing with one another and no one else.

▶ You and your partner agree that you are each other's **only sexual partners** ("sex" meaning everything from kissing to intercourse—whatever level you are participating in), and you agree to the sexual guidelines I discussed on page 116.

▲

If your partner refuses to make a Level 1 Commitment, I strongly urge you to say good-bye right then and there. **Your relationship will not be able to grow without monogamy, and if your partner doesn't respect and value you enough to offer you that commitment, he's not worth waiting for.**

COMMITMENT LEVEL

▼ ▼ ▼ ▼ *2* ▼ ▼ ▼ ▼

Commitment to Work Towards a Partnership

Once you and your partner are monogamously dating, you'll probably spend several more months deepening your knowledge of one another and testing your compatibility. This correlates with what we called a developing relationship in Chapter Ten. When you feel . . .

▶ your relationship is getting better and better
▶ you're sharing most aspects of your time and life together
▶ you're starting to think as "we"

. . . then you're ready for a Level 2 Commitment: working towards a partnership. **This means you acknowledge that you've become a couple, an entity within yourselves.** (When I was young, we used to call this "going steady.")

▼

COMMITMENT LEVEL 2 AGREEMENTS:

▶ You and your partner agree that **your relationship is special and worth nurturing.**

▶ You and your partner agree that your relationship has **the potential to be a lasting partnership.**

▶ You and your partner agree to work together, honestly communicating feelings, looking at your own blocks to intimacy, and learning to understand one another **in order to create that potential lasting partnership.**

▲

It's during this developing stage of relationships that a lot of us make the mistake of **not** getting a Level 2 Commitment. You assume you partner seeks a possible future with you—otherwise why would he be saying he loves you and spending all that time with you? You don't actually talk about your assumptions, and one day, months later, your heart gets broken when you bring up marriage or some-thing comparable and he responds by saying, *"I never said we would have a future together. I don't love you that way."*

DON'T STAY IN A DEVELOPING RELATIONSHIP FOR MORE THAN FOUR TO SIX MONTHS WITHOUT GETTING A LEVEL TWO COMMITMENT.

COMMITMENT LEVEL

▼   ▼   ▼   ▼   *3*   ▼   ▼   ▼   ▼

Commitment to Spend Your Future Together

Once you've agreed to work on creating a partnership together, you could spend six months to several years building that partner-ship, depending on how old you both are and the circumstances surrounding your relationship. **My advice is: The younger you are, the more time you should spend before agreeing to a Level 3 Commitment.** If you're in your early twenties, you proba-bly need several years of learning relationship skills and emotional maturity to give your love a strong foundation. If you're in your thirties, have had serious relationships, and are very clear about who you are and what you want, you may not need (or want to spend) this much time developing a partnership, and may be ready to commit to a future together within the first year. Each case will be different.

You're ready to make a Level 3 Commitment when:

▶ You've created a strong and healthy partnership that's functioning well almost all the time.

▶ You feel sure that you want to spend your future together, if not the rest of your life.

▶ You have no desire to investigate anyone else as a possible partner.

▶ You feel totally loved and appreciated by your partner almost all the time.

▼
COMMITMENT LEVEL 3 AGREEMENTS:

▶ You and your partner agree that **you want to spend your future together.**

▶ You and your partner agree to **formalize your commitment** by either
   1. becoming engaged to be married
   2. planning on becoming engaged as soon as you can
   3. deciding to live together

▶ You and your partner agree to continue working on yourselves and the relationship **to eliminate any remaining doubts or obstacles to a successful lifetime commitment.**

▲

You've probably noticed that a Level 3 Commitment is an agreement to spend the foreseeable future together, but not the indefinite future, as in forever. *You know you want to spend your life together, but for various reasons you aren't totally ready to formalize that desire (that would be a Level 4 Commitment).*

Making a Level 3 Commitment will look different from couple to couple, depending on how traditional or nontraditional your values are and on the circumstances surrounding your relationship. Here are some examples of couples and their Level 3 Commitments.

ANNIE AND CHRIS—BECOMING ENGAGED

Annie, twenty-nine, and Chris, thirty-one, have known each other for eighteen months. Neither of them has ever been married before, and both work at careers they enjoy. They've spent the past year sharing each other's lives, getting to know each other's families, and talking about the future they each want for themselves. From all this work they've created a strong, loving partnership that both want to maintain for the rest of their lives. Even though they've discussed marriage, they've never made any concrete decisions. So Chris decided to formally propose to Annie and they became officially engaged. They planned their wedding for a year later, giving them time to strengthen their bond further before they make that Level 4 Commitment.

Chris and Annie are both fairly traditional in their values. They decided not to live together until after the wedding, although they spend many nights at each other's apartment. **An engagement was the perfect Level 3 Commitment for them.**

JOAN AND KEITH—DECIDING TO LIVE TOGETHER

Joan, thirty-six, and Keith, thirty-eight, have been together for two and a half years. Joan has been married once before (no children), and both Joan and Keith's parents were divorced, so from the beginning they've worked very hard to communicate honestly and create the kind of relationship they both hope is possible. Their union is strong and healthy, and they know it's time to take it to a new level. Neither of them, however, is ready to get married. Joan has no plans to have children in the near future, possibly never, and *questions whether becoming legally married is the form she'd like her relationship to take. Keith agrees, and although he can't imagine his future without Joan, he knows he's still working through his negative views about marriage.* **After discussing their feelings, they decide to move in together.** This represents a powerful new commitment for them both, and a preparation for the next level of love.

Joan and Keith are not a traditional couple; therefore, becoming engaged doesn't contribute as much to their relationship as living together will. They're both comfortable with this option, since it serves two purposes:

▶ **It gives them a higher level of commitment.**

▶ **It gives them time to live together domestically and heal their fears and concerns about marriage or a similar arrangement.**

The Pros and Cons of Living Together Outside of Marriage

It would be remiss of me to talk about commitment levels without discussing living together. In the past few decades, millions of couples of all ages have chosen to live together, either as a prelude to marriage or in place of marriage. **Note:** *If you have strong judgments about living together due to your religious or moral beliefs, please understand that I'm looking at this issue purely from a psychological point of view.* For the rest of you, I feel it's important to understand both the positive and the negative consequences of living with someone you love.

THE CASE FOR LIVING TOGETHER

There is a part of me that feels, after having seen so many dysfunctional and incompatible relationships over the years, that all couples should live together before deciding to get married. I wonder how many unhealthy relationships would have ended if the two partners had tried being together twenty-four hours a day and come face to face with the issues they were avoiding by seeing each other only on weekends or a few nights a week.

Here are some of the benefits of living together:

▶ **You discover sides of your partner's personality you cannot know about unless you live together.** There is no way you can get to know a person whom you see intermittently as well as if you lived together. It's a lot easier for someone to be on his best behavior for three hours during a date than it is for him to maintain that behavior day after day when you live under the same roof. When you live with someone you uncover habits, attitudes, and behaviors you never see otherwise. You see him in his natural habitat, his home, and thus become exposed to sides of his personality that may be hidden from you if you're just dating. You see him when he's tired, sick, angry, frustrated, and grumpy. *Living together requires a sharing of power and control; it demands compromise and flexibility from both partners.* **You get exposure to the full range of his emotional reactions.**

I've heard so many nightmare stories about people marrying, and once they've moved in together, discovering things about their mate that are unacceptable. Marriage is tough enough without any unpleasant surprises.

▶ **You discover more about whether your life-styles are truly compatible.** Some men make great lovers in a romantic affair, but lousy husbands. Some women are fantastic part-time companions but terrible full-time wives. *You may enjoy loving someone but hate living with him.* The qualities that encourage you to fall in love with someone and have a great time seeing him may not be enough to create day-to-day harmony once you move in together. You may find out your partner's life-style doesn't fit with yours, something you'd never know unless you shared the same living space over a long period of time.

▶ **You discover how capable your partner is of true partnership.** Living together requires a sharing of power and control; it demands compromise and flexibility from both partners, since you're merging the habits and desires of two unique individuals. You may not find out how willing or capable your mate is of true partnership until you commit to living together. **Only when you have to make decisions together about finances, food, household responsibilities, acquisitions, etc., do you truly discover what kind of team player your partner is.**

THE CASE AGAINST LIVING TOGETHER

Here are some possible negative consequences of living together:

▶ **You can destroy the relationship by expecting too much from it when it's still developing.** Although I personally feel living together with a mate can be a valuable experience at a certain stage of the relationship, I also feel that *living together prematurely is a big mistake.* I've counseled too many couples who moved in together for the wrong reasons:

▶ to save money
▶ because one had a nicer place
▶ so they could spend more time together
▶ because one partner was afraid of losing the other

LIVING TOGETHER BEFORE YOUR RELATIONSHIP HAS REACHED A SIGNIFICANT LEVEL OF COMMITMENT, MATURITY, AND EMOTIONAL STABILITY CAN ACTUALLY SPEED UP THE DISINTEGRATION OF THE RELATIONSHIP.

If your relationship isn't ready to handle the pressures of living together, it might fall apart under the strain brought about by living together prematurely.

▶ **You can become emotionally lazy.** If moving in with someone feels like a goal to you, and you live together before you're ready, you risk becoming emotionally lazy in the relationship. You may avoid conflict in order to keep the peace, especially if you haven't learned to work through conflict together. You may give your partner less attention and appreciation since he or she is there all the time, or neglect the relationship in other ways.

YOUR LIVING ARRANGEMENT IS NOT YOUR RELATIONSHIP—IT'S ONLY ONE EXPRESSION OF YOUR RELATIONSHIP.

One of the most common mistakes couples make is becoming emotionally lazy, but this is even more of a risk for couples who live together before they've established a strong emotional bond.

▶ **You can avoid furthering your commitment to one another.** You may have heard the saying, *"Why buy the cow when you can get the milk free?"* I think it was used by many of our mothers in their attempt to convince us that boys wouldn't marry us if we had sex with them, since they were already getting what they wanted. I've heard this same argument about living together—**that if a man is living with you and enjoying the benefits of domestic life, he has no reason to ask you to marry him.** I have to agree that in some cases this may be true, especially if you haven't received a Level 3 Commitment before you move in together, and if you haven't known one another for a good length of time. *Some commitment-phobic men (or women) might hide behind living together to experience the intimacy they crave but also to avoid making the final commitment of marriage.*

I don't believe the solution is to refuse to move in with someone before you're engaged or married, unless that feels right to you. *If you're considering living with someone but want the formal structure of marriage somewhere down the road, you need to discuss all this before you actually move in together in order to avoid any misunderstandings. You may want to come up with a time projection—nine months or a year, for instance—at which point you'll reevaluate your relationship and decide whether you feel ready to marry.*

COMMITMENT LEVEL

▼　　▼　　▼　　▼　 **4** 　▼　　▼　　▼　　▼

Commitment to Spend the Rest of Your Lives Together

You are ready for a Level 4 Commitment when:

► You've had a Level 3 Commitment for some time (engaged, living together, etc.) and *have worked through whatever obstacles or emotional issues were in your way.*

► You have total trust and faith in your relationship and its ability to continue to grow and survive whatever adversity it faces.

► You feel excited about exploring deeper levels of love, intimacy, and surrender with your partner.

▼
COMMITMENT LEVEL 4 AGREEMENTS:

► You and your partner agree that you want to spend the rest of your lives together.

► You and your partner agree that as lifelong mates, your relationship becomes your creation, your "child," **and you will cherish, protect, and nurture that child called your partnership.**

► You and your partner agree to any other commitments you both feel are important to inaugurate your new level of oneness.
▲

For most people, a Level 4 Commitment is expressed by becoming legally married. For others who are less traditional, it may be expressed in a nonlegal ceremony, or in another private way in which they consecrate their relationship. Whatever form it takes, a Level 4 Commitment is the highest form of commitment you can make to another person.

The Real Meaning of Marriage

I believe strongly that it's not a wedding ceremony or a license that creates true commitment. **Marriage is not a piece of paper.** It's not wearing a ring or collecting photo albums of your vacations. It's not saying, "We've been married for twenty-five years."

▼

MARRIAGE IS A WAY OF LOVING, HONORING, AND CELEBRATING YOUR PARTNER DAY BY DAY AS AN EXPRESSION OF YOUR COMMITMENT TO ONE ANOTHER.

▲

In this way, marriage is an active, participatory process, not a static state. You aren't married because you had a big party, or because you sent in twenty-five dollars to the county, or because everyone thinks you are. *You are truly married when you and your partner resonate together mentally, emotionally, physically, and spiritually.* **I believe that the real act of marriage takes place in the heart, not in a church or synagogue or hotel ballroom. It is a choice you make, not just on one special day but over and over again, and that choice is reflected in the way you treat your partner.**

When a woman calls me on the radio, or writes me a letter and tells me she's been married for twenty years and is miserable because her husband is abusive, won't talk to her about their problems, cheats on her, or drinks and treats her like dirt, but she doesn't want to leave and "break up the marriage," I always respond in the same way: *"You don't have a marriage—you have a living arrangement."*

A marriage is a partnership, a union, not a battleground. **The moment you stop treating one another with love and respect, your marriage ceases to exist. Once you start living with anger and distrust of your partner, he is no longer your husband.** You may be living together, but you are not married. You may wait years to finally end the relationship, but *you were emotionally divorced when you closed your hearts to each other.*

I find that so many young people live with the dangerous misconception that when they get married, something wonderful will happen to the relationship. "When we finally get married, I know things will get better," they tell themselves. **I feel that deciding to marry invites a certain kind of spiritual acceleration or intensity into your life. Marriage becomes like a big**

magnifying glass—it will amplify or exaggerate whatever conditions existed before the marriage took place. If you have a fabulous relationship, marriage will make it better. If you have a rocky relationship, marriage will make it even more turbulent. Whatever problems you had before will seem more disturbing afterward. Whatever strengths you had will appear more substantial.

How do you know when you are ready to get married? Aside from encouraging you to work with all the checklists I've given you, I suggest you ask yourself:

"Do I feel married to my partner right now?"

If you already feel that oneness and resonance in your hearts, *then marriage becomes a celebration and consecration of the connection you have already worked hard to create.* Your wedding formalizes that celebration, but the state of marriage already exists between the two of you.

I don't believe anyone has the power to marry you any more than you already are. I *do* believe that offering your marriage to God or a Higher Intelligence for blessing is tremendously empowering. It's a way of honoring your Source for the gift of love you've found in one another, and asking for continued clarity and vision so you can expand that gift.

Naturally, your own beliefs are what's important. I wanted to share my thoughts with you since, over the years, people have told me my ideas have helped them clarify their views on marriage.

ANSWERS TO YOUR QUESTIONS ABOUT COMMITMENT

Here are some of the most common questions I'm asked about commitment, and my answers:

► "How can I tell if someone has a problem with commitment?"

You know by now that I strongly believe most relationship problems are surprises only because we didn't pay attention to warning signs along the way. Therefore, the best way to spot a commitment-phobic person is to follow the commitment-level guidelines in this chapter. *That means you should ask your partner how he feels about commitment during the new relationship stage, and pay attention to his answers!* Then make sure to get the appropriate commitments for each level as time passes. ***Don't avoid discussing it. Don't put it off.***

If your partner resists making the commitment you need and refuses to work toward it, it's up to you to end the relationship. **If he's really frightened of commitment and thinks he can get away with staying with you without making one, he will.** You need to honor your own needs and standards and stick to what you know is right.

> ► **"My partner says he wants to make a serious commitment to our relationship and our future but that he's 'not ready.' What does that mean? Is he just making excuses?"**

Your partner is telling the truth when he says he's not ready to make a commitment. The question you need to ask him is, *"Why aren't you ready?"* **If he doesn't know the reasons he's resisting becoming more involved, he can't do anything to improve or heal the situation.** His saying, "I don't know what it is" shouldn't be an acceptable answer to you. Your response should be, "Well, if you want to keep seeing me, find out!" Otherwise you can go for months and years living in emotional limbo while you wait for him suddenly to wake up one morning and discover that his fear of commitment is gone.

It's scary for someone to look at his or her emotional programming and old hurts. Let your mate know you understand his discomfort but that you also value yourself and your emotions too much to stay in a relationship indefinitely without knowing the direction it's taking.

Take some time to think about the circumstances in your partner's life. Are there genuine problems that prevent him from being ready to commit, such as a messy divorce he's just recovering from, or financial pressure he's under? Discuss these with him.

Another important step you need to take is asking your partner *when* he thinks he might be ready, and what it will take to get him ready. You have a right to know what kind of time period he's talking about. Ask him to do this revealing exercise—it might help him get in touch with his own feelings about commitment:

I'll be ready to make a serious commitment/get married when _____.

This is a fill-in-the-blank exercise. The person taking it should repeat the sentence at least ten times. Example:

I'll be ready to make a serious commitment/get married when:

► I own my own home
► I have $50,000 in the bank
► I'm thirty years old
► I never feel turned off by my partner
► I see an example of a happy marriage

► **"I've told my partner I need a commitment from him and he told me he's 'working on it.' How long should I wait?"**

That depends on what "working on it" means. For some people it means, "I'll tell you I'm working on it to get you off my back and buy some time." For others it might mean he is seriously examining his emotional programming in order to understand his fear of commitment. **You need to ask your partner what he means by "working on it."** Ask him HOW he is working on it. Is he going to therapy, reading books, attending a men's group, talking to other married men? **WHAT SPECIFIC, CONCRETE ACTION IS HE TAKING TO WORK ON IT?**

Don't just accept "I'm working on it" as an answer. You'll feel a lot better staying in the relationship while he's working on it if you know what that means. There's nothing wrong with a person confronting his fears of intimacy. In fact, it's healthier and more honest than someone who blindly throws himself into a relationship and then later puts up emotional walls. So support your partner in his self-analysis, *but make sure you're somehow included in the process and that you're kept informed of his progress.*

Make sure, however, that you're not looking for a premature commitment. For instance, *if you've only known one another a short while and are anxious to get engaged or married, you, not he, may be the one with the problem.* Reread the sections on premature commitment.

► **"My partner keeps promising me he'll buy me an engagement ring soon, but it never happens. Should I give him an ultimatum?"**

I don't know about you, but I wouldn't feel too thrilled accepting an engagement ring from a man I pressured to propose to me. What's the point? The real issues are: Why is he resisting, and what are his concerns? *Forcing him to buy you a ring is manipulative and childish.* You should be more concerned with solving the problems in the relationship. **On the other hand, if he cannot get clear on these issues and will not talk about why, you need to accept the fact that this relationship is not what you hoped it would be, and move on.**

I do believe in giving ultimatums when necessary, but only after you've exhausted all other possibilities. For instance, if you've known someone a few months and he's been frequently late in picking you up, you wouldn't say, *"If you're ever late again, don't bother coming over."* That's a very controlling form of behavior. On the other hand, if after a year of dating, your partner is still chronically irresponsible, you can say, *"If you don't agree to get some professional counseling starting within the next few weeks, I don't want to continue this relationship."*

Notice how specific that ultimatum was. The more specific you are when giving an ultimatum, the better your results will be. The other person knows what you expect of him, and will have an easier time complying with your demand. For example:

"If we don't get married soon, I'm leaving" (WRONG WAY).

"I need you to agree to go with me to a counselor to talk about why you won't set a wedding date, and I need you to do this within the next two weeks; if you won't, then I have to leave" (RIGHT WAY).

Ultimatums can be useful in waking us up to areas we've been in denial about, or forcing us to stop procrastinating about something we've been avoiding. But like any powerful tool, they need to be used sparingly and with sensitivity.

▶ **"How do I handle my relationships if I know I'm not ready for any kind of serious commitment? I'm only twenty-two and don't want to get married for a long time."**

If you are just interested in dating and learning more about yourself and people, you can be a lot more flexible with regard to how compatible you are with partners. Whereas a 70 percent compatible relationship might be unhealthy for someone who was ready for a long-term commitment, it would be perfectly acceptable for a young person enjoying himself or herself. It's still important, however, to pay attention to all the things we've talked about in the book so you don't get hurt and build emotional walls. **You don't need to be in ideal relationships, but you shouldn't stay in bad ones either.**

▶ **"I'm in love with two people at the same time. Is it possible to be committed to them both?"**

I could spend hours answering this question, but here's the short version:

AFFAIRS DON'T WORK. THEY END UP HURTING EVERYONE.

You may feel you're getting different needs met from each partner, but you aren't being fair to either one, even if they claim your other relationship doesn't bother them. *Don't use an affair to fill the holes in your primary relationship.*

If you're in love with two people, you need to take a serious look at what you want and need from a partner. **Use the tools I've given you in this book to make a choice.** Until you commit to one person, you won't be able to truly experience healthy love with either of them.

▶ **"It seems like my partner and I have been stuck between Commitment Levels 3 and 4 for a long time. We love one another and know we want to be together, but we're both scared of getting married. Will we be stuck here forever?"**

Some people have no problem making the transition from knowing they want a future together to actually doing something about it, while others struggle with their fears and doubts. *This might be especially true if you or your parents were divorced, or if you've been hurt very badly in the past.* **Rather than just waiting for the fears to clear, confront them head on.** Make a list of your fears and share them with your partner. Talk honestly about each one, together or with the help of a counselor. Work on understanding the real source of those fears. If they are largely due to your old emotional programming, they may not disappear until you actually take the plunge and make the commitment. If they are due to other factors, making concrete changes in your relationship will help. **You need to find a balance between a) ignoring your fears and blindly plunging ahead, and b) giving your fears so much power that they immobilize you.**

HOW TO KNOW WHEN TO BREAK YOUR COMMITMENT AND END A RELATIONSHIP

One of the most painful things in life is admitting to yourself that the relationship you're in isn't working and that it's time to leave. You wish you could go to sleep, wake up the next morning, and have everything be different, but you can't. You wish your partner would magically become the person you want him to be, but he won't. You know you've put off making the decision long enough and that it's time to say good-bye.

I believe that you should do everything in your power to salvage a troubled relationship. That includes using all possible sources of outside help, including *professional counseling, seminars, books, support groups, recovery programs, etc.* However, you may reach a point at which you feel you cannot or do not want to continue with your partner, and at that point you need to decide to stay or to go.

It's time to end your relationship when:

▶ **You realize you are incompatible.** If there's one thing you should understand after reading this book, it's that you and your partner must be compatible for your relationship to work. *If you aren't, your love alone will not be enough to overcome the inevitable problems. Only when you have found a new, compatible relationship will you realize how right you were to leave the incompatible one behind.*

▶ **You realize you have no sexual chemistry between you.** If, after reading this book, you recognize that you and your partner don't have enough chemistry to make your love more than a good friendship, you need to set both yourself and your partner free to find a complete union with a more suitable mate.

▶ **You and your partner have grown in two different directions.** I strongly believe that we often come together with a mate for a certain length of time in order to be each other's teachers, and when we have learned the necessary lessons, we need to go on. You and your partner may have grown tremendously in your years together, and given each other great emotional gifts. *However, you may have arrived at what I call the Divided Path, a point at which you are destined to travel in different directions.*

When your goals and styles of growing are too different, it will no longer be healthy or emotionally fulfilling for you to stay together.

The hardest part about reaching the Divided Path is that your love for your partner may not have changed, and that makes it even more difficult to say good-bye. I know, because I've arrived at the divided path several times in my life. All I can say to reassure you is that each time, my new path brought me greater happiness, wisdom, and love than I had ever known before.

▶ **Your partner has a Fatal Flaw he will not deal with.** There are millions of men and women who have had the heartbreaking experience of having to leave someone they loved because that person refused to face his or her own Fatal Flaws. We've seen how toxic Fatal Flaws are, whether it's alcoholism, drug abuse, addiction to pornography, or rage. **As I mentioned in Chapter Six, if your partner will not seek help in battling his problem, or is in total denial that he even has a problem, you have no healthy choice but to end the relationship.**

▶ **Your partner refuses to work on your relationship.** This is perhaps the saddest reason of all you may have to end a partnership, and the biggest waste. **If your partner refuses to face or discuss your problems and will not agree to any outside help in solving your conflicts, he has broken his commitment to your relationship as much as if he had an affair.** He may be scared; he may have had an abusive childhood; he may have a wonderful, loving heart somewhere inside him. *The fact remains that unless he's willing to be an **active participant** in your partnership, there is no partnership, and you must leave.*

If you're presently struggling with making the painful decision of whether to stay or leave, I hope the information in this book has helped you feel more certain about your choice, and given you confidence that, although it's not easy, you're doing the right thing.

PRACTICING RECOMMITMENT IN YOUR RELATIONSHIP

Some of the nicest requests I ever get are from couples who have been through my *Making Love Work seminars* and ask me to perform a remarriage or recommitment ceremony for them. Often I'll hear statements such as:

▶ "We've been married for fifteen years, but until we worked with you, we never really understood what commitment meant. Now we realize we've never really been married the way we want to be, so we need to have a new ceremony."

▶ "My husband and I were so emotionally shut down to one another and to ourselves that marriage was something we were doing because it was expected of us. We feel so much in love now, and really want to get married again because now we *feel* married."

I feel that practicing regular recommitment is an important part of any growing relationship. It reminds you of your agreements with one another and offers you an opportunity to make new ones. It helps you remember the true meaning of marriage as a continually renewing experience. *Yearly anniversaries are a perfect time to recommit to your partner.* Instead of just buying cards or going out to dinner, why not really honor your relationship by committing to him or her for another year? Remarriage or recommitment ceremonies are also wonderful events to share with your friends, family, and children. By demonstrating your love to one another, you are setting a wonderful example for others to aspire toward.

Whether you've just transformed your relationship into one that's more loving and want to celebrate it, or have survived hard times together and want a fresh start, or simply like the idea of regular renewal, recommitment as a ritual will add a new dimension of joy and intimacy to your partnership.

LIVING YOUR COMMITMENT

The other day I asked a group of people I was working with to share their definitions of commitment. The first few answers were what I expected: "giving 100 percent"; "surrendering"; "being there completely." Then a man stood up and told me if I really wanted to understand commitment, I should think about ham and eggs.

"Ham and eggs?" I asked.

"Yep, ham and eggs," he replied with a sly smile. **"Here's the difference between involvement and commitment: The chicken is involved, but the pig is committed!"**

After I finished laughing, I had to admit that he had a point. Many of us think we're committed to our partners, but we only give them pieces of ourself and our love periodically, like a chicken offering its most recent egg. True commitment isn't expressed in an occasional "I love you" or anniversary card. *Rather, it's a constant awareness of a sacred process you and your partner have entered into together to experience the highest joys and lessons that love has to offer.* This high commitment is reflected in every moment of your relationship, in the way you listen to one another, the way you touch, the way you give, and the way you receive. It transforms mere partnership into union and fills your every action with meaning. When you have the privilege of making this kind of complete commitment, you have truly given yourself a wondrous gift.

12

▼▼▼

THE ADVENTURE
OF LOVE

▼▼▼

I've always believed that reading a book on personal growth is like taking an exciting adventure with the author as your guide. The moment you open the book and read the first page, it's as if the writer reaches out her hand and says, "Come, let me share my vision with you and show you new ways of seeing life and seeing yourself. If you allow me to be your guide, I'll open doors to feelings and understandings you've never experienced before. I know the journey might be a little frightening at times, because I've taken it, too, but I promise to make it as safe as possible. I'll be right beside you the whole way." And as you turn each page, your fear of what you might discover about yourself becomes relief as you realize that you don't have to make the same mistakes you've made before. And suddenly you become excited about how many more choices you have than you ever thought you did.

Are You the One for Me? is meant to be just this kind of journey, and I hope it's been a rewarding one for you. I know that learning about your Love Myths, emotional programming, and all the wrong reasons to choose partners doesn't always feel good in the moment, but it empowers you by giving you the freedom to do things differently. So be proud of yourself for your willingness to grow, and find your highest dreams of love again. Trust your new ability, with the Compatibility Formula and the other tools you've received, to know when it's right, and create the partnership you've always dreamed of.

The adventure of this book is almost finished, but now, with all you've learned, an even more important journey awaits you, my favorite adventure—The Adventure of Love; for of all the exciting places we could visit, and exotic paths we could travel, love is the greatest adventure of all. The majestic sights it will reveal to us are not without, but within. It shows us the wonders of the heart and the magnificence of our ability to feel. It opens our eyes to the truth about who we are and who we are meant to be. As we allow love to touch us, it touches our very spirit, and we are blessed. It is a journey that, when taken, totally transforms us so that we will never be the same again.

Like all great expeditions, The Adventure of Love requires great emotional courage. It demands that you risk and change and grow, and just when you think you can rest, it demands that you grow some more. But through that growth you are rewarded with the experience of being fully and magnificently alive. *You feel more than you ever have before, and thus you become more than you have ever been before.*

The farther and deeper you go into your love adventure, the clearer it becomes that your true destination is not at some point in the future but is here and now, and that the goal is not to arrive somewhere but to be fully present where you already are. *You come to understand that loving isn't something you do to get a result— it's an action that, in itself, fills you with joy and therefore fulfills its own purpose at each moment.*

When you are traveling with someone who isn't right for you, the journey of love may take you down many difficult paths and offer you many painful lessons. **Only when you've found the right partner for your traveling companion will your journey, though always challenging, become one that truly brings you happiness. And only with the right partner can you use your relationship not to "fall in love" but to "ascend in love."** I believe, after all, that The Adventure of Love, in its highest form, helps us pierce the illusion of our aloneness in the world by offering us an opportunity to transcend the limits of our single self and experience a merging of selves, or oneness, with our beloved. *In this way, love is a doorway into the divine.* So choose your traveling companion with great care, since it is into his or her eyes that you will be gazing to catch a glimpse of God.

Thank you for allowing me to travel with you for a while. I wish you love and peace on your journey.

REAL

MOMENTS

✦

Barbara De Angelis, Ph.D.

This book is dedicated with love and gratitude
to my beloved husband,
Jeffrey James,
for blessing my days and nights with real moments
and helping me discover Heaven here on Earth,

and to my precious animal companion,
Bijou,
for being the embodiment of love and loyalty,
and for patiently teaching me how to walk slowly, play often,
and always be right here, right now. . . .

Acknowledgments

I would like to express my love and gratitude to the following people:

First, to my dear friend and literary agent, Harvey Klinger, for understanding why *Real Moments* needed to be written: Thank you for standing behind my vision, for supporting me in spreading my wings and flying to new heights.

To my publisher, Carole Baron: Thank you for your tremendous patience while I readied myself to write this book, and for your trust in my words and the message they contain. You continue to give me an opportunity to touch the hearts and souls of millions of people, and for that I am deeply grateful.

To Linda Riddle and Diana Soto, the directors of my companies: Thank you for letting me disappear for three months while I wrote this book, and for your phenomenal dedication to spreading our message of love and transformation.

To my personal assistant, Martha Cole, without whom I couldn't have finished this book in such a short time: Thank you for keeping the world out, keeping my life running, keeping me energized with your warm smiles and generous enthusiasm, and keeping me sane during some of the busiest months of my life. You have been my own personal angel.

To Mike Warren and Don Davidson of Inphomation, Incorporated: Thank you for believing in me and my work, and for giving me the tremendous opportunity to transform the lives of so many individuals and families through my television infomercial.

To Philip Saltonstall, for taking such a wonderful photograph of me for my book cover. Thank you for understanding why I wanted to shoot the cover in Sedona, Arizona, and for finding such a powerful and breathtaking spot to capture a real moment.

To Dottie Webster: Thank you for allowing Jeffrey and me to enjoy the solitude and sanctity of your home in Sedona so that I could write the last section of this book with a rested body and an inspired spirit.

To Elaine Reyna, my sister, my teacher, my friend: Thank you for your tender love and gentle guidance as I rediscover the ways of the Earth. Thank you for the gift of my name and for seeing who I really am. May our spirits always soar side by side.

And most of all, to my husband, Jeffrey: Thank you for respecting the silent inner journey I needed to take to write *Real Moments,* and for surrounding me with so much love that I felt safe to go deeper than I have ever gone before. Thank you for honoring my new direction and for always traveling by my side. Thank you for crying at all the right places when you read each chapter. Thank you for making me your bride. You are my greatest blessing.

Contents

Part Three
◆
REAL MOMENTS AND RELATIONSHIPS

Part Four
◆
THE PATH TO REAL MOMENTS
TOOLS FOR CREATING MORE LOVE
AND MEANING IN YOUR LIFE

Introduction

I wrote this book because I needed its lessons and reminders for myself. I wrote it because my life, like so many lives, needs more real moments. I wrote it because, as an author, I know that my most powerful path of self-discovery has always been to become silent, to listen to the silence, to write what I hear, and to know that the words which come through me onto the page are meant first for me to learn from, and then, for others to enjoy if they wish.

There are times in our lives that are ripe for reflection and transformation, and this is one of those times for me. Over the past few years, I have achieved much of the success I've always wanted. I've found the relationship I always dreamed of. I've created a rich and wonderful life. And yet, when I would ask myself, "Barbara, are you happy?" I found I did not know the answer. Friends would call to congratulate me on my accomplishments or my marriage, and say "You must *really* be happy *now*," and for days afterward, I would be haunted by their comments. I knew I *should* be happy with so much goodness in my life, but I suspected that I was not.

It was then I began to understand that what was missing from my life were more "real moments," moments when I was not trying to get somewhere or be something, moments when

I was fully experiencing and enjoying where I was, now. I had become very good at *doing*, but wasn't very good at just *being*, and of course that included *being* happy.

As I shared my secret handicap with friends and acquaintances, I realized that I was far from alone in my experience. "I'm writing a new book called *Real Moments*," I'd tell them. And everyone would respond in the same way: "Boy, do I need to read that!" I started seeing that I was not the only one standing at an emotional and spiritual crossroads in my life, that many of us are at that same crossroads, looking back on the life we have been living, questioning its meaning, questioning the choices we have made, searching for answers that will give us peace.

I believe too that, as a nation, America *itself* is in the midst of spiritual crisis, desperately trying to discover and define new values as it becomes apparent, in these violent and often frightening times, that the old values have somehow led us away from the very harmony and contentment our forefathers came here seeking. As we approach the twenty-first century, we are all, collectively, and alone, searching for more real moments.

In this book, I invite you to ask yourself the same questions I have been asking myself as I've stood at my crossroads:

"Am I happy?"
"What have I *really* been doing here?"
"Am I doing what I came here to do?"
"Do I have enough real moments in my life?"

I'll be honest with you—these are not always easy questions to confront. It takes courage to ask them, and often, even more courage to be willing to hear the answers that will emerge from your own heart. But your efforts will be rewarded by the new levels of love, peace, and revelation you will experience daily.

In the process of answering these same questions, I have discovered new and liberating truths about myself, and made powerful changes in my life, some quiet and invisible, and some quite dramatic. But the greatest change of all is that I am having many real moments now. More and more each day, I am discovering the peace I was searching for, and beginning to understand and experience what true happiness really is.

So even though this writing has been first for me, I offer it, in love, to you. My hope is that by sharing it with you, my fellow traveler, I will have enriched your journey toward your own real moments.

Barbara De Angelis
February 1, 1994
Los Angeles, California

Part One

THE HUNGRY HEART

Searching
for Real Moments

◆

· 1 ·

YOUR QUEST FOR HAPPINESS

"First I was dying to finish high school and start college.
And then I was dying to finish college and start working.
And then I was dying to marry and have children.
And then I was dying for my children to grow old enough for
  school so I could return to work.
And then I was dying to retire.
And now, I am dying . . . and suddenly I realize I forgot to live."

—ANONYMOUS

This is a book about the real moments that make life matter, and how to have more of them. It is about experiencing fulfillment and meaning in your life *now,* not when you have more money, or find the right partner, or achieve your perfect weight, but in this and every moment. It is about how to rediscover real moments with your mate and your children, real moments with your work and your play, and, most of all, real moments with yourself.

All of my previous books have been about the relationships men and women have with one another. *Real Moments* is about the relationship we have with the process of living itself, and the peace many of us have been searching for, whether we're aware of it or not.

◆

Look honestly at your own life. Are your days and nights spent doing things that are meaningful and make you smile? Or do you spend the majority of your time doing things that give you back the smallest percentage of joy? When your life is over, will you wish you had spent your time differently? If you had only one month to live, what would you change?

✦

Look deeply into your own heart. Are you happy? Is there something you think needs to happen *before* you can be happy? Are you sure that if that something occurred, you would truly be happy then? Would it be enough?

✦

Look closely at the values of your spirit. If you suddenly died tomorrow, and you looked back on your life, what moments would you cherish the most? What would you miss the most about your time on earth?

✦

In writing this book, I offer you an opportunity to begin finding the answers to these questions for yourself as I have been doing for myself. I believe that asking ourselves these questions is very important. It forces us to stop living our lives mechanically and unconsciously, and demands that we *pay attention.*

There's a famous Zen story about the student who approaches his Master and asks him to share some words of wisdom about life. The Master looks intently at the anxious disciple for a moment, and then writes one word with his brush: "Attention." The disciple is confused, and nervously asks the Master to elaborate and the Master writes again: "Attention." By this time, the young student is beside himself

with frustration—he can't figure out what his teacher is trying to tell him. And once more the Master patiently writes:
ATTENTION . . . ATTENTION . . . ATTENTION

> Paying attention to the moments in your life as they unfold is what having real moments means, moments when you are fully present, fully feeling, fully alive.

Sometimes they will be moments of great happiness. Sometimes they will be moments of profound sorrow. But always, when you pay attention to where you are and what is going on, right now, you will experience a moment that has meaning, a moment that matters, and that is what I call a real moment.

✦

"I find the question 'WHY ARE WE HERE?' typically human. I'd suggest 'ARE WE HERE?' would be the more logical choice . . ."
— LEONARD NIMOY
Mr. Spock in *Star Trek*

Are you fully here, right now, reading this sentence? Or are you reading and thinking about the work you should be doing, or what you're going to have for dinner? Are you kind of reading, but also worrying about the argument you had with your lover last night, or whether the guy you just met will call and ask you out? Most of us are not very good at giving all of our attention to whatever activity we're involved in, at surrendering fully to the experience of the moment. Having real moments is difficult when we spend so much time *NOT* being in the present, for part of what makes a real moment so powerful, so fulfilling, is that you are experiencing it one hundred percent.

Another term for this is *"mindfulness."* Mindfulness is a

concept that is an integral part of many Eastern spiritual traditions, particularly Buddhism. Simply put, it means to *pay complete attention to whatever you're doing, to allow your "mind to be full" of the experience.*

Mindfulness delivers you fully into the moment. It can turn an ordinary experience like taking a walk, putting your child to bed, holding your partner close, or even driving your car into a real moment. When you are being mindful, your intention is to fully experience where you are and what you are doing, rather than to have what you're doing now be another passing, forgettable moment which comes after what you just did, and before what you're about to do. Later in this book I'll share some tools for living more mindfully

The opposite of mindfulness is *mindlessness*, to do things without thinking, without feeling, automatically and unconsciously. I believe that it is our mindlessness that causes much of our suffering and the suffering of those around us:

- ✦ Mindlessness is what allows you to stay in a relationship that isn't nourishing you, and may even be harming you, and not notice how miserable you are.
- ✦ Mindlessness is what allows you to ignore messages your body is trying to give you when it has chronic indigestion or heartburn, and, instead, to pop an antacid into your mouth, until one day years later the doctor diagnoses you with a serious disease.
- ✦ Mindlessness is what allows you to smoke, or drink, or do drugs, and not notice, in spite of your chronic cough, your emotional inconsistency, or your mental ups and downs, that you are slowly killing yourself and hurting the people you love.
- ✦ Mindlessness is what allows you to know that there is injustice and cruelty occurring in the world around you, but not to speak out against it or do anything to stop it.

Mindlessness is an unhealthy mental habit many of us suffer from too much of the time. When we live our lives mindlessly, we miss all of the real moments. Psychology professor Ellen Langer, who writes about mindfulness, says people who live and act mindlessly run the risk of "being trapped in unlived lives." We move through our days, months, and years, focusing not on where we are, but on where we are going, and then wonder why we never feel we arrive anywhere that brings us lasting fulfillment.

How We Postpone Happiness

It is easy to be mindless in America, because dreaming of and living for a better tomorrow is the American way. America has always been a place where people come to chase their dreams. Dreamers from all parts of the world emigrated here, and were encouraged to dream even bigger dreams. The problem is, in the second half of the twentieth century, we have gotten so good at living for tomorrow that most of us spend very little time in the present. We plan for or worry about the future, and before we know it, our life is over and we realize that we were too busy being preoccupied with what had already happened or what we wanted to happen that we forgot to enjoy what was actually happening in each and every moment. *We become experts at preparing to live, but have a difficult time fully enjoying the process of being alive, right now.* We prepare for our careers, we prepare for the holiday season, we prepare for the weekend, we prepare for our retirement — when you add them all up, we are preparing for our life to be over.

The problem with being so good at living for the future is that we *get in the habit of not being in the moment,* so when those wonderful events we've planned for actually occur — the vacation, the promotion, the party, etc. — we have no idea how to enjoy them. We rush through these long-awaited experiences as if we can't wait to get them over, treating them like another task to be dealt with, and then wonder why we are left feeling so let down, so unfulfilled.

Recently, a good friend of mine got married. She spent almost a year planning her wedding, which was a very elaborate and beautiful affair. The morning after the ceremony, she called me from the airport on her way to her honeymoon. When I asked if she was happy with how things had turned out, she confessed that she was feeling strangely empty. "I hardly remember the wedding," she commented in a disappointed voice. "It seemed to pass by in a blur."

My friend's experience is not uncommon:

When we spend our lives preparing for the future, rather than enjoying the present, we end up postponing happiness. We lose our ability to appreciate and experience joy, so when we do have the opportunity for real moments, we miss them.

In America, we live in a culture that values *doing*, and not *being*. So it is no wonder that we are not good at creating and delighting in real moments. We have been concerned with quantity rather than quality, with the stimulation of constant activity rather than substance. We often judge ourselves and others on what we have accomplished, rather than on who we are. We are movers and shakers, achievement junkies, "a society of speed-worshippers," as Nina Tassi calls us in her book *Urgency Addiction*. "Bigger Is Better . . ." "All You Can Eat . . ." "Two for One . . ." "More for Your Money . . ." "Faster than Ever . . ." "New and Improved . . ."—these are concepts that make up the American psyche.

Since World War II, we have been in an era of frenzied

consumerism. We wanted to get as much stuff as possible as fast as we could. Consumption and accomplishment have been held up as the keys to happiness. We told ourselves that if we had the car, the house, the color TV, the right job, we'd made it. And if we had a newer model of these than the guy next door, or a more prestigious position, we were a success. Our heroes became those people who had the most. Our values focused on things. *Our goal was having and accomplishing instead of living.*

This "consumption consciousness" inevitably turned us into experts at postponing happiness. Postponing happiness means believing that, in order to be happy, certain conditions must be met. You think to yourself: "I'll be happy when . . ."

I'll be happy when I find the right partner.
I'll be happy when I lose twenty pounds.
I'll be happy when my kids are married and successful.
I'll be happy when I have my own business.
I'll be happy when I redecorate my living room.
I'll be happy when my boss finally gives me a promotion.
I'll be happy when I buy a new car.
I'll be happy when . . . you fill in your own blanks.

We believe that when we have a certain experience, or get a certain possession, or achieve a certain status. we will finally be happy and not until then. So we work hard, or allow time to pass, and eventually, what we thought would make us happy occurs. We finish school, or lose the weight, or open our own business, or buy the house. Then we wait to be overcome with joy—and we are disappointed. **We may feel a sense of satisfaction, but we don't feel happy.**

And so the process starts all over again. "Well, I know I said if I became company manager I'd be happy, but now I realize what will *really* make me happy would be to become a supervisor." And so once again, we postpone our happiness until we can achieve the next goal.

Like all addictions, the need to have enough and do enough requires increasingly larger doses to get you high, until you're just not getting off anymore. And for many of us, that is precisely what has been happening. We've bought our cars and our condos; we've launched our careers and climbed up the success ladder. We've tried to give our children the luxuries we didn't have growing up. We've gotten many of the things we wanted, and become many of the things we hoped for. But slowly, we have begun to suspect that something is wrong, *that the kind of dreams we've been following have delivered us into a spiritual and emotional dead end:* **We have been substituting the possessions we collected and the goals we achieved for real moments, and in spite of it all,** *many of us are not happy.*

What makes this process even more frightening is that the time in our life seems to fly by. Each Friday evening arrives and we wonder where the week went. Each New Year's Eve comes, and we wonder where the year went. We wake up one day and realize that we are turning thirty, or forty, or beyond, and wonder where all the time went. We watch our children graduate from school, or start families of their own, and feel like it was just yesterday that we rocked them to sleep or taught them to tie their shoes.

We cannot technically slow time down. We are changing, and ultimately aging and dying from the moment we are born. But by experiencing more moments completely and consciously, I believe we will also experience time in a more meaningful way.

The Longest Forty Seconds of My Life

You've probably had moments in your life that seemed to take hours, weeks that seemed to go on for months, months that seemed to last a lifetime. These are almost always times when you are fully feeling and experiencing what is happening to you—you are in labor giving birth to a child; you are waiting for test results to see if you or a family member is ill; you are sharing your first intimate kisses and embraces with a new lover; you're spending a night watching the phone, hoping your partner calls you to make up after a fight. In these situations, time appears to have slowed down, and no matter how much your intellect knows that this day, this night, is no longer or shorter than any other, you could swear that everything is moving at half speed. That's because you are intensely present, and intensely feeling, in each moment.

On January 17, 1994, at 4:31 A.M., I, along with millions of other Southern Californians, experienced one of the largest earthquakes in American history. I will never forget the terrifying sensation of holding on to our bed as it and the whole house violently shook and rumbled in the cold darkness. It felt and sounded like the end of the world had arrived, and we were certain that we were going to die. Thank goodness, we did not. And as we huddled together on the floor of our closet for the next few hours, riding out the aftershocks, we couldn't believe what we were hearing on the radio: All reports said the quake had lasted approximately forty seconds. "That's impossible," my husband and I said to each other. "It was *at least* three minutes." We thought the news reports weren't accurate. But they were. And in the days that followed, not one of the dozens of friends and neighbors I spoke with, nor the radio and TV commentators I listened to, had experienced a forty-second earthquake. They, like us, were certain that the initial temblor had continued for several minutes. Of course, we were all wrong. What we had experienced was the longest forty seconds of our lives.

The earthquake was, without doubt, the most frightening experience I've ever had. It certainly qualified as a real moment, though not the kind I choose to have often! However, like all real moments, it presented us with many gifts—couples became more intimate, having been reminded of what is really important in life; families drew closer together; friends and strangers reached out toward one another with true compassion and community. Experiencing that moment so intensely opened our hearts and woke up our spirits. **Because we were forced to slow down, we became completely present in each minute of that day and the days that followed, and as a result, we were able to feel more love.**

My Search for Happiness

For as long as I remember, I have been a seeker. Those who knew me would never have described me as a carefree, lighthearted little girl. My parents had a very unhappy marriage, and even as a child, I was looking for answers to explain the sadness I saw in my mother's eyes, the confusion I saw in my father's heart, and the pain I felt in my own. To the surprise of my teachers, my first poems written in third grade asked why there was so much unhappiness in the world. I had a burning need to understand the meaning of life, and felt lost without the answers I knew were missing.

As soon as I left home at eighteen, I began my search for truth in earnest. I found a spiritual teacher and began practicing meditation, spending months at a time in retreat, looking within for the peace and wisdom I longed for. After many years of focusing only on my inner world, I knew it was time for me to fully return to the outer world, and to discover my purpose for being here. That's when I went back to school to obtain my degrees, and began studying what I cared the most about—love, relationships, and the process of living.

I gave my first workshop in my living room for eighteen of my closest friends. I wasn't planning to become well known, or have a TV or radio program, or even write a book. I was just sharing what I'd been learning with people I loved. So I was surprised when thirty-five people showed up for the next workshop, and more for the next. Soon, it became clear that my path was being laid out before me, and that I should follow it, so I did. I felt very fortunate that I'd been blessed with the ability to communicate with people and remind them, along with myself, about the importance of love.

Once I made the decision to become a teacher, I committed myself to doing whatever I could to positively affect as many people as possible. I was not an overnight success, but I didn't expect to be. Nothing has ever come to me easily in life. I've always had to work very hard for whatever I got, and my career has been no exception.

Looking back, I think there are two reasons I have always tried so hard at everything I've done. The first is that when I was young, I had a lot less than most of my friends. Our house was the smallest of everyone in my crowd; my clothes were from the discount stores and had the labels cut out. I was never deprived of anything I really needed, but I did not know what it was like to have many of the things I wanted. So if I got something, it was because I had worked for it. The second reason I decided that I needed to try harder is probably because I felt so unattractive. Imagine a skinny, serious little girl with braids, sallow skin, and ugly white glasses, and you'll get the picture. I knew I wasn't about to impress anyone with my looks, so I figured I'd be smart instead. Even years later, when I got contact lenses, learned to style my hair, and knew there were boys who found me appealing, I had a hard time feeling like I looked O.K.

So as my career began to take off, I was too busy trying hard and working nonstop to notice that I was achieving a lot of success. Then, a few years ago, I had an experience that began to change the course of my life. It happened while I was being driven to the daily television show I was doing at the time. A friend from out of town was with me, and as we pulled up to the studio and she noticed some fans waiting for my autograph, her face broke into a wide smile. "You really made your dreams come true, Barbara," she said with love and admiration. "You must really be happy."

When I heard her words, it was as if a curtain had suddenly been lifted from my mind. In that moment, I saw that I had, indeed, achieved most of the dreams I'd always believed in: I lived in a home nicer than any of the ones my friends had lived in when I was little; I could buy myself all the things I couldn't have as a child; I could send my mother on all the trips she could never afford while she took care of me; I'd finally found a man who loved me as much as I'd always wanted to be loved (even when he saw me in my glasses and a ponytail!). And here I was, driving up to my own television show. But when I looked deep into my heart, I realized the frightening truth—*I was not happy.* **I was** *satisfied . . .* **I was** *fulfilled . . .* **but I was** *not happy.*

For the rest of that day, and many days afterward, it was all I could think about. "How had this happened?" I wondered. I believed so deeply in the work I did, and I knew that it was making a difference in people's lives. I *was* proud of all I had accomplished in my career. I had a wonderful, loving relationship. I was healthy. Why wasn't all this making me happy? Why wasn't it enough? What was missing?

Slowly, as the days and weeks passed, I began to see the truth. *I was not happy because I had not been allowing myself to experience enough real moments,* moments when I wasn't trying to achieve anything, moments when I wasn't working toward a goal, moments when I was simply being right where I was. **I was an expert at doing, but I was not very good at just being.** For so many years I had believed that I would be happy when I got what I wanted. Now that I had what I'd thought I wanted, I knew that getting more of it would never make me happy. *If it wasn't enough now, it would never be enough.*

I didn't want to forget this insight, so I wrote out a sign and put it up on my mirror where I could see it each morning. The sign said:

> W hen will I know I have enough,
> and what will I do then?

These are powerful questions to ask yourself. If you don't feel you have enough right now, when will you have enough? How much money or success would it take until you felt you had enough? And then, what would you do? What would your life be about? I've had people tell me that just asking themselves these questions started a self-discovery process that went on for weeks.

The Difference Between Happiness and Satisfaction

I know now, because I've answered these same questions, that I could write a dozen more successful books, appear in hundreds of TV shows, or, if I had children and were a full-time mother, I could raise the perfect kids, or if I were in business, I could buy every company I wanted, but that none of these would make me happy. *They would hopefully satisfy and fulfill me, but they would not bring me happiness.*

What's the difference between happiness and satisfaction? Satisfaction is a kind of **mental contentment.** *It marks a completion of something you started with a purpose in mind*—a project, an interchange, a meal. For instance, I feel satisfied when I finish writing a chapter of my book. I feel satisfied when I give a speech and it is well received. I feel satisfied when I clean out my closet. Something is complete.

Happiness is more of an **emotional contentment**. I feel happy when I praise myself for what I wrote in that book chapter. I feel happy when I allow myself to feel the heart of someone who comes up to share with me after the speech. I feel happy when I look at a garment in my closet and allow myself to recall how much fun I had the night I wore it.

I remember the day when my third book hit #1 on *The New York Times* best-seller list. My agent called me early in the morning with the news, and of course I was very excited. I'd worked very hard on the book, and felt very fulfilled and satisfied that it was doing so well. Later that night after Jeffrey got home from work, we lay in bed together. As he held me in his arms, he stroked my hair and told me how proud he was of me for putting so much of myself into that book, for doing such a good job of promoting it on tour, and for being so smart. My eyes filled with tears as I received his love. In that moment, and not before, I was happy. That moment of love was a real moment.

We all accomplish things in our lives that bring us satisfaction. But no matter how much we do, or how much satisfaction we experience, we need to learn how to create real moments in order to be truly happy.

> Happiness can only come from having
> enough real moments in your life.

✦

Right around the time I was going through these changes, I traveled out of town to give a lecture. I shared my new realizations, as fresh and unformed as they still were, with my audience, because I learned a long time ago that it's easier to give a good presentation when you're being totally honest. After my talk, a woman approached me and gave me a big hug. "What was that for?" I asked.

"It was a thank-you, " she replied. "Tonight you freed me from some guilt that has been plaguing my heart for months."

She went on to tell me that she was thirty-nine years old, married, and the mother of three children. She and her husband lived a very comfortable life, and although she was far from wealthy, she felt very blessed. "But something happened to me right after I turned thirty-nine, " she explained. "I woke up one morning and realized that I wasn't happy. I've been so confused, because I love my husband and I love my children, and I have everything I ever thought I wanted. I always believed that would be enough to make me happy. I began wondering if my feelings of emptiness and restlessness meant that I wasn't really as in love as I told myself I was. I've been afraid to even talk to my husband about it, but he's been worried sick, because he can tell something is wrong. Until I heard you tonight, I didn't know what it was. But now I do."

Like me, like so many of us, my new friend had created a full and good life for herself, but she'd been too busy *doing* to stop and experience the small moments of happiness that surrounded her. She had forgotten how to connect with her husband. She'd forgotten how to take time to savor all of the gifts she'd been given. The reason she felt so empty was because she wasn't filling herself up with the love and meaning that were already there in her life. Her heart was hungry for more real moments.

✦

Here is what I have discovered about happiness:

Happiness is not an acquisition — it is a skill.

We do not experience happiness because of what we get. We experience happiness because of how we live each moment. It is a skill, an ability we must master, just like learning

how to be a good painter, or an excellent athlete. Having an easel, a brush, and a palette of colors does not make me a painter—knowing how to paint does. Having a tennis racquet and ball does not make me a tennis player. Knowing how to play does. *Having certain experiences does not make me happy—knowing how to live them with full awareness and to mindfully be in each moment will make ..e happy.*

In this way, happiness is only possible and available in the present moment, and from moment to moment. It comes to us *not* when we are searching for it, for then we are somewhere else other than here and now, but rather when we allow ourselves to be mindful of exactly where we are and fully experience whatever we are doing.

The word *"happiness"* comes from the old English word *"hap,"* which means chance or fortune (either good or bad) that befalls a person—in other words, what *"happens"* to someone. Happiness, then, literally means *the experience of being with whatever is happening.* So although when we say "I want to be happy," we are usually projecting ourselves into the future, happiness, by definition, can only be found now, in this moment.

Thich Nhat Hanh, a world-renowned Vietnamese Zen Master, has written an enlightening book called *Peace Is Every Step.* In it, he says:

> *"Life can be found only in the present moment. The past is gone, the future is not yet here, and if we do not go back to ourselves in the present moment, we cannot be in touch with life."*

If you can't be happy now, with what you have and who you are, you will not be happy when you get what you think you want. If you don't know how to fully enjoy $500, you won't enjoy $5,000, or $500,000. If you can't fully enjoy taking a walk around the block with your mate, then you won't enjoy going to Hawaii, or to Paris. I'm not saying that having more money or more recreation won't make your life easier—it will. *But it will not make you happy, because it can't.* Only you can do that by learning to live with more real moments.

Imagine that you want to be a concert violinist. Someone gives you an old, poorly made violin on which to practice. Of course, you wish you had a Stradivarius, the best violin in the world, but you don't. So you study day and night, you pour your heart and soul into playing that inferior violin well. One day, a benefactor appears and hands you the Stradivarius you always dreamed of. Your hands shake as you pick it up, and then you begin to play, and you play exquisitely. The reason you can play so beautifully is not because you're using an instrument that is worth $250,000. You play so well because you had developed your *skill* as a violinist.

If you had not learned how to play that old, secondhand violin properly, you would not have been able to play the Stradivarius.

> If you don't develop your skill at enjoying what
> you have, you won't be any happier
> when you get more.

"And a Child Shall Lead the Way . . ."

Before you start thinking that this all sounds too esoteric and abstract for you to grasp, let alone put into practice, I want to remind you that you used to be an expert at happiness—when you were a small child. Children are masters at creating real moments. They haven't yet learned to postpone joy, so they practice it as much as possible! This is what makes each child so magical. They are totally present, totally alive in the moment. Their days and nights are filled with constant laughter and celebration. It's not just because they don't have jobs and bills and responsibilities—their priorities may be different, but they often play as hard and intensely as we work. Their contentment comes from their ability to discover and enjoy the pure wonder available in each taste, each flower, each cloud, each experience.

There are some people in your life you never forget, even if you encounter them just once. Several years ago I went to Disneyland with a group of friends. It was toward the end of the day, and we gathered on Main Street to witness the daily parade. As we waited for the characters and animals to appear, I noticed a woman push a little girl in a wheelchair up to the edge of the sidewalk so she'd have a better view of the festivities. She was about seven or eight years old, paralyzed from the neck down, and her wheelchair was more like a portable hospital with all kinds of boxes and devices attached to it that helped her body function.

Just then, the Main Street Parade began. Mickey and Minnie Mouse, Snow White and the Seven Dwarfs, and all the other colorful Disney characters danced down the street to the music of a marching band, followed by the star attraction—a huge gray elephant. But I hardly noticed the parade, because I could not tear my gaze away from the little girl. Her eyes were as wide as saucers; her mouth hung open in amazement; and on her face was the most radiant smile of joy I'd ever seen. She was spellbound by the spectacle passing in front of her.

My eyes filled with tears as I watched this special child, tears not of pity for her handicap, but tears of sadness for myself. I realized standing on that make-believe street that I did not know how to enjoy the magic of life as I saw her doing. I did not know how to be as happy as she was allowing herself to be. I did not know how to enjoy the parade with as much delight as she felt. I might be able to walk and run and do many things she could never do, but she had something far more valuable: **She possessed the gift of joy.**

I've never forgotten that little girl, or what she taught me, because that experience was a Real Moment for me. I had connected deeply with someone else's spirit, even though we never spoke, and it had infused the moment with meaning.

Barry Neil Kaufman, cofounder of the Option Institute, has a wonderful saying: "*We weren't born unhappy. We* learned *to be unhappy.*" That means we still have the talent for living in the moment within us, that we can unlearn our habits of mindlessness and begin to mindfully appreciate each experience of being alive. I believe that children are sent to us to be our teachers. When we witness them feeling and experiencing so fully, we should remember that they are demonstrating powerful spiritual techniques for our benefit! We need to honor them as they lovingly remind us of the path we must travel to reclaim our own joy and find our own real moments. "*Except ye be as little children, you cannot enter the kingdom of Heaven.*"

How I Learned to Stop "Climbing the Lake"

I did not find it easy to begin inviting real moments into my life. My old patterns of trying to **do** things kept getting in the way, and sometimes still do. A few years ago, around the time I first became aware of my difficulty in experiencing real moments, my husband, Jeffrey and I took a trip to New York City to do some business and have some fun. We arrived on the red-eye Friday morning, and as soon as we checked into the hotel, I found myself calling restaurants to make our reservations for the weekend, and scanning the paper for different activities we could enjoy. Jeffrey seemed to be a little annoyed with me, but I figured he was just tired. We went out for a while, and then came back to get ready for dinner. When

I took out my list of plans and began going over it with him,
I was surprised that he responded by acting disinterested
and aloof.

"What's wrong, honey?" I asked.

"I'm just feeling a little upset with you, that's all."

"Why, what did I do?" I asked defensively.

"I don't know, you're so frenetic, making lists and plans.
Why can't you just relax and stop controlling everything?"

My red flag went up—he'd said the "c" word—"control."

"I'm not trying to control things, I'm just trying to make
sure we have a good time!" I snapped.

"Well, stop trying so hard, Barbara, and maybe you will
have a good time."

Suddenly, I began to sob, from a place deep inside of me.
He was right: I was trying . . . trying to have a good time . . .
trying to make everything perfect . . . trying to make him
happy. I'd spent my whole life trying to control the outcome
of the events around me, working hard to accomplish my
goals, sincerely believing that the harder I tried, the happier I
would be. Now I had come face-to-face with the truth—that
*my trying itself was preventing me from experiencing the joy I
had been so desperately searching for.* **And so I wept, for in
that moment, I realized that I didn't know how to *not* try.**

Jeffrey came over and put his arms around me, and through
my tears I whispered: "I'm afraid if I don't try, I'll miss something."

I will never forget what he said next:

"If you keep trying, you'll miss everything. . . ."

The power of the truth Jeffrey spoke penetrated deep into
my heart. As he held me and kissed my tears away, I understood that I had to start learning how to live all over again.
One kind of energy had taken me to this point of fulfillment
in my life—the energy of doing: to push, to strive, to create.
This was not a bad energy—it was necessary to help me

achieve all I have. But I needed a totally new kind of energy to take me to my next level of fulfillment, a skill I wasn't very good at and hadn't known much about—the energy of being.

What my wise and sensitive man had seen that night in New York was that the very means I had used to get so far in my life were now getting in my way—that the more I tried to *do something* to be happy, the unhappier I, and certainly he, was going to be!!

Here is a story I wrote that night inspired by what Jeffrey taught me:

The Woman Who Tried to Climb the Lake

Once there was a woman who spent her whole life climbing a very high mountain. She began as a tiny child, and could not remember a time before the mountain. Year after year she would ascend the steep cliffs, and in the process she became very good at the motion of climbing. The muscles in her legs and her back grew strong, and after a while, climbing felt as natural to her as breathing. As time passed, and she went higher and higher, she didn't even have to try and climb any-more—her body did it automatically.

At last, one day, the woman reached the top of the moun-tain. She was overjoyed with her achievement, and couldn't wait to start out on the next portion of her travels, and to conquer her next mountain. As she looked out over the hori-zon, she saw a beautiful blue lake, stretching sideways as far as her eye could see. But being a climber all of her life, the woman had only lived on the mountains, so she had never seen a lake, and in fact, did not even know what a lake was. She watched the strange expanse before her, and concluded that it must be some unusual kind of blue mountain. Since the only way to continue her journey was to cross over the odd-looking blue form, she decided that was what she must do.

So the mountain woman walked up to the water, and began trying to "climb the lake" with the same motions she'd used to climb the mountain. At first, she couldn't understand why she wasn't making any progress, and, in fact, was exhausting herself. So she mustered all of the energy in her strong body and tried to "climb" even harder, placing one leg in front of the other, using her hands to attempt to grasp the "blue rocks." But her efforts were useless. She kept falling over, and wasn't going anywhere.

Just about this time, when the mountain woman felt like giving up, she noticed a person floating by on top of the blue lake, gentling gliding his body through the water with the slightest movements of his arms and legs.

"What are you doing, my friend?" he called out to her.

"What does it look like?" she answered, her face flustered with embarrassment. "I'm climbing the lake."

"Good woman," the man of the lake replied, "don't you know that you can't cross a lake by climbing it? The only way to travel through water is to swim."

"But I'm such a marvelous climber!" the mountain woman insisted. "I've spent my whole life learning to climb. I can climb any mountain, I can reach the top of any peak. Surely there must be some way I can climb the lake."

"I'm sure you are an excellent climber," the man of the lake answered politely. "But that skill won't help you here in the water. It took one kind of wisdom to get you to the top of the mountain—you had to make your power stronger than the mountain. Now you need to learn another kind of wisdom to get across the lake—you need to surrender to the power of the water and allow its force to be stronger than you. You don't have to try hard anymore. In fact, the less you try, the better you'll do!"

And so it was that the man of the lake taught the woman of the mountain how to swim. At first, she splashed and thrashed around in the water, for she was accustomed to using very strong energy in her climbing. But her teacher was very patient, and slowly she learned to float on the water's surface, and allow the waves and the wind to carry her gently forward, until she was hardly doing anything at all.

And that's how the mountain woman learned that the strength of surrender was just as powerful as the strength of pushing forward.

✦

As we learn to experience more real moments, we will be required to master different skills than those we've been using to live lives of list-making and goal-setting. **Climbing the lake doesn't work.** Throughout the rest of this book, I'll offer you tools for creating more real moments in every part of your life.

What Are Real Moments?

What is a real moment? How can you tell if you are having one? All real moments have at least three elements of experience that need to be present:

✦ Consciousness

Real moments occur only when you are consciously and completely experiencing where you are, what you are doing, and how you are feeling . . . *You are paying attention, so you will notice things you wouldn't normally perceive if you were not paying attention.* There is nothing else in your awareness but the experience you are having.

Only when your consciousness is totally
focused on the moment you are in can you
receive whatever gift, lesson, or delight that
moment has to offer.

✦ Connection

Real moments are always moments when you have made an emotional connection between yourself and something or someone else. It might be a connection between you and a loved one, or you and a stranger, or you and a tree you're leaning against, or you and God. *They are moments in which the usual boundaries which appear to separate us from one another are penetrated, and in that connection, a kind of magic occurs.*

We usually call this experience of melting
boundaries "LOVE." You and something else are
flowing into one another.

✦ Surrender

You allow real moments to happen when *you totally surrender into whatever you are experiencing, and let go of trying to be in control.* You are 100 percent engaged in what you are doing, whether it is taking a walk, making love, baking bread, or watching your children play. You are fully embracing, rather than resisting, the experience of the moment.

It is impossible to have a real moment
when you are trying to control or resist
a situation or emotion.

So, if I could give you a formula for having a real moment, it might sound something like this:

Become fully conscious of what you are perceiving or experiencing in this moment. . . .

Once you are conscious of it, allow yourself to break through the illusion of separation and make a connection with the person, thing, or feeling you've contacted. . . .

Then, surrender completely into that connection. . . .

Now, you should be having a real moment.

◆

Real moments are available in the things you already do every day. . . .

My brother is an expert windsurfer, and he has many of his real moments while he is standing on his board, riding the waves. All of his awareness is consciously focused on what he is doing. He feels totally connected with the sail in his hands, the fiberglass beneath his feet, and the water all around him. And he is surrendering completely to each movement of the wind and each spray of sea in his face. He feels fully alive, fully content. . . . He is one with the ocean.

My mother has many of her real moments in her garden. She focuses totally on each new flower she is planting, each patch of soil she is clearing of weeds, each old leaf she is plucking away. She makes a connection with the tiny, colorful lives that depend on her to be nourished and to blossom. And she surrenders to the feel of the earth between her fingers, the musky smell of the wet dirt that fills the air, and the sweet sensation of allowing Mother Earth to bring forth life through her.

I have many of my real moments while I walk my dog and best friend, Bijou. As I follow behind his small, furry body, I become totally conscious of every crack in the sidewalk, every bush and how its edges are shaped, every tree waiting to be visited. I connect with Bijou's relaxed pace of travel, and as I feel his rhythm, his needs become my own. And I surrender completely to the walk, knowing that there is nowhere else to go, and nothing else to do, for in that very real moment, Bijou helps me to remember that the purpose of life may be nothing more significant than to sniff each magical flower that we pass, and to enjoy the journey.

✦

Recently I received a greeting card in the mail, and I wanted to pass its message on to you:

Yesterday is history.
Tomorrow is a mystery.
Today is a gift.
That's why we call it "the present. . . ."

· 2 ·

THE CRISIS OF SPIRIT
IN AMERICA

"There must be more to life than having everything."
— MAURICE SENDAK

How did we lose our ability to experience real moments? What is the source of the restlessness we sometimes feel in the secret part of our hearts? Why is it often so difficult for us to find the fulfillment we are searching for? To find the answers to these questions, and to properly begin our journey toward what lies ahead, we must first look back to the past.

So imagine for a moment that you are a time traveler from eighteenth-century America. You set the dials on your Time Machine ahead to the future, push the button, and when the machine stops, you look at the clock and discover that you've magically landed in the last few years of the twentieth century.

As you step out of your Time Machine, you are greeted by America as it is in the mid-1990s. The first change you notice is the tremendous advancement in technology—cars, airplanes, televisions, fax machines, dishwashers, computers— these are all miraculous to you. "How much easier life is now than it was where I came from!" you marvel to yourself.

But as you move among your twentieth-century relatives, you begin to notice many things that confuse you. First of all, the people you see do not seem to be as happy or friendly as you remember their being back home. They do not say hello to each other but instead walk swiftly by with anxious looks on their faces as if they are all rushing off to an emergency. "Has something terrible happened?" you ask a passerby. He shakes his head rudely, and turns away, leaving you to wonder why everyone seems so disconnected and agitated.

Soon you notice that the streets and parks are filled with refugees of some sort, hungry, frightened-looking adults, even children, who seem to have no place to sleep. You assume these must be the surrendered enemies from a recently fought war with a distant land, until you hear them speaking English. "Why are so many Americans living on the streets with no homes?" you wonder in disbelief. "And why is everyone ignoring them?"

But it is when you begin to read the newspapers and magazines, and watch the magical box they call television, that you become truly alarmed. For this is what you see and hear:

- ✦ "New statistics were released today, stating that last year 2.7 million cases of child abuse or neglect were reported."

- ✦ "A new survey found that 43% of the population either are alcoholics, grew up in an alcoholic family, or married an alcoholic."

- ✦ "Police now estimate that a woman is raped every six minutes in America, and that three out of four women will be victims of one violent crime during their lifetime."

- ✦ "The majority of homicides are committed by one loved one or relative against another, and not by strangers."

✦ "New studies reveal that approximately one out of every two marriages ends in divorce, and infidelity, especially among women, is on the rise."

✦ "The government reports that we are losing the war on crime, and projects a need for hundreds of new prisons to house the growing number of criminal offenders."

✦ "Another drive-by shooting was reported today in a small, quiet town in the Midwest. Three people were killed, and four were wounded. According to witnesses, the suspects did not know the victims, and their only motive for the killings was that they were in the mood to 'kick some butt.'"

You watch the news reports with horror. Random violence . . . Parents beating and molesting their own children . . . Children murdering other children . . . Millions of men and women destroying their lives with drugs and alcohol . . . Broken families . . . People living on the streets . . . And fear, fear everywhere. . . . *"What has happened to America?"* you cry out in disbelief. *"How did it turn into such a self-destructive society? What happened to the hopes we had in my time for a better future, the dreams we had for a nation of prosperity and peace?"*

And you rush back to your Time Machine and set the dial for the century you came from, praying that it's not too late for you to return, and weeping for your great-grandchildren's grandchildren who will one day be born into this civilization of lost souls.

✦

As we stand on the threshold of the twenty-first century, our nation exhibits every symptom of being in a profound state of emotional and spiritual crisis. What has happened to America? **We are a society dangerously out of balance:**

✦ We have more material comforts than any previous civilization, and yet we also show more evidence of personal unhappiness. Our levels of crime, abuse, divorce, and addiction, to name just a few problems, are higher now than at any time in the past, and growing worse each year.

✦ Our ability to technologically master our world continues to expand at a breathtaking pace, while our ability to successfully enjoy living in that world seems to have been lost. Experiences that we were brought up to believe we could take for granted have, for many of us, become distant dreams we recall with longing: marriages that last a lifetime; neighborhoods that are safe which we proudly call "home"; the confident certainty that our children will have a better life than we did; and perhaps most of all, lots of time—time to walk, to be quiet, to enjoy the fruits of our labors, time to do nothing or anything at all.

The result is a people searching desperately, sometimes even dangerously, but often unsuccessfully, for meaning. Those of us in our middle years are disappointed by and disillusioned with the deterioration of the safe world we knew when we were young. Our elders look nostalgically back at the past, remembering when things were perhaps simpler, but definitely more sane. And our children, to whom we will leave this turbulent legacy, are a generation already characterized by fear, anger, cynicism, and a loss of innocence.

We are *not* a society that is doing better and growing happier each day, and that was the American dream.

And then there is the crisis of the land itself: The earthquakes, the hurricanes, the fires and the floods, the icy winters that last forever, the rains that won't stop—the very body of our nation is out of balance. Scientists will, of course, have their logical explanations for these phenomena. But if you listen closely, you can hear Mother Earth crying out to us for help.

✦

Some part of you already knows all of this. Like our time-traveling friend, you have read the statistics in the papers; you have seen the reports on television; you or someone you love has already felt the shadow of violence or abuse or addiction or divorce or joblessness darken your life. You know that our world is not the safe and hopeful place it used to be. But like me, and like all of us, you turn away from your fear and your sadness, and, in turning away, develop a protective layer of numbness that allows you to go through your days without succumbing to despair. *And it is that very numbness that makes it difficult for us to experience the real moments that we need now more than ever.*

I believe that our emotional and spiritual survival is dependent on our NOT becoming numb, and on our NOT turning away. Of course, I have only told one side of the story. There is also much goodness in our nation, many powerful voices of caring, many forces of change. But they are not enough. Our country is in trouble. We, as a people, are in trouble. Your happiness, and the happiness of your children and their children is on the line. We cannot each single-handedly cure all of society's ills, but we can contribute more kindness, more caring, and more consciousness to what is happening inside of us and around us. And that will begin to make a difference.

The need for more real moments in our lives is more important now than ever before in our history—*moments of compassion toward our fellow human beings . . . moments of connection with those we love and those who need love . . . moments of centering and healing for ourselves.* Yet ironically, it is more difficult to have real moments than it has ever been before. This is the dilemma we are faced with as the Millennium approaches.

How did we get from our nation's hopeful beginnings to this disheartening time? When we begin to understand the historic roots of the crisis of spirit in our country, we will understand the crisis of spirit in ourselves.

From Frustrated Pioneers to Novelty Junkies

America is a nation infused with a pioneer spirit. Many of our ancestors left their homelands in all parts of the world and traveled thousands of miles to this country, often braving tremendous emotional, financial, and physical hardships. African Americans, who unlike the original settlers did not arrive here of their own free will, but were brought to our shores in chains, have been forced to become pioneers of a different sort. They have taken the painful journey from bondage to freedom, moving out of the plantations and through the states as they searched for the dignity and equality their persecutors stole from them. Even the indigenous peoples of our land, the Native Americans, migrated across the plains in search of favorable weather and good hunting. *We have had a history of being movers, always fascinated with what is over the next hill, always looking for more*—more land, more water, more abundance, more freedom.

Around the beginning of this century, we realized that we had moved to the limits of our borders. There was nowhere else to physically go, no new cities to settle, no new space in which to spread out. We were *frustrated pioneers* who had run out of new frontiers. But we couldn't stop, because by this time, **we'd become novelty junkies.** The addiction ran in the family—it started with our grandparents or great-grandparents who first arrived here in the promised land, and had been passed down to us. Now it was in our blood. *We were hooked on wanting more.*

And so we refocused our hunger for more from places to things, and our fascination with technology and consumerism began. We made things work faster and more efficiently. We built things bigger and better. We created new rules about how to live, what to buy, what to wear, what was "in," and when we quickly tired of these, we rebelled against the traditions we ourselves had recently established, and made even newer rules. *Our constantly changing tastes were what fueled the American economy.* Even if our old car ran just fine, we still hungered for the new model. Even if our old shoes fit, we had to have the new ones with the higher heel, or differently shaped toe. Even if our old TV worked well, we needed the new version with the improved remote control and additional features. Anything old we discarded, anything new we fell in love with.

It is inherent in human consciousness to improve. So there is nothing unique about a people searching for and creating ways to make their life better—all civilizations throughout history have done this. *What is unique about us in America is the accelerated rate at which we continually search for novelty and progress.* More elements change in our modern culture during one year than used to change in European or Asian cultures for decades. And once other countries learn about what is "hot" in the United States, they often throw aside age-old traditions and embrace our latest fad with open arms.

In this way, America and its worship of the new has radically transformed the face of the world. Blue jeans, T-shirts, tennis shoes, movie stars, rock and roll, hamburgers—these have been our cultural exports. You don't hear American teenagers singing Italian or German pop songs. You don't see Americans rushing by the millions to see the latest French blockbuster. You don't watch Brazilian television shows subtitled in English. Yet the reverse of these occurs every day on every continent.

On a recent trip to Bali, my husband and I were witnessing a cremation parade and ritual, which to the Balinese is a very sacred and joyous occasion. As we watched thirty young Balinese men lifting up the platform on which the deceased rested, we were amazed to see almost half of them wearing T-shirts emblazoned with the names and logos of American rock groups. The Balinese culture is dedicated to its ancient traditions which are an integral part of everyday life even today. And yet somehow, rock groups like Pearl Jam and Aerosmith had even invaded the cremation ceremony of a Balinese rice farmer.

The Self-Indulgent Years

The baby boomers took a temporary vacation from materialism during the 60s, rebelling against the status quo and trying to live a "tune in, turn on, drop out" philosophy. But once we found out how much fun it was to make and spend money, the guys eagerly threw on their suits and tied back their long hair, the gals shaved their legs and got back into their bras. And as we traded in our old Volkswagens for shiny new Hondas and Toyotas, we followed the example of our now overjoyed parents and entered the American mainstream with a passion.

Starting in the late 1960s and continuing into the 70s and 80s, our frenzied consumerism peaked. *"You can have it all"* was our mantra, and we believed it. We'd always been a society enamored with the concept of freedom—that is what drew many of us here. Now, political and religious freedom weren't enough. We wanted financial freedom, sexual freedom, and emotional freedom. **We wanted as many things, as much pleasure, and as much self-discovery as possible.**

As consumers, we could not purchase enough, invest enough, or borrow enough to satisfy our hunger. Fortunately for us, technological advancement was peaking as well, and entire new industries were born, from computers to fax machines to cellular phones to CD players. How did we plan to pay for all of our new stuff? Why, we just filled our wallets with credit cards and took out second mortgages on our homes. The government printed more money, and we went on spending it.

In our personal lives, our pioneer mentality expressed itself in our passion for breaking through the old boundaries and experiencing more individual freedoms than ever before. "Let it all hang out" and "Do your own thing" were the mottoes. Open marriage, one-night stands, and swinging were born as we turned away from the old traditions with the same fervor with which we once left the old country and came to America.

Some observers call this period of our recent history "the self-indulgent years." We wanted to have more, do more, and be more. The phrase "self-improvement" was born, and along with it came industries to help us be the best. Now we could join health clubs to have the perfect body, take seminars and listen to tapes to understand and motivate ourselves, and read books to make sure we were doing it all correctly. Our most popular bestsellers taught us how to have better sex, how to be better parents, better tennis players, better managers, better at everything.

The more we did, the more we realized that it takes a lot of time to excel. And so we bought organizers, studied time management, and scheduled ourselves carefully. Even our children, busy with their gymnastics lessons, hockey practice, and computer clubs, needed kids' daytimers to keep track of their activities.

Perhaps we were too busy playing with our new toys and achieving new goals to notice the symptoms of burnout as they began to surface. At first, they were subtle: We'd realize it had been weeks since the whole family had eaten a meal together; we'd look at the calendar and discover that we had no free days or weekends during which we could, heaven forbid, do nothing; and the credit card bills kept piling up. But hey, we were having so much fun, slowing down was unthinkable.

It is apparent that most of us aren't having fun anymore. Why? *We didn't pay attention, and now we are paying the price for our self-indulgence.* All parties eventually have to end, and ours was no exception. The glitz and greed of the 70s and 80s is over, and now we are coming to terms with the social, spiritual, and emotional costs.

The crisis we face today in the United States reflects several political, technological, economic, and social changes that hit us all at the same time and, together, have taken their toll on the American psyche.

The Demise of the American Dream

Economically, reality finally set in during the latter part of the eighties. We'd had a wonderful time spending money, but finally, the time for paying the bills arrived. You don't have to be a financial expert to know what happened, and it doesn't matter what word we use to describe it—Recession, Depression, National Debt. The bottom line is that we ran head-on into an economic crisis that is affecting all of us.

Part of the fallout has taken the form of unemployment, not a new phenomenon in the twentieth century. But this time, it's *who's* unemployed that has us so frightened. People who never expected to be laid off are jobless—top level executives, professionals, managers. *Time* magazine reported that fifty-eight percent of Americans either themselves have lost a job or have a friend who has lost a job since 1991.

It's not uncommon to see men and women in their late forties and fifties showing up at job interviews and temp agencies looking for work. It was one thing to be between jobs as a twenty-year-old with no responsibilities. It's quite another to have three teenagers at home, a mortgage, piles of other debts, and to find that the position you've held for ten or fifteen years has suddenly vanished. Most men went into their middle years with the goal of achieving financial independence, or of retiring early so they could enjoy the fruits of their labors. Now they just hope they'll still have a job to eventually retire from.

For many older Americans, even the once glorious dream of retirement has tarnished, as interest rates plummeted, and the investments senior citizens had counted on to support them for the remainder of their lives have become less and less valuable. Millions of people over sixty, who'd carefully planned for their "golden years," working ten-hour days so they'd be able to enjoy the good life, find themselves having to postpone retirement indefinitely in order to simply survive. Others live in constant fear of not being able to pay medical bills, or they are faced with the disappointing reality of never being able to take that trip they always talked about, or burdened by the sense of failure that they will not leave any financial legacy to their children and grandchildren, because they must use their savings to live.

The effect our ailing economy is having on the twenty-something generation is no less frightening. It used to be that young adults went to college in the first place knowing that they would be able to get a much better job with a degree than without one. Now they are lucky to get a job at all. We have a whole new subculture of bellboys, waiters, and taxi drivers with bachelor's and master's degrees. The hopefulness the younger generation felt in the seventies, when college graduates were aggressively recruited by major corporations throughout the country, has been replaced with a dark pessimism about the future. No longer do they believe, as so many generations before have, that they will be better off than their parents were. Instead, their hearts are clouded with uncertainty.

And then there are the baby boomers, now with children of our own, facing the disheartening knowledge that our sons and daughters will probably not grow up to have more than we did—that, in fact, they will be lucky to have as much as we do. We watch our children struggle to find work, we open up our homes to them when they move back in order to save money, and we hurt as we witness their worries about their futures, remembering when we were their age and believed that nothing could prevent us from having it all.

We try to tell ourselves things are not that much worse than they used to be, that tough times come and go. But then we drive down the street, or walk out of our office and see the homeless men, women, and children, hungry, hopeless, huddled in the cold—they are the human reminders that we live, indeed, in a time like no other. Yes, there are the alcoholics, the ex-convicts among those who sleep on the streets or in cars. But there are also the single mothers, the unemployed airplane mechanics, the kids whose dads lost their jobs of fifteen years and didn't have any savings. Their faces reflect the human toll our economic crisis is taking. *It is not just about the loss of jobs, of homes, of opportunities—it's about the loss of the American dream.*

The Frantic Family Syndrome

Even for those of us who have jobs and can pay the bills, life is not what it was for our parents, or what we always thought it would be. Most families need to have two incomes in order to survive, and that means more women than ever before are working full- or part-time. Spending time with the children or with your partner, taking care of the home, pursuing hobbies or other interests, even doing the laundry—none of these are as easy as they used to be, because we are too busy surviving. This manic whirlwind of activity extends itself to our kids who, sensing that those who do more will get more, are scheduled weeks in advance for their own activities.

Psychologist John Rosemond has labeled this *"The Frantic Family Syndrome."* Mom, Dad, and the kids racing around from appointment to meeting, from school to work, occasionally stopping to eat, although rarely together. The home, which used to be a sanctuary of relative calm in the midst of our busy lives, has now, for many of us, become a domestic pit stop, the place we bathe, sleep, change our clothes, and grab some food before racing off to our next obligation.

Is it any wonder that we have lost our ability to have real moments when we are working so hard to hang on to what we still have? *We have been afraid to stop because we would end up with less . . .*

The Psychic Assault of Technology

If the American dream has been tarnished by our economic woes, then the American psyche has been equally injured by the explosion of technology. It is ironic that the very industry that brings us so much comfort and entertainment, and that has made our lives so much easier in a myriad of ways is itself responsible for much of the psychological dis-ease that has become a part of the American profile. From this point of view, the telecommunications satellite has been a weapon far more damaging than any of the warheads or missiles we once feared.

Modern technology has moved us out of the industrial age into the information age. Since we have become accustomed to our high-tech lifestyle, we rarely think about the impact it is having on us. I recently heard a sociologist on the radio share an amazing fact: *With the use of satellites, television, and computers, you and I receive more information in one day of our lives than our ancestors of several generations ago used to receive in 1,000 days!!* That means our brains have to process as much input in 24 hours as our brains used to process in 24,000 hours.

Fifty years ago, when World War II was fought, our parents and grandparents received their information about it through newspapers, radio, and film clips. Most of the news came without pictures, without sound, and often was days old. The death and destruction that accompanies all war lost some of its terrifying reality because there wasn't much **immediacy** to it. But today it is a much different story. **We don't just read about war, death, or natural disaster—we witness it as if we were there.**

In the past few years, I've had a front row seat at the crisis in the Persian Gulf, the war in Bosnia, the hurricanes in Florida, the floods in the Midwest, earthquakes in California and Mexico, and several shoot-outs between the United States government and various criminals. On just one day several months ago, I watched fires rage out of control in Los Angeles, a plane crash in Hong Kong, a bombing in Palestine, and children starving in Somalia. By pushing a button on my TV remote control, I've been able to be an eyewitness to tragedies that, in my own personal world, I would never encounter. This is too much pain for one person to absorb in a lifetime, let alone in one day.

What if our ancestors had been able to watch the dropping of the first atomic bomb in Hiroshima, or the executions during the French Revolution, or the spread of bubonic plague in the fourteenth century, or the crucifixion of Christ on TV?

Can we even fathom how this would have affected them and the decisions they made that determined our future?

America's Mental Meltdown

Observing even one of these horrific events would cause any human being great emotional distress. So how does it affect us when we are bombarded with them day after day? I believe it sends us into *major psychological overload*. The human psyche is only able to handle so much stress before it begins to malfunction, just as too much electricity flowing through a wire will cause it to melt, or even catch on fire.

Imagine a group of men in a room from which they cannot escape. Loud music blasts from dozens of speakers on the wall. Numerous television sets flicker with broadcasts from different channels. Lights constantly flash, and the room itself is vibrating. After just a short time, most of the men will begin to display severe changes in mood and behavior. They will become increasingly depressed, fatigued, and anxious. Soon after, they will start exhibiting signs of hostility and aggression. And eventually, the men will become violent. Nice guys will start screaming at one another, and even the most sensitive members of the group will get into physical fights.

What is happening here? *They are suffering from the effects of being overstimulated.* Scientific studies that investigate the effects of overstimulation on animals and humans reveal that when we are exposed to too much mental, emotional, or sensory input at once, our anxiety levels radically increase. **These high levels of anxiety need to express themselves somehow, and they often do in the form of hostility and violence.** It's as if our brains say: "STOP! I CAN'T TAKE IT ANYMORE. I FEEL LIKE I'M GOING TO EXPLODE!!"

All of us have experienced this in mild forms. Your phone rings, your tea kettle whistles, and your child asks you a question all at the same time, and you feel like screaming. Your mental circuits are overloaded, and your groan or curse indicates that you have just short-circuited.

We, in America, are suffering from *mental meltdown and emotional short-circuiting.* Our boundaries have been invaded by satellite television, fax machines, and cellular phones, and there are fewer and fewer places to hide. We can no longer ignore what is happening in other parts of the country or the world by retreating into our own private universe. **In our new global village, we are continually and relentlessly overstimulated, and this sentences us to living in a constant state of subtle but very real anxiety.**

Anxiety is not just a mental condition—it manifests itself in very powerful physiological changes. Our body gets hyped up when we experience fear or nervousness—blood pressure rises, heart rate increases, respiration becomes faster. It's as if our body releases its own brand of speed or uppers into our system. Perhaps we do not all become violent and show signs of overt hostility. But one side effect of constant stimulation is that *we get hooked on that hyped-up feeling, needing more and more of it to feel alive.*

Look at the trend in the popular television shows of the past few years: *Rescue 911, Emergency!, Cops*—we can't get enough of what we call reality-based programming. For anxiety junkies, it's not enough to be able to watch tragedies from around the world twenty-four hours a day on CNN. We want to see all the auto accidents, medical emergencies, heroic rescues, and dramatic arrests that we can. We need to keep that adrenaline pumping.

Of course, our other favorite type of program is the talk show, on which we watch everyday Americans vent their anger and hostility toward their mates who cheated on them, their parents who messed them up, and their neighbors whose dog is doing his business on their lawn. We see skinheads and African American separatists scream racial slurs at one another; we hear couples reveal the most intimate and embarrassing details of their unhappy sex lives. Ten years ago there were just two or three daytime talk shows on the air—now there are dozens. *It appears that we would rather become obsessed with other people's lives than fully live our own.*

Yesterday morning I turned on the television and watched a few minutes of a popular talk show. A couple sat on the stage yelling at each other. I could hardly understand what they were saying, since they were both screaming at the same time. The host of this program stood silently by, pretending to have lost control of the segment, but I know he must have felt some satisfaction as he pondered the high ratings this maniacal husband and wife would, no doubt, bring him.

I speak from experience, and with compassion for the hardworking hosts and producers of these programs, because I once hosted a talk show for a major television network. Day after day I would fight to produce a "quality" episode that would educate the viewer about relationships. I always received the same response—that "quality shows didn't get good numbers." I needed to book transvestite nuns, crossdressing dads, and women who only dated male strippers if I wanted to compete with the most popular programs.

The most recent contribution to our hunger for sensationalism is *Court TV*, an entire channel dedicated to live broadcasts of actual criminal and civil trials. Millions of Americans tune in each day to watch defendants sweat on the witness stand as they are grilled by the prosecution, and victims tearfully testify about their terrible experiences. We love speculating on people's guilt or innocence, and wait anxiously for each new development in these cases like a modern-day version of the lynch mob waiting for the horse to be kicked out from under the poor condemned man.

How America Has Numbed Out

What has technology done to our values, to our spirit?

By exposing us to so much human drama,
technology has desensitized us both to our own
pain and the pain of others.

As Vice-President Al Gore writes in his book *Earth in the Balance,* "Just as the members of a dysfunctional family emotionally anesthetize themselves against the pain they would otherwise feel, our dysfunctional civilization has developed a numbness that prevents us from feeling the pain of our alienation from the world." In other words, we've numbed out. Normal, everyday emotion isn't enough to make us feel passionate and alive anymore.

And so, we have become a nation of voyeurs. We get turned on by suffering and scandal. We get our kicks from watching physical and emotional violence, our entertainment from seeing strangers in psychological distress. We can moralize all we want about family values, but the bottom line is that, in late-twentieth-century America, *we are addicted to the shocking.*

Nowhere is this more apparent than in our nation's obsession with sex. Sex gets our attention like nothing else can, whether it's on the cover of a magazine, the plot of a television show, or the topic for a "tell-all" book. Journalist Neal Gabler believes that the increasingly graphic sexual explicitness found in our culture, from shock radio to MTV, is a *reflection of our frustration with the loss of the genuine."* "We feel a pervasive lack of authenticity in politics, art, religions, athletics, even human relations," he writes. "We no longer believe. Amid the fakery, we want something real. And just as the sex act itself rips through layers of inauthenticity to something fundamental, so, metaphorically speaking, does sexually explicit language . . . rip through . . . to something basic, primitive, and genuine."

What America Has Lost

I believe that we, as a nation, are not really numb at all. **I think we're in a state of psychological shock, exhibiting all the symptoms of post-traumatic stress disorder.** We have suffered many severe losses, all at the same time, and we are simply overwhelmed:

✦ *We've lost our confidence in the American dream.*

We can't count on the things we used to. We can't be sure that if we work hard all of our lives, we will achieve the financial security we want. We can't be sure that if we do well at a job, we won't be fired anyway due to the sluggish economy. We can't be sure that if we educate ourselves, we will even be able to find employment. *We can't be sure that if we play by the rules, we will be rewarded.* **Our sense of entitlement has been taken away from us, and that's what the American dream was all about.**

✦ *We've lost our belief in a better future.*

For the first time in centuries, the majority of us do not feel that the future will be better than the past. We don't believe that our children will be better off than we are. We don't believe that social conditions in our country will improve, rather than decline. Even the most idealistic of us has more dread and less hope than ever before.

✦ We've lost our sense of safety.

Even in small-town America, we no longer feel safe taking a walk at night, for fear that we will become yet another crime statistic. We don't feel safe driving our cars, for fear that we will be carjacked. We don't feel safe having sex if we are single, for fear that we will contract the AIDS virus. We don't feel safe sending our children to school, for fear that there will be a drive-by shooting, or an act of random violence. We don't feel safe leaving them in day care, for fear that they will be molested. We don't feel safe letting them ride their bikes to a friend's house, for fear that they will be kidnapped. We don't even feel safe in our own homes.

✦ We've lost our escapes.

When we lose our sense of safety, we also lose our traditional escapes from everyday stress and anxiety. Going out at night, taking a drive, having sex—all these were once ways we dealt with tension and focused on just enjoying life for an hour or two. Now even these activities can be dangerous, and we think twice before engaging in them. We feel trapped, prisoners in our own homes.

✦ We've lost our psychic privacy.

The old boundaries that separated our lives from those of the rest of the world have been invaded. Satellite technology has made it all but impossible to insulate ourselves from the world's tragedies and turmoil in our new, global village. It is difficult to "tune out" what is happening around us, even if we want to. And the phrase "I can't be reached" has all but disappeared from our vocabulary as cellular phones and fax machines make it possible for people to find us wherever we are.

✦ We've lost our protective distance from "the enemy."

Since our country was founded, Americans always knew who the enemy was. He was the British, the Japanese, the Germans, the Russians—that country and those people over there and far away. With the end of the Cold War, the downfall of communism, and widespread nuclear disarmament, our distant enemies have all but disappeared. Suddenly the threat to our home, our property, and our family is not coming from outside our borders, but from inside. The person with the gun out to get you is no longer around the world—he is around the corner. *The enemy has arrived—and he is one of us. . . .*

✦

Each of these in itself is a powerful loss. Together, they are psychologically devastating. And like all losses, these evoke intense emotions in us—feelings of anger and powerlessness:

We are angry because we are overstimulated.

We are angry because things were always supposed to get better, not worse.

We are angry because we have been working so hard to do things right, and it seems like someone changed the rules without telling us.

And we feel powerless to protect ourselves and those we love from harm.

In times of crisis, it is always the weakest elements in society that begin to break down first. Perhaps, then, the epidemic of violence in our nation is an expression of this same powerlessness by those who didn't feel empowered to begin with. Perhaps the randomness of the violent acts honestly reflects the generalized rage of those who commit these crimes. All of us are victims of the times, but some of us, who started out at a disadvantage, are falling apart faster than the others.

"Who killed childhood? We all did."
— JERRY ADLER
Newsweek magazine

If we as adults are experiencing high levels of anxiety and despair in these challenging times, then God help our children, who, as *Newsweek* magazine wrote in a recent cover story, are "growing up fast and frightened." When I went to elementary school, my biggest worry was whether or not I'd get picked for a volleyball team in gym class, or if I'd get invited to Emily Bell's birthday party. Now kids worry about getting killed. Six-year-olds watch children their age die in drive-by shootings. Junior high and high school students pass through metal detectors to make sure no one is carrying a gun. Childhood is not what it used to be—it has lost its innocence, and in this way, it isn't even childhood anymore.

Don't think your children or grandchildren don't know what's going on. They do. They may even be more honest sharing their feelings about it than we adults are. A recent Princeton survey of 758 children aged ten to seventeen from all economic backgrounds came up with the following results:

- ✦ 56% feared violence against a family member
- ✦ 53% feared an adult losing his or her job
- ✦ 61% worry that they won't be able to find a good job
- ✦ Only one third said they would be financially more successful than their parents
- ✦ 47% feared not being able to afford shelter
- ✦ 49% worried about not having enough money
- ✦ Only 31% in the cities and 47% in the rural areas felt safe at night
- ✦ One in six has seen or knows someone who has been shot

Safety and trust have always been the hallmarks of childhood. They insulate children from the harsh realities that will come with adult life so that they can grow and learn with confidence. When our sons and daughters wake up to a world they cannot count on, and go to sleep in a world they fear, is it any wonder that one in seven of them has contemplated suicide? "Increasingly they [our children] are left to fend for themselves in a world of hostile strangers, dangerous sexual enticements, and mysterious economic forces that even adults find unsettling," explains journalist Jerry Adler. At least those of us who are older have had time to develop some coping skills that help us deal with our anxiety. But what are our kids supposed to do with theirs?

Again, we come back to technology as one of the culprits for the emotional crisis our children are facing. When most of us reading this grew up, there were certain unpleasant parts of life we were not exposed to until we were old enough to handle them. *But with the uncontrolled and often uncensored flow of information our young people are getting, especially through television and movies, they know too much too soon.*

By the time the average child has finished elementary school, he has watched 8,000 televised murders and 100,000 acts of violence. He knows all about sex, including that having it can kill. He is aware that many children his age are being physically abused or sexually molested, and that some children live on the streets because their parents cannot find a job.

Last year a friend of mine told me the following story. She and her husband were making love one evening, and the next morning, her five-year-old daughter approached her at the breakfast table.

"Mommy, last night I heard you and Daddy making noises in the bedroom, " she said with certainty. "What were you doing?"

My friend, her mother, thought carefully for a moment, and then answered:

"Honey, you know when you are eating something you really like, and you're happy, so you make a noise like 'Mmm-mmmmm'? Well, Daddy and I were really happy, so we were making happy noises."

Her daughter seemed to accept this explanation, and my friend breathed a sigh of relief. But it was short-lived. That afternoon, her little girl burst into the kitchen after being dropped off from school.

"Mommy, you told a fib!" she said accusingly. "You weren't making happy noises like I do. **You were having an orgasm!**"

My friend was speechless. Obviously her daughter had gone to school, asked around to her other five-year-old friends, and discovered the truth. As her mother shared this incident with me, we commiserated about the fact that when we were growing up, we weren't even sure what orgasms were until well into our teens.

I often witness parents of small children sharing stories similar to this, and everyone responds by saying "Isn't that cute?" or "Boy, the kids these days!!" But when I listen to what's underneath the laughter, I hear nervous panic. "**How can I possibly protect my child from hurt and harm,**" the parents secretly question, "**when they have already lost their innocence?**"

The answer is *"You cannot protect them,"* and this is what has all of us, whether we have children or not, so frightened for the next generation. The rates of teen pregnancy, drug and alcohol abuse, and juvenile crime among American young people are the highest in the world. In fact, much of the random violence that has made us feel like prisoners in our own homes is caused by kids with guns. Like their parents, our children feel powerless and full of rage, and many of them aren't as good at repressing those feelings as we are.

There is a principle in metaphysics that says *"We are what we perceive."* If our kids have been raised on a visual diet of violence, it should be no surprise that they are behaving violently. And we must understand that their violence, their attraction to irreverence, such as is expressed in the popular MTV cartoon *Beavis and Butt-head*, and the slightly dazed look in their clear eyes are all cries for help. They are lost in the trauma of our time, and it is up to us to help them, and ourselves, find a way out.

✦

"We must all go and work in the garden."
— VOLTAIRE

America, our beloved homeland, is in crisis. We can no longer ignore its cries for help. And yet, we cannot turn back the clock and undo the damage that has been done. Nor can we or should we turn totally away from the technology and materialism that has brought us to where we are. What, then, is the answer? How are we to heal our psychic wounds, and the wounds of our children? Where is our garden now, and how can we make it grow again?

We must rediscover those real moments of love and connection that will give meaning to our existence, no matter how crazy the outside world becomes.

We must recommit to the compassion, caring, and gratitude that have always been at the heart of American values and, in this way, reclaim our country's spirit.

We must bring our lives back into balance.

As treacherous as the present may appear to be, I am deeply hopeful about our future. For all around us there are very distinct signs that a healing has started to take place in America, both in our values and in the way we define success.

Oriental philosophy teaches us that nothing in the universe can swing too far in one direction without eventually seeking balance by swinging back. *We, as Americans, sense how out of balance we have gotten, and we're beginning to shift from a consciousness of self-indulgence to one of self-discovery.* We're turning back to religion and spiritual practices in great numbers. Whereas we once measured success in terms of status, wealth, and accomplishment, now we're beginning to measure it in terms of how happy we are, and how much peace of mind we've achieved.

Instead of believing that more of everything is better, we're returning to a *back to basics* philosophy. Our social trends all reflect this movement: We've gone from uncomfortable spike heels and impractical miniskirts to work boots and baggy dresses; we're trading in our fancy foreign cars for four-wheel drives and vans; we're exchanging complicated gourmet foods for mashed potatoes and meat loaf.

With our new love of anything that reminds us of less technological times, we are also turning away from the sophisticated and toward the simple—Western style dress, earth-toned colors in our clothing, and Native American jewelry are the latest fashion fads, cowboy movies and TV shows our new favorites, as if we're attempting to turn back the clock, to recapture our pioneer roots and the values that we lost along the way.

We are also rebuilding our nests and, thus, hoping to recreate some of the privacy our technology has taken from us. We're going out less and staying home more, not simply because we don't feel safe, but because we want to be alone. There is a strong trend toward privacy as we try to carve out the time to rediscover who we are and what we truly want.

✦

As we approach the twenty-first century, we, as Americans, are beginning to undergo a deep spiritual and emotional transformation. It is this transformation that is going to save us.

There is a wonderful quote attributed to a Chinese general who lived centuries ago:

> If the world is to be brought to order,
> my nation must first be changed.
> If my nation is to be changed,
> my hometown must be made over.
> If my hometown is to be reordered,
> my family must first be set right.
> If my family is to be regenerated,
> I, myself, must first be. . . .

Now, more than ever, we need real moments that will regenerate our tired souls and bring real meaning back into our lives. As our expectations continue to be diminished by economic realities, and as our outer lives continue to be limited by the constraints of time, space, and circumstances beyond our control, we must turn to the inner life, where there are no limits. There we will discover our true freedom, in the ability to find fulfillment *not* over the next hill, or in the next accomplishment, but right here, right now.

In this way, moment by moment, America will come back home. . . .

HIDING FROM
REAL MOMENTS

"In a seeker's search for wisdom, he spent three painful and grueling weeks climbing a tall, rocky mountain. At the peak, he found a wise, old guru and asked, 'Wise man, how might I make my life happier?'

"The Wise Man responded, 'To begin with, the next time you want to come up here, go to the other side of the mountain and take the tramway.' "

— GARY APPLE

In our lifelong search for happiness, many of us are making the journey a lot more difficult than it has to be: we are looking in the wrong direction for fulfillment; we are avoiding the very kinds of intimate experiences that will satisfy our hunger for purpose and meaning; *we are taking the long way up the mountain.*

This chapter will give you an opportunity to look at how you may be hiding from real moments, and how much time you waste in the process. If you read this with an open heart, I believe you will come to understand how you have been standing in your own way, and preventing yourself from experiencing the peace and fulfillment you deserve. And that's the first step toward discovering the real moments that are already there waiting for you.

✦

To begin, ask yourself these questions, and think carefully about the answers:

What makes me happy?
How often do I experience moments of true happiness?
How do I know when I am happy?

Don't be surprised if answering isn't as easy as you expect it should be:

Often, we don't recognize real moments of happiness in our lives because we've been expecting something different—something bigger, flashier, and more dramatic.

To many of us, our pictures of how happiness should look and feel still have their roots in the "bigger must be better" mentality we were all brought up on. And so we have developed very unrealistic expectations of happiness—in our mind we see the word golden and glowing in capital letters: **HAPPI- NESS!!!!!!** The Big "H," the pie in the sky, the brass ring, the pot of gold at the end of the rainbow.

Thus, *we wait for happiness passively, as if it is something that will be bestowed on us at a particular time.* You just gave birth to your first child, and as you lie there exhausted from your labor, you think: "Now it's over and I should feel happy." You finally get the promotion you've been hoping for, and as you drive home to tell your wife, you think: "Now I can stop worrying about my job, and really be happy." You move into the new home you've dreamed of owning your whole life, and as you walk through each room, you think: "At last! My own home! Tonight I'll go to sleep happy."

But what if you don't? What if you feel good with a small "g," but not happy with a big "H"? "Something's wrong with me," you think suspiciously. "I *should* be feeling HAPPY, but I'm just happy." Or maybe you're not even feeling that— maybe you're actually feeling tired, or just O.K. Or maybe you're not feeling much of anything at all.

As we've seen, this is how we get hooked into believing that if we aren't feeling happy now, then happiness will surely be just around the next corner, or at the top of the next mountain. We know that big moment will come one day. On that day, you'll wake up and say . . . "Wait a minute . . . something feels different. Could it be? Could this be it? Oh my gosh, I think it is . . . I made it!! I'm finally happy!"

Waiting for Joy to Penetrate

I've spent much of my adult life working hard to try and be happy, and failing miserably at it. I could never understand what I was doing wrong, or why all the things I achieved and experienced weren't filling me up inside. One day about four years ago, I had an experience which gave me some of the answer. My husband and I had arrived at a small seaside town for a long-awaited vacation. We were exhausted from a year of long hours and very little free time, and I'd been counting the days until we got there.

The first two days passed quickly. Late one afternoon on the third day, I took a walk alone down a quiet road next to the ocean. The air was sweet and warm; the trees were filled with birds serenading the setting of the sun. And as I walked, I realized that I'd been feeling strange ever since our vacation started.

"What could possibly be bothering me?" I wondered. "It's perfect here. I'm swimming and sunbathing and making love and doing all the things I enjoy the most in the world. *I should be totally happy.*"

Then, it hit me. *I was waiting to be happy, as if happiness were some kind of condition that would descend upon me.* Like a child waiting anxiously for an expected surprise with her eyes closed, I was going through my days waiting for happiness to bang me over the head and announce its arrival. I'd wake up each morning and check . . . Am I happy yet? A little ache in my heart would respond: "No . . . not yet . . . check back later." And I'd go through my day, and periodically stop, as if to catch myself off guard, and think: "O.K.—how about now? Do I feel happy now?" Of course, the answer would always be "NO."

As I stood there on that beautiful road, a phrase appeared in my mind: "**Waiting for joy to penetrate.**" I realized that was exactly what I was doing. I was waiting for joy to penetrate my discontent, waiting for joy to make itself known. It's as if I wanted God to come down and announce: "Barbara De Angelis—Congratulations!! You are now officially happy! Enjoy it while it lasts."

I had happiness set up as being something *out of my control,* something that would or would not happen *to* me. When I went on vacation, I'd be happy. When I was relaxed, then I'd be happy. When I got a great tan, then I'd be happy. Of course, this meant that if I didn't go on the trip, or if I went and it rained for a week, then I wouldn't be happy, because those conditions I'd set up wouldn't be met.

So here I was, standing alone on a summer afternoon, waiting for happiness to announce its arrival in my life. And in that moment, I knew if I kept living as I did, I would have to wait forever.

I was waiting for happiness to come from the
outside into me, instead of creating it,
from the inside out.

I said in the beginning of this book that happiness is a skill, not an acquisition. *It is a choice you make in each moment about how you experience that moment, not a state you one day achieve.* By waiting for Joy with a capital "J" to penetrate me, I wasn't even recognizing the many real and happy moments that were available.

This, then, is the first way we hide from real moments—**we live in such a way that they are hidden from us.**

The Truth about Happiness

I believe that most people share a common and deadly misunderstanding about happiness—that is a fixed *state* we get to, like turning forty, or becoming engaged, or being in recovery from an addiction. I'm forty, I'm engaged, I'm in recovery, I'm happy. The truth, as I realized that day on my island walk, is quite different:

Happiness is not a state of being—it is a
series of real moments.

These moments don't just happen to us. We need to create opportunities for them to occur. *We need to stop hiding out from those very experiences that will bring us, from the inside, the experience of joy we're longing for.*

If happiness is not a state of being, that means *we cannot always be happy.* For those of us brought up in the "we can have it all" years, this is very disappointing news. I have seen myself and my contemporaries struggle against this reality, treating moments of pain, confusion, or unpleasantness of any kind like mud we've stepped in and can't wait to wash off. Anything that doesn't feel good we try to avoid, and if we can't, we attempt to rush through these undesirable experiences as quickly as possible, and get back to "normal."

I once heard someone from another country say "**The trouble with Americans is that they expect to live with ongoing euphoria.**" I can't say that I disagree. We are so enamored with perfection that we often have a difficult time dealing with dualism—good and bad, success and setback, joy and sorrow.

I've probably been more guilty of this attitude than most people. Until six years ago, I used to misinterpret pain or sadness as a sign of my own spiritual failure. I believed that *if I were truly living a good life, I would always be happy, and since I was not happy, I must be doing something wrong.* This belief caused me to live with a lot of denial. For instance, I felt that I should always be happy in a relationship, so I avoided facing problems, confronting controversial issues, or even admitting to myself that I was unhappy. And I missed a lot of real moments, because although they were powerful or meaningful moments, they were not particularly happy moments, and I ran from them.

If we want to find peace and live with authenticity, there is a truth we must face—**pain, sadness, unpleasantness, are an integral part of life**, and will inevitably occur from time to time. We cannot *always* be happy. Carl Jung said it this way:

> "There are as many nights as days, and the one is just as long as the other in the year's course. Even a happy life cannot be without a measure of darkness, and the word 'happy' would lose its meaning if it were not balanced by sadness."

Imagine that your child is ill, and you sit by her bedside late at night stroking her hair, soothing her frightened cries, waiting for her fever to go down. As you keep your watchful vigil, she is all that is important in the world, and nothing else seems to exist. You love her so much that it hurts, and the bond between you feels sacred. Are you happy? Of course not, but you can feel something deeply moving and meaningful about this experience, and you are right: *You are having a real moment.*

> At the end of our time on earth, if we have lived fully, we will not be able to say: "I was always happy." Hopefully we will be able to say: "I have experienced a lifetime of real moments, and many of them were happy moments."

In this way, it is only in learning how to experience real moments, *one by one,* that we will also be able to experience happy moments.

Symptoms of Not Having Enough Real Moments

Most people I know have a "real moment deficiency." They aren't experiencing enough real moments in their lives, and when we are deficient in real moments, we end up being deficient in peace, contentment, and joy. When dogs have a mineral deficiency, they start eating the dirt in the yard to fulfill their craving for minerals. When your body has a deficiency of energy because you haven't eaten for a while, you start craving a candy bar or something sweet to help you get your blood sugar back up. **In this way, when we have a real moment deficiency, we develop unhealthy cravings and behaviors in an attempt to fill up our spiritual and emotional emptiness in other ways.**

Here are some symptoms that suggest you may not have enough real moments in your life:

✦ *You need to constantly be doing something.*

When you aren't experiencing enough real moments, you live with a gnawing sense of restlessness and dissatisfaction that will not go away. **The only relief you get will be when you are busy doing something, because you are focused on your task on the outside, and not on what you're feeling inside.** You might become a workaholic, spending twelve or fourteen hours a day on your career, never unwinding long enough to forget about work. "I'd love to take some time off," you proclaim, "but this project is taking longer than I thought." Of course, it always will, because you set it up that way. If you're a woman, you might become a rescuer or professional giver, spending all your time helping your friends, your family, the local charity, or whoever needs you. "I don't know how I got so busy!" you complain. The answer is simple: *You didn't say no to anyone or anything.*

When you have a need to be constantly doing something, you will always be able to find someone to help, or a new project to take on, and despite your protestations about wanting more time to enjoy your life, you will not make the time. The problem is that you will get approval and accolades for your addiction to activity, especially if you end up achieving a lot for yourself or contributing a lot to others, and this reinforces your tendency toward overdoing.

People who do too much get very nervous when they aren't focused on doing something. *They are uncomfortable with a void, and feel the need to fill it as quickly as possible.* They're the ones who vacuum their house twice a day, or make lists about what lists they need to make. They don't do well doing nothing on unstructured, quiet vacations. Instead, they make sure to see every museum or every tourist attraction or read five books. If you fall into this category, you probably have your TV or radio on most of the time when you are home to fill up the silence.

Doing too much inevitably turns into a vicious cycle. Here's how it works:

You don't have enough real moments, so you feel empty → You feel compelled to fill up your emptiness by always doing → When you are always doing, you have no free time just to be → Since you have no free time, you don't experience any real moments → You feel compelled to fill up your emptiness by doing.

And the cycle goes on and on.

There is only one way to break the cycle, and that is to stop always doing, and create opportunities for the magic of real moments to occur: At night after the kids are asleep, turn off the television, sit quietly with the person you love and have a real moment of intimate connection; instead of scheduling every moment of your Saturday morning with errands, put aside twenty minutes to take a walk in the park and see what real moments with Nature you encounter; the next time you get together with friends, don't plan to do anything in particular—spend some time just being in each other's presence and enjoying the real moments that result.

Leave room in your life for real moments by having times when you aren't *doing* anything.

✦ *You have an addiction.*

All addictions have one thing in common—they numb you out to what is happening in the moment. They offer, instead, an intense sensory experience which either absorbs all of your attention or distorts reality. You may think you're having a real moment, but you are not, because your addictive activity, such as drinking or doing drugs, is actually disconnecting you from your true emotions and, therefore, making it difficult for you to connect with others around you.

People who are hungry for more real moments
often use addictions to get a temporary
hit of happiness.

But because the feeling of happiness that addictions provide is caused by the substance or behavior, and therefore is always temporary, you can't feel good without it. This is how you get hooked into wanting and needing more.

Addictions are so socially acceptable in America that, often, people don't even realize that they have one. I'm not talking about addictions to hard drugs like heroin or cocaine—those we have judgments about. It's the tolerated addictions—alcohol, cigarettes, recreational drugs like marijuana, tranquilizers and painkillers, gambling, pornography—that are so insidious, and in this way, so deadly, because we don't think of them as addictions at all. We call them *"habits."*

America has a real double standard about which "habits" we call serious addictions, and which "habits" we don't. Dad stands before his sixteen-year-old, waving his nightly martini in his hand as he berates his son for being a "pothead." A congressman sits puffing away on his fortieth cigarette of the day as he deplores the drug dealers who are ruining the youth of this country. Mom screams at her daughter for trying psychedelic mushrooms at a rock concert, and then retreats to her room to take a tranquilizer so she can sleep.

Whether it's full-blown alcoholism or watching TV ten hours a day, *regular use of addictive substances, or regular indulgence in addictive behavior robs you of your ability to fully feel.* Do whatever it takes and get whatever help you need to stop, and try getting high on living.

✦ *You are cynical, pessimistic, and sarcastic.*

I have great compassion for cynical people, because I know that underneath their armor of sarcasm and disdain, they are hungry for more real moments in their lives.

When we don't experience real moments, we
will have difficulty seeing the purpose and
meaning of our existence.

Without a sense of meaning, life is simply a series of random
events as we move purposelessly through each day. And when
we see no purpose, no sense to the way things are, it is easy
to become cynical and to stop caring.

Cynicism is a cover-up for pain, *an expression of angry
hopelessness that the world is the way it is. Cynics are often
frustrated believers who feel deep disappointment in people and
in life itself.* Think of someone you know who appears to have
a negative or pessimistic attitude. When you look into their
eyes, you will see a wounded spirit.

If you have lost your faith in why we are here and what
we are supposed to be doing, you aren't having enough real
moments. It is these moments that themselves will bring
meaning back into your life and make it all worthwhile.

✦ *You live your life through others.*

A grandmother sits alone in her apartment, watching soap
operas and talk shows all day long. She glances at the phone,
wondering if her granddaughter will call later tonight. She's
happy when she hears from her granddaughter—in fact she
lives for the calls and the occasional visits. She thinks back to
Thanksgiving when her granddaughter came to stay for three
days, and she smiles. Checking her watch, she realizes that
there are only four more hours until she should be getting
home from work. "Maybe I'll call her tonight," she decides.
"It's been a pretty uneventful week."

**If your greatest joy in the past few years has been the
success and happiness of your children or grandchildren, or
your mate, you are not having enough real moments in your**

life. You are living your life through someone else. I'm not talking about feeling happy with and proud of those you love. I'm talking about making other people the center of your life, and not having one of your own.

I have seen mothers do this with their children, rejoicing when a child succeeds, mourning when a child fails, becoming so enmeshed in their offspring that they are utterly dependent on their sons and daughters for validation. I have seen grandparents do this with their grandchildren, turning them into their only source of love, making seeing or talking to them their only purpose for living. I've seen wives do this with their husbands, losing their identity completely, gaining a sense of self-worth only through their husbands' accomplishments or their husbands' status in the community.

When we have lost a sense of our own purpose in life, we often latch on to someone else's purpose as a replacement. But it is never too late to find your own purpose again—in fact, knowing your own purpose is what will keep you alive longer.

> No matter what age you are, or what your
> circumstances might be, you are special, and
> still have something unique to offer. Your life,
> because of who *you* are, has meaning.

If you feel guilty reading this, perhaps it's time to take your life back, to release those you love from feeling you are living through them, and to rediscover your special purpose by having more real moments. You have your own special gifts to give, whether through volunteering your time at a retirement home or hospital, becoming a foster grandparent to a child who has little or no family, or helping out at a local day-care facility. *You do make a difference.*

✦ *You are judgmental.*

By definition, judging means *standing outside* of a situation, or a relationship, and criticizing what you see. You watch someone at work making mistakes and think "What a space case he is!" You feel frustrated driving behind an elderly person who's going fifteen miles an hour and think "How can they give licenses to these people?"

You can't be judgmental and have a real moment at the same time.

In order to have a real moment, you need to be totally in a situation, fully feeling it from the inside out. You need to be connected with the person you're with or the environment you're in. *When you are judgmental, you are disconnecting from that person or experience, thus making it impossible for you to have a real moment at that particular time.*

> When you let go of your judgments and create
> a moment of connection with another person,
> you take the first step toward being truly
> compassionate.

Here are two stories about how I learned to stop hiding from real moments, and learned some powerful lessons in compassion:

Learning Compassion on a Street Corner

Last year I decided to buy a new car, and set aside time one afternoon to visit a local car dealership. When I arrived at the lot, a salesman about fifty-five years old agreed to take me for a test drive in a car I was thinking about purchasing. Five minutes passed, ten minutes passed—he was still trying to find the keys, and I started getting annoyed. Things got worse when he couldn't remember a special alarm code used to unlock the car, and had to go back inside and look it up in a file. Now I was feeling incredibly tense, and resentful that he was wasting so much time. Finally, we got into the car and drove off the lot. But we'd only gone one mile from the showroom when the car stopped dead in the middle of the street.

"What happened?" I asked. "Did I do something wrong?"

"No," the perplexed salesman replied. "Maybe it just wasn't warmed up enough."

Then, I noticed the gas gauge was on empty. "Sir," I said in a frosty voice, "there is no gas in this car."

"Oh gee, you're right. I guess the mechanic forgot to fill it up."

Now I was fuming. I was going to be late for a meeting, and here we were stuck in the middle of a busy intersection, causing a traffic jam.

The salesman went into a nearby store to call the dealership and ask them to pick us up, and left me standing on the street corner. I was furious, and totally frustrated that I'd picked such an idiot to sell me a car. "What a moron," I cursed to myself. "Here I am wasting my whole afternoon because he wasn't smart enough to check and see if the car had gas. This guy has no brains!"

Ten minutes later, the embarrassed-looking salesman came out to wait with me. It was a very warm day in Los Angeles. His face was beet red, his shirt was drenched with sweat, and I started getting nervous that he was going to have a stroke. Taking pity on him, I decided to strike up a conversation.

"I didn't mean to seem rude earlier," I began, "it's just that I'm in a hurry to get to an appointment, and now my schedule is all messed up."

"Please don't apologize," he responded in a quiet voice. "It's all my fault. I'm having a horrible day—some personal problems—my mind just isn't working."

In that moment, I realized I had a choice. I could continue to judge him, which felt horrible to both of us. Or I could connect with him from the heart. And that's what I did.

"I'm sorry to hear you're having some problems," I said. "I know how distracted I am when I'm upset about something important."

That was all he needed to hear to feel safe. "It's my mother," he blurted out. *"I just got a call from the hospital—they were doing exploratory surgery and found out she has terminal cancer.* It's spread all over her body. After work, I have to tell her the bad news, and I don't know if I can handle it."

Tears welled up in my eyes as I felt this man's sadness. No wonder he'd been so distracted. No wonder he couldn't concentrate on selling me a car. Suddenly, running out of gas, being late to my appointment, and everything else seemed totally insignificant. Because I'd been willing to have a real moment with the salesman, I now understood his behavior, felt his grief, and was given a wonderful reminder that, to paraphrase a Native American aphorism, *we should never judge another human being until we've walked a mile in his or her moccasins.*

Seeing the Ghost of My Grandfather at the Wheel

Oddly enough, the second compassion lesson also has to do with an automobile. Several months ago, I was on my way to an important meeting when I found myself driving behind a car going about twenty miles an hour in a forty-five-mile-an-hour zone. There was no way to pass this car, so I was stuck following it as it puttered along, block by block. I tried honking my horn, hoping the person in the car would get the message, but it didn't help. As each moment passed, I became more and more agitated.

Finally, I caught a peek at the driver, and discovered it was an elderly man who looked about eighty years old. "I should have known," I thought bitterly. "Some old guy who shouldn't even have a license anymore." I was about to start honking my horn again at this hazardous slowpoke when suddenly and unexpectedly, my mind flashed on my grandfather, who'd died when I was nineteen. I loved my grandfather so much, and had been devastated when he passed away. I remembered how frail he'd been in his later years, his body betraying him with prostate cancer, his face creased with pain. I recalled how difficult it had been for him, having spent his whole life giving unselfishly to others, to face his failing health, and have to rely on friends, family, and strangers to take care of him.

Overcome with memories, my eyes filled with tears and my heart flooded with new compassion. I realized that the elderly driver of that car might as well have been my grandfather, and was probably somebody else's. He wasn't driving slowly in order to annoy me. In his last years, he was out taking a drive, savoring another day of life.

I watched the car moving carefully along in front of me, and silently apologized to the driver in my heart: "Please forgive me for becoming so angry with you, dear old man," I thought. "I'm glad you're still alive today, and I know that driving on your own might be one of the very last freedoms you have left. And forgive me for being so impatient with your pace and pressuring you to go faster. I now know that you're going as fast as you can. . . ."

I eased my foot off the accelerator, and allowed myself to tune in to the slow rhythms of the driver in front of me, respecting them, celebrating them. Finally he put on his blinker to make a turn, and as he disappeared around the corner, I help up a hand and waved in his direction. "Good-bye, Grand-Pop," I whispered. "Thank you for the reminder. . . . I miss you."

✦

Both of these events were precious, real moments in my life. *Each was unexpected, unplanned, and only existed because I was willing to stop and pay attention to what was really happening.* I could have hidden from the moment by criticizing the people involved, or condemning the circumstances. Instead, I followed the quiet impulses of my heart and *felt the moment rather than judged it.* In doing so, both times I received powerful gifts and necessary reminders.

> When you learn how to stop hiding from real
> moments you'll find that they are happening
> all around you, and can offer themselves
> when you least expect it.

How and Why We Avoid Real Moments

The first step in beginning to create more real moments in your life is recognizing how and why you avoid them.

✦ *We avoid real moments by being too busy or distracted to pay attention.*

Most of us frequently do two or three things at once. You're talking on the phone to your friend, paying your bills, and watching TV, all at the same time. How can you possibly have a moment of true connection and meaning with your friend? You can't. So you don't.

Watch yourself for the rest of today, or tomorrow. Notice how often you are focusing on several activities, but not fully enjoying or experiencing one of them. Maybe you're driving to work, listening to the radio, and thinking about an important project all at once. You're not really driving, listening, or thinking at all. You're not fully doing anything. So you miss the drive, you miss enjoying the music, and you miss getting deep insights into your project. And you definitely miss real moments.

✦

When I go from my home to my office, I drive down a long, wide road that starts out at the top of a hill, and ends up right at the coast highway next to the ocean. There's a traffic light at the bottom of this hill that's notorious for being very long—if you aren't lucky enough to get through it as you're coming down the hill, you can sit there at the light for six or seven minutes, waiting for it to change.

One day, soon after I decided to write this book, I was cruising down the hill, hoping to make the light, and just as the car in front of me passed through the intersection, the light turned red. I sat in my car and thought about how much I hated getting stuck here all the time, staring at the signal as if that would speed up the process. I looked anxiously at the clock every minute to see how much time had passed, and worried about all the things I had to accomplish that day.

All of a sudden, I was struck by the absurdity of the situation: Here I was, looking out on a beautiful sandy beach and beyond that, the ocean. The sun was shining in a perfectly clear sky, and the light shimmered on the water. *Millions of people traveled from all around the world every year to visit this very spot, and to look at this spectacular view that I wasn't even noticing or enjoying because I was too distracted and too much in a hurry!!*

I realized then that this was how I was living most of my life, **doing so much of everything that I wasn't paying complete attention to anything.** The stoplight was just a reflection of how few of my experiences, whether waiting at a light, having a conversation, or listening to music, I actually experienced. No wonder I'd decided to write a book called *Real Moments*—I needed to read it myself!!

I'd always considered having to stop at that intersection a nuisance. Now, I decided it was God's way of slowing me down when I was going too fast, and reminding me to pay attention:

"Stop . . . breathe in the fresh air . . . look at the ocean . . . it looks like it goes on forever, doesn't it? Isn't this a beautiful planet you live on? How lucky you are to drive by this lovely stretch of beach every day! How fortunate you are to be alive!!!! . . . Feel better? . . . Good . . . O.K., I'll change the light now. . . . Have a wonderful morning!!"

That day, I had a revelation at that intersection, and by the time the light finally changed, so had I. **By paying attention to the fact that I wasn't paying attention, I'd experienced a real moment that transformed the way I lived my life.** Now, each time I am met with a red light at the bottom of the hill, I smile and say "Thank you . . . I must have needed to stop and enjoy the view."

✦

Sometimes we avoid real moments because we are afraid of them. *We don't pay attention because, in the secret places of our heart, we suspect that by paying attention, we will discover some unpleasant truths about ourselves or our life.* This suspicion is correct:

> Real moments can be very confrontational.
> When you stop doing too much and take time to
> have real moments by paying attention, you will,
> undoubtedly, come face-to-face with emotions,
> revelations, or realities you weren't aware of.

Many years ago, I was in a very unfulfilling and incompatible relationship. I loved this man very much, but we were not right for each other, a fact I'd been trying to ignore because I didn't want the relationship to end. And so I filled my life with so much activity, so many projects, that I was literally working every day and evening, every weekend, and even on holidays. My work brought me tremendous satisfaction, and, unconsciously, I avoided paying attention to the relationship.

The time came for us to take a vacation, and for some reason, I decided not to bring any work with me. We had booked a room on a tiny island in the middle of nowhere, and for the first time since we met, we would be alone with no distractions, no agendas, no business to discuss. I remember getting on the plane with a hard knot in my stomach, not understanding why I felt so anxious. But I soon found out.

The second day of our trip, I spent an afternoon by myself on a deserted beach. It was a whole afternoon of real moments during which I could no longer escape from the truth in my heart—*I needed to end this relationship.* Until now, I had successfully avoided confronting the truth because I was so afraid of the pain it was going to cause him, and the drama it would create in my life. But there, on that island, there was nowhere and no way for me to hide from my feelings anymore.

It took me several weeks to get up the courage to tell the man I loved that I was leaving, but finally, I did. I often wonder what would have happened to us if I had not taken the time to experience some real moments with myself, if I had not faced the fear of confronting my truth. How much longer would we have lived together, not getting what we wanted and needed? We are both happily married to other people now, and have found out where we truly belong.

Sometimes, it does take courage to have a real moment, and to be open to whatever it reveals to you. But the alternative is avoidance, denial, and a life spent running from yourself. . . .

"What you bring forth out of yourself from the inside will save you. What you do not bring forth out of yourself from the inside will destroy you."

— GOSPEL OF THOMAS

✦

Later in this book, I'll share some techniques for creating real moments, but for now, just try an experiment—*Sometime in the next few days, do one activity with complete attention, and without distracting yourself.* It could be driving in your car and really paying attention to what you see around you, or preparing dinner and really paying attention to the fact that you are preparing nourishment for the people you love.

I tried this recently on an airplane. I decided to really experience flying in the plane for the full four hours my flight took, not to read a book or watch a movie, but to be in a speeding metal tube 35,000 feet up in the air. And that's just what I did. I sat next to a window and watched the earth pass beneath me for four hours straight. I witnessed tributaries turning into large rivers, plains bursting forth into mountains, and then sinking down into plains again. I saw small cities, large cities, and tiny towns, all looking so gentle from the sky. By the time we landed, I felt a love for the land of our country that I'd never experienced before, and I walked off that plane filled with peace.

✦ *We avoid real moments by putting up boundaries between ourselves and other people.*

Many of my most loving real moments have occurred when I was experiencing a connection with someone else—my husband, my dog Bijou, a close friend, and often, people I'm just meeting for the first time. What creates a real moment between two people? *Intimacy.*

Intimacy occurs when the boundaries between
you and someone else melt, and
your hearts touch.

If you have a problem with intimacy, and many of us do, you aren't going to be eager to create real moments with people in your life. You won't feel safe, because during real moments, your usual boundaries are penetrated. Your innermost feelings are revealed, leaving you feeling vulnerable, unprotected. *And if in the past, you allowed someone to get close to you, and it caused you pain, you won't find it easy to be intimate again without experiencing a lot of fear.*

This is one of the most common ways we hide from real moments—we give in to fear, and decide to avoid or resist intimacy. You become an expert at putting up emotional walls, psychic barricades around your heart. The walls keep out pain, but they also make it difficult for you to have real moments: since other people's love can't get in and your love can't get out, you don't experience intimacy. The boundaries that are there to protect you become an emotional prison, insulating you from the very moments of communion you need to be happy.

Magical Connections and Blessed Encounters

If you want to experience more real moments of intimacy in your life, you don't have to wait until you get into a relationship or marry. After all, we share this world with over five billion people. Unfortunately, we have so many rules about whom we can connect with, when connection is appropriate, and how much we should connect that we miss many opportunities for what I call *"magical connections and blessed encounters."*

In our society, we call people we don't know "strangers,"

and we go out of our way to avoid connecting with them. When you bump into someone in an elevator, you immediately apologize, as if you've done something wrong. When you notice someone looking at you for a while at a restaurant, you immediately assume either you have a run in your panty hose, or a stain on your tie, that the person is trying to pick you up, or that they're a psychopathic stalker and you're the next victim. Very rarely do you think, "Oh, there's another human being looking at me and making contact."

According to our "Boundary Book," there are certain "acceptable" subjects one can discuss with strangers: the weather, sports, entertainment, gossip. You can always complain with a stranger, since both of you simultaneously judging something else makes you feel safe with one another. And as long as each party respects the boundaries, you're comfortable. But none of these conversations will help you experience a real moment together.

If you're willing to share a real moment, you can learn things about yourself from strangers that you often can't learn from people you are close with.

> Strangers can be very pure mirrors of truth, reflecting back to you whatever you've been needing to see, delivering cosmic messages you've been needing to hear.

There is a safety in anonymity that allows us, when we don't know someone, to pierce through layers of ego and expectation, and open up to truths which are waiting to reveal themselves. I have had many spectacular real moments with strangers—while waiting in lines, meeting in a store, and especially on airplanes, since I travel so much. Let me share one with you. . . .

How I Met My Mirror in the Sky

I was tired when I boarded the plane in San Francisco that would carry me home to Los Angeles. I'd just finished two days of speeches and TV appearances, and felt talked out. So I was really looking forward to the flight, and planned to meditate and sleep the whole way—that is, until I got to my assigned row, and saw a little girl about nine years old squirming around in the seat next to me. "Oh no," I groaned inwardly, "not a child—I don't have the energy for it. Please let her be in the wrong seat." But I was out of luck. She was in the right place, and so was I.

I sat down and began strategizing about how I could avoid talking with her. "Maybe if I just close my eyes, she'll be afraid to say anything," I thought. "Or perhaps I should ask the flight attendant to find me a different seat." As we taxied down the runway, I was already counting the minutes until the flight was over.

All at once, I realized how unconsciously I was behaving. "Pay attention . . ." my inner voice reminded me. Throughout my lifetime, I'd learned over and over again that *there are no accidents in the Universe*—I'd been placed next to this little girl for a reason. If I was having such a strong negative reaction to the experience, there was probably a powerful lesson in it for me somewhere.

And so, I introduced myself to Bethany, who appeared to have been waiting for me to reach out to her. Once she saw that I was truly interested, Bethany shared herself without reservation. She began by telling me that she was very excited because this was her first flight in an airplane, and she was flying to meet her father in Los Angeles. Her parents had recently divorced, and her dad moved away with her brother and sister. Bethany was also given the choice of being with the rest of her family, but she chose to stay with her mother.

"That must have been a difficult decision," I told her, "to know you wouldn't be with everyone else."

"It was, but I felt like Mom needed me," Bethany explained with great solemnity. "She's going through a hard time." She went on to explain that her mother married and had kids at a young age, and was now feeling trapped and tied down. "She has lots of boyfriends, and goes out all the time," Bethany told me in a confidential tone, "and I don't like it because I'm alone so much."

"I'll bet you miss your dad a lot," I offered. Bethany's eyes filled with tears.

"I really miss him, and everyone else too. He calls me every day to see if I'm O.K."

"And what do you tell him?"

"I tell him I'm fine, but sometimes I'm not. . . ."

My heart hurt as I saw the pain and confusion in Bethany's bright eyes, too much pain for a nine-year-old to be carrying around. She was wise beyond her years . . . she had to be. And I saw the whole picture—Mom starts running around; Dad files for and gets custody of the kids, because Mom is unfit. But compassionate, loving Bethany doesn't want to abandon Mom. So she gives up a stable new life, the protection of her father and growing up with her brother and sister, to make sure Mom knows that someone still loves her. And night after night, she sits alone or with a baby-sitter, watching TV, waiting for Mom to come home from a hot date, and coping with her loneliness by convincing herself that she'd done the right thing.

And so we talked, Bethany and me. I told her about my own parents' divorce when I was eleven, how torn I felt trying to take sides, how I felt damaged and different because I didn't have a normal family like all my friends, and how I used to cry myself to sleep. "Me too!" she chimed in. I explained what I'd learned once I grew up about how parents are just people, and that inside of them, they are still little kids just like her. I tried to give her insight into why her mom was doing the things she was, and that just because she was the mom and Bethany the child, it didn't mean Bethany might not see things Mom didn't see. I suggested that she tell her dad how unhappy she was, and not worry that she'd make him feel guilty, because he needed to know. I reminded her that, above all, she needed to take care of herself first, even if it meant moving away. And then I told her how hard I'd worked to love myself, to know my parents' divorce had nothing to do with me, and to accomplish good things in my life.

"Look at what I've done as a grown-up," I said proudly, showing her several of the books I'd written which I happened to have in my briefcase.

"Wow—is this really you?" she asked, wide-eyed.

"Honest, it's me. And I've even been on television."

Bethany almost jumped out of her seat."Wait a minute . . . wait a minute . . ." she exploded. "I"VE SEEN YOU!!!! IT WAS ON SOME TALK SHOW, LIKE *OPRAH* OR *GERALDO*, RIGHT?!!!"

"Right."

"Oh my God, Oh my God, I am so excited!!!" Bethany began bouncing up and down.

"Do you know why I'm telling you all this? *So that you always remember that it doesn't matter where you came from—it just matters where you're going.* You're a very special, smart and talented person, Bethany. You can be anything you want to be. Hey, if I can do it, so can you."

Our flight was almost over. Bethany and I exchanged phone numbers, and I promised to send some books for her mother and father, and a special surprise just for her. She was quiet now, her face pressed against the window, enchanted by the scenery beneath her.

Suddenly, I got it. How could I not have seen the truth

sooner? **Bethany was *me*.** I had just spent an hour in an airplane talking to myself as a nine-year-old child, telling her all the things I wished someone had told me when I was in so much pain, showing her a vision of who she was destined to become someday, sharing lessons it took me thirty years to figure out. *God had placed me in a seat next to Little Barbara, with a different set of circumstances and a different name, but with the same troubled spirit, so I could heal that old wounded part of me.*

With Bethany as my mirror, I saw that, indeed, I had triumphed over my past, that I could forgive it even more than I had done before, and that part of my purpose was to share the lessons of my journey with all the big and little Barbaras and Bethanys and Bobs of the world. I shook my head, marveling at the perfection of the moment. Bethany had been my teacher in the sky as much as I had been hers, delivering a message I was meant to have, just as I delivered one to her. We were true sisters in spirit.

Just then, Bethany turned to me, and I saw her eyes were filled with tears.

"What's wrong?" I asked.

"Nothing—it's just that this is the happiest day of my life."

"Why, because you got to fly in a plane and you're going to see your dad in a few minutes?"

Bethany looked straight into my soul, and with a radiant smile she answered:

"No, **because I met you . . .**"

No honor, no award, no standing ovation I've ever received meant more to me than what Bethany said that afternoon. She rendered me speechless (not an easy task!). We've kept in touch, and the last I heard, she was still living with her mom, but her dad had moved back to be near her.

I will never forget Bethany. She gave me one of the most profound and healing real moments of my life. Soon after our meeting, as promised, I sent her a teddy bear so she could have a special friend to share her feelings and secrets with.

When I found out she named it Barbara, I cried. . . .

✦

"Just think how happy you'd be if you lost everything you have right now—and then, got it back again. . . ."

— ANONYMOUS

I hope you are having a real moment reading this. . . .

I hope I am helping you pay attention to forces and feelings inside you that you've been hiding from. . . .

I hope I'm getting through the layers of forgetfulness you've collected through the years, and that you're starting to remember why you are really here. . . .

I'm telling you all of this because I don't want you to waste any more time. You may not be aware that you are wasting time. In fact, your life might feel like you're squeezing forty hours of work and responsibility into a twenty-four-hour day. The time I'm speaking about that gets wasted is the time you don't spend in each moment, experiencing and appreciating it for what it is, the time that you lose because you live through it unmindfully, throwing away the opportunity for love, for connection, for learning, as if you have all the time in the world.

Several months ago I received a tearful phone call from a friend, informing me that she'd just been diagnosed with cancer. We spoke for a while, but even after I hung up, I couldn't get her off my mind. That evening, as my husband and I lay in bed, I told him the unfortunate news, and shared the strong emotions that had been coming up for me all day. I'd been thinking about my friend, who was my age, and how she must have been feeling that night, alone, except for her cats, in her dark bedroom. I knew that if I were she, I'd be wondering how much time I had left to live, and how I should spend that time if my cancer was not cured.

"How would I change my life if I found out I was dying?" I wondered aloud to my husband.

"I guess that would depend on how many years the doctors estimated you had left," Jeffrey said.

"I know one thing, I wouldn't waste even one day not fully feeling and enjoying every moment of life."

Suddenly, I was seized with a searing truth. Like my friend, *I too was dying,* perhaps not today or tomorrow, but thirty or forty or fifty years in the not-so-distant future:

Why would I need to know I was about to lose everything to really enjoy it?

Why do so many of us only get motivated through fear and loss?

Why do we wait until we're ill to appreciate the miracle of our bodies?

Why do we wait until our partner is walking out the door to realize how much we need him or her?

Why do we put off living the way we want to live, as if we have all the time in the world?

Our time here on earth is so short. If we are fortunate, we have approximately 80 years, 29,200 days to experience life and all it offers. How many of us, as we breathe our last breath, will truly be able to say *"I feel fulfilled with who I was, and with what I did. I enjoyed all the moments God gave me"*?

Often, it is only those who are on death's doorstep that can see clearly enough to remind us of the precious gift each day of life truly is. The late actor and director, Michael Landon, shared this message in an interview just a few weeks before his death several years ago:

"While life lasts, it's good to remember that death is coming, and it's good that we don't know when. It keeps us alert. It reminds us to live

while we have the chance. Somebody should tell us that we are dying. Then we might live life to the limit, every minute of every day. Do it! Whatever you want to do, do it now. There are only so many tomorrows. . . ."

We need to stop wasting time hiding from real moments and, instead, seek them out, not next year, not when you finish reading this book, but NOW. And that is an easy thing to do. Because:

Real moments are always available.

We do not have to look far to find them.

. . . They are as close as the person sitting next to you in an airplane, or the waitress who brings you your coffee each morning before work, or the friend going through a difficult time who reaches out to you.

. . . They are there whenever and wherever you decide to pay attention to what's in front of you.

. . . They are blessed encounters and magical connections just waiting to happen, if only you will give them the chance.

Part Two

REAL MOMENTS
AND LIVING

♦

GIVING BIRTH
TO YOUR SELF

"Where am I? Who am I?
How did I come to be here?
What is this thing called the world?
How did I come into the world?
Why was I not consulted?
And If I am compelled to take part in it,
Where is the director?
I want to see him."

—SØREN KIERKEGAARD

In the process of living out the years of our lives, there comes a time when we realize that, somehow, we've gotten lost along the way. We've lost our own sense of purpose and direction. We've lost the ability to live by our own values and beliefs. We've lost our capacity for uninhibited joy and celebration. We move through each day with a buried uneasiness, a silent suspicion that something is not right. But no matter how hard we search for the source of our discomfort, we can find nothing apparently wrong. We are chasing a ghost who will not reveal himself.

We try doing more, going to new places, changing the way our bodies look, buying something different, or loving someone new, and perhaps for a while, we feel better. But then, the shadow of discontent returns, stronger than ever, and we begin to wonder if something is seriously wrong with us. Maybe this is the mid-life crisis we've heard about. Maybe we're just ungrateful for what we have, and will never be satisfied with anything. Maybe we're just not meant to be happy.

What are we looking for? **We are searching for the pieces of ourselves that we've lost, and without them, it is difficult to experience real moments.**

What happened to these pieces?

- ✦ Some of them were taken away by our parents or caretakers, in an attempt to turn us into what they thought we should be.
- ✦ Some of them we've given away to others in an attempt to be accepted or loved.
- ✦ Some of them we've hidden away, frightened of what others might think if they knew our secret selves.
- ✦ And some of them we've simply forgotten about, because we've been trying so hard to be something other than who we really are.

Without those pieces, we will never experience the wholeness we crave and the peace we are searching for. We will find it difficult to have the real moments we need. How do we get the pieces back? How do we return to a state of wholeness? We must pass from the cramped, yet familiar womb of who we have been into the person we are meant to be. We must take the journey from our old life of sacrifice and limitation into a new life of authenticity and freedom. **We must give birth to ourself again.**

"There came a time when the risk to remain tight in a bud was more painful than the risk it took to blossom."

—ANAÏS NIN

What we, in our country, have been calling a mid-life crisis is really a spiritual crisis. *If, by the time we reach an age at which we expected to feel content, whether it's thirty, forty, or beyond, we are not living with purpose, meaning, and many real moments, we will find ourselves dissatisfied and unfulfilled.* One day, we wake up and look at who we've become, and we don't like what we see. All of our hard work, all of our efforts have not given us the happiness and peace of mind we thought they would. The values and priorities we believed in have led us to an empty fulfillment. *"Is this all there is?"* we ask ourselves. This condition has been misinterpreted as everything from a fear of death, a yearning to be young again, or boredom with routine and predictability. But it is none of these. *It is a state of spiritual panic.*

W hat allows us, as human beings,
to psychologically survive life on earth,
with all of its pain, drama, challenges,
is a sense of purpose and meaning.

Purpose means that there is a reason for you to be here, that you have something to do that matters, *that your existence is significant.*

And meaning implies that your experience of living brings you fulfillment and joy from moment to moment, *that living your purpose is worth it.*

When you lose your sense of purpose and your experience of meaning, you lose those things that fuel your spirit, and enable it to make its presence known in your life. You become disconnected from an inner source of serenity, and feel compelled to search in vain for something or someone to fill the void. You're alive, but you're not fully living. You are missing out on real moments.

Maybe you are experiencing this right now. Maybe you've been feeling trapped in a life or a relationship that isn't giving you what you thought it would. Maybe you've worked for many years to get somewhere, and now that you've arrived, you aren't sure you want to be there in the first place. Maybe you think everything should be fine in your life, because you have what you've always wanted, but it doesn't feel fine. Maybe you've been feeling unsettled for a while, and haven't known what it was until this moment. Or maybe you're young, and suspect that if you don't stop and pay attention now, you'll end up in the same rut your parents did.

✦

Giving birth to yourself requires that you ask yourself difficult questions:

Who am I?

Am I living as the person I want to be?

What have I really been doing with my life?

Am I happy?

What brings me joy?

What do I need to let go of to be free?

These questions are the contractions in your rebirth process that will push you through to a new, liberated existence. Asking and answering them requires great emotional courage. It means seeing parts of yourself you've been ignoring, facing truths about your life you have been evading, confronting dreams you have been avoiding. Birth is never easy. But the reward for your having taken the journey will be life as you've never lived it before.

So if you, like me, are in the process of giving birth to yourself, know that this is a powerful and sacred time of your life. A force of transformation has seized hold of you. Like a strong wind at your back, it will help propel you in the direction you need to go. Surrender to its currents, and if you get a little frightened of the speed at which you're traveling, whatever you do, don't try to turn and go back the other way. There's no where to go but out. And as the poet Robert Frost said:

> "The best way out is always through."

Where You Got Lost Along the Way

When did we first start to disconnect from who we really are? When did we give the first piece of ourselves away? It began the moment we were born. From the time we are small children, we collect other people's values and beliefs, and make them our own. It started with your parents. Through their words and actions, they demonstrated their values and traditions, and passed them on to you. You learned how to express or not express feelings, how to deal with conflict, how to treat those different from you, how to give affection, how to practice your spiritual beliefs, how to celebrate holidays and special occasions, how to bring up children, how to cook, what to cook, how to set the table, how to take vacations—the list goes on and on. You did not study formally—*you watched, listened, and learned.*

Most of us don't consciously choose to think, behave, love, walk, talk, or eat like our parents. It just happens, sometimes so subtly that we don't even notice the similarities until someone else points them out. "You're kidding!" we respond with disbelief. "But I'm so *different* from them." Maybe yes, maybe no. *It's how you are the same that's the issue.*

How We Abandoned Our Dreams

There is another way we lost ourselves: **We adopted our parents' or social group's hopes, dreams, and expectations, leaving little or, in some cases, no room for our own.** You became a doctor because your father was a doctor, and from the time you were little, it was just assumed you would be too. You still live in your hometown, and belong to the same church as your parents, just because no one in your family has ever left. You went to college and joined a sorority just like your mom did, and volunteered for the same causes, because that's what all the girls in your high school crowd did. You got married at twenty-three and had two children right away, because all your older brothers and sisters had families early.

Sometimes, taking the path others expect you to follow may truly coincide with your own dreams as well. But more often, it is a path that takes you far away from your vision, far away from the possibility of your own adventures, far away from yourself. *Years, even decades later, you wake up and face the fact that you did what others considered right or wanted you to do, not what you wanted to do.*

Maybe you became a doctor like your parents wanted you to be, but you've always dreamed of being an architect, and now, at forty-seven, you're burned out and miserable. Maybe you secretly longed to leave your hometown and move to the other side of the country, and now, years later, you've started a family and have no hopes of getting out. Maybe you didn't want to go to college at all, but wanted to study meditation and yoga, and now you find yourself living a life just like your mother's, married to the same kind of man, going to the same kinds of parties, with your spiritual self buried deep inside. And maybe you found the husband and had the kids right away because that was the thing to do, and now you're only thirty and you feel like your husband is a stranger, your children are a burden, and you dream of running away from them all.

> As long as you have not reexamined your belief systems, and discarded the portions you never actually choose as an adult, you will never fully grow up.

Taking on the values of others affects our relationships, our personal philosophy, our work ethic, the way we raise our children, and the way we treat ourselves. No wonder so many of us feel something is not right with our lives: Our authentic self is covered up with layers upon layers of other people's "you should's," "you must's," and "you really ought to's."

Paying the Price for Fitting In

When you think about the cultural consciousness in the United States, it's not surprising that many of us have worked so hard to belong—it is part of the American psyche to be politically and socially correct, to know what's in, what's out, what's acceptable, what is taboo. **We are brought up in this country to fit in rather than find out who we are.** And those who are different and do not fit in are made to suffer and feel like failures.

When I was twelve years old, I was not cute and blond like the popular girls. I did not wear the right clothes, because I could not afford them. I was the only kid I knew whose parents were divorced. I had the ugliest pair of white glasses in the world. I did not fit in.

Once a month after school, I went to a dance called a Cotillion, sponsored by a local club. There in a large country club ballroom, instructors would teach all of us how to do the foxtrot or the cha-cha, and then they would line all the boys up on one side of the room, and all the girls on the other. The idea was that each boy would approach a girl and ask her to dance.

Each month, the same thing would happen: I would watch as, one by one, each girl would be chosen, until I was the only one left. And then, a very overweight boy named Martin, whose face was literally covered with freckles and whose hands were coated with sweat, would stumble across the empty floor and ask me to be his partner while the whole room watched and snickered. And as the music began, and Martin grabbed my unwilling hand, I would curse myself for being so different and so unacceptable, and wonder if I'd ever know what it was like to fit in.

I soon found out. By the time I was in junior high school, and continuing into senior high, I'd become one of the most popular girls in our class. I finally felt accepted. But like anyone desperate for approval, I was petrified of losing my status by making a social mistake. And so I only befriended the other popular kids, regardless of what kind of people they were, or how uninteresting they might have been, and ignored the kids I really wanted to get to know—the artists, the musicians, or the quiet, unassuming young men and women in my honors classes who had great minds. I am ashamed to say that I became exactly what I had hated so much when I was the social outcast. *I didn't want to be friends with someone who did not fit in.*

When I look back on this time of my life, I feel tremendous regret for my behavior. **I missed out because I was so afraid of being left out.** I was so hungry to belong, to be accepted, that I was willing to lose myself in order to have a few people

I could call friends. Of course, they did not know the real me. They only knew the part of me I thought they would approve of—the rest I hid carefully away.

When we graduated, everyone wondered why I chose to attend a college in the Midwest when all of the kids in my crowd were attending the Ivy League schools on the East Coast. I myself wondered why I made the decision to head toward Wisconsin, away from everything familiar to me—that is, until I got there and found something I hadn't even realized I was looking for: FREEDOM! Suddenly, I was free from everything and everyone I had ever looked to for approval. For the first time in my life, I began to explore who Barbara really was, and that was the beginning of the first stage of my rebirth. I know now that I could never have found myself if I had stayed in Philadelphia. My desire to belong, with its roots in that awkward, unattractive little girl on the Cotillion floor carrying around so much pain, was greater than my desire to be me.

So Martin, wherever you are: *Forgive me for not seeing that you felt just as ashamed and rejected as I did, that we were kindred souls back then. I hope, like me, you've finally found your dignity, and that whoever your dancing partner is now always looks proudly up at you when you take her in your arms.*

✦

"It takes a lot of courage to release the familiar and seemingly secure, to embrace the new. But there is no real security in what is no longer meaningful. There is more security in the adventurous and exciting, for in movement there is life, and in change there is power."

—ALAN COHEN

Each time you gave up a dream, a belief, a desire, or a habit because it wouldn't be approved of, or you wouldn't fit in, or it wasn't what was expected, or it just wasn't done, or because of what the neighbors or your mother or your relatives would think, you gave away a piece of yourself. *The more pieces you gave up, the less of yourself was left.* In some cases, you might have become so buried under piles of other people's values, that when you attempt to find yourself, there is no one there. And when you don't know who you are, you cannot experience real and meaningful moments either alone or with others.

> When you compromise your dreams and your values for someone else's, you give your power away. The more you have sacrificed your authenticity, the more disempowered you will feel.

How do you begin to take your power back? You start by rediscovering your own truth, your own values, your own voice, and living it every day.

When a child is born, she leaves behind her mother's womb, and is cut free from the cord that bound her, by breath and blood, to her first home. This exodus is necessary for the infant's survival. She can no longer grow while she is still enclosed within those walls, and that which once nurtured her will soon become that which destroys her, unless she breaks free.

In this way, giving birth to yourself means leaving behind parts of yourself that no longer nourish you, and cutting your connection to all of the beliefs, values, and obligations you've taken on that were not yours to begin with. It means saying good-bye to the person others have expected you to be, and reinventing yourself as the person *you* want to be.

✦

"Nothing is at last sacred but the integrity of your own mind."
— EMERSON

On the road back to yourself, the first stop is integrity.

Living with integrity means that who you appear to be is who you really are. Your beliefs, your values, your commitments—your inner realities— are all reflected in how you live your life on the outside. The more you live as who you truly are, the more peace you will invite into your life.

Living with integrity means:

✦ Not settling for less than what you know you deserve in your relationships
✦ Asking for what you want and need from others
✦ Speaking your truth, even though it might create conflict or tension
✦ Behaving in ways that are in harmony with your personal values
✦ Making choices based on what you believe, and not what others believe

Living without integrity takes a lot of energy. It is intellectually and emotionally exhausting, because who you are on the inside and how you behave on the outside are not **congruent** with one another.

Imagine that you are standing on a river, with each of your feet in a different boat. One boat represents your values, and the other represents your behavior. You start floating down the river. As long as the two boats remain close together, you're fine. But when one starts to drift farther away from the other, it will become difficult to straddle both craft. The farther apart the two boats get, the harder it will be for you to keep a foot in each, until at one point, the two boats become too distanced from one another, and you fall into the water.

The farther your own behavior drifts from your values, the more difficult it will become for you to function happily each day, and the more internal anxiety you'll experience. You will have to stretch too far to stay psychologically and spiritually afloat. At some point, your system will just break down. This can take the form of physical illness, mental stress or collapse, and emotional turmoil.

Running an Integrity Check

Here is a simple way to begin noticing all of the places where you are out of integrity with your values, and it's something you can start practicing as soon as you put down this book:

Each hour, on the hour, check with yourself to see if anything you've done or said in the past sixty minutes was not congruent with who you are.

Replay the past hour in your mind as if you're watching a movie, and *wherever you feel an uncomfortable feeling, stop the movie and notice what was happening.* Were you pretending the sarcastic comment your husband made didn't bother you? Were you silently listening to a friend judge someone you care about, without defending that person? Were you eating something you know was unhealthy, that you promised yourself you'd stay away from?

You will be amazed at how many times a day you betray yourself by smiling when you are really hurt, holding back love when you want to reach out, agreeing to do something that does not feel right to you, or showing the parts of yourself that someone is comfortable with rather than being who you truly are.

Let's say you do this integrity exercise, and find you're averaging five incidents an hour during which you are not being 100 percent authentically who you are. Now multiply the number of hours you are awake (say, sixteen) by five and you get eighty. Take the eighty little acts you perform or communications you express each day that are not congruent with your inner self, multiply them by 365, and your total is 29,200. That means, **29,200 times each year, you betray your own values and beliefs, you do or say something that doesn't feel right inside.** And each time this happens, you create physical and emotional stress in your system.

Now, let's say you are forty-five years old. We won't count the first eight years of your life in our equation, since most children are quite authentic until they "mature" and begin editing themselves in order to get approval. So you would subtract 8 from 45, which leaves 37, and then multiply *37 years × 29,200 incidents.* That equals: **1,080,400!!!** 1,080,400 times in your life so far when you've been untrue to yourself, **1,080,400 times when you were not living on the outside as who you are on the inside.**

> N o one betrays us as much in our lives as we betray ourselves.

Is it any wonder then, that by the time we reach even our late twenties, we begin feeling uneasy with ourselves, and by our thirties and forties, we are often in the midst of spiritual turmoil? And what of real moments? How can we experience them when we, *the experiencers,* are not even fully experiencing ourselves?

If you start today doing an Integrity Check each hour, you will soon notice that you are behaving much more congruently in all areas of your life. You'll catch yourself about to betray your values, and in that moment, you'll have the freedom to choose to be authentically who you truly are. By the end of just one week of Integrity Checks, you will feel more powerful and more peaceful than you have in a long while.

You will be ready to discover the real moments that have always been there, waiting to bring you joy.

✦

"The important thing is this: To be able at any moment to sacrifice what we are for what we could become."
— CHARLES DU BOIS

Right about the time I began working on *Real Moments,* I made a business trip to New York. One afternoon I found myself stuck in bumper-to-bumper traffic in the backseat of a taxi cab. The driver and I began talking, and when he found out I was an author, and that I was writing a book about living life with meaning, he lit up. "This is right up my alley!" he proclaimed. And he proceeded to tell me his story:

The Taxi Driver's Secret for Finding Happiness

"You know, I didn't always drive a cab," he explained. "I used to be in sales. I drove then too, but I was away from home most of the week. Didn't see my wife and kids much in those days. I was making good money, and going on a fast track, you know, to try and keep up with the other guys in the company. I guess I thought I'd made it. You know, my dad was a pipe fitter—came over from Poland when he was sixteen, before the war. He really never got the hang of English, but he was good with his hands. I knew he always wanted better for me, and so I felt pretty good driving around in a nice suit and closing deals.

"Well, one day about ten years ago, my youngest son got hit by a car while crossing the street. Oh, he's O.K. now, but he was really bad for a while. The thing was, my wife couldn't find me. I was out on the road, driving between some town and another, and didn't call in until the day after the accident happened. When I finally reached her, she was hysterical. She told me our son might not make it, and how could I not be there, and she couldn't live like this anymore.

"I hightailed it home from Ohio in seven hours—a record. And when I walked into that hospital room, and saw my little boy lying there with tubes stuck in him, all wrapped up in white bandages, I fell apart. My wife looked like hell, my youngest daughter wouldn't stop crying, and in that moment, I realized that things hadn't been right for a while with all of us. I was never home. That kind of says it all, doesn't it? Sure, we had nice things, and sure, my pop was proud of me, but we didn't have a life together. Jeez, what if my son had died when I was away? It could have happened, you know. Right then and there, I made a decision. I didn't care what it took, I was going to get my life back again.

"That's when I quit my job and bought the cab. A real glamorous promotion, right!! Hey, but you know what? The last ten years have been the best of my life. I got to see my kids grow up, and all three of them are doing great. My wife and I got our marriage going again. Now she's my best friend, and I sure as heck wouldn't have said that ten years ago. And we saved up enough to buy a little cottage on a lake upstate. It's not much, but every Friday we drive up and spend the weekend. I'll tell you, when I'm sitting on my porch looking out at the trees and the water, I feel terrific, you know what I mean?"

I did. I had just met a truly happy man. He had lost himself, like so many of us have, and then he had given birth to himself again, finding his own way home.

I told him that I was so impressed with his story, I was going to put it in my book, and he was thrilled. "My wife won't believe this!" He laughed.

"Tell me something," I said. "If you had one piece of advice based on all you've learned about how to be happy, what would it be?"

He was quiet for a minute, and then he replied:
"To be happy, you have to say 'no' to things."

The Power of "No"

I am sure that God placed that cab driver in my path for a reason. I needed to learn the power of "no." I'd been living my life by a different aphorism:

"To be successful, you have to say 'yes' to things."

I said "yes" to all the projects that came my way, "yes" to all the opportunities to give a speech, "yes" whenever my staff asked me to put on another seminar that would help people, "yes" whenever a friend needed advice, no matter what time of night or day. My phone rang constantly, my schedule had no free sections, and listening to the driver describe his cottage on the lake, I felt like giving up everything and buying a cab myself!! He had made real moments a priority in his life, by recommitting to his own new values, and saying "no" to values that no longer served him.

> We need to find the courage to say "NO" to
> the things that are not serving us if we want to
> rediscover ourselves and live our lives
> with authenticity.

I can tell you from experience that this is not as easy as it sounds. Saying "no" can mean cutting ties you have had for a long time to people, places, things, and ideas. It can mean making decisions that others do not approve of. It can mean letting go of old values and identities before you've quite developed the new ones, and being in a state of emotional limbo for a while—you know you aren't who you used to be, but you aren't quite sure yet who you are becoming.

But hidden within every "no" is a "yes." When you say "no" to doing something that does not feel right anymore, you are saying "yes" to strengthening your own integrity. When you say "no" to remaining friends with people who do not support your growth or new direction, you are saying "yes" to the new friends who will soon be arriving in your life. When you say "no" to selling out your principles and ideals in order to get ahead in business, you are saying "yes" to a new level of self-respect. When you say "no" to not being treated as you deserve to be in a relationship, you are saying "yes" to loving and protecting yourself.

As I look back on my life, it has always been saying "no" to something that has been the first step in each of my most powerful emotional and spiritual transformations.

My First Big "No"

I was a senior in high school before I learned to use the power of "no." It was 1969, and our school had a strict dress code—no pants for girls, and no blue jeans for boys. Everyone thought this was stupid—in the winter, the temperature would go down to fifteen degrees, and the girls would be trudging through two feet of snow wearing stockings and little short skirts. And the boys were allowed to wear black jeans, and green jeans, but not blue. God forbid someone should think we had a bunch of farmers attending our school. As secretary of the student council, I tried for months to talk with the principal and have the dress code changed, but he wouldn't budge. So I decided to organize a strike!

I don't recall why I chose this issue on which to take my first stand. Perhaps it was because we were in middle of the Vietnam War, and I felt helpless to do anything that would prevent my friends from being drafted. Perhaps it was because I knew I'd be leaving for college in a few months, and didn't care anymore what people thought of me. Or perhaps I was just tired of always saying "yes" to everything and trying so hard to get everyone to like me.

For weeks, in secret, I planned our tactics. On one particular Friday morning, we would all show up wearing pants or jeans. I figured if enough kids did it, they couldn't suspend us all. The word spread through the grapevine, and finally Friday arrived. I could hardly wait to get to school to witness the uproar we would cause. So you can imagine how devastated I was to discover that *most of the students chickened out at the last minute and wore their regular clothing. Only about one hundred of us had dared to defy the dress code.*

Within fifteen minutes after the first bell rang, the principal called a special assembly. The whole school, 1,800 of us, gathered together in the auditorium. "Apparently some of you do not know the meaning of the word 'rule,'" he began in his droning voice. "It has come to my attention that a radical group of students attempted to lead a strike this morning in protest over our dress code. Naturally, this infringement of school policy will not be tolerated. Those students will be asked to return home and come back to school when they are properly attired. The rest of us will resume class as usual. If anyone has any information about the instigators of this plot, please see me or the vice-principal."

When I remember this now, I laugh at how ridiculous the situation was—our principal trying to exert some last measures of control over us before we went off to college, the students being too afraid to defy him, and me feeling abandoned by everyone who had promised to lend their support. But at the time, I wasn't laughing. I was angry—angry at those in authority for not respecting my values, and angry with my friends for not being more courageous.

None of us ever got suspended for our strike. But I paid the price for organizing it. At our graduation ceremony several months later, I didn't receive any of the awards and scholarships I'd been told by my teachers I would get. All of them were given to another girl who never questioned school policy or took a stand on anything. I remember sitting on the stage in my cap and gown with the other three elected student council members, and watching people whisper to one another as this girl's name and not mine was called over and over again. I could just imagine the parents using this as a lesson for their children: *"See what happens when you go against the rules?"*

I can't say I was not hurt and disappointed that I didn't receive the honors I'd worked so hard for. However, what I did get was far more important: **I found my voice, and a piece of myself that had been buried for years under my hunger for acceptance. By speaking out for what I believed was right, I had taken an important first step in giving birth to myself.**

In the end, the power of "no" triumphed after all. A year after I graduated, the dress code was finally changed so the students could wear what they wanted to school. But that's not the end of the story. Four years ago, twenty-one years after I graduated, I received a letter from my high school announcing that they wanted to elect me to the Hall of Fame, along with other famous graduates like baseball great Reggie Jackson, since, and I quote, **"you have become someone we can all be proud of."** I called my mother and laughed for ten minutes on the phone!! I haven't made it back there yet to attend the ceremony or receive my award in front of the present student body, but believe me, when I do, I will make sure to say what I never got a chance to say twenty-five years ago in that same auditorium—*that education would serve us better by teaching us to give birth to ourselves as individuals, rather than trying to get us to conform to other people's ideas of who and what we should be.*

✦

As we journey toward wholeness, rediscovering our own values and standing by them is one of the most significant ways we can live authentically and experience more real moments. Here is one of my favorite stories about integrity. I don't recall where I first heard it, but I pass it on every chance I get:

Once there was a young Jewish boy who lived in a small town located in what was then the Russian Empire around the turn of the century. This was a time when there was great persecution of the small population of Jews in each village by the Cossacks, the Czar's soldiers. Every day during market hours, as the townspeople gathered in the main square to do their business, the Cossacks would ride into town on their powerful horses, scatter the goods and wares of the Jews, read the latest edict from the Czar limiting the Jews' freedom, and then ride off.

Now, this young boy was exceedingly fond of his grandfather, who happened to be the old Rabbi of the village. All the Jews in town agreed that their Rabbi was as wise as Abraham or Moses. Every day, the young boy would walk with his grandfather from their modest home to the center of the city. The Cossacks would come riding in, dust flying, and the soldier in charge would read the daily edict: "From today on, no Jews can buy more than five potatoes at a time," or "The Czar has ruled that all Jews must sell their best cows to the state at once."

And each day, the same thing would happen: The old Rabbi would listen along with everyone else to the edicts, and then he would raise his walking stick, shake it in the air at the Cossacks, and in a loud voice proclaim: "I protest!! I protest!!" And then one of the Cossacks would ride into the crowd, and strike the Rabbi with his riding crop yelling, "Silence, you old fool!" before riding off. The Rabbi would fall to the ground, his followers would rush to pick him up and brush the dirt from his coat, and his grandson would help him back to their house.

Day after day, month after month, the young boy watched in horror as this scene repeated itself. Finally, he could hold his tongue no more, and one day, as he escorted his bruised grandfather from the town square, the boy got up the courage to address him. "Beloved Rebbe," the boy asked in a trembling voice. "Why do you keep speaking out against the Czar each day, when you know the soldiers will just beat you? Why don't you just keep quiet?"

The Rabbi smiled kindly at his grandson and answered:

"Because by not speaking against what I know is wrong, I would become one of them. . . ."

Speak your truth—it will always lead you back home to yourself.

Making the Passage to Wholeness

Turning away from who you have been should always be done with love. After all, the birth process begins nine months earlier with an act of love. So too must your passage to wholeness begin not as a negation of your past, but an affirmation of your future. *It's not a question of determining what is good or bad in your life, but rather, what is serving you and what is holding you back.* Just because you choose a new path does not mean the old path was a bad one. Just because you take a new direction does not mean the old way was the wrong way. Just because you take on new values does not mean the old values were corrupt. **We must learn to say no without having to make what we are leaving behind wrong, or make ourselves wrong for having not left sooner.**

Leaving without judgment is especially difficult to do

when, in order to grow, you must say no to people or activities for which you feel a lot of love. Sometimes the love is so strong, you become afraid that you cannot leave if you still feel it, *so you try to kill the love in order to get the courage to break away.* I see many people do this in relationships—they know it's time to go on, but it hurts too much to do it while they still feel so much emotion. So they talk themselves into hating their partner, or in the case of work, hating their job. Then, leaving is easier, because they don't feel the pain of loss. But in the end, they robbed themselves of the love they nurtured for so long.

Nothing has to be wrong with what you've been doing for you to make changes in your life. It can just be the right time.

Saying Good-bye Over the Airwaves

One of the hardest things I've ever had to was quit my job as a radio talk show host. For two years, I had a daily show in Los Angeles. Each day, I'd try to help callers deal with the problems they'd present to me, and the program became a huge success. I had a very special relationship with my listeners—I felt protective of them when they were being mistreated, I cheered for them when they made breakthroughs, I cried with them when they experienced tragedy. They were my family, and I was theirs.

One night, I had a dream that the radio station changed its format to all news, and fired all of the talk show hosts. In the dream, I told my husband what was happening, and said, "This is great, because now I don't have to quit, and no one will be angry with me for leaving." The next morning when I woke up and remembered the dream, I knew immediately that it was time for me to let go of the show.

My dream had revealed that it was my fear of disappointing

my audience that was holding me there, along with the fact that I loved what I did so much, and couldn't imagine letting go of something I'd worked that hard to achieve. Leaving would have been easy if I hated my job. *But I knew that although staying on the air would continue to serve others, it would not serve me.* I longed for the time to write more, travel more, and challenge myself in new ways, and the job was not structured so that I could do that.

When I said good-bye during my last show, I cried and my audience cried with me. I received thousands of letters pleading with me to return. Some people even picketed the station, demanding that they do whatever it took to get me back. My office even received a few angry phone calls, accusing me of abandoning my loyal following. I watched all of this go on, knowing in my heart that I'd made the right choice, because although everyone else felt I belonged there, I knew I didn't anymore.

This was not the first or the last time in my life that following the voices which call me down my road angered people who wanted me to stay right where I was—*not because it would be good for me, but because it would be good for them.* And so I have gotten used to the labor pains that often accompany each new life I birth myself into; the tearing away that is often necessary; the forces tugging on me to stay; the temptation to give in to the voices that call: "*We won't love you if you go.*" However, each time I follow my heart, I emerge from my new metamorphosis with more wholeness and more freedom than I ever imagined before. And it is these rebirths that have given me some of my most precious real moments.

✦

"The only life worth living is the adventurous life. Of such a life, the dominant characteristic is that **it is unafraid.** It is unafraid of what other people think . . . It does not adapt either its pace or its objectives to the pace and objectives of its neighbors. It thinks its own thoughts, reads its own books, it develops its own hopes, and it is governed by its own conscience. The herd may graze where it pleases or stampede where it pleases, **but he who lives the adventurous life will remain unafraid when he finds himself alone."**

— RAYMOND B. FOSDICK

I hope that reading this chapter has made you restless— restless to examine your life and discover where you are not living in integrity with your own values, restless to make some of the changes and take some of the risks you've been avoiding, restless to begin searching for the lost pieces of yourself, restless to begin dreaming again, restless for more real, authentic moments.

You are free to do this, you know. **You** *can* reinvent your life. There is no waiting period. You can begin now, right after you put this book down.

Will you feel better if I tell you that reinventing your life doesn't necessarily mean that you have to quit your job, or get a divorce, or sell everything and move to the country? *It may mean that you do the same things differently.* It may mean you take a different road to work, or that you feed your family when *you* want to, and not at 5:30 because that's when your mother always fed you. *Dozens of opportunities will come your way today, or perhaps tomorrow, to make a different choice*—to give one of your lost selves a voice, or to reveal a part of you no one has seen before, to wear or do or say something that you would have said just wasn't like you.

Who Are You?

Here are some of the questions to ask yourself as your re-birth begins. They are designed to be more like keys that will open doors to hidden places, rather than simple questions with precise responses. Think about each one carefully. Plant them deep inside of you, as you would plant a seed deep into the earth. And then be patient. Don't be in a hurry for the answer to grow.

These are good questions to talk about with people you love. They are also good to write about. As you change and rediscover more of who you really are, the answers will change. Know that just by asking these questions, your journey back to yourself and to more real moments has begun.

Who Am I?

1. In which areas have I inherited behaviors and attitudes similar to those of my family members, that are keeping me from being authentically my own person? (Communication, expressing love and affection, health habits, work ethic, political and spiritual beliefs, etc.)

2. How did my family treat (or judge) people who were different from us? How do I treat people who are different from me? Am I comfortable with being different?

3. Which of my own dreams or beliefs have I sacrificed, diminished, or put aside in order to fulfill the expectations of others?

4. What parts of myself, both in the past and the present, have I hidden from others for fear they would disapprove of me? What parts do I bury even from myself?

5. In what ways have I tried to fit in that have resulted in my compromising my values or editing myself, both now and in the past?

6. What things have I done in my life in the past that I felt I should do, even though I did not fully want to do them?

7. What things am I doing now in my life that I feel I should do, even though I do not fully want to do them?

8. What habits and traditions do I still practice that are more a reflection of other people's values rather than my own?

9. What are *my* values and beliefs? If I lived them 100 percent, how would that look in my life? How would the people close to me react?

10. Am I living where and how I want to live, or where and how someone else wants me to live? What would I have to change to have my lifestyle congruous with my desires?

11. What must I do in order to unearth the buried parts of me and bring them back to life?

12. What do I need to let go of to finally grow up?

13. Am I happy? What would make me happy?

14. What do I need to do in my life to be free?

✦

"When you die and go to Heaven, our Maker is not going to ask, 'Why didn't you discover the cure for such and such? Why didn't you become the Messiah?' The only question we will be asked in that precious moment is 'Why didn't you become you?' "
— ATTRIBUTED TO ELIE WIESEL,
author and Holocaust survivor,
paraphrasing an old Yiddish story

You are one of a kind. There has never been, and never again will be a human being like you. There is nothing ordinary about you. **If you feel ordinary, it is because you have chosen to hide the extraordinary parts of yourself from the world.** Maybe you have even forgotten that they are there, because it's been so long since you've last seen them.

But listen . . . they are calling to you . . . voices from within yourself . . . crying out to be recognized, to be reunited with one another. *"Set us free,"* they whisper, *"and we will show you the way back to wholeness."*

You have heard the call, you have felt the movement, so you understand that the time for your rebirth has come. Now your labor begins:

> Empty yourself of everything you
> no longer need.
> Make space for your emerging spirit.
> Then just let go and enjoy the ride.
> Remember: You already *know* how to do this.
> That's how you got here in the first place. . . .

REAL MOMENTS
AND WORK

"Your work is to discover your work, and then, with all your heart, to give yourself to it."

— BUDDHA

Real moments aren't just for weekends. They aren't meant to be saved for a special occasion, like a favorite article of clothing you only wear on Saturday nights, or holidays. They shouldn't be limited to walks on the beach, early morning bike rides, or cozy cuddles with your beloved. They need to be woven through the entire landscape of your life. And that includes your work.

You spend at least one half of your waking life at work, whether work means a job outside your home, such as a salesperson, or a job inside your home, such as a mother. That is a lot of time to spend doing something unless it makes you happy. This explains why so many of us return from work at the end of the day, or finish our household duties, and look like we've been run over by a truck. **It's exhausting to do something you are not fully enjoying, especially when you know you will have to do it all over again the next day.**

The spirit feeds on joy, love, and celebration. . . .

W ork without real moments dries up your
spirit, and leaves it hungry.

You know you have a hungry spirit when you sit in front
of the television at the end of the day, clicking from one channel to another, or when you open your refrigerator and stare
blankly at what's on the shelves, or when you go directly from
work to the bar down the street to have a drink and "unwind."
What you are looking for will not be found on any TV program, or in any food box or carton, or at the bottom of a glass
of beer. *Your spirit is hungry to know that the hours of this
precious day you just spent working were not spent in vain, that
they counted for something, that they had some purpose and
meaning.*

It is hard to come home and share love with your wife
when your spirit is hungry. It's hard to embrace your husband
with passion when your spirit is hungry. It's hard to sleep
deeply and dream peacefully when your spirit is hungry.

You would not neglect to feed your body during the day.
So, too, you must not neglect to nourish your spirit.

Finding Your True Vocation

Sometimes, we feel it is difficult to have real moments filled
with meaning during the day because of the kind of job we
do. "I'm a cashier at a supermarket," you think to yourself.
"How can my job feed my spirit?" The answer is: *Doing your
job cannot bring you real moments, but doing your Work can.*

A ll of us are here on this Earth with Work to
do, but your Work has nothing to do
with your job.

◆ Your **job** is what you do to survive physically, and to support yourself and your family. It is the profession you choose, the skills you develop.

It is being a painter, a plumber, a computer programmer, an archeologist.

◆ Your **Work** is what you do to survive emotionally, and to support your spirit. It is the lessons you are here to learn, the wisdom you are here to gain. It is the map for your personal Earth adventure.

Your Work Is Your Purpose.

It is learning to treat others with compassion, learning to love yourself even with your imperfections, learning forgiveness, learning courage, learning trust, learning love.

◆

"You need not wait until you are older, wiser, and mature enough to accept a wonderful job from God."
— MARCELLA DANIELS

Another word for Work is **vocation**. Most people think "vocation" refers to the job you have or the career you've chosen. But the word vocation is derived from the Latin *vocatio,* which means *call* or *summons*. So your "vocation" literally means **your calling**.

Each of us has a calling, something unique to contribute to the world, something valuable to share with the people we love and live with. **Your calling is your job from God**, Job with a capital "J"! What kind of jobs does God give us as humans?

◆ To be kind to one another
◆ To take care of the Earth
◆ To enjoy God's marvelous creation as fully as possible

✦ To learn everything we can while we are here about being good human beings
✦ To love and accept ourselves and others as much as God loves us
✦ To remember who we really are

You do not need to prepare for these jobs, or even qualify for them. **The fact that you are here and have a physical existence means you obviously got the job!** And as for learning how to do your Work well, that's what on-the-job training is all about.

When you don't know your Purpose, or your true Vocation, you might resent your everyday job, or think you have the wrong one, because you'll expect it to fulfill your spirit, and it cannot. A job is a job. Of course, some are more suited to you than others — it's up to you to find the most enjoyable job you can. But just because you have what you consider to be an "ordinary," "boring," or "unglamorous" job, doesn't mean you cannot do the Work you are here to do. You don't have to be a minister, or a teacher, or a writer to live your purpose.

Remember my friend the cab driver? His job was to drive a taxi. His Work, his calling, was to share love with his family and all those he came into contact with, and to remember, in this life, what was truly important. From what I saw when I met him, he was very successful at both. And it was doing his real Work *while* he was on his job, as he did when he reached out so honestly to me, that gave his job meaning.

When you know what your true Work is, you can do it anytime — when you are building a house, or selling shoes, when you are cooking dinner for your family, or helping your child with her homework. And you can do it anywhere — in a store, over the phone, on a street corner . . . even in a taxi.

✦

"How many cares one loses when one decides not to be *something,* but to be *someone.*"

— C O C O   C H A N E L

Each of us has a Calling, not just the teachers and preachers of the world. I can't tell you what your Calling or your true Work is. That is for you to discover. In fact, **that's the first stage of your Work—for you to figure out your Purpose, your Calling, your gift.** But I'll give you a hint about how to begin: *Look at what is unique about you, those characteristics or abilities that distinguish you from other people, and there you will find your Vocation.*

Maybe your uniqueness lies in your ability to express yourself well with words, or to have a calming effect on others, or to make people laugh, or to understand and simplify complex situations. Maybe your gift is your voice, your strong hands, your eye for beauty, your talent for seeing the best in people. And if you aren't sure what your gift is, ask the people who know you.

Sometimes other people see our gift and Purpose before we do. Where else should you look to find your calling?

Look at what you love to do.
Look at what brings you joy.
Look at what gives you peace.
There is your calling, waiting for you to
embrace it.

Nothing in our Universe was designed without a purpose. An eagle's wing was shaped so that he could fly. A rose was given color so it would attract the honeybee. Our bodies need to rest for several hours a day, and it just so happens that the

Earth turns away from the Sun, our source of light and heat, for that same amount of time, and when we are rejuvenated, the Earth has turned back toward the Sun again. From the movement of the planets, to the movement of blood through our veins, every detail of our physical existence reflects a Higher Order.

You are a part of Creation. You are part of that Order. There is a reason for your being who and what you are. There is purpose in everything about you. *You have been given your particular and unique gifts and abilities so that you could do your particular and unique Work. It is not an accident.*

> You have exactly what you need to fulfill your Purpose here. Your wings are shaped perfectly.

✦

Why do so many of us ignore our Calling, and refuse to take up our true Vocation? *Because we make the mistake of thinking that we have to earn money doing something for it to be worth our time and energy.* It's as if we think that being paid for what we contribute is a cosmic sign that what we contribute has worth.

> Receiving money for what you do is not a validation that you are living your Purpose and doing your real Work—receiving joy and contentment is.

I have a friend who works as a manager in a large corporation. His job consists mostly of paperwork, meetings, and more paperwork. It pays well, but he doesn't find it fulfilling. What does satisfy him, however, is what he's always called his "outside interest"—working with underprivileged children. For ten years he has volunteered as a Big Brother to many young boys, taught basketball on weekends to kids from the inner city, and once a year he helps raise money used to sponsor poor children for a week at camp.

We spoke on the phone recently, and he told me he was thinking of quitting his job. "I feel like what I do at this company is useless, that I'm not contributing anything to society," he complained. "Maybe I should go back to school and become a social worker, or a teacher. I mean, I'm thirty-seven years old, and I'm not happy with my work."

"But you're already a social worker and a teacher and a basketball coach," I reminded him. "You're just not getting paid for it. Would it make that much of a difference if you were?"

My friend was stunned. He'd never thought about the fact that he really was living his Purpose, **because he wasn't being rewarded for it financially.** He thought about his job at the company as what he really did, and his Work with the kids as a hobby. But it was really the other way around—*his Work with the kids was his real profession, and his day job, which helped him earn a living, was his hobby.*

"So what you're saying is, everything I'm doing is fine," he proposed. "It's the way I look at it that needs to change."

"Right, " I agreed. "If it helps, think of your job at the company as what you do to pay the bills so that you can be free to fulfill your Calling as a guardian angel to those boys."

Like my friend, you may have a job that has little or nothing to do with your real Work, except that it gives you the financial freedom to do it. You are an executive secretary, but your real Work is organizing your church choir. You are an accountant, but your real Work is raising your children. You sell real estate, but your real Work is motivating your friends to be the best they can be.

Let people know what your real Work is. When you meet someone new, and they ask "What do you do?" tell them the truth: "I work at learning how to be good to myself and other people, and for a job, I cut hair," or "My real Work is being a mother and a wife, and to support myself, I am an investment counselor."

Real Moments happen
when you do the Work you came here to do.

If the first part of your Work is figuring out what your Work is, the second part is learning how to do your real Work every day. *The more opportunities you create to participate in your Purpose while you do your daily job, the more real moments you will experience.* Maybe you are a teacher, and at some point during your day you reach out to a child who is carrying a lot of personal pain, and let him know you understand, and that you care. Your day suddenly becomes meaningful, not because you went to work, but because you practiced your true Vocation while you were there. Or maybe you work in a large factory, and one afternoon you take ten minutes to convince your employer to hire a friend of yours who hasn't been able to find a job and is having a difficult time supporting his family. You go home that evening with a smile on your face—at your job, you found a way to do your Work. You feel complete.

If what you do for a living involves relating to people, then you will always be able to conjure up a real moment or two during every day. Anytime you transcend the usual, superficial way of connecting with others, and share from the heart, you can have a real moment.

Whenever you're sharing love,
you're living your Purpose.

Here's something that will help you experience more real moments during your regular work day: **Make a list of activi-**

ties, behaviors and attitudes you can incorporate into your job at work or at home that will help you live your Purpose. These will serve as reminders, so that whenever you are feeling in need of a real moment, you can pull out the list, choose to put one of the items into practice, and create an instant sense of purpose.

I suggest that you carry a copy of the list around with you, post another on your desk or refrigerator, and read them often. Here are a few items from my own list. Perhaps some of these will give you ideas for yours.

✦ Share a moment of love with someone
✦ Appreciate beautiful things in your environment
✦ Learn something new
✦ Look for an opportunity to make someone feel valuable
✦ Play with the dog
✦ Spend a few minutes in the garden watching the flowers grow
✦ Lie in the hammock and let the breeze rock you back and forth
✦ Stop and remember *why* you're doing what you are doing

When Your Job Is Bad for You

What you do as a job isn't as important as *how* you do it. If you do it with caring, if you do it with contentment, then it will be a good way to earn your living. Your job doesn't have to be an activity where you can fully express your real Work or Calling. *But it should not be an activity that goes against your Work.*

When you have a job where you must
compromise your values, hide your true self, or

> participate in actions which are out of integrity,
> then your job is a place your spirit dies
> eight hours a day.

You cannot compartmentalize different portions of your life from one another. You can't have a job that is toxic to your well-being, and prevent it from affecting your relationship, your health, and your peace of mind. *If your job takes you that far off your Purpose, it will be difficult for you to get back on track at the end of the day, and after years of living incongruently, you may not be able to even find a sense of Purpose anymore.*

As I write this, I think of a woman I know who works in the entertainment industry in Los Angeles for a very well-known personality. Her job is flashy and high profile, and she makes a lot of money. There's just one problem—her boss treats her like dirt. He is rude, abusive, immature, and inconsiderate. Every time my friend calls me or we have lunch, the conversation revolves around the same two topics: how much she hates her job, and how frustrated she is that she can't meet any nice guys and get married.

For years I've listened to her complain about both sides of her life. Finally, last week I couldn't take it anymore. "Have you ever considered that the reason you can't find a nice guy may have something to do with your staying in an abusive relationship at work?" I asked her.

"I don't like what you're saying, but don't stop," she said with a grimace.

"Well, no matter how much you feel 'It's just a job,' what you spend eight hours a day doing, year after year, affects your self-esteem and what you expect from the rest of your life. I can't see any way you can attract a really loving relationship when the one you're in at work is so unhealthy."

"But it's such a good job . . . " she replied.

"No matter how much money it pays," I reminded her, "no job is a good job if it isn't good for you."

If your job isn't good for you, get a new one. *In the end, the price you'll pay staying in a situation where you are cut off from yourself and your own integrity will be much higher than what you will temporarily lose by leaving.*

✦

"I think most of us are torn. We have at least two people at war in our body. One person wants to retire and grow fabulous tomatoes, and the other wants to stand up on a pedestal and be worshipped and get bigger and bigger and bigger until she explodes."
— BETTE MIDLER

When you mistake your job for your Purpose by taking it too seriously, you can get really messed up. You will work too hard, and have a difficult time saying "no" to anything. And when you start believing that your job is more important than someone else's, or that you're the only one who can do it, or that the world can't survive without your incredible contribution, then it's time for you to retire and grow tomatoes—or at least take an extended vacation—in order to get back in tune with what you're really here for.

Taking your job too seriously means that you either don't know you have a Purpose other than your job, or you have temporarily forgotten what it is. You will not enjoy your job when you mistakenly think that it's your Work, because then you will make every small event that occurs in the course of a day a big deal. I'm not saying that you should do your job carelessly, or without one hundred percent excellence. You shouldn't. *Just don't lose your identity in what you're doing.*

If you sell twenty-five houses this month, or close three big deals, or beat out someone else for a contract, or manage the kids and the chores effortlessly, it does not mean you are any better or more deserving inside than if you had sold nothing, lost a contract, or had kids who were out of control. Knowing that, perhaps you can be a little more forgiving of yourself and those you work with and for, when things do not go as smoothly as you wish they would.

How I Got Lost on the Way Home

I am speaking from painful experience. For many years, I confused my job as a spiritual and emotional teacher with my Purpose, and it caused me a lot of unnecessary anxiety and unhappiness. In all fairness to myself, I understand how I could have fallen prey to this misconception: *some of us are given jobs that look suspiciously like a Calling.* Health-care professionals, teachers, priests, politicians, gurus, poets, motivational speakers—we all are tempted to believe that we are among the lucky few whose job and Calling are one and the same. None of this weekend Purpose stuff for us. We get to live our Purpose through our job. How blessed we feel to have been chosen to be so important! What would the world do without us?!!!

From the time I began teaching, I believed with all my heart, and with all sincerity, that my job and Purpose were to help as many people heal emotionally as I could, and to open them up to experiencing more love in their lives. I saw great suffering around me, and wanted to use my talents and gifts to help alleviate that suffering, and make a difference in the world.

What I didn't see was that by believing my Purpose was to help people, and having a job where I did exactly that, I set myself up for a lot of pain and spiritual torment. For instance, what if I couldn't help someone? Did that mean I wasn't good at my Calling? What if someone didn't want my help? Would that mean that *they* were off purpose? What if I didn't help enough people by the end of my life (whatever "enough" was in my mind)? Wouldn't that mean I had failed to fulfill my Purpose? Wouldn't I have failed God?

And so I became an *overzealous prophet of love*. I didn't just want people to grow, they *had* to, and if I saw them resisting, I became frustrated inside. Didn't they recognize the gift I was offering them? How could they turn away from an opportunity to find their own freedom? And if I felt the people I taught were growing too slowly, or not moving through their resistance quickly enough, I became impatient inside. What was taking them so long? Didn't they realize that the fate of the world rested on their getting enlightened? Why couldn't they go as fast as I could?

Of course, I rarely shared these emotions with anyone, but I know people felt them. Once in a while someone would tell me they were afraid no matter how hard they worked on themselves, it would never be good enough for me. When I heard this, I would be shocked. Where had they gotten this idea? I loved everyone, I rejoiced at seeing them grow. How could they say they felt judged? What I did not see and what my students did not understand, was that **because I thought my Purpose was to save the world, I took any sign that I wasn't doing that not just personally, but as a cosmic disappointment.**

Naturally, when the world needs saving, one can't take time off, so I became a workaholic. How could I take long vacations when there were people in pain? How could I cancel a seminar when it might mean a couple would end up getting divorced because I hadn't been there to save them? After all, this was what I came here for, to help, not to sit around enjoying myself while other people suffered. And so I worked and I worked, and because I got such approval and gratitude for everything I was doing, I took this as a sign to keep on working.

In the beginning, I was so intense about my mission that I

didn't even enjoy the work I did. I was too uptight to have a good time. This should have been a sign that something was wrong, but I didn't know enough back then to interpret it correctly. "The reason I'm not happy," I concluded, "is that I haven't helped enough people yet."

Looking back, I guess you could say that I sometimes acted like a *cranky guru.* I'd get annoyed at one of my assistants if they didn't put the chalkboard on the stage at the right time. I'd be critical of an employee for missing the deadline for an ad. I'd be upset with someone I was helping for not taking my advice. When I look back on this period now, I cringe with remorse, even though I understand the source of my unpleasant behavior—*I couldn't figure out why, when I was doing such serious important work as saving the world, other people weren't taking it as seriously.*

Fortunately, I mellowed tremendously after the first seven years of this phase of my career, learning to be gentle and loving as I shared my message, and teaching from a place of compassion. But inside, the turmoil continued, and as I wrote in my first chapter, despite the success and good fortune I was experiencing, I still was not happy. That's when I knew it was time for me to become a student again, and to find some new teachers of my own who I hoped could help me understand why living my Purpose was not fulfilling me.

Up Against the Wall

I never expected to have an awakening that would so completely change my life while hanging from a fifty-foot wall by a rope, but I did. Here's the story of how it happened:

My husband, Jeffrey, is a chiropractor. Several years ago, he began talking about a well-known chiropractic lecturer and motivator he'd recently met. His name is Dr. Guy Riekeman, and he travels around the world teaching doctors about how to find and live their Purpose. "You have to meet this man," Jeffrey kept encouraging me, "and I really want to do his ropes course with you."

A ropes course is a series of physical challenges such as standing on top of a telephone pole and jumping off, walking on wires fifty feet off the ground, or climbing a sheer wall with only tiny crevices in which to place your hands and feet. Safety ropes are used, such as those used by mountain climbers. The purpose of a ropes course is not to master the physical feats, but to face the psychological and spiritual "walls" we all carry around with us, and to experience breakthroughs by triumphing over those limitations.

I've always had a lot of emotional courage in my life, but not much physical courage. So I wasn't thrilled with the idea of leaping off a telephone pole and trusting that the people on the ground would pull my rope taut in time. But it scared me so much to think about it that I knew I had to go. Besides, I was hungry for some new breakthroughs.

✦

It was snowing that day in the Colorado mountains as we began our ropes course, led by Guy. As I put on my safety helmet and my special mountaineering vest with hooks and cables running through it, I was scared to death. I didn't think I'd even be able to climb halfway up a telephone pole, let alone leap off it. So I can't describe how proud of myself I was when, several hours later, I jumped off the pole into midair, or walked a few steps on thin wires high above the ground while holding hands with Jeffrey. And as the day progressed, and I was able to accomplish each challenging exercise, I thought I was doing great—that is until we got to The Wall.

Imagine a fifty-foot wall rising from the ground, totally flat except for a few dozen tiny cement protrusions scattered randomly over the surface. Three people are connected together with about six feet of rope separating them. The idea is for all of them to get to the top of The Wall, and obviously, either they all make it or none do, because they're tied together. I remember standing in the freezing cold, my parka pulled tight, and watching the first team strain to climb up The Wall, finally making it to the platform on the top. It looked hard, harder than anything we'd done all day.

Guy tied me and my two teammates together, me in the middle, and the climb began. I stretched my leg up in front of me, and barely reached the first tiny peg. With all my strength, I grabbed on to another peg also almost out of reach, and pulled myself up the first few feet. Already, I was out of breath—we were 10,000 feet above sea level, and the air was thin and icy. Out of the corner of my eye, I noticed both of my teammates were much higher up than me, as high as they could go while they were still attached. For the next fifteen minutes I worked harder than I ever had in my life at anything to make it up about fifteen feet.

But now I was in trouble. My body was trembling uncontrollably. My legs were cramping. My hands were so cold that I could not feel them anymore. I still had thirty-five feet to go, and my teammates had been patiently waiting for me to catch up. I looked around desperately for pegs to grab, but they all seemed too far away. I would summon all my energy, and lunge at one of them, only to fall off the pegs and dangle in the air by the safety ropes my team on the ground were holding tight.

The group had been coaching and cheering me along throughout, and now they intensified their efforts. "Come on, Barbara," they shouted from below me, "You can do it. Don't stop now. Just try going up one more peg." The more they encouraged me, the worse I felt. I made a few more pathetic tries at pushing my body up higher on the sheer wall, and each time, I'd fall back as the crowd below gasped.

I began to cry. "I can't go any farther," I moaned. "I don't have the strength. I'm so sorry. I know I'm ruining it for my partners." This only seemed to fuel my supporters, who intensified their cheering, which only made me cry harder, hot angry tears. *Why couldn't they see that I was finished? Why didn't they understand that I just couldn't do it?*

Then I heard Jeffrey's voice. "I know you can do it, baby," he shouted. "Don't give up. Don't give in to your fear! Just dig deeper and find your strength, and try to go a little higher. "

"I can't," I shrieked back in a choked voice. "I want to come down."

"Yes you can," he insisted, the crowd agreeing with him. "You can do it!"

I began to sob hysterically, because I knew Jeffrey was wrong—I now realized, probably for the first time in my life, that no matter how hard I tried, how much I pushed myself, how intensely I wanted it, I could go no farther. I couldn't make it. I couldn't even move one muscle anymore. I was completely paralyzed. I clung to The Wall, overcome with a sense of failure that I had never known before. *I had let my partners down, and held them back from reaching their goal. I had let Jeffrey down. Most of all, I had let myself down.*

How I Learned to Stop Pushing People and Start Loving Them

It seemed like an eternity that I hung there on that lonely mountaintop, my lungs screaming with pain, my body cramped and frozen, my heart breaking. Finally, I heard Guy's voice say "I think she's at her limit. Let's get her down."

I hardly remember letting go of The Wall, and being lowered down to the ground in my harness. But when I felt the earth once again beneath my feet, I collapsed onto the snow, weeping, and felt Jeffrey reaching for me, and then cradling me in his arms.

"I'm here, sweetheart," he whispered. "I won't leave you."

"I'm sorry. I'm so sorry. I just couldn't do it. Please forgive me. I'm so sorry." That's all I could say through my tears, over and over again.

"Shhhhhhh," he comforted me. "You did great. I'm so proud of you for even trying. I saw how much you pushed yourself, honey. You have nothing to apologize for."

"I feel so terrible," I sobbed. "I didn't want to disappoint you. I wanted so badly to make you proud of me. But I just couldn't do it. I just couldn't go any farther. *I just couldn't keep up with the others."*

Jeffrey looked at me with tenderness and compassion, and softly said: **"Barbara, that's how everyone else in your life always feels around you."**

When I heard his words, it was as if a veil lifted from my eyes. In that moment, I got the truth about myself as a teacher and as a person, realized how I'd been misunderstanding my Purpose. Jeffrey was right. That was how everyone felt around me—*like no matter how fast they went, I could go faster; like no matter how hard they tried, I would push them to try harder; like they were always slowing me down, and would never be able to keep up.*

On The Wall that afternoon had been the hearts and souls of all my students, my lovers, my friends, who, so many times, in so many ways, had cried out to me as I had to my team that day, "I just can't go any farther. I can't go any faster." And the voices that came from below, urging me on with the best of intentions even as they ignored my pain represented my own voice, as I had been using it to motivate, to push, to implore the people I served to go farther. And as I lay in a cold bundle on the ground, I saw the truth:

. . . *That everyone in my life had always been growing as*

fast as they could, and that what they had needed from me all along was exactly what I'd needed that day from my team and from Jeffrey—not judgment, not disappointment, but love.

. . . I needed Jeffrey to love me, even though I couldn't climb to the top of The Wall.

. . . I needed to know that wherever I got to was enough.

. . . I needed to know that it wasn't reaching the destination that made my climb a success, but just the act of climbing itself.

I learned more about being a teacher that day, clinging to The Wall, than I had during all my years of giving seminars. I learned that a teacher respects The Wall, and the process every climber goes through. A teacher knows when to say "keep climbing," and when to say "come down." *And a teacher knows that, ultimately, there is no up or down, high or low, no better or worse—there's just The Wall and what the climb teaches you.*

I will always be eternally grateful to Guy Riekeman for facilitating such a crucial breakthrough in my spiritual growth, and to Jeffrey for so wisely and lovingly telling me the truth in a moment when I was finally ready to hear it.

Saving the World as a Hobby

Facing my own wall of misunderstanding changed me profoundly. After my experience in Colorado, I taught from a level of unconditional love and compassion I had not previously reached before. And I was happier than I'd ever been in my life. But I knew my rebirth was not complete. I still felt compelled to work seven days a week and overschedule myself, because I still felt responsible for "saving the world."

And then, I began to write this book. I knew when I chose the book's topic that writing it would force me to examine myself in a way that only writing does. *For me, working on a book is like a twelve-month seminar.* Every day, every night, every waking moment for a year is spent thinking about, talking about and writing about a topic—in this case, real moments and the search for meaning.

So each day as I wrote this for you, I'd read the pages and think about myself. **Was I happy? Was I hiding from real moments? What was my Purpose?**

Slowly, powerfully, I began to understand. As long as I, with my intensely passionate personality, believed that my Purpose, or even my job, was to do my part to save the world, I could not relax in my life, or focus on my own happiness. After all, I take whatever job I do very seriously. But now I saw that my job and my purpose were two different things:

My job was to be a teacher.

And my Purpose, my true Work, was to learn to celebrate my existence here on Earth, to love myself and others fully, and to be happy.

As for saving the world, as a friend of mine suggested, I could do it *"as a hobby!"* But my first responsibility was to save myself, and to experience as many real moments as possible.

This new understanding gave me the gift of freedom. I could do my job, which is teaching, *when* I was actually teaching, not twenty-four hours a day. *My acts of contribution to others, my moments of vision for our planet, could now become acts of love, and moments of joy, rather than full-time burdens, and cosmic obligations.* **I had finally given myself permission to be happy, no strings attached.**

✦

I am aware that most people do not live their lives with the same emotional velocity as I do. *I am also very certain that there is a purpose in my life having been as dramatic and intense as it's been, and therefore, a purpose in the sharing of my story.* Teachers often use metaphor to convey their message, and in many ways my life has been structured as a living metaphor to assist me in guiding others on their journey toward love and wholeness.

You may not feel the same proportion of spiritual responsibilities as I've felt in my life, but you have your own battles which interfere with your happiness that are just as significant—battles between the obligations you've taken on to your company, your family, or whatever is important to you, and your own need for time, for joy, for peace. And although you may never have been stuck on a fifty-foot wall in the mountains, unable to go up and afraid to come down, I know you've faced your own walls of fear and disillusionment. Perhaps you are even facing one right now.

May these stories comfort you in your search for meaning. May they remind you that you are not alone. May they give you the courage to reexamine your job, to discover your real Work, and to infuse them both with real moments. You may realize that you want to sell your business and move to the country, or find a healthier company to work for, or go back to school to become a veterinarian. *Or it may be that the adjustments you need to make in order to be happier are, as they were for me, adjustments in your **thinking** rather than in your **doing.***

✦

In the end, your Work is about creating real moments by choosing to do the simple things each day:

Greet the Sun.
Breathe deeply.
Marvel at the wonder of your body.
Make someone smile.
Scratch your dog's tummy.
See the soul behind someone's eyes.
Appreciate an everyday miracle.
Thank the land for your food.
Wave to a bird.
Tell someone you love them.
Say good night to God . . .

REAL MOMENTS
IN DIFFICULT TIMES

"Sometimes we turn to God
when our foundations are shaking
only to find out that it is God
who is shaking them. . . ."
— ANONYMOUS

There are moments in your life that are so sweet, living on the earth seems like a blessing and a privilege — when you first set eyes on your newborn child; when you're lying in your lover's arms early in the morning listening to the rain fall against the window; on that first day when you notice Spring's arrival, and the air is filled with promise and anything seems possible. And there are times in your life when it all seems to make sense, when things happen the way you planned them, when it is easy to believe in God and a magnificent Intelligence, for who or what else could have created a world so abundant in miracles.

Then, there are the difficult times — times when you've lost something you worked hard for, or someone you loved, times when your faith in goodness is tested, times when you just want the pain to go away. And nothing makes sense, and none of it seems worth it, and it's hard to believe in anything.

If you are old enough to read this, you have already gone through many difficult times in your life. Perhaps you're even going through one right now. One thing is for sure: *As long as we are alive, we will move in and out of crisis and adversity, and our joys will live alongside of our sorrows.*

Life on our earth is about change. In fact, you are alive because you are changing continually, and change always contains death and rebirth. At this very moment, there are cells dying and being reborn in every organ and muscle of your body. When your physical body stops changing and re-generating itself, it ceases to exist—that's called Death.

This cycle of destruction before creation is omnipresent in our physical universe. The orange blossom on a tree has to die before the fruit can grow. The seed must die before a plant can emerge as wheat must die in the making of bread. As the late Joseph Campbell emphasized so insightfully, *"You can't make an omelet without breaking eggs."*

W hat went before must change form in order
to rebirth itself, and in the process, the old form
needs to be discarded.

It's easy to be philosophical and even accepting of change when you're talking about fruit and wheat, but it's a lot more challenging when you're talking about your own life. *As human beings, we cherish the familiar.* We cling to our routines, our daily rituals, our favorite chair, our parking spot, our side of the bed, in an attempt to give ourselves some sense of certainty and control over what we secretly know is a totally unpredictable universe. *And so we are frightened of change*—it **robs us of the safety we are accustomed to and plunges us into emotional free-fall.**

This is our dilemma—for as sure as the earth continues to turn, change will come. And it will always come in the form of loss—when we lose our youth, our hair, our figures, when we lose our jobs, our dreams, or our energy to make them come true. The loss will come when our children grow up and we lose their innocent, unconditional love, when we grow apart from those we were once close with, when death takes our grandparents and then our parents from us, and suddenly we are the elders in the family. The loss will come when our friends or our beloved passes from the world, and we are agonizingly alone. The loss will come as we age and are no longer the vital, molten core of our society, but the softer, quieter edges. The loss will come, ultimately, as we slip out of the harbor of our body and sail back into the realm of spirit.

Life is a series of painful good-byes, and good-byes are never easy. But on the other side of good-bye is hello; on the other side of releasing the old is embracing the new.

> The journey in between what you once were and who you are now becoming is where the dance of life really takes place.

In this way, difficult times are usually those times when the greatest amount of change is occurring. They may not be enjoyable times, and they certainly aren't comfortable times, but they are potent with opportunities for great awakening. And they are ripe for real moments.

✦

Difficult times make real moments more available to you because they open doors to your inner world that you may normally keep locked. When you are faced with crisis or trauma, the pain is so great that your usual filters which numb you to your emotions don't work. It is impossible to be distracted from what's going on inside of you. *You are forced to feel everything. And it's in fully feeling whatever is happening to you right then that you experience a real moment.*

Think back to a painful time in your life. Perhaps it was when you were going through a divorce, or when you were ill, or when someone in your family was in trouble. If you are like most people, you will be able to reflect back on that difficult period and say: "As much as it hurt, that *divorce, illness, tragedy, accident, etc.* was one of the best things that ever happened to me." From where you stand now, you can clearly see the gift that was hidden inside the problem. You learned things you needed to learn.

Crisis forces you to pay attention, to your life, to your relationships, and to yourself. It acts like a high-powered searchlight that focuses its beam so intensely on something, illuminating it in every detail, that you can't see anything else. And it is in those moments of powerful self-reflection and personal revelation that real moments happen.

◆

"Out of every crisis comes the chance to be reborn."
—NENA O'NEILL

From the womb of darkness, each day the dawn emerges. From the womb of adversity, you emerge with added wisdom and strength. *This is the power of difficulty—it forces you to tap into reserves of courage, hope, and love you weren't aware you possessed.*

Pain helps you to unfold yourself, to discover
the hidden treasures of spiritual wealth you did
not know existed within you.

Dan Millman, who's written several wonderful books about what he calls the "peaceful warrior," has a great saying about difficult times: *"Tragedies serve as an express elevator to Spirit."* With nowhere else to turn, we turn within, and find new connections to a source of comfort and clarity. Would we have discovered those inner realms eventually? Perhaps. But our pain and desperation accelerated the process. I've often talked to friends going through hard times who reported this same experience—that as much as they hated the awful circumstance in which they found themselves, they simultaneously felt new levels of personal power, and even peace.

W̶e̶ don't develop courage by being happy
every day. We develop it by surviving difficult
times and challenging adversity.

Pain nourishes courage. Mary Tyler Moore, who has faced and surmounted many serious personal and physical difficulties in her own life, said it very simply: *"You can't be brave if you've only had wonderful things happen to you."*

Whenever I'm interviewed by a reporter, or speak in front of a large group, I am frequently asked the question: "What has contributed the most to your having so much knowledge about life at such a young age?" My answer is always the same: "PAINFUL EXPERIENCE!" And it's true. As I look back on the times in my life that taught me the most, they were the difficult times. By surviving them, I gained a confidence in myself I never could have achieved if I'd led a totally happy life.

It is not easy to accept difficult times as gifts rather than unjust punishments. When you are in the middle of tragedy or heartbreak, it feels like God has singled you out for misery. "I don't care if there is some cosmic lesson in this," your spirit screams from within, "I just want the pain to stop!" I don't think you'd be human if you didn't recoil from unhappiness. *But never judge yourself for how you endure your suffering—*

there is no right or wrong way to experience hardship. Disliking difficult times does not mean you have less faith, or are less enlightened. It just means you haven't completely unwrapped the gift yet . . . *What's miraculous is that, in spite of your attitude toward adversity, and regardless of how willingly or unwillingly you move through it, move through it you will—and on the other side, new strength and wisdom will be waiting.*

Whenever I am faced with difficult times, I remember something my first guru taught me in a meditation course twenty-five years ago:

> "The wind blows strong and hard on the
> tender young trees, not to harm them, but to
> teach their roots to hold firmly to the ground."

My life has been very windy. And there have been times when I have cursed the wind for the disruption it's caused me. But now I have grown into a tall, strong tree, with powerful roots. I bless the painful moments in my life, and I thank the wind. Its relentless force has molded me into the woman I am today.

Learning to Dance with Your Pain

I once heard a saying: *"You can't stop the waves, but you can learn to surf."* Surfing means learning to ride the waves, to move in the direction the current is taking you. **And that's the best method I've discovered for dealing with pain and crisis—to move deeper into it, rather than away from it.**

> You can create real moments in difficult times
> by surrendering to your pain, rather than
> resisting it.

I call this *learning to dance with your pain,* to find the rhythm of the challenging time you are in, and to attune yourself to it. Learning to dance with your pain means not avoiding your feelings of discomfort or fear, but choosing instead to consciously explore them. It means talking about the very thing you would rather forget. It means giving yourself the time and space to indulge in the sadness or grief.

About nine years ago, just before Christmas, the man I loved and was living with at the time walked out on me. He didn't give me any logical explanations—he just packed up and left. I suspected that he was cheating on me, which I later found out was true. But when it happened, all I knew was that he was gone, I was alone, and my heart was broken.

For several days I battled the overwhelming pain and terror I felt. I talked on the phone incessantly to anyone who would listen; I wrote him letter after letter, and then tore them up; I reread all the cards he'd ever sent me, searching for a clue as to why he'd left. Each night I would cry myself to sleep, praying that the next day would somehow be better, and each morning I would wake up, and as soon as I remembered what was happening, I'd be swallowed up by the pain all over again.

I don't know what made me decide to go away by myself for Christmas. I suddenly knew I had to get away to somewhere isolated from my friends and the television and all other distractions. I spent several days researching the right spot for a retreat. Then I heard about a tiny cabin set on some hills in Cambria, California, a little town halfway between Los Angeles and San Francisco. The owner of the cabin told me that it was beautiful but rustic—no heat, no electricity—just wood and glass looking out onto a grove of trees. "It's the perfect place for solitude," he agreed. And that's exactly what I wanted. *I needed to be alone with my pain.*

I packed up my car and drove up the coast. And for the next four days, I didn't speak to a soul. I wrote in my journal,

I meditated, I walked in the woods and along the beach during the day, I sat by candlelight surrounded by total silence at night. **I stopped resisting what was happening to me, and instead, surrendered to my pain and loss completely.**

And an amazing thing began to happen—I started to fill up with a deep, comforting sense of peace. I felt my own spirit, and experienced once again my connection to the Whole. I felt protected and soothed, as if I were being watched over in my time of trials. And as my vision cleared, I saw truths about the relationship I had not wanted to face before, and I finally let go. The intense pain began to disappear, and in its place was a dull ache, the kind you have when you've been wounded, but are now healing.

Many years have passed since that Christmas in the cabin, but I still consider those four days when I learned how to dance with my pain some of the most meaningful and precious real moments in my life. *By surrendering to my time of crisis and moving into it, rather than away from it, I rebirthed myself into a new level of clarity and serenity.* I passed through the dark night of the soul and emerged into light.

Joseph Campbell writes:

> *"The dark night of the soul comes just before revelation. When everything is lost, and all seems darkness, then comes the new life and all that is needed."*

Finding Love in the Darkness

Times of crisis draw people together. They bring out the best in our human nature. They elicit our compassion, our generosity, our innate kindness. They help us transcend our differences and celebrate our oneness. We see this every time there is a flood or an earthquake or a hurricane. *The forces of love always rally to guide us through the dark days.*

Dİfficult times always create opportunities for
you to experience more love in your life.

Finding love in the darkness is simple. Reach out to others
in your despair, and they will reach back. Say "I need help,"
and miraculously, help will appear. You have so many more
resources in your life than you realize—friends, acquaintances, people who love you. "I didn't know so many people
cared," you think to yourself as you receive cards or phone
calls, or offers of assistance. Sometimes it takes a tragedy or
loss for us to acknowledge how loved we truly are. This is one
of the reasons difficult times can be rich with real moments—
because they are rich with love.

✦

Last year, a friend of mine died of the AIDS virus. His name
was Jon Gould, and he was only thirty-nine years old. Jon was
a gentle, kind man in the truest sense of the word, and his life
was dedicated to service and self-discovery. When his family
and companion asked me to conduct Jon's memorial service,
I felt honored, but I was a little nervous about how it would
turn out. I wanted to do justice to Jon's beautiful spirit, but I
knew there would be a lot of intense feeling at the service.
Both of Jon's parents, who were divorced, would be there,
along with many of his past lovers and a very diverse group
of people. And I knew that Jon's sister had just lost her own
little girl to a tragic death, and that the family had gone
through more pain in the past few years than most families
do in a lifetime.

The service was held in the home of Jon's mother. His partner had decorated the entire house with huge yellow sun-
flowers, Jon's favorite. Pictures of Jon were displayed everywhere. Over a hundred of us crowded into the living room,

and as Jon's favorite music played in the background, I began by sharing these words:

> *"Many traditions believe that at the time of passing on, the soul has a chance to evaluate its life and its choices, and that a gathering together of those who loved him will help the soul see his value, celebrate himself and, wrapped in love, go on toward the Light and the beautiful adventure that awaits."*

Suddenly, I could feel the relief in the room as we all realized that our purpose in coming together was to celebrate Jon, not to mourn him. The death of a loved one leaves those who are still alive feeling so powerless, and at a loss as to what to do with all the feelings that can no longer be shared directly with that person. But as we sat close together on that special evening, **each of us felt purposeful, even in our grief, for we knew we could do something—we could love.**

And that is what we did. We spent several hours loving Jon, through sharing cherished experiences, telling funny stories, remembering the fabulous food he cooked for his customers and his friends, and acknowledging how he had touched our lives. We laughed, we cried, we prayed for the peaceful journey of his spirit. And when it was all over, we each lit a floating candle and placed it in the swimming pool as we said our special good-byes.

Driving home by myself that night, I thanked Jon for the priceless gift he had given me by allowing me to facilitate the celebration of his passing. I had been reminded, once again, of the healing power of love:

> When we bring enough love into the darkness,
> it will illuminate our hearts with light
> and soothe our pain.
>
> When we bring enough love to our difficult
> times, it will reward us with real moments.

✦

There are times like these when, for just a moment, we open our hearts and share the best of ourselves. *We remember how to love.* Just after the big earthquake in January 1994, I stood trembling on the street outside my house in Los Angeles. Neighbors in bathrobes offered one another food, comfort, and extra batteries—it reminded me of Woodstock, or the gatherings I used to attend in the late 1960s. For a few days, we of so many races and dialects in Los Angeles were one family. You could feel the love. And then the intensity of the crisis was over. And the love went away.

Why does it take tragedy and difficult times to bring us back to love? Why do we need nature's close calls to make us realize how much we love our mates, our children, our friends? Why do we forget to love until it is too late? How much pain and destruction will it take for us to remember?

There is a beautiful portion of *A Course in Miracles* which reads:

> "Trials are but lessons that you failed to learn, presented once again."

I often wonder whether we would have fewer difficult times if we remembered to share more love and find more real moments during the easy days.

> Perhaps crisis forces us to return to our center when we have drifted away from our true values, and to put our lives in perspective when we have forgotten what is really important. . . .
>
> Perhaps it is the Universe's way of getting our attention fast, and refocusing us on love. . . .
>
> Perhaps this is the hidden gift that difficult times hold for us.

✦

My wish for you is that you have
many happy days,
and few sorrows. But when those
difficult times come,
may you meet them with surrender,
and move through them with love.

Part Three

REAL MOMENTS
AND RELATIONSHIPS

✦

· 7 ·

REAL MOMENTS
AND LOVING

"There is only one path to Heaven. On Earth, we call it Love."
— KAREN GOLDMAN

Of all the wonders life on Earth has to offer, none is greater to me than Love. Love infuses life with meaning. It performs magic and miracles. It brings light where there was darkness and hope where there was despair. It is your greatest teacher, and your most constant blessing.

Love is a force more formidable than any other. It is invisible—it cannot be seen, nor measured, yet it is powerful enough to transform you in a moment, and offer you more joy than any material possession could. Once love is yours, no one can take it away from you. Only you can relinquish it, if you wish.

Love is the magician of the Universe. It creates everything out of nothing. One moment, it isn't there, and the next— POOF—it appears in all its splendor, and you greet it with amazement. And what delights it produces out of thin air— smiles, laughter, goose bumps, hot flashes, tender words, silly names, happy tears, and, most of all, life. Love produced you. Without it, you wouldn't be here at all.

Love's greatest gift is its ability
to make everything it touches sacred.

Love sanctifies life. *Where love is, you are given a glimpse of the sacred.* You rise above your humanness and see the world through heavenly eyes. Your child, your beloved, your dog or cat, your garden, or whatever it is that you love appears adorable, precious, supremely beautiful, and somehow perfect in spite of its imperfections. And love also consecrates time and place and possession, bestowing special stature upon them: The day you first met your husband; the anniversary of your wedding; the special bench in the park where you go to talk; the rocking chair in which you nursed your child; the old afghan your grandmother made you; your little girl's first note that said "I love you, Mommy"; these become sacred artifacts commemorating the presence of love in your life.

But most of all, I believe that love offers you an opportunity for deep, spiritual awakening, for when you love, the usual boundaries which separate you from something else dissolve; you transcend the illusion of separation which defines human existence, and you experience Oneness. Suddenly, you are no longer alone in the Universe. There is a flow between your being and the being of whomever you are loving. All that is you is pouring out into them, and all that is them is pouring out into you. Your souls are dancing together.

Perhaps you have had moments like this, but not known exactly why they moved you so much. . . .

You and your husband stand above the crib of your newborn child, watching her sleep. Her tiny body rises and falls with the rhythm of her peaceful breathing, and you turn to your husband and his eyes meet yours. All at once, you feel a force of love circling from you to him to your daughter and back to you again, and as you flow in the fullness of the energy, you are aware of a timeless bond that connects you together. Nothing else exists. You feel totally complete.

✦

It's late at night and you're sitting outside on your back porch listening to the crickets and watching the stars. Your faithful dog who's been your best friend for ten years pads up alongside of you, and nuzzles his head under your arm. As you hold his warm body close to yours, you suddenly feel a surge of love for him, and the unconditional devotion he has always shown you. He raises his head and, for a long moment, looks at you as if to say, "Yes, I feel it too." The night swallows both of you up into an eternal peace, and it seems you are the only two beings in the world. This moment is all yours.

This is the power of love—*it takes you on a journey from separation to Oneness.* It penetrates the normal boundaries in which you live, the boundaries that make you feel like "you," distinct and unrelated to anyone or anything else. You know that you are not your husband or wife or dog or friend or the sky. And yet, in those very real moments of love, "you" turns into "us," something infinitely more fulfilling than you alone.

In this way, love creates an unlimited experience with no boundaries, no edges. It allows you to travel out of yourself.

All love is an out-of-body experience.

You may not have ever considered yourself a spiritual person, *but every true experience of love is spiritual,* as your spirit touches the spirit of someone or something else. **Love becomes your doorway into the divine.**

Love is the ultimate method for creating real moments, because love forces you to practice mindfulness. It pulls you into an eternal present. It focuses all of your attention on what you are experiencing, and it requires that you surrender to it.

The better you become at loving, the more real moments you will be able to create.

✦

"Every deep love relationship is a path of initiation, a journey involving many tests and trials."
— BARRY AND JOYCE VISSEL

An intimate relationship is a sacred opportunity for you to use love as a path for personal and spiritual transformation. It forces you to open where you were closed, to feel where you were numb, to express what was silent, to reach out where you would retreat. *It's easy to feel like you are a loving and enlightened person when you are alone, but when you get into a relationship, you come face-to-face with every emotional limitation you possess.*

Relationships are an instant and continual training ground. They insist that you look in the mirror at yourself, they reveal all the parts of you that are not loving. They show you your dark side. They knock on the door of your heart, demanding that you open the places you've kept locked. And then, every day and night, they give you an opportunity to practice love, to stretch yourself beyond what is comfortable, and to keep doing it better.

Using Your Relationship as a Path

I chose to follow the path of love at a very early age, for I knew it would lead me to the real moments of meaning I was searching for. It has been an exciting, mysterious, often painful but always liberating journey. For a long time, I wasn't very good at loving. I made many mistakes; I hurt myself and I hurt others. But slowly, I learned how to use love and relationship as a sacred path of learning and transformation. And

I was finally blessed to find a man who was willing to travel that same path with me, and share the adventure.

All great creations begin with a vision. Before an artist paints, he has a vision of the picture in his mind. Before an architect designs a building, she has a vision of what it should look like. Before a musician writes a piece of music, he hears the finished piece in his head. Vision fuels the birth of all that is produced with love.

> If you don't have a vision of where you want your relationship to go, it won't go anywhere.

Being in a relationship without both of you agreeing on its destination is like trying to take a long road trip without a map—you're going to get lost over and over again, and you're not going to enjoy the ride. To use your relationship as a path, both you and your partner must create a shared vision of the purpose of your being together, and then make a sincere commitment to living that vision.

Vision helps us get through difficult times. It focuses our awareness on the destination, and encourages us to keep going, even when we feel lost or disheartened. It is the vision of the career you want to have that helps you study, write papers, and work hard through college. It is the vision of holding your newborn baby in your arms that gives you, as a mother, courage to get through the pain of labor. **It is the vision of your relationship as a transformational path that will give you and your partner the strength, patience, and perseverance to travel the High Road of Love together.**

Here are several truths that make up the vision my husband and I share of our relationship:

1. **We have been brought together for the purpose of helping each other grow, and will be each other's teacher.**

2. Our relationship is a precious gift—it will take us through whatever we need to learn to become more conscious, loving human beings.

3. The challenges and difficulties we experience will always illuminate our most needed lessons.

Because we have made a commitment to accept this purposeful vision of our love, we experience the struggles and problems we encounter in a sacred context. When we argue, we are angry at one another, when we get frustrated and feel like turning away, our vision shines like a beacon of light in the fog, reminding us that there is a higher purpose to the everyday difficulties we're challenged by. *We remember that we have chosen to travel together for a reason, and by remembering, we can more quickly release the anger, move beyond the hurt, forgive, and find our eternal bond of love that is always present underneath.*

It is easy to forget the true purpose of your relationship when you are busy with work, children, and family obligations. And when you forget your purpose as a couple, you lose your way. A relationship that has lost its way will stop moving and growing, for it won't know where it is supposed to go.

If you and your partner have lost your way, seek out real moments together. In them, you will find your way back home to the heart of your love.

Feeding the Soul of Your Relationship

You need real moments of intimacy, of oneness, to nourish the spirit of your love so that it will continue to grow. Sharing these moments with your partner reminds you both of your timeless connection, your purpose in finding one another, and thus gives you renewed vision and courage to get you through the challenges of living together.

> Real moments are the life blood of intimate
> relationships.

Without real moments, the soul of your relationship will die. You may still choose to ignore your lack of fulfillment and stay together, but your relationship will exist as an empty shell, an arrangement of convenience you make in order not to be alone.

Having real moments of intimacy doesn't mean just being with someone. It's what *happens* when you are together that makes it a real moment of love. You can be physically together and be emotionally a million miles away because you are not in the moment. Or you can create a real moment on the phone, even though you're calling from 1,000 miles away, simply because you are letting the boundaries go and sharing the deepest parts of your heart.

Most relationships I see around me are suffering from real-moment deprivation. It's not that the two people don't love each other—they do. But *they don't feel the love as deeply as they should,* because they aren't giving the love opportunities to surface and be experienced without distraction. *They aren't having enough real moments together.*

✦

Earlier this year, my husband and I spent an hour with a wonderful woman named Robin, picking out our wedding invitations. Jeffrey left her store first to get back to his office, and I stayed to finish up the details.

"He's wonderful!" Robin remarked. "You two make a great couple. You seem like best friends, and I loved watching you interact together."

"Thank you," I answered. "Believe me, we've worked really hard to get our relationship to be as good as it is."

"Do you want to hear something sad? I must see twenty couples a week who come in here to pick out invitations, and I'd say on a good week, maybe one couple actually seems to be happy together, and behaves lovingly toward each other. It makes me wonder why they're even getting married."

Robin's comment didn't surprise me. I know from teaching seminars for so many years that her observation is sad but true. Most people look at a relationship like a possession—"I have a car; I have a job; I have a relationship." The relationship becomes something to *get*, and once that goal has been obtained, they don't put much time or energy into it.

> Marriage is not a noun, it's a verb. It isn't something you get, it's something you do.

Marriage is not a wedding ring, or a piece of paper that proves you are husband and wife, or a party that says you've been married for twenty-five years. Marriage is a *behavior*—it is how you love and honor your partner every day. You aren't married because the county or your family thinks you are. *The real act of marriage takes place in the heart,* not in ballroom or a church or a synagogue. It is a choice you make, not just on your wedding day, but over and over again, and that choice is reflected in the way you treat your husband or wife.

Your marriage is renewed and reconsecrated every time you share a real moment together.

✦

"Every moment of your life,
you are offered the opportunity to choose—love or fear—
to tread the earth, or to soar the heavens.
Fear would walk you on a narrow path,
promising to take you where you want to go.
Love says, 'Open your arms and fly with me.' "
            — E M M A N U E L , as told by Pat Rodegast

We avoid real moments in relationships because if we aren't used to them, they can be frightening in their intensity:

Have you ever sat with someone you loved late at night, sharing your thoughts, your hopes, your secret feelings? At first, you're just talking, but at some point, enough doors have been opened, enough connection has been made, and something greater than your two individual selves is created. It is tangible. You both can feel it. It is a space you occupy together, a sacred space that emerges when enough truth has been spoken, and acknowledged. Suddenly, you feel your connectedness as strong as anything you've ever felt. You are experiencing a real moment.

All at once you realize that you are out of control. Your boundaries have melted, and the usual protections you have are dissolving, leaving you uncomfortable in your vulnerability. You are being seen without your masks, your innermost emotions are being witnessed by someone else. The sanctity of your personal space has been penetrated.

Ironically, this is actually the definition of love, when you allow your soul to touch someone else's. If you are not good at trusting and letting go, you will pull away from the moment, and turn away from the love, for fear that you will lose yourself in it. You will crave retreat from your partner, maybe even from the relationship. Or perhaps you will just avoid intimacy and relationship entirely, knowing that without it, those terrifying moments of vulnerability cannot happen.

What are you running from? Your own nakedness. What are you afraid of? Losing your edges, your ego, and being swallowed up by a force more powerful than you. It is a kind of death—the death of your separateness, the death of your illusions about yourself.

Many of us spend our life playing hide-and-seek with ourselves—we do whatever we can to avoid facing our truth, and exploring our shadows. *If this has been your agenda, you will be terrified of true, deep love and the real moments of surrender it requires of you.* And you will find ways to flee from them.

Clarissa Pinkola Estés, author of *Women Who Run with the Wolves*, says that: "Fear is a poor excuse for not doing the work. We are all afraid. It is nothing new. If you are alive, you are fearful . . . **To love means to stay when every cell says run!**"

Loving may appear to be an emotional risk, but in reality, it isn't a risk at all.

Y ou never lose by loving.
You always lose by holding back love.

 . . . The real risk is in living with someone year after year without truly knowing their soul, or their knowing yours.

 . . . The real risk is having a marriage based on materialism and superficiality, and avoiding those kinds of human connection that are truly significant.

 . . . *The real risk is being in a relationship without real moments.*

Finding Your Ability to Feel Again

Experiencing intimacy with your beloved requires that you open yourself totally to the moment, not just by showing up physically, but by *showing up emotionally*. You aren't pretending to listen, but thinking about something else; you aren't reading the paper while she is trying to reach out; you aren't going through the motions of loving, but feeling numb—you are fully present with him or with her. After all, if *you* aren't *there* in the moment, then who is there to love, to connect, to be intimate with?

Being there emotionally in the moment means knowing how to fully feel your feelings.

The ability to feel love is based on the *ability to feel* . . . period. *You can't feel love or happiness or contentment if you have forgotten how to feel.* Many of us were robbed of our ability to feel as children. Now, as adults, not feeling has become an old habit—we suppress, edit, and deny our emotions on a regular basis. We respond to requests for connection with phrases like: *"Not now," "I don't want to talk about it," "Nothing's wrong," "Aren't you ever satisfied?"* We drink alcohol, take drugs, eat junk food, work incessantly, and watch too much TV, all in an attempt to numb ourselves. Thus we carry years of frozen feelings inside of our hearts, and when it comes time to connect, to be intimate, even if we want to, we don't know how.

> Finding your ability to feel again is the first step toward experiencing true intimacy with your partner and creating real moments in relationship.

To do this, you need to defrost the ice around your heart. Cry all the tears you never shed; release the old rage from your body; find your voice and give it permission to say all the things it has kept silent for so long. *The more you work on healing your emotional wounds, the easier it will be for you to love.*

I've spent my whole life developing powerful and effective

techniques to break down emotional walls. I needed them first to heal myself, and then to share with my students. There are many other teachers and therapists who also offer their own methods for emotional healing. **Use us. We are here to help you find your way back to yourself.**

✦

"You learn to speak by speaking, to study by studying, to run by running, to work by working; and just so, you learn to love . . . by loving. All those who think to learn in any other way deceive themselves."

— SAINT FRANCIS DE SALES

How do you begin to experience more real moments in loving? **You begin.** No putting it off until your next vacation, or Saturday night, or until you finish this chapter. *Now* is the time. No waiting until it feels right, or until you think you'll be better at it. *It will never feel right until you do it, and you won't get better at it until you start.*

Loving well is a skill, just like playing an instrument, or operating a computer, or cooking—the more you do it, the better you get. Creating real moments of intimacy takes practice. You could listen to every tape I've recorded, or attend every seminar on relationships that is available, but you still wouldn't be good at loving. **Loving is the only way to get good at loving.**

Many years ago, before I even became a teacher, I was married to a well-known magician. He was a master at creating exquisite illusions on stage and doing miraculous sleight of hand with coins and cards. Whenever anyone would ask him how he made his magic look so effortless, he would explain that he'd spent years practicing, and he'd share his favorite saying:

"The difficult must become habit, the habit easy, and the easy beautiful."

It's been over fifteen years since I've heard that phrase, but as I write today, I haven't been able to get it out of my mind. It *is* difficult to love well, but the more we work on it, loving becomes a habit. You no longer have to remind yourself to tell your partner how much you appreciate him—you just find yourself doing it; he doesn't have to be asked to share his feelings—he volunteers them on his own. Suddenly, it feels more natural for you both to love, to give, to open, than it does to not love and to hold back. And the more you each give, the easier it gets, until there's no more effort. Finally, what's become easy begins to deepen as you and your beloved step out of the way and allow love to simply flow through each of you to the other. Your love has become beautiful.

✦

In the first section of this book, I said happiness is a choice, and so is love.

> Love is a choice you make from
> moment to moment.

You *choose* to love, to express it, to share it, to show it. You do not wait to be seized by an overwhelming feeling of love that propels you into action. You don't wait to say "I love you" until the words are bursting out of your mouth. You don't wait to give your wife a hug until you can't physically control yourself. *You make these gestures because you remember that you love this person, and because you know that by choosing to love, you will not only make your partner happy, but you will focus your own attention on the love you feel and bring yourself joy.*

Creating Real Moments in Your Relationship

Real moments will not chase you down as you race busily through your life. *You must invite them into your relationship by setting aside the time and space in which they can occur.*

- ✦ Set your alarm clock to go off ten minutes earlier so you can cuddle in bed
- ✦ Meet for a picnic lunch in a park
- ✦ Take a silent walk holding hands
- ✦ Go for a long drive to nowhere
- ✦ Sit together on the couch by candlelight
- ✦ Share your deepest fears and wildest dreams
- ✦ Turn off the television, start talking, and see what happens

Many couples insulate themselves from the intimacy of real moments by always having other people around—their children, their relatives, their friends. They rarely go out together alone. They use the excuse of being there for the kids to avoid each other. And when they do take a vacation, it is always with one or two other couples. Does this sound familiar to you? I hope not, because it is a dangerous way to live. You will wake up one day, look at your partner, and see the face of a stranger.

You need to be selfish in order to have real moments together. Do whatever it takes to find the time. And don't worry about neglecting your children or your friends. They will feel your renewed love and rejoice in it.

The greatest gift you and your partner can give
your children is the example of an intimate,
healthy, and loving relationship.

✦

Every couple must follow their own road to their own real moments. But here are some things that can help if you're not sure where to begin.

Feeding Your Partner's Heart—The "3 × 3 Formula"

Most people I see are walking around *love-starved*. Their hearts are hungry for love, and they aren't getting enough. Ask yourself right now:

"Am I getting enough love from my partner?"

"Is my partner getting enough love from me?"

I've developed an *Intimacy Formula* to help you feed your partner's heart: Our bodies need to eat three meals a day, with a few snacks in between. Our hearts needs to be nourished in the same way. **Feeding your partner's heart means feeding him/her three Love Meals a day. That means three times a day when you choose to actively love your partner, for at least three minutes.** I call this the "3 × 3 Formula," three minutes of intimacy three times a day to feed your partner's heart. Maybe it's three minutes in the morning together before you get out of bed, three minutes on the phone in the middle of the day, and three minutes after the kids go to sleep.

But Love Meals aren't enough—your partner also needs little **love snacks.** A love snack is a kiss on the neck, a compliment, a note you leave him, a thank-you, a phone call to say "I love you." Love snacks may only take a few seconds, but they create instant connection, and *mini-real moments.*

What do you feed your partner during these Love Meals and Love Snacks? Just like we have the four basic food groups in nutrition, I've come up with three basic emotional food groups, that I call **The Three A's: Attention, Affection, and Appreciation.** You *pay* attention, you *show affection,* and you *express appreciation.* When you give your mate these three ingredients during your three minutes, you will be nourishing his or her heart.

Attention: *Paying attention means being there 100 percent,* totally in the moment with the person you love. You are not doing anything else other than being there for them. When you give your partner all of your attention, even for a few moments, they have the opportunity to really feel you, and to receive your love. Look into their eyes; ask yourself what they need from you. You already know the answer. Remember—it is when we fully pay attention that real moments can occur.

Affection: *Showing affection means giving physical inti-macy—touching, holding, being physically close together.* This kind of affection is not particularly sexual. Rather, it is loving. Physical affection soothes and heals our body and soul. It's even been shown to strengthen our immune system. It will help connect you and your partner emotionally by linking you on the physical dimension first.

Appreciation: *Expressing appreciation means demonstrating your love verbally, telling your partner what you love about them, what you're grateful to them for, what they've done that has made you proud.* Most of us don't get enough appreciation, and are starving for gratitude. Notice that I did not say *show-ing* your appreciation by doing something, like making the bed for your wife, or getting your husband's car washed. This part of the formula needs to be verbal. You need to say the words: "Thank you for being so patient with me this morning when I was in a bad mood." "I am so proud of you for getting that new account at work." "I love the way you made our son feel so special for getting all A's and B's on his report card—you're really a great mom."

Three times a day, for at least three minutes, use the Three A's to feed your partner's heart. You will be amazed at the results. You will see your mate begin to glow right before your eyes. You will feel more in love. And you will have many more real moments.

Don't forget those Love Snacks. Ever since I came up with this whole concept, Jeffrey and I have been practicing it diligently, and several times a day, one of us will approach the other with a smile and announce: "Love Snack!" That's our cue for a quick hug or kiss. When any of our friends see us do this, and we explain how it works, invariably the wife will turn to her husband and say, "Hey, I want a Love Snack too!"

The purpose of this Intimacy Formula is to get you in the habit of having real moments of love and connection with your partner. It may sound like a cute little idea, but the effect it can have on your relationship is transformational.

Love Processes

Here are some structured ways of expressing your love called "Love Processes" that can create instant intimacy and real moments. You use these processes when you and your partner are alone together and have some uninterrupted quality time. It's helpful to sit across from one another, or next to each other, and hold hands. In each Love Process, you and your partner take turns going back and forth, each of you saying the key phrase, and then filling in the blank. The more specific you are in your response, the more powerful the exercise will be. After you are finished with one phrase, your partner should respond by thanking you, and then take his turn.

Here are a few examples for each Love Process. Your responses will probably be longer than these samples. You can spend as much time as you like doing a particular exercise. I suggest a minimum of ten minutes, and even longer is better.

The Appreciation Processes

✦ "Something I love about you is . . ."

"Something I love about you is how attentive you always are to me when I come home from work, making me feel like I can relax and let myself be taken care of for a while." (Thank you.)

"Something I love about you is what a great sense of humor you have—you always make me laugh when I'm being too serious, and I need that!" (Thank you.)

"Something I love about you is how hard you work on this relationship, and how much you reach out to me when I try to shut down. You never give up on me and you make it safe for me to open up." (Thank you.)

✦ "I love you because . . ."

"I love you because you always listen to my feelings, even when I know it's uncomfortable, and you make me feel like what I have to say is important." (Thank you.)

"I love you because you believe in me and my dreams for our family, and no one has stood by me before in my life like you have." (Thank you.)

"I love you because when I watch you play with our children, I see the little girl inside of you come out, and she is the sweetest, most loving person in the world."

The Gratitude Process

✦ "I'm grateful to you for . . ."

"I'm grateful to you for accepting my daughter as your own when we decided to get married, and being the father she never had." (Thank you.)

"I'm grateful to you for not giving up on us when I was so afraid of making a commitment, and helping me learn to trust love again. You saved my life." (Thank you.)

"I'm grateful to you for being so patient with me while I worked out my anger at my ex-husband, and loving me even when I took it out on you." (Thank you.)

The Forgiveness Process

✦ *"I'm sorry . . ."*

"I'm sorry that I make it so difficult for you to get through to me sometimes, and that I go so far away from you. I don't mean to make you work so hard to love me. I just get scared. *Please forgive me.*"

"I'm sorry that I criticized your ideas for remodeling the house last week, and made you feel like you weren't doing anything right. I'm so sorry I was so thoughtless, and didn't see how much you wanted to make things better for us. *Please forgive me.*"

"I'm sorry that I don't always let you know how much I need you, and get so busy with work that you feel neglected. I'm sorry I don't tell you every day that you're the most important thing in my life. *Please forgive me.*"

✦

I have seen these Love Processes create miracles in thousands of relationships, including my own. They work because they open the doors to your heart, and allow the love that has been waiting there to flow out, and, at the same time, invite your partner's love to flow in. I hope they lead you to many real and treasured moments together.

Making the Choice to Love Now

It is an unfortunate part of our human nature that we take what we have for granted until we lose it, and then weep for what can no longer be ours, and berate ourselves for the time we wasted.

If you have someone special in your life, don't wait to start loving them.

Do not put it off for even one day. Make the choice to love now. You do not, as your mind would like you to believe, have all the time in the world. Whoever loves you is only on loan from God, and he or she could be taken from you at any moment. I don't say this to frighten you. Believe me, I don't like this setup either. But that is the way it works, and why it is so important to make every day of loving count.

Let me share two stories with you. On the surface, they are both about death, but their real message is about life.

In Memory of Bobby

About eight years ago, I was teaching my Making Love Work weekend seminar in Los Angeles as I used to do each month. One of the course participants was a very successful man in his fifties. He'd accumulated great wealth over the course of his life by working eighteen hours a day. In the process, however, he had neglected his wife and three sons, and now, after twenty-five years of marriage, she was asking for a divorce. This man was devastated—he thought he'd been a good husband and father, and couldn't understand what he had done wrong. Even his therapist, who'd sent him to my course, hadn't been able to get through to him.

For two days in the seminar, this man did something he'd

never done in his life—he looked inward. There, deep within his heart, he found feelings he didn't know he'd had: love he had never expressed to his wife and sons; anger at his father for driving him to be successful from the time he was a small child; and tremendous grief that he was discovering all of this when it was already too late to salvage his relationship. For the first time since he was a little boy, he wept. On Saturday night, he shared that although he had failed in his marriage, he was determined to start new, caring relationships with his sons. "I can't wait to tell them how much I love them," he announced triumphantly, and we all cheered for his powerful breakthrough.

The next morning, just after we began our session, one of my staff members interrupted the class with an emergency. "There's a woman and her two sons in the lobby," she whispered. "They need to find their father who's taking the class. It seems that their brother was killed early this morning in a bicycling accident in Europe."

I caught my breath. Right away, I knew who the man they sought was. We escorted him out of the room, and then we all held each other as we heard his sobs and screams of anguish when his wife told him the tragic news. Suddenly, the door opened, and he approached the stage and asked me if he could address the group before he left.

I will never forget that moment as long as I live. He stood before us, tears streaming down his face: "I want to say two things," he began. "First, I thank God that I was here this weekend, because I learned how to feel, and if I hadn't gone through this seminar, I wouldn't even have been able to cry for my son. I would have been numb like I've been my whole life.

"And second, you all know how excited I was about the future, about finally being able to tell my boys how much I loved them, how proud I was of them. But now I'll never be able to tell Bobby that, because he's gone. I lost my chance. So please, if I can give you anything, let it be this: *Don't wait until it's too late, like I did. If there are people in your life who you love, tell them, show them, and do it today. Because you don't know if they will still be here tomorrow.*"

All of us in that room wept along with our friend as the truth he spoke penetrated our hearts. Our minds turned to our own husbands and wives and brothers and fathers and children we took for granted, assuming they would still be alive by the time we got around to telling them how much we loved them.

As the man turned to leave, I made him a promise—that Bobby's death would not be in vain, that I would share this story whenever I could for the rest of my life, as a reminder for whoever heard it to *love now.* So this was for you, Bobby. . . .

In Memory of Ellen

Ellen Baron was my rabbi's wife, and my friend. She died three years ago after a long and painful battle with cancer. Ellen was my age. At the time of her death, she was forty years old, and her son, Jonathan, was five.

When I first met Ellen, it was hard to imagine that she had cancer, because she was so physically beautiful. She had a radiance about her that was impossible to miss. She exuded life and love, and we all were sure that if anyone could conquer the disease, Ellen could.

Ellen's strong and courageous spirit did conquer her cancer, as she used it to move into even higher levels of consciousness and propel her through tremendous personal transformation. But Ellen's body could not fight off the physical assault of the disease, and after years of agonizing treatment, she knew it was time to go, and she passed on.

No death is ever welcome, but Ellen's illness and death seemed especially incomprehensible. She and David, her husband, were a rare couple completely in love with each other, and in her support for his work as a rabbi, her kindness and gentle spirit touched thousands of people every year. When she died, those who loved her were devastated.

Ellen's funeral was a standing-room-only affair. One by one, Ellen's many friends, her doctors, her son, and her husband got up to share their cherished memories, their pain, their loss, and, more than anything else, their love with all of us, and with Ellen's spirit which we could feel hovering nearby. For several hours, with laughter and with tears, we celebrated the woman that had been Ellen Baron, and acknowledged her passing into a different form.

I remember at one point looking around the chapel and seeing everyone, even strangers, holding hands with each other. The love in the room was overpowering. Suddenly, an enormous wave of sadness washed over me. *"Why do we wait until the people we love die to celebrate them?"* I asked myself. *"Why is the day on which we love and honor a person the most, a day when he or she can no longer hear our words? Why don't we share those stories and memories and feelings with the same depth of passion while that person is living?"*

Ellen should have been standing before us, surrounded by baskets of flowers, as we paid tribute to the magnificent wife, mother, and woman she was. She had always been well loved, but I couldn't help thinking that it took death to finally put her fully in the spotlight.

Do the people in your life really know how much you love them, and how deeply you need them? Don't wait to celebrate them until they pass from the earth. Don't save up your words for their funeral. Don't put off loving them with abandon. **Do it now.**

Give a "life party" for someone you love. Invite that person's friends, family, and neighbors, and allow each of them to take turns sharing their appreciation and gratitude.

We need to start memorializing life instead of
death, and create real moments today, rather
than real memories tomorrow.

✦

"The distinction between human and spiritual is made only by human beings. They are not separate. They are woven together. If you do not open your heart to human beings, you will find it difficult to open your heart to God. If you do not love human beings, including yourself, you will find it difficult to love God. Your spiritual path begins in your humanness, with the simple day-to-day willingness to be honest, kind, and loving, to the best of your ability."
—RON SCOLASTICO AND THE GUIDES

Ultimately, loving is a spiritual practice. When you love a person, or an animal, or a tree, you are loving a piece of God. And each real moment in loving gives you a chance to bring the sacred into form, and, thus, participate in creating a little more Heaven on earth.

Look around you—
you will see someone who needs your love.
Offer it to them,
In that moment, you will be their blessing.
And God will be smiling.

WOMEN AND
REAL MOMENTS

"O Great Mother, mother of us all, oldest of the old,
come to me through the labyrinth of time
to help me remember the wisdom of my forebears,
the eternal life-giving power of woman."
— HALLIE IGLEHARD AUSTEN

I write this chapter as a woman, to you who are also women, so that we may find the real moments we need to nourish ourselves. I write this too for all men who love women and seek to understand us.

Women, you see, know about real moments in the very core of our being. *Real moments are our natural territory.* We are at home with them, like a bird that catches the wind and allows it to take her wherever it is going. *Flying requires surrender, and that is why women are so good at soaring through the valleys and canyons of our inner world—we understand how to surrender.* Our bodies are made for it. We surrender when we make love, and receive our beloved. We surrender each month to our moon cycles, and release the blood which we do not need. We surrender during childbirth and allow our son or daughter to emerge into the world. And when we let ourselves, we surrender easily into real moments.

Women are alchemists.
We transmute the ordinary into the miraculous.

We can make a walk down the street with our child an enchanted adventure. We can take an empty room, put some plants here, some curtains there, and make it into a place that feels like home. We know how to turn a quiet conversation with the person we love into an opportunity for true communion. We can transform the simple act of arranging flowers, wrapping a gift, or giving a hug into a sacred moment filled with feeling. Herein lies our power, as well as that which frightens men most about us—*we see the potential for magic and love in everything.*

Since the beginning of time, and until recently, women have had more access to real moments than men simply because of the way our roles in the world were structured. Society would not let us out, and so we turned inward. We stayed at home with our children. We had more quiet, more solitude, more moments of connection. We baked bread and worked in our gardens, we read, we knitted, we prayed.

In this past century, we have gained our freedom to live as equals with men, but in the process, we've lost our spiritual center. We have taken on men's stress-related diseases, men's physical and emotional exhaustion, men's lack of peace. Our freedom is killing us. We are missing our real moments. And we desperately need to get them back.

✦

Women are the nurturers and givers of the world—we are genetically and psychologically programmed to take care of everyone. We can tune in to another person's needs before he can. We know when our baby is about to cry. We know when our husband needs to cry. If someone sneezes, we offer them a tissue. If someone is angry, we offer them a smile. We want to do whatever it takes to make everyone happy. We are pleasers. We love to love.

The problem is that when we make pleasing others a priority, we often do it at the price of neglecting to please ourselves. By being so self-sacrificing, we deprive ourselves of the time and opportunity to have the very real moments we seek and are so good at savoring. *We become disconnected from the core of who we are.*

Do you know what the worst thing you can call a woman is? SELFISH. . . . Most of us would rather be called anything than that. Call me a wimp, a pushover, a coward, a love addict, but don't call me selfish. Selfish means I am not thinking of your needs. Selfish means I'm not taking care of you. Selfish means I am a bitch. Selfish means I am not a woman.

We are taught from the time we are little girls that to be loving means to take everyone else's feelings into account. No father says to their daughter, as they do to their sons, "Go out there and kick ass, honey. Make them all look like nothing compared to you." Instead we are told to be nice, to share, to understand, to apologize, to forgive. These are good behaviors. Men need to practice more of these. *But as women, we do these too much.* We give when we should insist on receiving. We forgive when we should state our ultimatum. We apologize when we should demand an apology.

> Women need real moments of solitude and self-reflection to balance out how much of ourselves we give away.

For women, taking the time for real moments is a matter of psychological and spiritual survival. If we do not, we will be sucked dry by everyone and everything that needs us. We need to create a day, an hour, even five minutes, when we give to ourselves only, and not to anyone else. We need to regularly replenish our generous spirits, so we can continue to give without resentment and without emotional burnout. We need silence. We need space. We need to listen to the pleas of our own heart, and no other.

But let us confess the truth—we are not good at this, at being self-ish. We are uncomfortable doing things just for ourselves. *It makes us feel guilty.* We suspect we are abandoning everyone, the husband, the kids, the dog, the friend in crisis. And so we feel the need to apologize when we take care of ourselves, whether it's going off for a day alone, or closing the door and reading for two hours, or attending a class and leaving the family with take-out food. "Look, I'll only be gone for four hours, and when I come back, I'll play games with you all night, O.K.?" "Honey, I know I'm leaving you with a lot to do when I go away to visit my friend, but I'll make lists of everything." Bribery, submissive behavior, we'll do anything—just don't be mad at us for leaving you.

Men have no problem being selfish, and I say this with admiration, at least in this context. If they want to ignore the family after dinner and read the paper, they do it. They don't apologize, they don't keep sneaking glances at you to see if you're "O.K." with their decision. They forget about you and everyone else. Why then, as women, are we compelled to make excuses when we nourish ourselves? Why do we feel we need to "make up" for our real moments alone by giving twice as much when we return?

> To have real moments and find your center
> again, you have to stop worrying about what
> other people think.

If you have been giving on command and living selflessly, some people in your life who have come to depend on you for their emotional sustenance, moral support, car pooling, regular meals, clean laundry, free advice, and whatever else you've been handing out will probably not like it very much when you start taking time for you. They may openly express their displeasure, or they may just get grumpy. Ignore them. They will get used to your special personal times, even encourage them, once they see the new light in your eyes and feel the new calm in your heart.

Even before I began writing this book, I realized I wasn't having enough real moments with myself. Over the course of a few months, I made some dramatic changes in how I was spending my time. I gave up teaching many of the regular seminars people had always relied upon. I stopped going out to social events I wasn't interested in. And now, as I am in the middle of my writing process, I'm not even answering my phone, but having my assistant inform people that I'm in seclusion until the book is done. This is sure upsetting some of my friends and acquaintances. It's hard for them to believe that I am not there for them when *they* want me to be, which is the story of my life. Of course, no one has come out and actually said: "How dare you take time for yourself, you selfish bitch," but I can feel a few of them thinking it.

And how am I feeling? Absolutely wonderful. I am coming back into balance. Having given and given and given some more, I desperately needed to replenish my own source of inner sustenance.

✦

"Is this then what happens to woman? She wants perpetually to spill herself away. All her instinct as a woman—the eternal nourisher of children, of men, of society—demands that she give. Her time, her energy, her creativeness drain out into these channels if there is any chance, any leak."
—ANNE MORROW LINDBERGH

Men are entities unto themselves. They know where their edges are, where they end and the world begins. But the boundaries between women and the world around us are not solid—they are permeable. Our edges are blurred, our perimeters porous, and through the holes, our spirit leaks out. *We are in a constant process of give and take with what is outside of us.*

Women are all moonchildren. Our bodies change with the cycles of the moon—it pulls on us, just as it does the ocean, creating invisible tides within our soul that no one else can see, but we can feel. *In this way our body is never completely our own.* Each month, it belongs to the moon. When I am pregnant, it belongs to my child—for three quarters of a year, someone else is actually living inside of me. After I give birth, it is not over—my breasts belong to my son or daughter as my milk flows forth to feed them.

In relationships too, we have been designed to be permeated—in order to join together sexually, it is I who must open myself and receive my lover. He enters inside of me, and with a part of himself, he touches a dark, hidden place that I cannot even touch myself. What before was me alone now includes another.

But it is not just our bodies that give and receive so naturally—it is our psyches as well. When we walk down the street, or walk into a room, or talk on the phone, we feel feelings that are not our own, and pick up on other people's angers, hurts, and yearnings we don't even want to know about. A child cries somewhere—a part of you leaps out psychically to hold it. There is a crisis or tragedy thousands of miles away—you find your day is ruined, because a part of you is there, comforting, helping. These are not decisions that we can control. They are instincts that are bred into our feminine fiber. Forces pull on us, and without thinking, we respond.

Our permeable nature is what makes women so wonderfully flexible, so able to heal quickly after defeat, so capable of picking ourselves up and starting over. *But we live in constant danger of becoming overly adaptive and overly responsive to what pulls on us from the outside, and thus being pulled off center and losing ourselves.*

> Women need times when we close off our
> borders to everything but ourselves.

We need moments when we shut all the doors of our being that are perpetually open and retreat within. *We need times when we are not physically, emotionally, or psychically accessible to anyone or anything but our own hungers and dreams and voices. We need real moments with ourselves.*

Close down the store for inventory. Don't worry about the customers. They'll be there when you open up for business again.

Gathering the Scatterings of Your Soul

Most women I know have spent their lives giving away pieces of themselves, one after the other. We give a piece to our lover, a piece to each of our children, pieces to friends, parents, in-laws, bosses, employees, committees, and just about anyone else who asks, and even those who don't. We scatter fragments of our soul around like careless offerings, and yet we are surprised, at some point, to find ourselves so empty and emotionally depleted, and we can't quite seem to figure out how it happened.

> Coming into wholeness as a woman isn't so
> much about discovering who you are, but about
> taking back the parts of yourself you gave away.

If you think other people took your power from you, you can never get it back, because you never relinquished it. When you

*see that you gave your power away, then you can begin the
process of retrieving it.*

My real awakening as a woman began when I started the
process of retrieving lost pieces of my Self. These were the
scatterings of my soul, pieces of my integrity, my self-respect,
my truth, my trust, that I had given to my father, my ex-
husbands, my lovers, my employers, my gurus, my business
partners. Some pieces I had given when I was just a child,
hoping to be loved, hoping to keep Daddy from leaving, and
when he left anyway, hoping to get him to come back once in
a while. Some pieces I gave when I fell in love, hoping to
avoid conflict, hoping to make everything look good, to make
a man feel I was so perfect for him, he couldn't possibly
choose someone else. Some pieces I gave away by not speaking up for myself when I should have, by pretending I had
enough when I needed more, by crying when I should have
shouted, by smiling when I should have walked away.

**These are soul bribes. We barter pieces of our soul, and
in the process, betray ourselves** . . . but for what? So we can
say we are in a relationship? So we have a ring to prove we
are loved? So we don't have to be alone on Saturday night?
So we can have a nice house and nice things, even though
we're miserable? So our kids can have a father around, even if
he is a real jerk?

*Each woman has her price. Each of us is seduced into
betraying herself by different temptations.* For me, it has always been *belonging.* I used to pay any soul price to lovers,
to friends, to teachers—anyone who would act like they
were there for me, anyone who would stay. For many
women, it is security. I can think of at least ten of my
friends right now who are only staying with their husbands
because they are so "comfortable," and don't want to give
up their lifestyle. They are willing to live passionless, dis-

honest lives so they can still drive their nice car and keep their big house with the live-in maid.

I grieve for every woman who sells her soul and gives up her name just so she can feel like somebody. I grieve for every woman who is willing to change her values, her opinions, and even her breast size just so she can get a man to accept her. I grieve for all of us everywhere who have scattered our souls.

A time will come in your life when you cannot go forward without putting yourself back together. A time will come when you realize you can't achieve any kind of peace if you leave those orphaned parts of yourself behind. You suddenly awaken, and know you must go and gather the scatterings of your soul.

How do we do this? It is different for each of us. Some of us who have very little soul power left need to leave where we are and whom we are with in order to get ourselves back. Some of us need to stop running from love and settle down. Some of us need to start saying all the things we have been hiding to all the people we have been hiding the truth from. Some of us need to stop talking so much and start listening to our own silence. Some of us need to quit our jobs. Some of us need to get jobs. Some of us need to make new rules with everyone in our life. Some of us need to break the rules. Some of us need to shut the door, turn off the phone, and become a hermit for a while. Some of us need to get out of the house and stop hiding.

Slowly, piece by piece, we put ourselves together again. Each time I have brought a piece of myself back home to my heart, I have felt my soul rejoice, like a mother welcoming back a long-lost child. And with each new homecoming, I emerge into my life with more courage and less fear.

There is a story I have heard many times in many different versions about sticks. If you take one stick and try to break it, you can do it easily. But if you put that stick together with many others, and then try to break the sticks, you cannot do it. The bundle is too strong. A woman without her missing pieces is like a solitary stick. She can be easily broken. *But a woman with all the pieces of her soul bundled together has the power of wholeness, and is unbreakable.*

Letting Your Spirit Out to Run Free

A woman's journey back to wholeness is not an easy one. At least mine hasn't been. Sometimes we don't know where to begin, or how to take the first step toward real moments, because we have not experienced true emotional freedom in so long. Have you ever seen documentaries about animals who are brought up from birth in cages? When the cage door is finally opened, the animal almost always refuses to come out. You would think it would run from its cage, relieved to finally be free, but that is not what happens. In the animal's mind, the cage door is still there, because it has always been there. And so it sits passively in its little prison, frightened to move beyond what has become a safe habitat.

> Sometimes the habit of losing ourselves is
> stronger than the habit of being ourselves and
> so we aren't sure how to run free.

Here is a true story about how I learned to let my spirit run free:

✦

Several years ago, I began to experience a powerful restlessness. This restlessness was no stranger to me—since I was sixteen, it had moved in and out of my life like the wind, and each time it appeared, it would stir up everything I had neatly arranged and cause trouble. Or more accurately, I would cause trouble, for when I felt the wind of restlessness begin to whirl inside of me, I would go into a kind of spiritual heat, and begin madly searching for something to appease my sudden hunger for change. When the feeling wasn't that strong, I would do things like clean out my entire house, or trade in my car for a new one, or plan an exotic trip. But there were a few times when the restlessness would overtake me so completely that I would feel swept away, and end up doing something quite dramatic like having an illicit love affair, or getting a divorce, or changing careers. This restless wind never really blew me off my course, and everything would always work out as it was meant to in the end, for I never made changes that weren't overdue anyway. But the suddenness of the process was often exhausting, painful to others, and frightening to me in its intensity.

When Jeffrey and I began our relationship, I felt like someone who has a disease they are keeping a secret. What could I say to him: "Look, this thing happens to me sometimes—I go a little crazy, and this other part of me emerges, but if you should see me go through this, remember that it's nothing personal"? I was so frightened of blowing it, of sabotaging our relationship and losing the best thing that ever happened to me. Of course, I had no intention of doing this, but then again, I never did. *"This time,"* I vowed to myself, *"when it happens, I will be ready."* And so I waited for the wind.

And it came, a delightful little breeze of everyday adrenaline at first, and then gusting into the old familiar urge to break free—but of what? This time, I was happy. This time, I knew I needed to stay right where I was. This time, I didn't need the wind to liberate me from a relationship or situation I had been stuck in.

And so day after day, I fought the forces inside of me that whispered: "Run . . . run . . ." Who was it that was calling to me, I wondered. What did they want me to run from? Where did they want me to run to? I prayed for the answers to these questions, and asked that I be shown the truth, given the wisdom to win my battle.

My Teacher, Crystal

Spiritual teachers come to us in many forms. They are not always dressed in white robes. They don't necessarily have to even know they are teachers at all. They show up in your life when you need a reminder, and point the way.

My teacher during this turbulent time was a dog named Crystal. Crystal was a beautiful Siberian husky that lived across the street from me. I had spent my whole life being scared to death of all dogs, especially large ones, until I got my own dog Bijou. He helped me make friends with all of the dogs in the neighborhood, and introduced me to the magical world of animals. So when my neighbors brought Crystal home as a little puppy, I knew it was my chance to know a big dog from the time it was small, and conquer my fear completely.

As soon as Crystal was ready for visitors, Bijou and I began going over to her yard to play. I was her first friend outside of her family, and Bijou, as it turned out, would be her first and only dog friend. She was still quite small, so even little Bijou could manage to romp with her without getting trampled, but each day she grew by leaps and bounds, and I knew it wouldn't be long before she weighed almost one hundred pounds.

One day during the summer when Crystal was just four months old, my neighbor told me they would be leaving for a few days, and Crystal would be alone except for a friend of the family who would stop in to feed her. I remember being quite concerned. "She's only a puppy," I thought to myself.

But she had already grown to be quite a big dog, and I was reassured that she would be O.K. Late that night during my sleep, I was awakened by an eerie sound. At first I wasn't sure what I was listening to—I just knew it pierced my heart. Then, I realized it was Crystal. She was howling like a wolf, crying out with loneliness.

I crept out of bed and walked in the dark to my neighbors' empty house and through the back gate. There was Crystal, sitting on the porch shaking, her thick fur shining silver in the moonlight. I ran over and hugged her. "Poor Crystal," I crooned. "Everyone left you, and you don't understand that they're coming back. Poor baby." I held her muscular body and rocked her back and forth as she nuzzled against me. When I left, I promised to return the next day to make sure she was all right.

To my surprise, we had a huge rainstorm the following morning. It rarely rains in Southern California in July, but it did that day. I realized that Crystal was unprotected. Naturally her owners didn't think it would rain, and so she had no covering over her porch. I quickly gathered up dry blankets and plastic garbage bags, and ran over to Crystal's house. She was standing there waiting for me, soaking wet and shivering. And again, I held her, made a dry place for her to lie down, and told her everything would be fine.

In a few days, her owners came back and thanked me for what I'd done, but things were never the same between Crystal and me. *We were connected now, linked together by a powerful bond I didn't quite understand.* It was more than the fact that I'd taken care of her. There was a mysterious force that joined us. I began to feel very unhappy seeing Crystal locked up behind her gates. She had a big backyard to run around in, but she was never taken out for walks, and hadn't seen the world outside her home. Each time I passed the house with Bijou, Crystal would poke her head through the fence and begin to cry. Tears would fill my eyes, and it was all I could do to not grab her and run for the hills. "I don't know what it is about that dog that moves me so much," I'd comment to Jeffrey. "I know her family loves her, and she loves them. I just keep wanting to get her out from behind the fence." I couldn't stop thinking about Crystal, and I didn't know why.

Crystal's Escape

One day, as I sat at my computer writing, I thought I heard a knock at the front door. I went downstairs, and when I pulled the door open, to my utter amazement there was Crystal, sitting politely on my porch, her tail wildly wagging. "How did you get out?" I asked in disbelief as I gave her a hug. I walked her back across the street, and my neighbor was just as surprised as I was that she had escaped. "Maybe someone left the gate open," she suggested as she put Crystal back inside. I wondered if I was imagining Crystal smiling at me as I turned to go home.

Then, Crystal started digging a hole next to the gate. I knew what she was doing. She was trying to get out so she could run free. And it worked. Every few days, I would find her at my doorstep again, a wild, joyful look in her beautiful dark eyes, her paws caked with dirt, and her now huge body rippling with excitement. My neighbors kept filling up the hole and Crystal kept digging, and repeating her escape ritual. And I silently cheered her on.

One evening before bed, I began reading *Women Who Run with the Wolves*. Clarissa Pinkola Estés writes beautifully about *La Loba*, the One Who Knows, the Wild Woman in each of us who needs to be resurrected and allowed to run free. That night, I dreamed about Crystal. I saw her furtively digging to escape her carefully fenced-in yard. I heard her calling to me with an ancient howl. And when I awoke the next morning, I understood everything:

Crystal was my mirror, the embodiment of my own Wild Woman, the passionate, mysterious, instinctual part of myself that I had kept locked behind closed doors throughout my entire life. She had been crying out to me from her comfortable yet confining prison, the cry of one who longs for the freedom to move without restriction, to run with abandon, to sing with her soul-voice. Her cry had summoned me, and without knowing why, my own restless spirit had howled back. *We were sisters, we belonged to the same pack. And she knew this before I did, for in her wise wolf way, she had looked into my eyes and seen my soul pacing back and forth, digging at the dirt under my self-erected gates, yearning to run free.*

Each time Crystal showed up at my door, I had celebrated her escapes because that is what I needed to do—to dig myself out of my own emotional fences, the shoulds and should nots by which I'd been living my life, the limits I put on which parts of me I could show my husband, my friends, my public, and which parts I had to hide. Now I understood the restlessness. Now I understood the voice that would suddenly appear in my head and whisper: "Run . . . run . . . " It was my Wild Woman, emerging from beneath the dirt where I kept trying to bury her, warning me that I would suffocate unless I broke through my own barriers. No wonder I would go wild every five years or so, and do something shocking and unconventional! I was like a chained dog who finally escapes, and tears up every trash can in the neighborhood with all of her pent-up energy.

Crystal had shown me the answer:

> It was not escape I was looking for, it was
> freedom. I didn't want to run away.
> I just wanted to run.

After each of her adventures, Crystal always obediently returned home. She didn't want to leave permanently. She just wanted to leave sometimes. And that was my truth as well. I knew I would no longer need to leave where I was to find my freedom. *I just needed to let my Wild Woman out for more runs.*

So that is how Crystal taught my spirit to run free. I do not have the storms of restlessness like I used to, just breezes. When they come, I know I am overdue for a run, and I take a day for myself, or write poetry, or spend time with women, or go to a Grateful Dead concert and dance my feet off. And then I come home.

How do you know when you need to take your spirit out for a run? *You become irritable, annoyed, bored, critical, confused, tired, or a little crazy.* You want to eat bad things, give your children away, tell your husband to find his own damn car keys, check into a hotel by yourself, order room service, and watch romantic movies all night. All this means is that your Wild Woman is calling to you. Go to her. Find out what she is really hungry for, feed her, then take her out to play.

Soon after my awakening with Crystal, her family moved back East and took her with them. Their new home is on several acres of land, and Crystal now runs wherever she pleases. I miss her very much, and think of her every time I pass that old gate, but my heart smiles to know she is happy, for her spirit has told me so. She will always be one of my most treasured teachers.

> *Run free, my Wolf-Sister.*
> *The land beneath your feet rejoices to feel you dancing upon it.*

Finding Real Moments for Ourselves

Here are some ways that we can create real moments for ourselves as women.

✦ *Seek solitude.*

Women need quiet times when the only voice we hear is our own. We are so used to making everyone else's voice more important than ours. This is a habit with most of us, especially if we grew up thinking that God is male.

> If we were taught that the doorway to God
> is through a male,
> we look outside of ourselves and our femaleness
> for spiritual connection, and not within.

For a long time, I depended upon men to give me direction and guidance, and did not trust my own inner voice. I spent most of my life setting men up as one sort of savior or another. Most of them did not object to the status I conferred upon them. I've had a guru, a husband who thought he was a guru, and business associates who wanted me to think they were my guru. I was so busy listening to their opinions that I never had time to discover my own.

Give yourself times of silence, so your voice of wisdom can emerge. It needs to become strong so it won't be shouted down by all the other voices in your life that may try to talk you out of your feelings or your knowing. Keep a journal where only your voice has a say. Take a walk in a quiet place. Listen. Soon, you will hear your own spirit talking to you.

✦ *Give birth to something.*

When a woman gives birth, she is tuned in to her magic, the ability to change the form of things. So anytime you want a real moment, give birth to something. It doesn't matter what you give birth to—a garden, a cake, a innovative idea at work, a bedtime story for your children, a letter to a friend, a healing for yourself, or a clean kitchen. You will feel the creative life force flowing through you, connecting you to Mother Nature herself.

I believe that we need to give birth regularly or we lose our connection to real moments. There are some women who keep getting pregnant over and over again, not because they are ready for or want another child, but because they are addicted to the process of giving birth as their only connection to their personal and spiritual power. Often, it is their own rebirth they are unconsciously seeking. They desperately need to give birth to themselves, to the lost pieces of their spirit, to their creativity.

We need to see all of our creative acts as ones of giving birth, not just those when we physically produce a child. I don't have any children of my own. But I am a mother. I have brought forth life in many forms. I have given birth to much love.

> All women are mothers, because we bring forth
> life and love wherever we go.

✦ Seek the company of other women as teachers, sisters, and friends.

Women need feminine mirrors in which to discover their own beauty. When we come together with other women, we are empowered in our wholeness. We remember who we are. We recall the steps to our Dance.

Throughout the ages, women have always had female teachers, grandmothers, and wise elders from whom they sought protection and Initiation. They guided us on our path and reminded us of our grace and dignity. But for many centuries now, we have been living in a patriarchal society. We have given men the power to define us, to teach us, to tell us our place. We have lost our connection to the Ancient Mothers from whom all life has sprung. We have forgotten our magic. We have lost our way.

Since I began my spiritual journey at age eighteen, I have had only male teachers. I honor them for all they taught me about strength and about silence. But they could not teach me about being a woman. And so for the past few years, as I have struggled to come back to wholeness, I have longed for a female teacher and guide. I prayed to find her, and I knew that until we met, I would not be complete.

Earlier this year, Jeffrey and I were in Big Sur, California, making arrangements for our wedding, which was to be several months later. One of the women helping us approached me and said, "This may sound a little strange, but I found the names of a Native American couple in the back of a book I happened to be reading this morning, and I wanted to tell you about them. They are cofounders of a nonprofit organization called 'One Earth, One People Peace Vision,' which is dedicated to restoring respectful relationships between humanity and all living things. For some reason, I thought of you and the work you do, and felt you should have their address and phone number." I thanked her, and when I took the paper from her hand, something told me I needed to call right away.

And so I did, and we arranged to meet the next day in the little historic town where they live, San Juan Bautista, one of the original California missions. Their names are Juan Jose Reyna, Jr., who everyone calls Sonny, and Elaine Reyna, who is known as Bluebird. Sonny is a writer, environmentalist, and Native American spiritual leader. Elaine is an artist/visionary and designer of traditional and contemporary ethnic clothing. When Bluebird walked up to me in their store and art gallery, and looked into my eyes, I suspected that she was the woman I had been searching for.

We sat outside in a sun-filled courtyard and began talking,

not about superficial subjects, but about who all of us really were, because we already felt a powerful connection. Jeffrey shared with them about his life, his dreams, his healing work as a chiropractor. Then I spoke about my path as a seeker, the lessons I had learned along the way, and my longing to know more.

Bluebird listened intently, and when I was finished, she looked deeply into me and said: "You know, Barbara, what you need is a Big Sister." My eyes filled with tears. I have never had a sister, not even a woman older than myself to guide me. And in that moment, I knew I had found her, and that she had found me too. "Welcome home to our indigenous family!" she proclaimed. "We are related in the spirit, and I am so happy to be reunited with you again, Little Sister."

Since that day, Bluebird has been my Big Sister, my teacher, my friend. "Women need to remember that we are sacred, that we are life givers," she reminds me. "Thank the Creator for the experience of Life, and celebrate it as the most precious treasure, the sorrow and the joy." This beautiful and humble woman is teaching me how to honor the Earth and all it produces, how to honor myself as a woman, and how to have real moments every day.

✦

My own female spiritual teachers, Crystal and Bluebird, have not come in very traditional forms, because I am not a very traditional woman, but yours do not have to be so unusual. You have many teachers waiting to guide you, many beautiful female spirits to help you on your journey back to real moments. Look around you to your grandmothers, your aunts, your friends, your daughters, and you will find them. Ask, and their presence will be revealed to you. You do not have to take the journey alone.

I dedicate this chapter to my Big Sister and
teacher, Bluebird,
whose spirit sits gently on my shoulder and
beckons me to follow her,
over the earth,
into the river,
above the sky.

"Fly, Little Sister," she whispers.
And I do. . . .

MEN AND REAL MOMENTS

"I have now reigned about fifty years in victory or peace, beloved by my subjects, dreaded by my enemies, and respected by my allies. Riches and honors, power and pleasure, have waited on my call, nor does any earthly blessing appear to have been wanting to my felicity. In this situation, I have diligently numbered the days of pure and genuine happiness which have fallen to my lot: They amount to fourteen."

—ASCRIBED TO ABD ER-RAHMAN III
OF SPAIN, A.D. 960

I t is not easy for men to have real moments and they are suffering greatly because of it. The women who love them are suffering. Their children are suffering. The world is suffering.

I cannot write about men as a man, as I can about women. But I can tell you what I've seen as I've loved and worked with the men in my life, and what I've learned from the men who've asked me to be their teacher. These observations are careful but admitted generalizations—they may not be accurate for all men, but they do express a truth that I believe is relevant to most men.

That truth is this: that men are dying because they don't have enough real moments—they are dying emotionally because they deprive themselves of the love and intimacy they need; they are dying physically because, in their hunger for accomplishment, their lives are often so out of balance that they don't know when to stop and rest, so their bodies just give out; and they are dying spiritually because they aren't sure how to turn within and begin their journey toward the sacred.

If you are a woman who loves a man, you probably already suspect this about him. Something is missing. You can't quite put your finger on it. It has nothing to do with how hard he works, or how much free time he has. It doesn't matter how old he is. It is not a material thing. Rather, it is about a place inside of him that he rarely goes to, the place of just being there, of silent, receptive feeling, of opening to the mystery of love. This is the place where you long to meet him. You arrive. You wait. He doesn't show up.

If you are a man, you may experience this hunger for real moments that I speak of in different terms, men's terms. It is a longing to take a rest from the incessant, pounding rhythm of movement that permeates your life. It is an uncomfortable yearning to go somewhere, be somewhere different from where you are, a yearning you know will not be satisfied by changing jobs, cars, or women. It is the sound of something calling to you from within that you want to answer but don't know how. It is a restlessness that never goes away.

Here is the thing about men and real moments:

> Real moments are about being, they are not
> about doing. And men are doers.

Men have been trained since the beginning of time to be good at doing—they hunted, they built, they protected. That was their role, and thus it was through their work, their toil, and their accomplishment that they defined themselves, and found their value. Women, on the other hand, were required to be good at relating—we pleased, we nurtured, we connected. We became skilled at feeling and being.

In our twentieth century, these roles have begun slowly to change, but we cannot forget that they have been in place for a long time. Habits die hard. And genetic memory influences much of our values and behavior. I always remember my mother telling me how different I was from my brother when we were babies. "You were content to sit and watch people, to color, to play with paper dolls," she'd explain. "But Michael always had to be moving. He never stopped." And she's right. We called my brother "The Furniture Mover," because even as a little boy, he was always trying to move things from one place to another. If he couldn't move the objects in our house, he would keep himself moving. We have old films of Michael, before he could even talk, running around and around in circles.

Men are movers. It's in their blood. *And so when men look for meaning, they look to their work, to what they are doing, whether that activity is completing a project, building new shelves for the garage, or playing a good hand of cards.* This is where they think they will find satisfaction.

But the nature of men's work has changed radically. From a conqueror, an adventurer, a soldier, men have been transformed into accountants, salesmen, and computer programmers. They are displaced warriors and unemployed explorers. Their work does not always provide them with the instant satisfaction that building a house for the family, fighting off the enemy, or plowing a field gave their great-great-great-grandfathers. It is often so removed from obvious meaning that it does not allow them to have many real moments.

✦

Men are at home in the physical world, the world of the concrete. They feel comfortable with what they can see and touch and measure. **They are goal-oriented.** That is why they put such a high value on *doing,* because it produces a result that fits into their model of what is worthwhile.

The kinds of experiences that offer you a real moment are not, as we have seen, necessarily moments of obvious achievement or accomplishment. They are quieter, subtler, and *their benefits are not so much tangible as they are invisible.* So these aren't experiences that men naturally value, because they can't easily measure how they could be meaningful. If I'm a man and I work two extra hours and get overtime pay, that's a benefit I can put in my pocket—that's meaningful. But if I spend those same two hours talking with my wife, or walking by myself, where's the benefit? **I can't measure it, and so it doesn't appear to hold as much meaning and value for me as working overtime did.**

This difference in values produces constant conflict and frustration in relationships between men and women. You mention to your husband that you'd like to spend some time just talking with him. "About what?" he responds. Suddenly, you feel annoyed, confused. Why do you have to give him an agenda of what you'd like to discuss? Isn't it enough that he knows you want to talk? No, it is not. Just talking together and sharing intimate time probably does not hold the same value for him as a man, who places a great deal of importance on doing, as it does for you as a woman, who places a great deal of importance on relating and being.

Women, when we stop taking care of everyone else and get around to focusing on ourselves, are good at just being. That is why we crave nondoing experiences, especially with our partners. We know they will produce delicious real moments.

Men need to find nondoing experiences as
meaningful experiences.

Men need to stop looking for the instant benefit they will receive from an experience, and feel what is actually going on in the moment, right here and right now. *Real moments are in the realm of the timeless and the invisible. Their value cannot be calculated or measured.* If you try to measure it, you aren't having a real moment anymore.

✦

"To be on a quest is nothing more or less than to become an asker of questions."

— S A M K E E N

The journey back to real moments is a journey characterized by questions, as we talked about in Chapter Four— questions like "Who am I?" "Am I living the life I want to lead, or the life others want me to lead?" "Am I happy?" "Do I give enough love? Do I get enough love?" In order to ask questions, you have to conquer the fear of not knowing, and discover the courage to live with uncertainty for a while.

This is not an easy task for men. Men are of the earth. They need the solid, the certain, the well-marked path. *They are often uncomfortable with, even frightened of, the unformed, the vague, the fluctuating, the mysterious . . .* (and of course that is a good description of the female psyche!). This can make it difficult for them to question, to search, to explore the unknown—it is unfamiliar territory.

Women like asking questions.
Men like having answers.

To ask a question implies that one doesn't know the answer. Women, as a rule, are not afraid of "I don't know," which is a form of intellectual free-fall. After all, we are good at surrender and letting go. We practice this every time we

make love, menstruate, give birth, and kiss our children good-
bye as we send them off to school. You will find more women
involved in personal growth, belonging to support groups,
buying self-help books and seeking therapy because we are
comfortable, even stimulated by asking questions, and we
aren't usually in a hurry to get to the answers.

Men, however, *like to know. To men knowing is a form of
doing, a show of mental strength.* I have seen men go to great
lengths to avoid saying the words "I don't know." Instead,
they utter statements such as *"I don't want to talk about it,"
"Why aren't you ever satisfied?" "Don't you ever shut up?"* or
"Just relax, everything is under control." They do not want to
admit that they do not have the answer clear in their minds
just yet, so they stall, avoid responding, or, if you are insis-
tent, try scaring you off with anger in order to find the time to
figure things out and get to a place of knowing and certainty.

> Being unwilling not to know hurts men.
> It keeps them stuck where they are.
>
> It prevents them from moving forward, from
> breaking through to new levels of emotional and
> spiritual freedom.

In his important book *Fire in the Belly,* Sam Keen describes
a man's sacred quest for himself as a journey of passages . . .
*"from cocksureness to potent doubt . . . from having the answers
to living the questions."* Living the questions means living in a
constant state of surrender and loss of control. This is the
antithesis of what men have been trained to do. Instead, they
have been taught to dominate, conquer, hold out, prevail, and
not give in. I say this with tremendous respect. It is these
same qualities that have enabled a man to fight off his enemy,
kill to protect his land and family, venture into dark forests to

hunt for food so those he loves can survive, stand with his brothers against the oppressors who want to take away his freedom, climb up one more mountain in order to find a safe spot for his new home.

But in his quest for real moments, a man has to muster up the courage to turn his back on the ways of the warrior, for they are destroying him and his relationships. It means learning to say to your lover: *"I'm not sure," "I need time to think about it," "Could you slow down? I'm not sure what you mean," "What do you need that I'm not giving you?" "How can we do it differently?"* and *"I'm sorry."* It means being willing, at times, to live with uncertainty, to open to the mysterious and unexpected, to enter into a moment with no agenda other than to fully experience it, and to know through it all that you are still a man.

That is all we, as women, want from you. **We want you to take the journey with us.** We want to explore together. We want to be spiritual comrades. We want to discover new territories of intimacy, new realms of physical passion, and new levels of happiness. We want ascend together in love. We don't want to leave you behind.

And in spite of all of your conditioning and every cell in your body that screams: *"But if I let go, I won't be a man,"* know that, in our eyes at least, **you will be our most honored champion and our most brave hero.**

Frozen Feelings and Sacred Tears

Now, the part you men have been dreading, where I talk about feelings. You knew it was coming, didn't you? Of course. Because, in order to have real moments, whether with your lover, your children, or yourself, you have to be willing to fully feel. And that is difficult for most men to do.

For centuries, men have lived as strangers to the emotional

world where we as women thrive. **You had to become an expert at *not* feeling in order to survive.** How could you strangle a man with your bare hands if you were feeling compassion? How could you hold up your spear and face a wild animal charging at you full speed if you were feeling fear? How could you follow orders to throw a grenade into an enemy village, knowing innocent people would be killed if you did, but that you would be killed if you didn't, and allow yourself to feel anguish?

It is no different in the twentieth century. The modern business world can be just as vicious and demoralizing as any battlefield. Men are rewarded if they are tough and ruthless and diminished if they are perceived as "too soft." If you show fear, you are not respected. If you demonstrate unshakable confidence, you are called a leader. The weapons have changed, but the rules of the game are the same.

This is the price you paid for your manhood: *What has been required of you to "be a man" has also required you to numb yourself to feeling.* And herein lies your dilemma. You cannot kill your ability to feel terror, shame, and grief without killing your ability to feel joy, love, and compassion. And so many men walk around in a state of secret despair, their hearts full of frozen feelings that they will not or cannot release. Your woman, your children reach out to you, begging you to join us in the dance of emotion, and you shake your head "No!" We turn away and weep, concluding that you do not love us, never guessing your carefully hidden secret: You have forgotten the steps.

If you are honest with yourself, if you turn your attention inward, you will feel the psychic scars you inherited along with your manhood, those ancient wounded places that keep you from living as joyfully as you deserve to, that keep you from dancing with wild abandon alongside of those you love, that keep you from having real moments. **These scars, these** wounds must be your new landscape to conquer if you wish to live authentically and fully as a human being and a man. Sam Keen again says it in a male voice: "*Men have much to mourn before they can be reborn.*"

> To conquer a wound, you must heal it, and to heal it, you must feel it.

Facing your wounds, and melting your frozen feelings requires courage, forgiveness, and tears. *I believe that all tears are sacred, that they let us know the ice around our heart is melting.* Tears are not easy for men, but they will give you back pieces of yourself you didn't even know you had lost. I am proud to have been present, throughout my many years of teaching, when thousands of men have cried again for the first time since they were little boys. These are sacred occasions, just as birth is sacred—a new being is emerging into the world. It helps to have an understanding, caring midwife there to catch you when you break through your veneer of numbness—any open, loving woman will do, preferably your own!

> Some of *women's* most treasured real moments with the men we love occur when you give us the gift of sharing your tears.

When Jeffrey trusts me enough to show me his pain, and allows me to hold him and comfort him while he navigates through it, I am overwhelmed with gratitude. He has opened the door to the inner sanctum of his heart, and invited me in. There is no greater intimacy.

Do the emotional work you know you need to do. This is the most important commitment you can make to your marriage, to your children, or to yourself.

The Curse of the Pack: Male Loneliness

Men like being part of a pack. They like watching sporting events in packs, drinking in packs, talking around the water cooler in packs, going on a fishing trip in packs. In the pack, they feel safe. In the pack, they get to not feel alone, without being pressured to reveal anything of themselves. **In spite of this, most men I know are lonely, not because they lack companionship, but because of their inability to experience real moments together.**

This is not an obvious loneliness—it is more like a deep sense of isolation. Men share the unimportant things, like who won last night's game, how much they paid for a new muffler, and what they think of the new secretary's legs. But they keep their dreams and secrets carefully hidden from each other. It is not uncommon for "best" buddies to not even know that their friend is unhappy in his marriage, worried about an aging parent, has a sexual problem, or is months behind on paying his bills. They just don't talk about this stuff.

A recent McGill report on male intimacy found the following:

- ✦ Only one out of ten men has a male friend with whom he discusses work, money, or his relationship.
- ✦ Only one out of more than twenty men has a male friend with whom he discusses his feelings about himself, sex, and other more intimate topics.

What this means is that most men never talk about anything truly important or personal with other men in their life. They never experience real moments with someone of their own sex, with their brothers in spirit.

Last month, Jeffrey and I were discussing one of our

friends, who happens to be one of Jeffrey's best friends. "It's too bad that he and his wife are going through so much right now," I commented.

"What are you talking about?" Jeffrey asked with a puzzled look on his face.

"You know, how much they have been fighting about money, and not getting along very well." I realized as I went on that Jeffrey had no idea what I was referring to. "Honey, hasn't he even mentioned this to you?"

"No," he replied in a surprised voice. "I just talked to him yesterday, and he said everything was fine. When did you talk to him?"

"Today, and he broke down and cried on the phone with me."

We both shook our heads in amazement, realizing that Jeffrey didn't even know what was going on in the personal life of such a close friend. So what was my secret for getting him to open up? It was simple . . . I asked him how his marriage was doing, and when I heard the hesitation in his voice, I reached out and invited him to talk about it, something most men would feel too uncomfortable to do. I violated the male taboo that says "Don't get too personal," but because I am a woman, I got away with it.

✦

There is a certain comfort level men exhibit when they are in a group that disappears the moment they are alone with just one other man. That is because the dynamic between two people demands intimacy, and if you think intimacy with a woman is frightening to a man, you can begin to imagine the secret panic he feels when faced with the prospect of being intimate with another man.

If you are a man, imagine for a moment that it's late at night, and you are sitting by a fire talking with another man.

You are sharing your deepest feelings, your most private thoughts, and he is doing the same. You feel understood in a way you haven't for a long time, a way that even the woman you love can never understand you, for she is not a man. The connection between you and your friend feels alive and powerful. There is a tangible force flowing between you, of brotherhood, of sameness.

Suddenly, you become uncomfortable. You are experiencing love with another man. If you are heterosexual, you panic, thinking "I shouldn't be feeling this way. What does this mean?" and you will do something in that moment to sever the intensity of the connection—make a joke, get up and stretch, change the subject. Perhaps you will even avoid the person afterward, going out of your way to diminish any importance the experience might have had for you. I've known some men to actually create an artificial reason for ending the friendship because they became so frightened at feeling love for another man.

This is all fear-based, homophobic behavior. *It is a total misinterpretation of a powerful moment of love for sexual attraction.* You make the mistake of trying to give the experience significance and consequences beyond what it is—**a real moment of love**. Most men don't even let themselves get this far in sharing intimacy with one another. In unconscious anticipation and avoidance of such a horrifying experience, they keep all men at arm's length. And in the process, they end up with no truly intimate friends of their own sex.

> The fear most men have of experiencing
> intimacy with one another makes male
> friendship awkward.

I'm not letting women totally off the hook here. We, too, have our tolerance level for feelings of love with a girlfriend before we get uncomfortable, but it's way past where most men would have already run out the door screaming.

✦

"Having no soul union with other men can be the most damaging wound of all."

— R O B E R T   B L Y

Every man needs to bond with other men from the heart. He needs replacements for the kind of brothers and fathers he always wanted and perhaps never had. He need to fulfill his needs for intimacy with someone other than his lover, so she isn't his only outlet for feeling (which will eventually drive her crazy and make him resentful). He need mirrors of his own quest to understand his masculinity, soul buddies who can validate his journey like no woman ever can.

Find a friend. Take off your mask. Show him who you really are. Don't be afraid of how close you feel . . . it's just love.

✦

A word to men who love women: This is what your lover wishes she could say to you:

"Do you want to know the secret for making me truly happy? Share real moments with me. That is what I am hungry for. That is what I have been trying to tell you. The sudden embrace after dinner, the kiss in the bathroom for no reason at all, the call from work just to say 'I love you,' the moment during love-making when you hug me tight as if to say 'Yes, I am here with you, right now, the only place in the world I wish to be'—this is what I need.

"When I seem angry or melancholy or anxious, it is not because I need a vacation, or because my hormones are acting up—it is because I cannot find you. I'm reaching out to you through the darkness, but your hand does not reach back to

grasp mine. I'm calling to you in my heart, but my plea is greeted only by your silence. Where have you gone? I miss you, not your body, or your conversation, but your precious spirit.

"This is what I want from you—to meet me at the place where love resonates in your heart. For just one moment, feel how much you love me, feel it until you want to burst, and right then, gently take my face in your hands, look into my eyes, and drown me with your love."

✦

"If you observe a really happy man you will find him building a boat, writing a symphony, educating his son, growing double dahlias in his garden, or looking for dinosaur eggs in the Gobi desert. He will not be searching for happiness as if it were a collar button that has rolled under the radiator. He will not be striving for it as a goal in itself. He will have become aware that he is happy in the course of living life twenty-four crowded hours of the day."

—W. BERAN WOLFE

Some final tips before you begin your journey toward more real moments:

. . . Take regular quiet time away from everyone
where you can be alone with yourself.
. . . Start a journal. It may seem corny, but
women have known the secret power of writing
down their thoughts for centuries. No one needs
to read it but you.
. . . Cultivate a special buddy you can grow with.
. . . Do less.
. . . Question more.
. . . Walk the land.
. . . Listen to your heart.

. . . And when in doubt, ask the woman in your
life to help you practice having more real
moments.
. . . It will be our pleasure . . .

· 10 ·

REAL MOMENTS
AND THE FAMILY

"Fifty years from now,
it will not matter what kind of car you drove,
what kind of house you lived in,
how much you had in your bank account
nor what your clothes looked like.
But the world will be a little better
because you were important in the life of a child."
— ANONYMOUS

Everything I have written so far in this book about experiencing real moments can be applied to your relationship with your family—your parents, your children, your brothers and sisters, and your chosen family of friends. This chapter contains some additional thoughts about families with children, because there are special and important things we need to remember about loving our children, and because in these challenging and often frightening times, our children need our love and support more than ever before.

◆

Children are powerful seeds that grow up into gardens. What we plant into the mind and heart of one child will one day

211

affect thousands of people. That is why children have always been associated with hope—they are our opportunity to break free from the cycle, to throw off the chains of the past and make the future better. They are a doorway into healing and new beginnings.

What your children become will ultimately reflect back on you. You will always be one of the most powerful influences in their lives, because it was your job to nurture the seed so it could become the garden. Instinctively, you know this, and so you try to give your children all the things you never had, and to take care of them in every way possible. But in your sincere efforts, you may have forgotten one crucial truth:

Y ou cannot be a good parent if you don't take care of yourself.

If your job is to water the seed-souls of your children, you need to make sure *your* watering can is full. You need to keep your own heart filled up. You need to make sure you are giving yourself enough love, support, and real moments first before you can give to your kids.

Filling ourselves up first is something many parents fail at miserably, in the name of forfeiting our needs for the needs of our children. The baby-boomers of the fifties and sixties are particularly guilty of this pattern. We have attempted to become superparents, to offer our children all of the recreational activities, educational opportunities, and material possessions our parents couldn't give us. True, there are many neglectful parents out there as well, who use the television as an electronic baby-sitter, and don't even notice when their own children are attention starved. *But the majority of us feel guilty when we take time for ourselves,* fearful that one day when they are grown up, our children will point at us accusingly, saying "It's all your fault—if you hadn't taken that vacation [gone to the gym, spent that afternoon with your friend, gone back to school], I wouldn't be the mess I am today!"

I know a woman who lives for her children. She has given up every hobby, interest, even her friends, if it means taking any time away from her two girls. Recently, I convinced her to meet me for lunch, not an easy task. I stopped to pick her up, and from the good-bye scene at her house, you would have thought she was leaving for a three-week trip to Africa — she went over five lists with the baby-sitter, told the kids over and over again that she would only be gone for two hours, and apologized for even leaving at all. No sooner had we arrived at the restaurant than she called home to see how the children were doing.

"Marlene," I said, "it's only been twenty minutes since you left. Do you really need to call them now?"

"Well, they aren't used to me being gone," she responded, shaking her head. "They get upset when I'm not around."

"But they aren't little babies anymore," I reminded her. "They're five and seven years old. How will they ever learn to be independent?"

"Maybe I do go overboard a little bit, but I don't want them to ever feel neglected like I did when I was a child."

This was not an easy conversation for me to have with my friend. How could I tell her how much she had been neglecting herself? How could I let her know how insecure I saw her children becoming, because they hadn't learned to let go of her, even a little bit?

✦

"Nothing has a stronger influence psychologically on their environment, and especially on their children, than the unlived life of the parents."

—C. G. JUNG

When you neglect yourself for the sake of your sons and daughters, you are not doing them any favors. *If you are living*

for or through your children, and ignoring your own needs, all
you are teaching them is how to sacrifice who they are in order
to make someone else happy, a value which never works in the
end. Perhaps when they are still very young, they will love
being waited on hand and foot. But this will render them
spoiled and unimaginative, and when they're older, they will
look at you and see an unhappy figure with unfulfilled
dreams. And they will feel guilty that you threw all of that
away for their sake.

I can promise you one thing: Your kids will never grow up
and say *"Mom, Dad, I am so grateful that you totally sacrificed*
your own happiness, intimate relationship, and growth as a hu-
man being so I would never hear the word 'No.' I'm glad you
were miserable so that I could have everything I wanted. Thank
you for not fully living your lives. I plan to follow in your foot-
steps and give up all the fun and personal satisfaction in my life
when I have children."

Children learn from watching you live.
If you take the time to have real moments for
yourself, they will learn to do the same for
themselves.

If you take the time to feed your own heart, your children
will learn to feed theirs, and not to run on emotional empty.
Instead of sacrificing your life for your children, live your life as
a model for them to emulate.

✦

"The best thing to spend on your children is your time."
— LOUISE HART

What do children really want from us, the grown-ups in
their lives?

✦ They want to feel loved and valued.
✦ They want to feel like they make a difference in our lives.
✦ They want to feel they are O.K. just the way they are.
✦ They want to feel like we are proud of them, and don't wish they had been born to someone else.

Every child needs to know his or her parents feel this way in order to develop a healthy level of self-esteem and self-love.

Sharing real moments with your child is the best way to show him how important he is to you and to give him a powerful experience of feeling your love

Love, not toys, makes children feel worthwhile. Unfortunately in our society we shower our children with material possessions in an attempt to make up for the real moments of connection we are lacking. For many parents, it is easier, less time consuming, and less confrontational to buy their child a new toy than to share some honest, loving moments together.

One of the most amazing stories I heard in the days following the Los Angeles earthquake had to do with this very same confusion of values. The earthquake hit at 4:31 A.M. on a Monday. A few hours later, a television reporter was out with a camera investigating the damage, when he saw an enormous line of people winding around a building. He assumed that these people were lining up to receive emergency aid, water rations, or to buy flashlights, since most of the city was without power. But this was not the case.

Why were thousands of people standing in line only hours after a major disaster? They were anticipating a new delivery of Power Rangers, the "hot" toy of the moment, to a local toy store!!! These parents had left their frightened children at home with friends or relatives amidst the broken glass and during repeated aftershocks, to wait for three hours until the store opened so they could buy plastic warrior midgets!

I'm sure those parents had good intentions. Certainly, many of them were thinking "*I'll bet this Power Ranger will make little Jimmy feel better.*" But plastic fighting men were not what the terrified children in Los Angeles really needed that morning. They needed to know they would be safe if an earthquake of that size or greater happened again. They needed to talk about their terror; they needed to be held; **they needed love.**

> When you give your children material things
> as replacements for love,
> you teach them that it is objects, not love,
> which will bring them happiness.

It is a tragedy that so many children end up with lots of things but have few real moments of intimacy with their parents. Intimacy isn't a word we usually associate with children—we use it to describe the experience of closeness we have with a lover. The word "intimacy" comes from the Latin, *intimus*, which means innermost. So really, **intimacy is the experience of connecting with the innermost part of another person. Experiencing intimacy with your children happens when your souls touch—and that is the most lovely of real moments.**

Your children crave these real moments with you. They want intimacy. They want your time and your complete attention. When you pay full attention to a child, he feels important, as if who he is and what he has to say has value. Ten minutes spent giving a child your undivided attention and love is worth ten hours of dragging him around from one attraction to another, but not really paying any attention to the person inside of him at all.

How many of us, now that we are adults, love our parents, but feel they do not really know us? How many of us feel they never took the time to understand the person we are inside, with all of our hopes and all of our fears? How many of us who were given "things" look back in vain for a memory, any memory, of a moment of true connection and unconditional love? *How many of us still weep because our mother or father doesn't get who we really are?*

Sit down with your child. Look deeply into his heart. Listen carefully to his words. Discover the unique and beautiful spirit he is inside. There is no one else like him in the world.

Children are on loan from God. Pay attention
to who has been sent to you for caretaking.

Guilty Love: The Dilemma of Being a Divorced Parent

Bringing up children is always challenging, but it is even more so for single and divorced parents. They often feel consumed by the guilt of the failed relationship, and terribly frightened that this failure puts their children at risk for developing emotional problems down the line. So they become good at what I call "guilty love," a smothering, selfless, nonstop kind of attention they focus on their kids. It's as if they sentence themselves to a form of penance: *"I've ruined my children's lives by getting divorced, so now I can't have any more fun. I won't date, I won't see my friends, and maybe that will begin to make up for my sins."* These parents find it even harder to take the time for their own personal real moments, or to have them with their children.

You know you are a victim of guilty love when, as a parent, you feel almost ashamed and defensive doing something just for you. You find yourself constantly apologizing to your children for things you shouldn't have to make excuses about:

"Mommy has to go out to the dentist for a few hours today, but I promise for the rest of the week we'll be together every second, O.K.?" The message this gives a child is that you exist for the sole purpose of being their slave, and that anytime you fulfill a personal need, you are breaking the rules.

I have a friend who is a divorced father. He refuses to get into a new relationship because it "might not be good for the kids." When his children visit for the weekend, he won't even take phone calls from friends. "I don't want them to feel abandoned by me again," he explains. Can you imagine what his children are like? They are self-absorbed, selfish, whining little people with no sensitivity to anyone's feelings but their own. They demand constant attention and entertainment. They don't know how to be quiet or alone for five minutes. And why shouldn't they be this way? This is what their father has unintentionally taught them by always giving up his needs and desires for theirs.

Our high divorce rate has bred a whole race of *"Disneyland Dads,"* weekend fathers like my friend who attempt to fit two weeks of loving and recreation into the two days they have with their children once or twice a month. They arrive at the house armed with bribes in the form of toys and gifts that say "I brought you this so you won't be mad at me for not living with you anymore." They indulge their kids with all the junk food, scary movies, and late nights that Mom refuses to let them have. They become smiling sugar daddies, leaving all the hard work and discipline to her.

Let me tell you something as someone who was one of those children many years ago—we secretly hate those guilt gifts, those frantic visits that are supposed to make up for the fact that you aren't there to tuck us in at night, that you made Mommy cry, that our family is forever broken. We hate that proud look in your eyes when you thrust those games and dolls and dresses upon us, waiting for us to make a big deal over this latest offering, as if you really think we're too little to know we're being bought. And we feel contempt for you when, at the end of the day, you sigh with relief after feeding and entertaining us like a favorite pet, so satisfied with yourself that you were a good dad, and that everything's O.K.

And as you walk to the car and wave good-bye, we want to scream at the top of our tiny lungs: "IT'S NOT O.K.!! THOSE STUPID TOYS AND TREATS DON'T MAKE IT O.K.! WHY DON'T YOU REALLY TALK TO ME? WHY DON'T YOU NOTICE HOW MISERABLE I AM? WHY DON'T YOU JUST HOLD ME AND TELL ME HOW MUCH YOU LOVE ME?"

This is what your children want you to know, whether they are five or fifty with children of their own, whether you as their parents divorced or stayed together: **All we have ever wanted, and all we want now, is real moments with you, when you see us, accept us, and love us. That's all.**

◆

"The year my son Kevin was eight, one of our car-pool drivers was often delayed picking the kids up from school. One afternoon, when Kevin was dropped off at home particularly late, I asked him what had happened. He said that school personnel had told him to wait for his ride in the room next to the principal's office. Hadn't he been awfully bored for that half hour? 'No,' he said, 'I kept busy finding the pictures in the wallpaper.' "

— SUSAN K. PERRY
Playing Smart

Children naturally know how to have real moments. They live in the timelessness of the present. They see the everyday world as full of wonder and mystery, and with this perception, they infuse the most ordinary things with magic. The abstract designs on the wallpaper become fascinating pictures. The old scarf becomes a ball gown. The family dog becomes a fierce lion protecting the young prince. Every object, every act, takes on significance and meaning.

My fondest memories of childhood play have nothing to do with store-bought toys, but of magical moments my brother and I created together. One of our favorite things to do was to build a cave of large red cardboard blocks, take an old chiffon paisley scarf of my mother's and hang it over the entrance, and then sit in the cave for hours. We would pretend we were in an exotic Arabian tent in the desert, and with the basement light filtering through the sheer purple scarf, the inside of our hideaway was filled with a luminous glow. This was our special place to share our secrets, our fears and tell stories of how we wanted our lives to turn out.

> All children know how to open the door to the kingdom of wonder.

If you need to experience more real moments in your life, ask a child to take you on a tour of his or her world. Follow in their footsteps for a few hours, or a day, do whatever they are doing, play at whatever they are playing and you will remember how to see the world through a child's eyes. If you pay close attention, you will notice that children are constantly inviting you to enter their magical world, but you're refusing the invitation. **They are offering you a precious gift—the opportunity to have some real moments.**

Last week while I was taking my morning walk, I passed by a little friend of mine who lives down the street. Her name is Alex, and when I stopped to say hello, she told me she was collecting old flowers to dry and make into pictures. My first instinct was to finish my walk and rush back to my computer, since I was in the middle of writing an intense section of the book. Then I remembered that my book was entitled *Real Moments,* and that I needed to have more of them. So I asked Alex if I could help her find flowers for her collection, and suggested we look in the big garden behind my house for suitable candidates.

For the next hour, Alex and I wandered around my back-yard, looking for flowers with broken stems, blossoms that were about to fall off, and petals that already lay on the ground. She showed me how different colors would look beautiful together, and how mixing twigs and leaves with the flowers would make a nice effect. After about ten minutes, I noticed that the tension I'd been feeling all day was beginning to dissipate, and soon I was feeling very centered and joyful as I collected dying flowers with my nine-year-old friend. It was a lovely afternoon.

Every few weeks, I make a point to share real moments like this with the kids in my neighborhood. Bijou and I will sit on the curb with two or three children and I'll just talk to them—about school, about their friends, about what they think and feel. They allow me to enter their world, and remind me how to make everything meaningful: we lie on our backs and notice how the clouds change shape, and see what forms they're showing us; we watch the dogs and cats play together and imagine what they are saying to one another; we talk about our favorite foods and movies. *I often feel that the time I spend on the street enjoying real moments with my small friends is probably more important for my well-being than all the books I could ever read or seminars I could ever take.*

If you have children, then you have built-in opportunities for real moments right at home. If, like me, you don't have kids of your own, borrow someone else's for a half hour, and allow them to be your guide on the road back to innocence and wonder.

Y̶ou have as much to learn from children
as you have to teach them.

✦

"If you're happy, you can always learn to dance."
— OLD BALINESE SAYING

Imagine that your child is drawing abstract pictures on white paper and cutting them up into pieces. You approach and ask him what he is doing. He looks at you with annoyance—isn't it obvious what he is doing? He's drawing pictures and cutting them into pieces. What you really mean by your question is: *What is the purpose of what you're doing? What is the goal of your activity? What do you hope to accomplish?* **You are imposing your goal-oriented values on your child, thus taking him out of the moment.**

We ask children the wrong questions all the time:

"What is that for?"
"What are you going to do with that?"
"Why are you doing that?"

If we could remember back to our childhood, if we were having more real moments, we wouldn't have to ask the questions, because we would already know the answers: **"I'm just doing what I'm doing. I'm being where I am. Maybe in a moment, I'll decide to do something different with this, but right now, I'm perfectly happy doing things exactly as I am."**

It is good to teach children the importance of setting goals for themselves. But in our attempt to help them become "successful," we often rob them of their natural knowing and intuitive values, and interfere with the real moments they spontaneously create for themselves.

> By always asking our children to explain the purpose of everything they do, we are teaching them that their value is in *doing*, not in *being*.

Many of our problems as adults stem from our distorted system of values that emphasizes what we accomplish, rather than who we are, as a measure of self-worth. We need to support children to break this cycle, and remind them that it is *who they are as a person, and not what they achieve, that makes them special.* Unfortunately, we cannot rely on our present educational system, which is purely goal-oriented, to teach this to our kids. **It is up to us to tell our sons and daughters, through our words and our behavior, that we love and admire them not because of what they do or do not achieve, but for the pure goodness we see shining from their hearts.**

Stop worrying about what your children will become. Stop trying to develop them into something. Your job is to help them be happy, and as the Balinese saying goes, if they are happy, they can always learn to dance, or be a doctor or an artist or whatever they want to be, because they will have mastered the most important job in life first.

Creating Real Moments with and for Your Children

Here are some other suggestions for experiencing more real moments with your children:

✦ *Allow them to fully feel their emotions.*

Children intuitively know that the way to release an uncomfortable emotion is to fully feel it first. They cry and wail, and five minutes later they are smiling. They have a tantrum, and in a half hour, they have forgotten what they are angry about. It is we adults who mistakenly try to get our kids to suppress their emotions by telling them "You shouldn't be upset," "That's a silly thing to cry about," "Why are you laughing so hard?" or "You have no reason to be angry." *By doing this, we pull them out of the moments in which they are being with their pain, or their joy.*

Let your children feel their feelings. Help them find words

for the emotions bubbling inside of them. Show them you understand what they are going through, and ask if there is anything you can do to help. Often, there isn't, and you need to let them be, realizing you are more upset by their pain than they are. Of course, it will help if you practice these same guidelines in your own life!

◆ *Encourage your children to keep diaries or journals.*

When we write down our thoughts and feelings about a day or an event, we get to step back, look at them clearly, and learn from what we see. Keeping a diary or journal is a marvelous way to create real moments for yourself as an adult, and it works just as well for children. The diary becomes a special and secret friend, an outlet for their emotions, and an opportunity to practice being mindful and paying attention to what's going on in their world. If your children are too young to write, you can have them dictate their thoughts or feelings to you, and perhaps draw pictures to go with the words. And as they grow older, they will be able to use their writing time as a form of meditation and personal exploration.

◆ *Create family rituals for experiencing real moments together.*

The same Love Processes I described at the end of the chapter "Real Moments and Loving" are wonderful to practice within a family. I have taught thousands of parents the *Appreciation, Gratitude,* and *Forgiveness Exercises* and heard how fulfilling it was for them to share these with their children. Some people like to set aside some time once a week, perhaps on a Sunday evening, when they sit in a circle as a family and do a Gratitude and/or Appreciation Process. Join hands, and take turns sharing "Something I'm grateful for," or "Something I really love about you," etc. Other families like to incorporate shorter versions of these exercises at the dinner table just before eating once or twice a week. And whenever there has been any upset or tension in the family, a Forgiveness Exercise is a must. Don't forget—these are not just for the children, but must include the adults as well.

In the next and final section of this book, I'll be sharing many ideas for creating real moments in your life. I encourage you to teach all of these to your children, and to make loving rituals an integral part of your family tradition.

✦

"Children are . . . very ancient souls in tiny bodies."
— MASTER ADALFO

Your children are not your children. They are your teachers, your guides, your challengers, your lesson-bringers, your truth-tellers, your heart-healers, your spirit-polishers. They are connected to a source of wisdom and love that most of us have lost in the process of growing older. They see angels, they practice unconditional love, they have cosmic connections.

All children are little mystics. They travel easily between the visible and invisible worlds. They have not yet gotten caught up in the boundaries of time and space. They know how to fly.

Until we inhibit them with our ideas of what is real and unreal, all children possess a natural spirituality. They *remember things we have forgotten, and sadly, when we don't respect and acknowledge their natural knowing, we force them to forget as well.*

There's a beautiful story I heard some time ago about a mother who'd just had her second child, another little boy. It seems that one night, as she approached the baby's room, she saw her first son, who was three, standing next to his little brother's crib, staring at the tiny figure lying there. Not wanting to disturb whatever was happening, she remained outside by the door. Then, she saw her older son lean toward his newborn brother, and in a conspiratorial tone whisper: **"Psssst. Hey . . . Jimmy. It's me . . . your brother Danny. Tell me what God looks like . . . I'm starting to forget."**

The mother's eyes filled with tears as she witnessed this sacred and real moment. She realized that Danny knew little Jimmy had just come from the world of spirit, a world Danny vaguely remembered, but was losing touch with as he identified more with his physical body and his role as a male human being called Danny. In this secret conversation, he was reaching out to Jimmy in hopes of recapturing some of the truth he could feel slipping away more and more every day.

I love this story. It says everything there is to say about who our children really are:

> Welcome them into your life as your teachers
> and your blessings. . . .
> Allow them to show you how to find meaning
> and celebration in every moment. . . .
> And if you, too, have forgotten what God looks
> like, ask a child to help you remember. . . .

Part Four

THE PATH TO REAL MOMENTS

Tools for Creating More Love and Meaning in Your Life

◆

· 11 ·

EVERYDAY SPIRITUALITY: Real Moments with Yourself

"The distinction between human and spiritual is made only by human beings. They are not separate. They are woven together. If you do not open your heart to human beings, you will find it difficult to open your heart to God. If you do not love human beings, including yourself, you will find it difficult to love God. Your spiritual path begins in your humanness . . ."
— RON SCOLASTICO AND THE GUIDES

Once, long ago, the peoples of the Earth knew the truth of Oneness: that matter is just the joyful song of spirit; that the human is just a playful dance of the Divine; that the Earth, the animals, the wind, the sun, and the stars are all brothers and sisters sharing one heart that beats in a cosmic rhythm. And their knowledge of Oneness blessed the days of their lives, for it made everything they experienced sacred.

But over time, the truth was forgotten, and The Way of Separation was born. And the people came to believe that God was different and outside of them, and that Nature was a word for inanimate objects like mountains and rivers and trees here to be man's servants. And they decided that some people, like priests and sages, and some places, like churches and temples, were infused with more spirit than others, and therefore were better. They placed heaven above them, and no longer saw earth as a sacred place. *Thus their everyday lives became ordinary, for they had lost their connection to the Divine.*

✦

We are the great-great-grandsons and -granddaughters of those who followed The Way of Separation. **We have separated the spiritual from everyday living, and thus separated ourselves from experiencing everyday spirituality.** The spiritual has become associated with Sunday church services, or the Sabbath, or yoga and meditation, or a trip to India, or a tour of a famous European cathedral. We think praying is more spiritual than riding a bicycle, reading religious literature more holy than making love. We are living secularized lives and yet wondering why life often feels so meaningless and devoid of purpose.

We have even separated from our very home, the Earth. We have disconnected from its rhythms. We try to tame them with technology as if the planet itself were a wild animal we are determined to dominate. We treat the Earth with hostility. If a mountain is in our way, we move it. If a tree blocks our view, we cut it down. We poison the waters and pollute the air, and *because we foolishly think of ourselves as distinct and separate, we do not see that by hurting our Mother, the Earth, we are hurting ourselves.*

The search for real moments and everyday spirituality must begin with a return to The Way of Oneness.

> Everyday spirituality is not an escape from your usual life in search of some special, exalted experience, but a surrender into the fullness of every experience.

It is not a path that leads you away from the human to the spiritual, from the Earth to Heaven, but rather one that leads you back into the ordinary and everyday, and invites you to find the spiritual within it. It begins and ends where you already are, right here, right now. There's nothing else to look for, nothing else to acquire. You already have everything you need.

♦

"We are not human beings having a spiritual experience. We are spiritual beings having a human experience."

— RAM DASS

When I became a seeker, I began what I called a "spiritual path." In my longing to know God, I turned away from worldly things. I practiced meditation for hours, sometimes days at a time. I spent whole years in retreat and silence, living in the mountains, seeing only other meditators. I viewed my physical body as an obstacle to enlightenment, my human desires as impediments to achieving a pure, spiritual state. And I looked at my life on Earth as some sort of prison sentence I was serving that kept me from going back "home" to my Divine origins.

I had many beautiful and uplifting experiences during those years, but I could only be happy when I was doing my "spiritual practice." After searching and searching for answers to my dilemma, I finally had the important realization that *all of human life was a spiritual practice—I was supposed to be practicing being human!!* And thus far, I hadn't been doing a very good job. In fact, I'd attempted to avoid being human entirely. No wonder I was so miserable: I was in the water, but trying not to get wet!

Since that time, I have worked on embracing my humanness, not running from it, and looking within it for the very same spiritual experiences I used to seek elsewhere. I know now that my presence here on Earth is not a sentence—it is a gift; **that being human is not a loss of spirit, but an opportu-**

nity for spirit to enjoy itself on the physical plane. I am here because I am loved.

In order to experience everyday spirituality, we need to remember that we are spiritual beings spending some time in a human body. We are not separate from spirit. This would be impossible. We are simply spirit disguised in human form. *In this way, we are connected to all life.* The flower is spirit disguised as a flower. The tomato is spirit disguised as a tomato. The rock is spirit disguised as a rock. This book you are holding is spirit disguised as a book. We all share the same source. We are all made of the same invisible particles of matter. We are all One.

As parts of the whole organism called Life, we are utterly dependent upon all of physical creation for our survival. Your body does not end at the edges of your skin—it reaches beyond the physical boundaries into the air around you, which feeds your lungs; it stretches out through space to the Sun, which nourishes the soil with light and gives you food; it extends deep into the Earth, which offers you wood and rocks and earth to create shelter. In this way, your body goes on forever in all directions, and contains all things.

Your very existence is a product of an eternal cosmic courtship between Heaven and Earth. Can you not see how loved you are by your Father, the Sky, and your Mother, the Earth, who come together in every moment to bring you life? There is a meditation I teach my students in one of my seminars:

> "The Earth is my Mother,
> The Sky is my Father.
> I am a child of Universal Love . . ."

The next time you feel disconnected from the world around you, or you're looking for a real moment, go outside, sit down on some grass or dirt, and repeat this to yourself silently, or aloud, with your eyes open or closed. Between each repetition, take a deep breath, filling up with the gift of air. Soon, you will feel your connection to wholeness, and you will know peace.

◆

"People see God every day. They just don't recognize him."
—PEARL BAILEY

When we separate the spiritual from the everyday, we limit our opportunities for real moments. We miss ordinary miracles and wonders because we are looking for something flashy, something that screams "I am special, I am holy." We are so distracted by our search for the extraordinary that we don't even recognize the sacred when we encounter it.

The other day a good friend and I were talking about our own growth process, and he asked me if I believed that there were any truly holy people in the world. I thought for a minute, and answered that I believed *anytime a person was coming from a place of love and kindness, they were holy.* The Greek root of the word "holy" is *holos*, meaning complete or whole. **So holiness really is wholeness, and holy people are people in touch with their wholeness and the intrinsic wholeness of the Universe.**

I have learned that you don't have to look far for real moments of holiness. They are everywhere. All you need to do is to pay attention. . . .

One night a few months ago, my husband and I were coming out of a restaurant when we heard someone singing. We looked up and we saw a middle-aged man walking slowly along the sidewalk, carrying several shopping bags and crooning a lonesome song to himself. I thought perhaps he was just someone in a melancholy mood until he got closer—then I noticed that his clothes were threadbare, he appeared thin and hungry, and was shivering in the cold. "He probably doesn't have a home," I thought sadly. I realized that he had no intention of stopping and asking us for money. He was just passing by.

Something in this man's song touched my heart deeply, and I decided to reach out to him.

"You have a beautiful voice," I called out. He stopped and smiled at us.

"Thank you kindly," he answered. "It used to be better, but the damp air isn't too good for it."

"Would you sing some more for us?" we asked. And so he did, soft and shy at first, and then forgetting where and who he was, he sang boldly, belting out a hymn with all his heart and soul. For a moment, he was no longer a forgotten face on the boulevard, looking for a doorway to sleep in. He was an artist with an audience, sharing his gift with us, the only thing he had to share—the joy of song he had somehow managed to hold on to even though he had lost everything else. And as his voice soared, it filled the night with an ancient holiness, for in it, I heard the voices of every human being who had ever sung to God in delight, or darkness, or despair.

When he was done, we applauded and told him how good he truly was. Andy, for that was his name, apologized for only knowing a few verses of the song. "I haven't been too well lately," he explained. "I've had a lot of bad breaks, lost my job and my apartment, but I still try to keep a good attitude." As I listened to Andy talk about his unthinkably difficult life with a cheerful smile, I knew he had succeeded at something most people, including myself, find very difficult. In spite of everything, he still celebrated his joy in being alive. He was moving through life singing. He was having real moments.

Before Andy left, we gave him some money and wished him well. I know that we made a difference in his life, not so much because of the dollars we put in his hand, but because we allowed him, for a moment, to be somebody special and make a difference back to us. That night, we got the better half of the deal. *Andy was our teacher, our sidewalk angel, our unlikely but genuine holy man.* His unfailing spirit filled me with humility as I was reminded that with all the blessings in my life, I don't walk around singing joyfully as he does.

✦

Real moments of holiness happen when we experience moments of wholeness with ourself, our environment, or another person. **As you go through your day, look for holy moments and everyday miracles**—the hug your child gives you for no reason at all; a flock of birds flying past a cloud; the beautiful array of fruits and vegetables the earth has produced that are waiting for you at the supermarket; the song playing on the radio that gives you just the message you've been needing to hear; the lone yellow dandelion bursting through the crack in the concrete sidewalk.

When you stop and pay attention to holy moments and everyday miracles, you will start living with awe and wonder, and participating in a Divine love affair with God.

Living Each Day with Reverence

My husband and I recently spent several weeks in Bali, an island which is part of Indonesia. The Balinese have a reputation for being the friendliest people on earth, and after getting to know some of them in our travels, I would say they are also the happiest. This is not because of what they have, because they have very little in terms of material possessions: The average income is around three hundred dollars per year; most Balinese live in open-air homes with no glass windows or solid doors; and the majority of them bathe and wash their clothing in the rivers and streams that surround the lush, green rice fields. But I would never call the people of Bali poor, *for they possess a rare gift of knowing how to truly enjoy and find sacred meaning in every moment of life, and this is the secret to their happiness. They are masters at creating real moments.*

Each morning Jeffrey and I would go to breakfast in the hotel restaurant, and there we would be greeted by Putu, our smiling waitress. Putu was one of the most content people I have ever met. Her eyes sparkled with joy, her manner radiated warmth and peace. When I first met her, we had just arrived from the United States, and in her presence I became even more aware of how tense, hurried, and agitated I was. I watched her move with grace, I listened to her laughter as she handed me a glass of juice, and I realized that Putu knew something that I did not. In spite of all my success, and the luxurious comforts we live with daily in the United States, I had to admit that Putu was a much happier person than I was. And she knew it too. "It is hard for us to understand," she shared with me in her careful English, "why all of the people who come here from America have so much, yet look so unhappy."

Putu told me this without judgment. She simply could not figure out what we tourists were doing in our everyday lives that had caused our hearts and spirits to be so much more closed than those of her friends and family who lived simply on the island. But after spending time on Bali, I knew the answer. I learned it from watching a tiny, withered couple in their eighties cheerfully working their rice paddy one day, as they had done for over sixty years, stopping to wave gaily at me as I walked by. I learned it from our guide Adi, who told me that every morning he woke up excited, waiting to discover what interesting people and beautiful sights God would put in his path as he drove us around. I learned it from a master wood craftsman in a tiny village, who treated each of his carved Buddhas like they were Lord Buddha himself, polishing their wood bellies with love.

All of these kind people have one thing in common—**they live each day of their lives with joy and reverence.** They thank the rice for growing as they harvest it; they thank the sun for rising as they walk out into its warmth; they take delight in each new person they meet; they celebrate each new day as a sacrament. *They are masters at everyday spirituality. The whole Earth is their temple, and their very existence reason enough to rejoice.*

My wonderful trip to Bali was a humbling and inspiring experience. Since I returned, I've been trying to live with more reverence for all life around me, and when I do, I find myself blessed with many more real moments.

✦

"A man asked his Rabbi, 'O wise one, how can I best serve God?' and waited for a profound reply. The old Rabbi thought for a moment and answered: 'You can best serve God with whatever you are doing in the moment.' "
— OLD HASIDIC STORY

Real moments with yourself do not occur when you do anything special or out of the ordinary, but, as the great sage Yogananda said, *when you do little things in an extraordinary way.* Do whatever you already do, but pay attention:

It is mindfulness that transforms the ordinary
task into the extraordinary experience.

The "Right Now Meditation"

I want to share with you my favorite technique for living mindfully, but first, let me explain how it came about. One day about a year ago, I took my dog Bijou out for his afternoon stroll. I'd walked almost four blocks when I suddenly stopped and realized that I wasn't on the walk at all—I was thinking about a phone call I'd just finished with a TV producer; I was worrying about meeting my book deadline; I was wondering whether or not I should hire a new employee. I was everywhere but walking down the street. "Happiness can only be found in this moment," I reminded myself, "but how do I get myself back to this moment, and how do I stay once I get here?"

Suddenly, two words popped into my head: *"RIGHT NOW . . ."* I decided to use this phrase and fill in the sentence with whatever I was actually doing in the moment. This is how my thoughts went:

"Right now, I am walking Bijou up the hill. . . . Right now, I am placing one foot in front of the other onto the pavement. . . . Right now, I am watching Bijou's cute little body prance in front of me. . . . Right now, I am taking a deep breath of summer air. . . . Right now, I am looking up at the blue sky. . . . Right now I'm admiring that red flower. . . Right now, I am right here, right now. . . ."

As I practiced my *"Right Now Meditation,"* my mind relaxed, and my breathing deepened. I stopped trying to rush Bijou along, and enjoyed stopping whenever he did. I began to feel very centered in each moment, and a quiet sense of peace began to permeate my whole being. By the time our walk was over, I felt as if I'd just had a mini-vacation, and I wore a smile of contentment on my face.

Since that day, I practice *"Right Now Meditation"* all the time, especially when I am looking for a real moment.

Some Hints for Practicing "Right Now Meditation"

✦ Try doing it at least once a day.

✦ You can use this technique when you are driving, cooking, eating, people-watching, building something, taking a walk, making love, or doing anything at all.

✦ Do your series of "Right Now's" for at least five minutes to get the most benefits.

✦ Always end with the phrase:
"**RIGHT NOW, I AM RIGHT HERE, RIGHT NOW. . . .**"

✦ It's good to take a deep relaxing breath between each "Right Now," because breathing always places you instantly in the moment.

✦ I've found the technique works best when you think your "Right Now's" silently to yourself, rather than saying them out loud. You may want to experiment.

Using "Right Now" as a Breathing Meditation

One variation of this mindfulness technique is to use it with your breathing when you are sitting quietly with your eyes closed. Find a comfortable place where you will not be disturbed. Close your eyes, and become aware of your breathing as you inhale, and as you exhale. Then begin your "Right Now Meditation" silently as follows:

AS YOU INHALE: "**Right now, I am breathing in.**"
AS YOU EXHALE: "**Right now, I am breathing out.**"
REPEAT . . .

You will notice that your breathing begins to slow down, become more even, and that the spaces between each inhalation and each exhalation are filled with a timeless peace. **Do not concentrate as you think your "Right Now's"** . . . just *gently* have the thought about breathing in and breathing out.

If you would like to use your "Right Now" breathing for some emotional healing, you can use these phrases:

AS YOU INHALE: "Right now, I am breathing in love."
AS YOU EXHALE: "Right now, I am breathing out fear."
REPEAT . . .

I've used this in seminars with wonderful results. You may even notice old buried emotions surfacing and clearing away, or long-unshed tears emerging from your eyes.

Other Techniques for Creating Real Moments with Yourself

✦ *Keep a Journal or Diary.* Don't write down events, but rather, record your uncensored feelings, your observations, your real moments. It's not necessary to write each day—even a few times a week will be valuable. *The more you put your attention on real moments you've just experienced, the more of them you will recognize the next time.*

✦ *Have an Inner Guidance Session with Yourself.* A variation on keeping a journal is to imagine that you are connected to a powerful source of wisdom and truth, whether you see it as a Guide or Teacher, or just an energy, and *ask it to send you messages you need to hear through the process of your writing.* Open yourself to whatever pops into your mind, and write down whatever you "hear" in your head. *Don't stop to analyze or understand what's coming out.* When you are finished, read what you've just "received"—you will be amazed at the quality of wisdom and inner guidance that poured through you onto the page.

✦ *Take a Mindfulness Walk.* Even if you don't have a dog, you need to take yourself for a walk once in a while. Instead of just going somewhere, make it a mindfulness walk by using the *"Right Now Meditation"* as you stroll along. You will notice things inside of you, and outside of you, that you hadn't been aware of before.

> "Just to be is a blessing.
> Just to live is holy."
> — RABBI ABRAHAM HESCHEL

Yesterday, approximately 200,000 people throughout the world died. Their time on Earth is over. They did not wake up this morning. They did not feel the sun on their face, or feel the wind on their skin. They did not hear laughter, or singing, or birds calling to each other. They could not eat an apple or drink a glass of water. They were not held or kissed or smiled at. They cannot see the stars twinkling in the sky tonight. They cannot gaze at the moon. They cannot read these words, close the book, turn out the light, and snuggle into the covers, only to dream and wake again.

You are alive.
You are here *now.*
You have another day.
That is a blessing.
Enjoy the ordinary everyday miracles that make
up your life. . . .
They will be your most sacred real moments.

· 12 ·

SILENCE AND
SACRED SPACES

"We need to find God, and he cannot be found in noise and restlessness. God is the friend of silence."

—MOTHER TERESA

It is often in silence and solitude that you will find your most meaningful real moments. Silence nourishes the soul and heals the heart. It creates an insulated space between you and the noisy, demanding world you live in, a womb of still-ness in which you can be reborn over and over again. Silence has a regenerative power of its own. It is always sacred. It always returns you home.

Solitude is very necessary for silences which go deep. You must make time to be alone. Aloneness is not the same as loneliness. The word *alone* is derived from the Middle English phrase *"all one."* When you are alone, you are not simply away from others, but you are *with yourself,* **you are all one**— you are at one with your own essence; you come back to wholeness with yourself. In this way, you are not aware of the lack of the people from whom you've temporarily retreated— *you are aware of the fullness of you.* And it is in your *all oneness* that you can listen to your own inner voices, invite direction from your own guides, and recapture your own dreams.

The ancients knew the value of the solitary journey, the silent vigil by a fire, the vision quest. But we live in a time when technology has stolen our silence and solitude from us. It is increasingly difficult to find a truly quiet place. Even mountain stillness or desert tranquillity is regularly disturbed by the roar of jet planes overhead and the rumble of passing cars with radios blasting. It is hard to be completely alone with over five billion of us living on one planet.

Most of us have very little silence in our lives. Try recalling the last experience you had, excluding your sleep time, of being in silence for an hour or more. You wake up to your clock radio blaring, you watch television while you dress and eat, you drive to work listening to the morning talk show, you eat lunch in a noisy restaurant, and so the day goes. We get so used to the lack of silence that we become uncomfortable when faced with it. I have a friend who lives in New York City and travels quite frequently. He never leaves home without one item—his "noise machine," a device that emits a constant background noise that people play in order to sleep. Whenever he stays at my house, which is in the mountains outside of Los Angeles, he complains that "it's too quiet here—silence gives me the creeps." Then, he plugs in his little machine, and as he listens to the "noise," he falls easily asleep.

My friend's "creeps" come from the discomfort he experiences when the silence removes all of his distractions, draws his attention inward, and forces him to be with himself.

Silence and solitude are confrontational.
They plunge us instantly into truth,
and it is for this reason that they are so essential
to the health of our spirit.

Silence allows you to pay attention to everything, to watch the flow of mental garbage that goes through your mind. It's like sitting for a while on a riverbank and watching debris float by on the river. When you choose to be solitary and silent, you witness the thoughts, reactions, and emotions that have been interfering with your ability to make clear decisions, or to discover the answers to problems, or to know what your true feelings are. You can observe all of this emotional debris, notice what isn't serving you or is actually causing pain and turmoil in your life, and decide what you want to throw out and what you want to keep.

Imagine that you are hanging pictures in your living room. You become so absorbed in your task that you don't take time to stop, stand back, and notice if the pictures are hung correctly. You just keep banging those nails into the wall. Taking times for silence means standing back far enough so you can determine if the pictures in your life are crooked or straight. Silence will help you see clearly, sometimes for the first time, exactly what is out of balance in your life.

> Going in makes coming out much
> more powerful.

When you make the time for the apparent nondoing of silence and solitude, your doing will become much more effective and meaningful. Great sages, shamans, saints, and warriors have always known this. They retreated into silence before undertaking a journey, a battle, a ceremony, a quest. They took their solitude on hilltops under the full moon, in hidden groves deep in the forest, in sweat lodges, in chapels. There, they would empty themselves of their limitations and burdens, and open to the sacred mystery of the void. They would be transported beyond the constraints of time and space. They would be embraced by the life-giving power that is the Source of all creation. And then, they would emerge to perform their earthly responsibilities, infused with power and vision that can only be acquired from contact with the Unbounded.

In my own life, it is the silences that have formed the foundation for the creations and contributions I am most proud of. When I was in my twenties, I spent months at a time on meditation courses in Europe with other meditation teachers. We would often practice days, and even weeks of silence along with our regular meditations. For weeks at a time, I wouldn't utter a sound, nor would I hear one—no conversations, no greetings, no jokes . . . just silence. The deeper I went into silence, the more profound my spiritual experiences became.

Looking back, I know that these were some of the most powerful and transformational moments of my life, preparing me for the work I was to do in the years to come. My husband teases me and says, "Yes, but once you came out of silence, you started talking, and haven't stopped since!!" In some ways he is correct. I went so deep within myself, like pulling an arrow back on the bow, that I often feel I am still flying through the air in the other direction. I do know that without those opportunities to travel deeply inward, I would never have been able to come out into the world with such determination and focus, and I wouldn't have known how to listen to the forces that have guided me.

◆

> "The more you talk about It,
> the more you think about It,
> the further from It you go.
> Stop talking, stop thinking,
> and there is nothing you will not understand . . ."
> — SENGSTAN

The power of silence lies in its emptiness. *Silence is a receptive space. It creates a sacred void, an opening through which you can receive: truth, perspective, strength, healing, revelation.* In silence, you transcend words, and contact the wordless. You transcend form, and contact the formless. You fill up with a peaceful knowing.

Silence is not the same as prayer. Prayer is a way of directing your feelings and thoughts, focusing them and sending them toward a source. Silence is listening, receiving, being. One is trying to reach the source or communicate with it; the other, silence, is allowing yourself to hear the source within yourself, to become one with it. Prayer is directed outward. Silence is directed inward. **In prayer, you are the sender; but in silence, you are the receiver.**

I believe that God, Goddess, Cosmic Intelligence, The Higher Power, or whatever force you believe in is there to be called upon, thanked, and appreciated. **But I also believe that communication with Spirit is like a two-way radio, that you can receive messages as well as you can send them out.** *If you aren't feeling as connected as you'd like to Spirit, and you've been praying in the traditional way as hard as you can, perhaps you need to pray less and listen more. Maybe God's been waiting for a chance to talk to you, but hasn't been able to get in a word edgewise . . . !*

Learning to Listen to Silence

Navigating through silence is like navigating the ocean—it is a skill. It takes practice, and the more you practice, the better you get. *The first step is to quiet your mind, to leave behind your usual thought processes.* That's like getting into a boat that takes you away from the shore and out to sea. Just as there are many kinds of boats, there are many methods for quieting the mind. You can use any one of a variety of meditation techniques and breathing exercises. Take the time to find one that works for you. After all, if you don't like your boat, you won't want to go out sailing very often.

Once you have your vehicle for traveling away from your everyday landscape, you will need to learn to become a master at grabbing on to the currents and riding the waves. There are different "waves" or levels of silence:

. . . There is surface silence, a quiet, gentle calm that lulls you into a centered space.

. . . There is deep silence, a powerful swirling rush of love and knowingness that sends your spirit rocking and rolling into new levels of consciousness.

. . . And then, there is the tidal wave of silence, an overwhelming force that engulfs you completely, swallowing up your ego and identity, and plunging you into a swirling mass of Light and Bliss, until you become one with it.

Start wherever you are, and let the Silence itself become your guide. It will take you wherever you need to go.

✦

If you aren't used to going within, you will need to be patient with yourself while you learn how to navigate inner space. It will take you some time to get used to its rhythms and melodies:

Imagine you are walking through the woods with a friend who happens to be carrying a portable tape player that's blasting loud music. You won't be able to hear anything else but the music. If your friend turns the tape off, at first you still won't hear much—your ears need to adjust to the quiet. Soon, you will start to notice sounds that were always there, the rustle of leaves in the wind, tiny animals moving through the brush, the creak of massive tree branches. The more time you spend listening, the more you will hear.

It is the same with taking journeys inside yourself. At first, it may seem like nothing is happening, like you are just sitting there breathing or meditating. Soon, however, you will learn to pick up feelings that are very quiet, but were always there beneath the everyday noisiness of the mind.

> When you and the silence become friends, it
> will speak to you as loudly as anything you could
> ever hear from the outer world. Soon, you will
> not be able to ignore its voice, which, after all,
> is the voice of your own spirit calling to you.

Here are a few other very simple ways to experience more silence in your life:

✦ **Drive with your radio turned off.** *Cars are great moving meditation centers.* You can't be bothered, and you can't really get up and leave. Some of my greatest revelations have come while driving in my car. For twelve years I gave a weekend seminar once a month in Los Angeles, and each Friday night on the way to the workshop, I would drive in total silence, allowing my mind to empty and to tune in to my inner broadcast. I've also taken many wonderful long car trips in silence, especially when I'm traveling out of town. By the time I arrived at my destination, I had received guidance I needed and answers I'd been searching for.

Make your car into a sacred space: When you are alone, try driving silently, or listening to gentle music that has no lyrics. Keep your eyes on the road, but listen for the sound of your inner voice.

✦ **Sit in silence by firelight or candlelight.** Build a fire in your fireplace, or simply light some candles, place them close to you on a table or desk where you can see them, and turn out the lights. Make sure the TV and radio are turned off, and that you won't be disturbed. Sit and watch the flames. Listen to the logs crackle, or watch the wax drip down the side of the candle. Imagine the light illuminating all of the dark or hidden places inside of you. Pay attention to what you see. Or if you see nothing, just enjoy the simplicity of the moment.

✦ **Take a silent walk with the person you love.** This is a way of sharing your silence. Find an enjoyable place to walk, the quieter the better. Hold hands. Feel the rhythm of each other's footsteps, the warmth of their skin touching yours. Pay attention to everything you see, and everything you feel. Soon, you may notice that your hearts are speaking a silent language with one another.

✦

"Your sacred space is where you can find yourself again and again."

—JOSEPH CAMPBELL

I believe that each of us needs a sacred space, a symbolic environment which draws our awareness in and focuses it on our true journey. Having your own sacred space will help you experience more real moments in your life. It will call you back to the real moments you have had before, and make your pilgrimage within easier.

A sacred space can be a pillow in the corner of your bedroom where you pray or meditate, a shelf or dresser where you place objects that have special meaning, even a wall where you hang reminders of your growth process. It should be someplace you can sit or kneel in front of, or if that's not possible, a place you can stand in front of. It doesn't have to be big—it might only be a six-inch by six-inch section of your night table.

A space is made sacred by your intention that it be so.

That is it. You do not need fancy statues or the perfect piece of furniture. All you need is whatever you would like to have there, things that will help center you and stir your spirit. Your sacred space might include:

- ✦ Photographs of people you love—your mate, children, friends, family, pets
- ✦ Photographs of beloved relatives who have passed on
- ✦ Religious or spiritual symbols that have meaning for you
- ✦ Pictures of your guides and teachers
- ✦ Mementos from your life that remind you of special real moments
- ✦ Your favorite inspirational books, your Bible, prayer book, etc.
- ✦ Objects from nature that will remind you of your connection to the Earth: rocks, crystals, flowers, shells, etc.
- ✦ Candles

My sacred space is in my writing room at home. I am looking at it right now. It is on the top of a low cabinet against the window. It contains many of the items I listed, and others that are precious to me. It is the place where I pray, where I center myself, where I ask for guidance, where I express gratitude for my blessings. I have my own special, private rituals I perform there, rituals that are designed to help me turn within and remember who I really am and what I am here for. Whenever I feel lost or frightened, whenever I move off center, I come upstairs to my sacred space, kneel or sit before it, and use it to guide me back home to myself.

Even when I'm traveling, I create a little sacred space wherever I am. The first thing I do when I arrive in a hotel room is to take out a few special objects and place them next to my bed. Now the room is mine, now I am at peace.

Some people like to have another sacred space outdoors. If

you are fortunate enough to live in an environment where this is possible, your outdoor sacred space might be a special tree behind your house, or a spot by a lake, or a rock overlooking the ocean. You can bring important objects with you on your visits, or you can come alone and simply allow the sanctity of Mother Nature herself to help you return to center.

Don't be in a hurry to create a sacred space where you live if you don't already have one. Just hold the intention of inviting it into your life, and then wait for a while. *Let your sacred space tell you where it wants to be.* Slowly, it will manifest itself as one object after another finds its way there. Some will be things you've had for a long while. Some will be unexpected gifts. In time, you will construct your own unique rituals and real moments in your sacred space.

The more you visit your physical sacred space, the more you will get into the habit of connecting with your inner sacred space, until soon, you will carry your sacred space with you wherever you go.

✦

"Come out of the circle of time
And into the circle of love."
—JALALUDIN RUMI

The easiest way to make any space a place where you can experience real moments is to bring love to it. **Love makes every space sacred, and every moment meaningful.** When you and your partner lie in bed at night and hold each other close, you are in a sacred space. When you are brushing out your daughter's hair, you are in a sacred space. When you offer a hug to a friend who is filled with sadness, you are in a sacred space. Love ushers us into a timeless place of rapture. While we are immersed in loving, love is all there is. Nothing else exists.

After you read this, close your eyes.
Breathe gently and deeply, until you have pulled
your awareness from the outside in.
Navigate past your thoughts, and around
your feelings.
Keep going, until you find the Silence.
Dive in . . . go deeper and deeper.
Now, float in the Silence.
Let it permeate every cell of your being.
Know it as Peace.
Know it as Love.
Become the silence. . . .

· 13 ·

RITUALS AND
REAL MOMENTS

"When humans participate in ceremony, they enter a sacred space. Everything outside of that space shrivels in importance. Time takes on a different dimension. Emotions flow more freely. The bodies of participants become filled with the energy of life, and this energy reaches out and blesses the creation around them. All is made new; everything becomes sacred."

— SUN BEAR

Rituals create powerful opportunities for you to experience real moments. They transport you from the regular everyday world into the world of the sacred, and help reconnect you with the wholeness of life. When you practice a ritual or personal ceremony, you instantly become conscious and mindful. You create a sacred time and space, as each act is rich with significance. You are right here, right now, remembering your true purpose, nourishing your heart, and renewing your spirit.

For as long as human beings have walked the earth, we have made ritual a part of our lives. Those ancient ones who came before us and lived in harmony with the earth understood the importance of the sacred ceremony as a path for creating connection, and for infusing what was often a harsh and challenging existence with higher meaning. There were rituals for planting the crop, and rituals for celebrating the harvest. There were rituals to honor the change of seasons, and rituals to honor the changes in our bodies. Dancing, singing, chanting, feasting, purifying, and praying were not practiced at random—they happened at prescribed times for a particular purpose.

Slowly, as the centuries progressed, we disconnected from the earth and shifted from living a spiritual existence to a more secular existence. And in the process, we removed much of the ritual from our lives. We were too busy trying to achieve more and become more to stop and perform ceremonies that did not create the instant results to which we had become addicted.

Some rituals were left, but especially here in America, they too were tainted by our materialistic values. Birthdays, Christmas, and anniversaries became about receiving gifts and eating and drinking too much, not about celebrating love and renewal. Weddings became about having a lavish party, not about consecrating the union of two hearts. Even death doesn't escape this siege by commercialism as we spend large sums of money on elaborate coffins and headstones, but don't take the time to fully honor and bless the spirit of our friend or relative.

When our life is devoid of ritual, we rush through it. *We don't stop to reflect on the meaning of the events that are happening to us. We find it hard to remember our purpose in the bigger scheme of things. We forget who we are. We lose our way.*

> When our rituals turn away from the spiritual
> and emotional and focus only on the material,
> our spirits lose the roads on which they can
> travel homeward.

✦

I had to travel thousands of miles across the world to witness an example of the life-enhancing power of ritual, on our recent trip to Bali. The Balinese have rituals and ceremonies for everything—there are rituals for opening your place of business each morning, rituals for blessing the bridges so that vehicles will travel safely across, rituals for the moment when your child takes his first steps. As our gentle and kindhearted guide, Adi, drove my husband and me through the lush rice fields and hills of the island, he explained all of the special prayers and ceremonies to us with reverence. "*Rituals give us the opportunity to focus our attention on what is important,*" he said humbly.

The spiritual peace one feels on Bali comes from the strong sense of meaning with which the Balinese do everything in their lives. Unlike many of us in the Western world, they do not wait for a few days a year on which they celebrate their children, or the food the earth provides, or the love of their family—they honor the blessings in their simple, harmonious existence daily. **Each day becomes a series of very real and significant moments.**

✦

What are rituals for?

✦ *Rituals give rhythm to life.*

They are the drumbeat keeping time as you walk on your path. They provide continuity. They offer predictable intervals in an unpredictable world. In this way, your acts of observance serve as a single thread that weaves itself through your days and nights, connecting you with the familiar. The prayer you say each morning as you greet the dawn, the ceremony of recommitment you and your beloved have on each anniversary, the solitary walk you take each Sunday—these become the milestones by which you measure your journey. *They stop and demand that you pay attention to the place where you are, the emotions you are feeling, and the moment you are in.*

On the last day of every year, Jeffrey and I celebrate a special ritual. We spend several hours sitting together in a quiet place and expressing our gratitude for everything that has happened to us in the past twelve months. We acknowledge each other as well as the other people who have given us love; we share our appreciation for the events that have occurred, the lessons we've learned, the challenges we've faced and the new wisdom they brought. Month by month, we go through the year and recall significant moments, lovely memories, and wonderful blessings. By the time New Year's Eve arrives, we feel fortunate and full of grace.

It is sad that so many people choose to pass through life's significant moments by getting so intoxicated that all they are left with the next day is a hangover. This, too, is a sort of ceremony, but *one that is based on becoming unconscious, not more conscious.* Our New Year's Eve ritual leaves us feeling complete with the year that has passed, and excited about the new year to come. We end the year with some very real moments, which is the best natural high of all.

◆ *Rituals are for celebrating rebirth, for marking passage from one stage of life to another.*

They are important for honoring the crossing of a symbolic threshold. We use them to acknowledge the obvious life changes—birth, marriage, and death—but there are so many other significant occasions that go unnoticed, and therefore, unsanctified: *the formation of a step-family; the changing of a career; moving from one home to another; the triumph over an addiction; the healing of a disease or accident; the onset of men-struation, and, later, menopause; divorce or the letting go of a relationship; the last child leaving home; the accomplishment of a long-sought-after goal.* By marking these experiences with ritual, they become intensely meaningful real moments.

A few years ago, when Jeffrey and I began talking about getting married, I found myself feeling very anxious and afraid. I knew the reason why—I still carried so much pain from my failed relationships that I felt "ruined," like damaged goods. I wished I'd never been married before, that I could come to him as if it were the first time. Turning the clock back was impossible, so I decided to create a passage ritual for myself, to officially end the cycle of pain I'd been in for so many years, and mark the new cycle of fulfillment.

I went to a special spot on a hill overlooking the ocean, where I could sit by myself. With me, I brought pictures of each man I'd loved, and some mementos from those relation-ships. I also brought some special objects from my sacred space at home that always help me connect with the higher truth. And then, I had my own "letting go" ritual, where I thanked each of those men for the lessons they taught me and the love they gave, took back whatever pieces of myself I felt I'd given each of them, and said good-bye to the past. I tore up the pictures and letters, and burned them in a little bowl until they were just ashes. Taking the ashes in my hands, I offered them back to the earth and the wind, and asked that my heart be healed of any fear of commitment, and be made whole again so I could offer all of it to Jeffrey.

This ritual marked my passage from the woman I had been to the woman I had become. *It gave me a moment to fully acknowledge my transformation, and to formally release the past.* Afterward, I felt like I'd shed one thousand pounds of fear. Of course, I continued to work on building up my trust in myself and strengthening our relationship, but that ceremony was a turning point in my healing process.

Perhaps you've passed through many life stages without stopping to honor your journey, or perhaps you are passing through an important stage right now. Take the time to create a meaningful ritual for yourself, and to celebrate your rebirth.

✦ *Rituals are for healing and renewal.*

They can be used to purify and strengthen your connection to God, your partner, your work, and yourself. You can create a renewal ritual when you feel the need for new clarity and strength, when you need guidance and direction, or when you and someone you love want to go to a deeper level of intimacy together, but feel there are some things in the way.

I do renewal rituals before I write a book, when I notice myself feeling spiritually disconnected and too caught up in my work, and when I come up against some old emotional pain that I am moving through too slowly. Sometimes I create them in my sacred space at home; sometimes I do them in the bathtub if I want to feel really "cleansed"; sometimes I go out in Nature to a mountaintop, or, when I can, to one of my favorite power spots like the one in Sedona, Arizona, that's pictured on this book cover. I always emerge from my renewal rituals feeling centered and protected.

✦

> "Only within burns the fire I kindle.
> My heart the altar.
> My heart the altar."
> —POEM OF A BUDDHIST NUN

All rituals begin and end in the heart. They are not about places; they are not about objects. They are about love, respect, and remembering.

Anything done with mindfulness and intention is a form of

ritual. In creating your own rituals, don't get caught up in the material trappings and forget your purpose—to create a moment of spiritual connection and meaningful awareness. You don't need to be surrounded by candles and incense, or be in any particular locale, or use some special formula if you choose not to. All you need is your decision to make the time and place you're in significant, and the experience you are having sacred.

> What makes a moment into a ritual? It is your intention that your time be ritualized and purposeful. It is your decision to give meaning to what you are doing.

Each of us needs to rediscover and redefine our own rituals. Some you will practice daily, some at special times. Here are a few *concepts* that will bring meaning to some of our traditional occasions for celebration. What kind of rituals you use and how you structure them is up to you.

Birthdays—Celebrate the birth of the person you've become in the past year. Give gratitude for another year of life, and for all the blessings you received. Release everything you don't want to take into the new year ahead. Honor your parents for coming together and giving you a passage onto the Earth.

Relationship Anniversaries—Celebrate the growth you've made as a couple in the past year. Honor each other for the love and devotion you've given. Acknowledge the changes you've seen in your partner. Recommit to your relationship, renew old vows, and create new ones for the coming year.

Baby Shower—Each person can share their wishes and wisdom for both mother and child, giving gifts of knowledge, as opposed to mere physical offerings. Tell the unborn baby how much it is loved and its birth anxiously awaited.

Thanksgiving—Share your gratitude for the blessings of the year. Make gratitude calls and write gratitude letters. Thank the Earth for providing you with a home and for sustaining you with its food.

Christmas/Hanukkah/New Year's Time—Celebrate the blessings of the year, the love you have received, and the light that has guided your life. Share your gratitude and love with those you care about. Give. Usher in the new cycle with joy.

Easter/Passover—Release anything you want to let go of, those parts of you that you no longer need or that don't serve your highest good. Say good-bye to the part of your old self that is dying, and welcome the resurrection of your new self as it begins its journey toward more freedom.

Vacations—Set goals for personal and spiritual renewal. Have the intention of not returning with certain burdens, tensions, or emotional blocks you left with. Use your time away for healing and reconnection with yourself and your loved ones.

◆

Our planet, our home, knows the secret of ritual and celebration. Each morning, the sun rises in a blaze of reds and oranges to kiss the Earth with light and warmth; birds sing their first jubilant song thanking the day, and gardens open in a colorful greeting. Each evening, the sun sets, painting the sky with a dramatic good-bye, and making way for the darkness; crickets chirp their rhythmic lullaby, and the Earth sleeps. Each winter, the Earth humbly sheds the old so the new can grow. Each spring, it proudly celebrates its renewal with an abundance of life.

The Earth does not allow its changes to go unheralded. It honors them with glorious and dramatic ritual. We must learn from the Earth, and honor our own cycles with sacred celebration. *It is showing us the way.*

If you live life in a sacred and mindful way,
every moment can be a ceremony
that honors your connection with the Creator
and with all living things. . . .

· 14 ·

GRATITUDE AND
ACTS OF KINDNESS

"We can do no great things—only small things with great love."
—MOTHER TERESA

Several years ago, a woman named Anna Herbert from Marin County, California, became aware of a phrase running through her mind:

"Practice random kindness and senseless acts of beauty."

She began sharing this thought with friends, calling it a form of "positive anarchy," and decided to experiment with its philosophy by doing kind deeds at random. She would plant flowers in an ugly vacant lot; she'd pay the toll on the bridge for several cars behind her. Soon, the idea spread onto automobile bumper stickers, and across the country, and the "guerrilla kindness" movement was born.

Acts of kindness create instant real moments. They are the living rituals of everyday spirituality. They connect your heart with the heart of another person, and create pathways through which your love can flow.

The wonderful thing about practicing random kindness is that each day, you will be presented with thousands of opportunities to do so. A car will be waiting to be let into your lane of the highway; a person will be running to catch the elevator you're standing in; someone will drop some things and need help picking them up. You have children who need to be told they are special, a mate who needs to be told he/she is loved, friends who could use a one-minute phone call just to say you treasure them, dogs and cats who crave a hug, scratch, and a kiss, and hundreds of strangers to whom a smile would mean they were not invisible.

✦

Two years ago, Jeffrey and I rented a little cottage on a small island for our annual end-of-the-year vacation. The first day after we arrived, I had just sat down outside to read when I heard the pitiful "meow" of a cat who sounded like it was crying. When I looked in the bushes, I saw her—a scrawny stray black kitty that was more skin and bones than fur. She looked like she hadn't eaten in weeks, and was shaking from fear and hunger. I knew if I fed her, she wouldn't leave us alone for the next ten days, but my heart broke as I thought of her starving. I went inside, got a can of tuna fish, and placed it where she could see it.

For twenty minutes, the cat cried and whined, but wouldn't come near the food. She was terrified, I realized—she had gotten used to being yelled at and chased away by all of the local tourists, and didn't trust that I wouldn't hurt her as well. I sat on the ground and talked to her in a soothing voice, promising that I would take care of her if she would give me a chance.

Finally, my kitty friend cautiously approached the tuna, wolfed it down as fast as she could, and ran off into the bushes. But I knew she'd be back, and she was . . . later that day, just in time for dinner. I was prepared. I'd gone to the local store and stocked up on cat food, and it only took her five minutes to feel safe enough to eat it.

For the next week and a half, I took care of my small black friend. She spent much of her day lounging in the sun with us, and a few times at night when it rained, I'd hear her calling to me, and I'd unlock the door to our porch so she could have a dry place to sit out the storm. I looked forward to getting up each morning and seeing her little face peeking out from behind a bush. Jeffrey kept reminding me that when we left, the next tenant would probably chase her away again, but I didn't want to think about it.

The fateful day finally arrived when we were scheduled to leave and return home. Kitty watched us pack, walking in and out of my legs as if to say "Please don't go." I wrote a note for whoever was coming to the cottage next, begging them to feed the cat, and leaving them extra cans of food. But as we stood by the front gate with our suitcases, and Kitty planted herself in front of me, her green eyes staring into mine, I began to cry. "I'm abandoning her," I thought bitterly to myself. "I know I can't bring her back to the United States, but now that I've given her love, I'm being cruel by taking it away. Maybe she would have been better off if I hadn't given her a taste of kindness at all."

Suddenly, I heard a voice in my head whisper: *"You showed her what kindness was for the first time in her life. She will always take that with her. She will always know that she was loved. Love is never wasted."*

I'll never know what happened to my little black kitty friend. I hope she was cared for by someone else. But I do know this—with her help, I experienced many real and precious moments during that vacation. My love and kindness, however briefly they were shared, did make a difference in her life. And her love made a difference in mine.

Love and kindness are never wasted.
They always make a difference.
They bless the one who receives them,
and they bless you, the giver.

There are innumerable ways to create real moments by sharing your kindness: You can make sandwiches, drive by a city park, and give them out to the homeless people who live there; you can leave a daisy on a stranger's windshield; you can tell the person who is waiting on you in a restaurant that they are doing a great job. You don't even have to do anything physical—just sending people your kind thoughts and surrounding them with love will also affect them positively. When you see someone who appears to be unhappy or alone, visualize them surrounded by light and love. When you think of someone who is suffering or lost, wrap them in loving energy.

Never underestimate the healing power of everyday kindness. One loving word can lift a person out of the depths of despair and offer them hope; one smile can help them believe that they matter; one caring action can even save their life. I've personally met dozens of people who've confided to me that they were seriously contemplating suicide until a stranger said hello to them in an elevator, or a friend called to say "I was thinking about you." One real moment of love was enough to make the difference.

If each of you reading this practiced just one random act of kindness a day, starting tomorrow, our world would be transformed.

✦

"We are all connected to everyone and everything in the universe. Therefore, everything one does as an individual affects the whole. All thoughts, words, images, prayers, blessings, and deeds are listened to by all that is."

—SERGE KAHILI KING

Yesterday, I climbed a mountain. When I reached the top, I sat on a flat place between two tall stone spires, and looked out across the horizon. The day was clear, and I could see for miles: ancient red rock canyons, monuments to the massive earth changes that formed this beautiful part of the Southwestern United States; rolling hills alive with cactus, desert brush, and wildflowers; and sky—turquoise blue that seemed to stretch forever. The wind blew in strong gusts, kissing the mountain and me with its warm, sweet breath. Two hawks hovered almost motionless in the air above my head, their wings spread wide to catch the breeze, as if they, too, were awestruck by the glory of this place and this perfect afternoon.

I had come to the mountain looking for a real moment, and I had found one. Everything else but where I was and what I was experiencing dissolved, and I was left only with gratitude as I beheld the marvelous grace of the Creator. I was grateful that a spot such as this existed. I was grateful that my legs were strong enough to climb the steep hills to bring me here. I was grateful that I had eyes clear enough to see such an exquisite display of divine handiwork. I was grateful for my beloved husband and spiritual traveling companion, whose presence I could feel on a nearby ledge. I was grateful that I had been guided and protected thus far in my life so that I could arrive at this very moment.

My heart filled with quiet joy. My mind emptied and opened to peace. And one phrase echoed through my body: *"Thank you. . . ."*

> Ultimately, real moments are always
> moments of gratitude.

You cannot have a real moment without feeling truly grateful. Just the fact that you here, that you are able to experience a real moment doing whatever you are doing, will fill you with gratitude. *Your very existence is a miracle, as is the world you live in.* You do not have to be on a mountaintop to feel grateful. Anytime you stop for a moment, and pay complete and mindful attention to the fact of your presence here on Earth, your spirit will whisper "Thank you."

✦

If you want to experience a real moment, and remember nothing else you've read in these pages, simply begin focusing on your gratitude. Find something you feel grateful for, and then let yourself really feel it. Maybe you're grateful that your children are healthy and safe. Maybe you're grateful for the love a friend continually shows you. Maybe you're grateful that you woke up in a comfortable bed and had something to eat. Maybe you're grateful that you've survived this long in spite of your own efforts to self-destruct. Surrender completely to the feeling of gratitude, and you will be having a real moment.

When you live with constant gratitude,
your life will become a living prayer.

We often think of prayer as an asking, a plea to a higher power for a favor or blessing. And there is a time and a place when we need to request guidance and strength. But the word *pray* really means *"to praise."* From the beginning of time, man and woman have known the power of prayer as a means to give thanks for the wonder of creation, to honor the gift of life. This kind of prayer, then, becomes a vehicle through which our gratitude can flow forth. It connects us with our love for living, and reminds us of the abundance of real moments that are continually bestowed upon us.

Sun Bear, a sacred Native American teacher and author, says that prayer is a way "for humans to give back to the creation some of the energy they are always receiving." The Earth gives us a home on which to place our feet; the air allows us to breathe; the water sustains us; the Sun keeps us warm and illuminates our path with light. Gratitude allows us to put life back in balance.

How can our prayers and praises affect the Universe? They are an energy, a vibration of love, and all vibration affects everything else in creation. *When you feel gratitude in your heart, you are loving creation in a very concrete way.*

The Earth is a living, breathing organism. Like you, like anything that is alive, it too needs to be treated with love and kindness. How easily we forget that we are guests on this planet, that Mother Earth generously gives of herself for our comfort and pleasure. *If a friend invited you to be a guest in her home, would you throw your trash on her floor? Would you put poison in her water supply? Would you tear down her walls so you could make room for your own possessions? Would you kill her pets so you could have more space to yourself, or because you thought it was fun?*

This is how we have been treating our planet, like rude, insensitive house guests who mistakenly think we can leave whenever we want to. But this is our home. There is nowhere else for us to go.

We must stop taking our loving host, Mother Earth, for granted. We must behave like any decent guest would—*we should respect the space we have been given; we should clean up after ourselves; we should offer our help where it is needed; and most of all, we should learn to say "Thank you."*

✦

Begin by saying "Thank you" to creation whenever you can. You can start right now. . . .

. . . If you have a window nearby, look outside, notice the trees, or the other people who keep you company here on the

Earth, or the daylight that allows you to see all of this beauty, and say "*Thank you.*" Say it out loud. It will feel good. It will make you smile.

. . . If you are at home, and have a refrigerator full of food that the Earth has generously provided, open the door, look at the amazing variety of delicious nourishment, and say "*Thank you.*"

. . . Walk into your children's bedroom. Watch them sleeping. Somehow they were created out of your body, through the brilliant design of divine intelligence. Kiss their foreheads, pull up their covers, and say "*Thank you.*"

. . . Take a deep breath. Feel the air slide into your lungs, feeding your body with life. Exhale, and everything you don't need is released. Breathe in again—there's enough air for every breath you need to take, and it's the perfect formula to keep you alive. Exhale again, and say "*Thank you.*"

Thank you for reading my words, and receiving the love behind them. Thank you for traveling with me, and coming this far on our journey. We are almost home. . . .

· 15 ·

FINDING YOUR WAY
BACK HOME

"I searched for God and all I found was myself.
I searched for myself and all I found was God."
—SUFI QUOTE

W hat is your true destination on your journey Home? It is nowhere but here, no time but now. It is in this moment alone that you can find yourself. It is in this moment alone that you can find God. *That is because there is always nothing else but this moment, and this moment, and this moment.*

I have spent my whole life learning how to get back to this moment, to where I already am. Slowly, slowly, more and more of me is arriving here as I reclaim the pieces of my spirit that ran away from home. One by one, they return from their quest for what they thought would make me happy, only to find that happiness cannot be acquired—it can only be learned.

W hen I look for happiness, I lose it. When I
stop looking, and surrender to where I am,
I find it.

Like this, we are all forgetting who we are, and remembering, and forgetting over and over again. That is the journey, not a straight line from here to there, but a circle, from here to here, and back around. But each time, the forgetting becomes less painful, and the remembering easier.

Someone once explained to me that our spiritual growth unfolds in the same way an eagle rises from the ground toward the sky. He does not fly straight upward. He circles, passing over the same territory again and again, but each time, from a higher vantage point. This is how we come home—we slowly rise into the fullness and freedom of who we truly are, until finally, we become one with the Truth.

The Talmud says *"Every blade of grass has its angel that bends over it and whispers, 'Grow, grow . . .'"* **You, too, are being guided and protected on your journey home.** Teachers will appear when you need them, and when you are ready. They already have. Some you will recognize, others you may not. Don't forget that teachers come in all forms, and some of the best ones may not look like teachers at all.

The task of your teachers is not to take you anywhere, but to help you pay attention to where you are. Know that the more you surrender into each moment, the sooner you will be able to experience all of the love and peace that is waiting for you right here.

✦

"What would it be like if you lived each day, each breath, as a work of art in progress? Imagine that you are a Masterpiece unfolding, every second of every day, a work of art taking form with every breath."

—THOMAS CRUM

It is evening, at dusk. I find myself drawn to the backyard of my home from where I can watch the fog float in from the sea, following the valley that lies between my hill and the wilderness across from me. The sky is violet and flame. The only sounds are the night birds chanting in rhythm like contented monks. Everywhere there is stillness.

I sit with my dog in my lap and marvel at nature's exquisite way of saying good night. And then, I think to myself: *"It will always be like this here, even in forty or fifty years when I am no longer alive to witness it. The same fog will appear at sunset on hot summer days, and fill the night with mist. The same sea will lie quietly in the distance. The same trees will send shadows across the lawn. The same moon will rise through above the clouds, painting the valley silver with its light. All of this will be here, but I will be gone."*

For several minutes, I am overwhelmed by the eternality of nature. I feel small, frightened, and hopeless in my insignificance. What can possibly have meaning in my life? What can I possibly do or accomplish that will make sense?

My dog shifts on my lap to get a better view. Suddenly, I remember that all I am supposed to do is what I'm doing:

To stop, sit back, and witness the glorious spectacle of creation. . . .

To receive the privilege and blessing of being alive. . . .

To be fully present, right here, right now. . . .

To love. . . . To be grateful. . . .

To celebrate life, moment by moment. . . .

I am part of the sacred ritual taking place. . . .
I am part of what makes it beautiful. . . .

M̲ay your life be rich with real moments
and
may you travel your path in peace. . . .